GEORGE LOHMANN

PIONEER PROFESSIONAL

GEORGE LOHMANN

PIONEER PROFESSIONAL

Keith Booth

Published in Great Britain by
SportsBooks Limited
PO Box 422
Cheltenham
GL50 2YN
Tel: 01242 256755
email: info@sportsbooks.ltd.uk
www.sportsbooks.ltd.uk

First Published May 2007

Front and back cover photographs of George Lohmann and the Oval pavilion in 1888 courtesy of Surrey County Cricket Club.

A catalogue record for this book is available from the British Library.

ISBN 978 1899807 50 5

Printed and bound in England by
Cromwell Press

To Norman

CONTENTS

ACKNOWLEDGEMENTS

I am grateful to the following institutions and their staff for the help they have given in the provision of and access to source material for this book:

British Library
British Newspaper Library
Family Records Centre
Guildhall Library
Kensington Central Library – Local Studies Section
Liddell Hart Centre for Military Archives, King's College London
London Metropolitan Archive
Melbourne Cricket Ground Library
Minet Library, Lambeth
National Archives
National Library of South Africa, Cape Town
Surrey County Cricket Club
Surrey History Centre
Trent Bridge Library
University of the Witwatersrand, Johannesburg (William Cullen Reference Library)
Wandsworth Local History Centre, Battersea

Many people have been extremely generous in the provision of their time and expertise. My gratitude goes in particular to the following: David Ainsworth for information on schools in the Wandsworth area; Dean Allen for sharing his knowledge of James Logan, Matjiesfontein and imperialism in South Africa and for his trawl of South African newspapers and James Logan's scrapbook; Robert Brooke and Steven Shean for sharing their knowledge of the Quaife family; Carol Fletcher and Reg Quaife for information on the Quaife family; Paul Bush of Sunsport Tours for making the travel and accommodation arrangements for my research trip to South Africa; Clarke's Bookshop, Cape Town, and its staff for allowing access to its stock on South African social history and the Boer Wars; Brian Cowley for drawing my attention to his letter to *The Cricket Statistician* giving details of Lohmann's participation in match-winning sides; Jeff Hancock and Trevor Jones for access to the Surrey County Cricket Club Library, in particular photographs and correspondence on Lohmann between former librarian, Peter Large, and Geoffrey Howard; Chris Harte for drawing my attention to the article by

R R Langham-Carter in the *Australian Cricket Journal*; Millicent Mashiyane and Benny Phaladi of Rand Water for pointers on Lohmann's time at the Johannesburg Waterworks Company; Randall Northam of SportsBooks Limited for his conscientous attention to the detailed editing of the manuscript; Professor André Odendaal, Chief Executive of the Western Province Cricket Association and formerly Professor of Social History at the University of the Western Cape, for sharing his expertise on South African cricket history; Michael Owen-Smith of the *Cape Times* for sharing his knowledge of early South African cricket; Roger Page for providing me with publications on Australian cricket not available in the UK; Andrew Preece for information on Joshua's branch of the Lohmann family; Professor Liz Stanley, Research Professor of Sociology, University of Newcastle upon Tyne, for information on the letters of Olive Schreiner; David Studham, Librarian of the MCG, and his staff for advice on sources and very kindly making available unique resources during my brief visit to Melbourne when the Library was closed because of ground redevelopment; Max Tyler of the British Music Hall Society for information on Charles Pond; Carol van Vuuren of the Western Province Cricket Union for helping arrange contacts in Cape Town; Bernard Whimpress for information on early Australian cricket; Jonty Winch for helping identify the Wanderers players of 1897/98; Peter Wynne-Thomas for providing me with the 'Logan' and 'Lohmann' sections of his, as yet unpublished, Index to *The Cricketer* and allowing me access to the letters of Arthur Shrewsbury in the Trent Bridge Library; and, finally, to my wife, Jennifer, for her invaluable help with the detailed research, illustrations and proof-checking, and not always successful attempts to keep the cats out of the supermarket baskets which served as a filing system. Without her, much of this book would have remained unwritten, but had she been allowed free rein, none of it would have been, as research angles several removes from the George Lohmann story would continue to be assiduously pursued.

PREFACE

Lohmann, whose great performances were so many that a book might be written about them
W A Bettesworth *Chats on the Cricket Field*

WHEN PAKISTAN were demolishing England in Lahore in December 2005, a member of the Sky Sports commentary team mentioned that, in the whole history of Test cricket, Shoaib Akhtar's strike-rate had been bettered only by those of George Lohmann and Sydney Barnes. It was one of those trans-generational statistical comparisons which rarely have much meaning because of differences in climatic conditions, the nature of pitches and the quality of opposing batsmen. Lohmann played his cricket in a totally different social and political environment. It was the era of Gentlemen and Players, the high noon of Empire, half a century before Pakistan appeared on world maps. Yet both he and Shoaib are part of cricket's continuum. In each case, there is a reliance on variation of pace and although Lohmann's quicker ball was about the same speed as Shoaib's slower one, the two bowlers stand at either end of a tradition of what Richard Daft called the 'head bowler', the kind who applied brain as well as brawn to an art which has been refined over three centuries, but one pioneered by George Lohmann and his contemporaries.

As well as having the lowest strike-rate in Test cricket with a wicket every 34.19 balls, Lohmann also has the lowest average, 112 wickets at 10.75. His position is likely to remain unchallenged. The opposition batting was not of the strongest, the pitches were uncovered and some of the matches subsequently deemed to be Test matches would not have stood up to the sterner criteria of later years, but constant throughout 130 years of Test cricket, every match has begun with twenty opposition wickets available. Lohmann averaged more than six of those per match, a statistic bearing comparison with those of any of his contemporaries or successors and well ahead of most. It is not as though he was accompanied by bowling nonentities. Around at the same time were Lancashire's Johnny Briggs, Yorkshire's Bobby Peel and for one match, his Surrey colleague, Tom Richardson. In sixty per cent of his 293 first-class matches, Lohmann had five wickets in an innings, in almost twenty per cent ten in the match. His average of 13.19 for his county is the lowest for any 'serious' bowler in the County Championship era.

Almost a century elapsed between Walter Bettesworth's speculation in 1896 that a book might be written about George Lohmann and the appearance in 1991 of Ric Sissons' *George Lohmann: The beau ideal,* an offshoot of *The Players: A Social History of the Professional Cricketer,* winner of the Cricket Society Literary Award for 1988. A year earlier, when former Surrey Secretary Geoffrey Howard was contemplating a biography of Lohmann, Librarian Peter Large wrote to him '...may I wish you every success with the book; one on Lohmann is long overdue'. Sissons' book is a 65-page limited edition and Howard's intentions were eventually condensed into an article in the 1991 Surrey Yearbook. Both leave one with the feeling that Lohmann's place in cricket's firmament deserved something bigger and better. *George Lohmann – Pioneer Professional* is certainly bigger; whether it is better I shall leave to the judgment of others.

My interest in George Lohmann was first kindled while preparing my last book *The Father of Modern Sport: The Life and Times of Charles W Alcock.* Among the many hats Alcock wore were those of editor of the magazine *Cricket, A Weekly Record of the Game,* secretary of the Surrey County Cricket Club (to be eventually succeeded in that rôle by Geoffrey Howard) and joint editor of the first definitive history of the club. He was a major figure at The Oval for all but the first seven years of Lohmann's short life and while his writings on Lohmann are invariably complimentary, even at times verging on hagiography, he was in direct conflict over pay in 1896 and subsequent contractual negotiations for the following year. History tends to be angled from the point of view of the establishment. The opposite position is also worth exploring.

Accounts of Lohmann's life and cricketing achievements in standard histories and reference books have tended to be anglocentric, based as they are on contemporary accounts in *Cricket* and *Wisden.* So the Surrey years have been well documented, his South African period less well, particularly the years after the rift with Surrey in 1897. Yet Lohmann was idolised on three continents and, even in the years of his failing health, exerted an influence on South African cricket that was to last well beyond his lifetime. The strides made in the early part of the twentieth century owed much to his influence on the game in his adopted country. Some of the most powerful men in South African society were not only his cricketing and business colleagues but were also his friends in a way which would not have been possible in his native land.

Some of the primary source material for this period is not available. Lohmann does not seem to have kept a diary and although the evidence is that he regularly wrote letters, few have survived. Publication of the Johannesburg newspaper *The Star* was suspended during the Boer War and the records of the South African Cricket Association before 1898 were destroyed by fire. Those that remain are incomplete: the minutes of the meeting of 31 August 1899 were approved on 21 January 1903 with no indication that anything had gone on in between. Yet a tour of a South African team to England of which Lohmann was assistant manager had been arranged for 1900, then deferred for a year. Newspapers in the Cape, however, continued to be published and there is sufficient evidence there to suggest that Lohmann was the yardstick against which contemporary South African cricketers were measured.

The principal world of George Lohmann was that of global professional cricket, a world in which he exerted a major influence in making that professionalism respectable and acceptable, but to suggest that is all he did is to underestimate the man. His world of cricket was interlinked with other worlds of the extended family, business, politics, medical science and humanity generally.

Keith Booth
Sutton, Surrey
April 2007

Throughout the book, there are references to money which, given the difference in the purchasing power of the pound, are meaningless in isolation. Methods of calculating the Retail Price Index have become progressively more refined, but as a rough rule of thumb, multiplication by a factor of 70 will give an approximate translation of late nineteenth century pounds into early twenty-first century ones. So the professionals' wage claim in 1896 was equivalent to £1400 instead of £700, still less than half of what their successors receive for a Test match nowadays.

Where bowling figures are given, it should be noted that overs were of four balls before the 1889 season during and after which they were of five. The exception is the Australian tour of 1891/92, when six-ball overs were the norm in Test matches and first-class matches against South Australia and Victoria. New South Wales remained at five.

CHAPTER 1

HOME AND FAMILY LIFE AND EARLY CRICKET (1865-1883)

From quiet homes and first beginning
Hilaire Belloc

Kensington

GEORGE ALFRED LOHMANN was born in the respectable west London district of Kensington on 2 June 1865, the second son of George Stewart Cundell Lohmann and his wife, Frances, née Watling, widow of Daniel Pattle and, aged only 31, a mother of five sons and a daughter at the time of her first husband's death.

The period of mourning was by Victorian standards fairly brief, almost akin to Hamlet's funereal baked meats coldly furnishing forth the marriage tables. There were only sixteen months between the death of her husband and Frances's subsequent remarriage and under two years between the births of Charles, her last child by Daniel, and Stewart, her first by her new husband, who was also generally known as Stewart. The Pattles had lived in Adelaide Road, Hampstead where Daniel is described on the 1861 Census of Population as a wine merchant. On his death certificate, he is a Dining Rooms Keeper[1], having been at the Queen's Arms Public House in Haverstock Hill[2] and later, as part of the partnership of Stearn and Pattle, at an establishment of the same name in Bird-in-Hand Court, Cheapside. So the likelihood is that there was money in the family and though this may have been part of the attraction, Stewart Lohmann was of solid middle-class stock and it would not have been overstretching his resources to support what eventually became two families merged into one.

Recent research shows that the changing pattern of family life has resulted in seventeen per cent of men born in 1970 being stepfathers, twice as many as among those born in 1958.[3] So perhaps society is on its way back to a situation which obtained a century and more ago. The reasons, however, are different, remarriage and repartnering arising in the twenty-first century from higher separation and divorce rates and in the nineteenth from shorter life expectancy.

Stewart Lohmann could trace his descent to one of a number of German families who came to England with George I, the first ruler of the House of Hanover, on the death of Queen Anne in 1714. He was the youngest of four children of Johan Diedrich Gottfried Christian Lohmann and his wife, Elizabeth Cundell. His elder siblings were in 1851 a governess, a clerk to a corn factor and a student at the Royal College of Music. After Johan's death, his widow Elizabeth kept a lodging house in St Pancras – a respectable one where the lodgers were merchants' clerks and insurance clerks.[4]

Campden Hill Road, Kensington where George Lohmann was born, was part of the Phillimore Estate, inherited by William Phillimore in 1779 and left in trust to his younger son, Charles. William had died in 1829 and by the 1860s Charles had commissioned 315 new residences for the estate. On Campden Hill Road these were 'large houses for wealthy men who came here for their health'.[5] They still stand today, their bay windows, balconies and proximity to Kensington High Street making them 'much sought after' in the estate-agent speak of the area. Further north, on Campden Hill proper (erroneously given as Lohmann's place of birth by both Sissons and *Cricket Archive*), beyond Duchess of Bedford's Walk were several lodges – now all demolished – occupied by the aristocracy, including the Marquess of Bute, and not far from Kensington Palace Gardens, locally known as 'Millionaires' Row'.

The 1861 Census of Population shows the road occupied by respectable professionals such as accountants, architects, barristers and retired army officers, all with live-in servants. Violet Hunt and Ford Madox Ford were to hold a salon there at the beginning of the following century, a meeting place for H G Wells, Arnold Bennett, Joseph Conrad, Henry James, Ezra Pound, Wyndham Lewis and John Galsworthy who lived there for a few years between 1897 and 1903. That scenario, however, is applicable only to numbers 7 and upwards and not the southern end of the road which runs at right angles to what is now Kensington High Street (then Kensington Road). Numbers 1 to 6 were part of Lower Phillimore Place, running parallel to the High Street and comprising much smaller houses occupied mainly by the builders and other artisans involved in the construction of the estate. The houses were demolished in 1931/32 and replaced by shops and flats. The Lohmanns lived at no 3, now the site of Pickwick's Gifts, flanked by a branch of the Bradford and Bingley Building Society and the Palms Bar Grill.

It was respectable enough and certainly not part of the slum properties that covered much of Victorian London at the time. In the 1851 Census of Population and on his marriage certificate, George's father is described as a 'Merchant's Clerk', on Stewart's birth certificate as a 'Banker's Clerk', then on George's and subsequent ones as a 'Stockbroker' or 'Stock and Share Dealer', so there is evidence of a solid professional and educated family background, perhaps not far enough up the social scale to give the option of becoming a gentleman amateur, but stable enough to give George the support required by a young upwardly mobile professional cricketer.

Battersea and Wandsworth

THE FIRST son of Stewart and Frances, Stewart, had been born north of the river in St Pancras, but by the time the third child and first daughter, Julia, came along, the family had moved across the Thames to the first of a number of addresses in the Battersea–Clapham Common–Wandsworth Common area.

Ric Sissons in *George Lohmann, the beau ideal*, suggests this may have been a down-market move, caused by the stock market crash of May 1866 precipitated by the collapse of Overend, Gurney and Company[6] and David Kynaston suggests much the same in his biography of Bobby Abel.[7] That is a possibility, but unlikely, given that at the time George's father held a relatively junior position as a stockbroker's clerk and was less prone to be affected than more senior members such as brokers and jobbers.[8] He had previously been a merchant's clerk[9], then a banker's clerk[10] and was later to become a stockbroker in his own right, so in professional terms, the movement was up-market rather than down.

There is a photograph of George Lohmann, as a boy aged 8,[11] attributed to Southwell Brothers of Baker Street. The family portrait at this time was the prerogative of the middle-classes and above. So, if the move was down-market, it was certainly not too far or it was a downward movement from which the family did not take many years to recover.

It is more likely that the move was simply to larger premises to accommodate the needs of a growing family. The ages of Frances's children from her former marriage ranged at the time of Julia's birth from five to thirteen; the total was now eight (daughter Frances was no longer with them) and while that size of family was somewhere near the norm for the time, it did necessitate more spacious living accommodation.

Parts of the Battersea area to which the family moved from Kensington are now yuppie territory, parts are suffering from inner city blight, but in the latter half of the nineteenth century, they were the essence of

Victorian respectability. Their first residence in Mayfair Villas, Falcon Lane [12] where George's younger sister, Julia, was born in June 1867, has long since fallen victim to the bulldozer and inexorable advance of commercialism in the shape of branches of the multiples, Asda and Boots. The Falcon Inn still stands on the corner and the ease of commuting into the City from nearby Clapham Junction railway station was doubtless part of the area's attraction. In 1868, Octavius, Frances's eighth son was born prematurely and died in infancy aged three weeks.[13]

The next move was one stop down the railway line to Wandsworth Common, more specifically to 2 Hope Villas, a large family house, still standing, but now renumbered and readdressed as 137 St James's Drive, and it was here that Augusta, the second daughter, was born in 1869. The house is in an attractive area of the metropolis, overlooking the Common in what was a century later to become Margaret Thatcher's poll-tax free flagship London Borough. It remains a popular residential area for a number of Surrey's professional playing staff and others whose financial position allows them to live in an area where very few properties are advertised under the half-million mark. On the end of the terrace beyond what were then stables stands *The Hope* public house which still retains much of its Victorian atmosphere notwithstanding recent attempts, soon abandoned, to modernise it into the *Faith and Firkin*.[14]

School

GEORGE'S EARLY schooling was at the Louvaine Academy, a small private school for boys, opened in 1865 at the newly-built property of 16 Louvaine Road.[15] It was run firstly by Caleb Kerby, then after his death by his widow, Jane, with their daughter and two sons as pupil-teachers and two assistant teachers.[16] However, after James, the eldest son, left to acquire an MA and later become a clergyman at Alston in Lancashire, the school closed in 1875. A Mrs Meggeson moved to 16 Louvaine Road[17] which by 1881 was occupied by Samuel Bone, a draper, and his family.

No information has been traced on George's subsequent education. He certainly continued it somewhere, as the evidence of his later life points to a literate, numerate and articulate man and the Elementary Education Act of 1876 made education compulsory until the age of twelve. One possibility is the Holy Trinity School, Upper Tooting, which by 1878 had 81 boys, 49 girls and 65 infants on its register. The annual treat was a trip to the Crystal Palace Grounds. If George was at that school, then over a quarter of a century the wheel was to come full circle as it was there that he was to spend a few days of his last season in cricket when the South African touring team he managed in 1901 played against W G Grace's London County.

The 1871 Census of Population finds the family of George and Frances at 2 Hope Villas, their two boys and two girls, now aged seven, five, four and one, along with five sons from Frances's earlier marriage, Henry, Zachariah, Frank, Walter and Charles aged seventeen, fifteen, twelve, nine and eight. The eldest two are stockbroker's clerks, the remainder still at school. The household was brought up to a round dozen by Elizabeth Linsey, a seventeen-year-old live-in servant, presumably kept well occupied by the demands of a large growing family.

The census reveals among George's five half-brothers, Joseph Pattle – as he was to be known later, though at this stage he is recorded as Zachariah J – Frances's second son by her first marriage. Joseph was George's senior by ten years and, under the stage-name of Charles Pond, was also to distinguish himself in the world of professional entertainment, but in his case, in music hall. Sissons has assumed that George's father remarried after Frances's death in 1886 and that Charles Pond was a step-brother. Consequently, the part played by Joseph in George's life has perhaps been underestimated. He was not a step-brother, someone whom George met on his father's second marriage, but a half-brother, a contemporary sibling.

The Stock Exchange

STEWART LOHMANN was a stockbroker's clerk before becoming a member of the Stock Exchange in his own right, following his application in March 1869. He was clerk to Edward Bland who, along with H D Bland was also one of his guarantors, a requirement for the first two years of membership. However, Murray Richardson replaced Edward Bland for an unexpired portion of the two year term.

As Bland's clerk, he had been based at 3 Crown Court in Threadneedle Street, but now established a base at Throgmorton Chambers in Throgmorton Street and continued as a member of the Exchange for the next ten years. Applications for renewal of membership were made annually. By 1879, his residence had become 2 St James' Road – clearly the same house as Hope Villas, possibly a Post Office redesignation – and by 1880 he had moved to Battersea Park Road and the following year to 24 Orbel Street.[18] After that, there were no more applications for membership and Lohmann senior reverted to being a clerk.[19]

By this time, George had followed in his father's footsteps and, along with his elder brother Stewart, was a stockbroker's clerk, as their elder half-brothers Henry and Zachariah had been ten years earlier.[20] Henry continued to work as a stock exchange clerk and by 1881 had married and was commuting to the City from Dorking. Neither Stewart nor

George worked directly for his father,[21] but each would have developed financial literacy and business sense that would stand them in good stead in later life, Stewart as a commercial traveller and George as a professional cricketer, better educated than most of his colleagues, aware of his commercial worth and determined to ensure he was rewarded accordingly.

Church Institute

IT WAS in 1876 that the eleven-year-old George became attached to the Church Institute – the Upper Tooting Church Institute to give it its full title – in Wiseton Road, a couple of streets from his home; an organisation, founded by C H Baker around 1868 and supported by Thomas Bates, Vicar of Balham, which was the educational, sporting and social arm of the Anglican church of St Mary Magdalene and, like the Boys' Brigade, Church Lads' Brigade and the Sunday School movement, epitomised the Victorian spirit of muscular Christianity. It ran evening tuition in the 3Rs and other subjects in association with the Science and Arts Department, South Kensington. It also provided facilities for hockey, swimming, rambling, rifle shooting and, significantly, cricket. In 1881 it had 1,100 members on its books and distributed 73 prizes,[22] so by the thirteenth year of its existence it had become an organisation providing major services to its local community.

In a profile in *Cricket* in 1885, when at the age of 20 he had already begun to make an impression on the county scene, Lohmann's early years at the Institute are recalled and it is recorded that he won prizes for both batting and bowling in his pre-teen years of 1876, 1877 and 1878. The club played on Wandsworth Common and the likelihood is that it was that part of the Common bounded by Trinity Road and Burntwood Lane, marked on nineteenth century Ordinance Survey maps as a cricket ground and now used as a sports ground by Old Grammarians and Old Sinjuns (Sir Walter St John's Football and Cricket Club).

In between matches, Lohmann delighted in frequent visits to The Oval.

> During my holidays I used to come to the Oval as often as my pocket money allowed, and, taking a few sandwiches with me, sat down to enjoy the cricket; I doubt whether I have ever enjoyed anything so much in my life as I did in watching those matches – except in actually playing. The first time I came to the Oval was in 1876 or 1877 when I was about 11 or 12 years of age, and I remember seeing W W Read and A P Lucas batting.[23]

The activities of the Institute, which in its early years shared a modest room in a small house in what is now Tooting Bec Road before moving to its present home in Wiseton Road, continued well into the twentieth century and, reporting the 67th Anniversary celebrations in 1931, the *Wandsworth Borough News* recalls,

> Those present were then invited to remain after the service for a cup of tea and a chat over old times and scenes. A representative 'picture gallery' had been arranged in the stage of the hall comprising photographs of the various cricket, hockey, swimming, rambling, rifle and other clubs included in the activities of the Institute extending over a period of more than half a century. Many of these caused considerable amusement as the boys and youths depicted in their 'teens' in the photograph are now middle-aged and elderly men with sons and grandsons of their own connected with one or more branches of the Institute's life and work.[24]

The building still exists and the twenty-first century activities of badminton, indoor bowls, short-mat bowling, table-tennis, billiards and snooker reflect those of their nineteenth century predecessors, though the muscular Christianity concept has gone and operations are conducted under the auspices of the considerably more secular Wiseton Leisure Activities.

There were two sides, Church Institute and Church Institute Junior, which played regularly on Saturdays throughout the summer. It was for the latter that George first played. It is probable that 'Junior' is indicative less of an age limit than a 2nd XI. Few other sides carry the suffix, so the likelihood is that the membership of the Institute was such that they were able to raise two teams. Later reports which refer to a Church Institute (1st Eleven)[25] would support this interpretation and it is improbable that at this stage in the game's development at this level the concept of an age limit had been considered. There was no league system and opponents were other church and church-affiliated sides who beyond arranging fixtures and grounds were not over-concerned with administrative niceties. The purpose was to play for fun in the spirit of muscular Christianity. Organised coaching would have been minimal or non-existent and to judge from the scores, the quality of the pitches and the batting left scope for improvement.

The incidence of three-figure totals was under one in ten, the average innings score being between 40 and 50. It was not unusual for the innings of each side to be completed in time for a second innings to be played. The standard of play was not particularly high, nor was the recording of it to the standards of modern scoring requirements. The scores of individual batsmen usually add up to the team total, give or take the occasional misprint, but bowling analyses are not given (though, at the time that is far from unusual, even at first-class level) and the newspaper scorecards have entries such as 'played on' or 'thrown out' and on one occasion a 'substitute' batting, some 130 years or so before the ICC got round to allowing such flexibility. Sometimes the bowler is given credit for run outs, but to counterbalance this generosity often does not receive it for catches and stumpings. Nevertheless, more coverage is given to local cricket than is the case today where, certainly in London, full scorecards of local matches are rarely seen and that given by the local newspaper the *Wandsworth and Battersea District Times* allows an insight into George Lohmann's very early days as a cricketer.

Aged just eleven, he was already beginning to make an impact on the scene in 1876[26] and by the following season, he was opening the batting regularly and taking his fair share of wickets, including, doubtless, several not attributed to him when catches were made from his bowling. In his first appearance of 1877, he made three, but it was a significant three representing exactly the difference in the overall totals of the Institute Junior's 30 and their opponents St James' 27. More important, however, was Lohmann's impact on the St James' top order. The scorecard read:

Page b Lohmann	0
Garratt b Lohmann	0
Short b Lohmann	0
Foskett b Lohmann	4

He later took a catch and there were two other catches and a hit-wicket not attributed to the bowlers. The other two wickets were run out, so it is known for certain that he had a hand in at least half the wickets and more than likely that he contributed to some of the others. It was his twelfth birthday.[27]

The next Saturday, against St Mary's Balham, the Institute Junior, having made a rare 101, dismissed their opponents for 18, the first four batsmen making just two singles between them, two being bowled by Lohmann, one being caught by Lohmann and the other an unattributed 'played on', quite probably also to Lohmann.[28] In the next fixture against Parochial, he had a 'six for', all bowled.[29]

And so it went on. Two matches were lost by narrow margins. Most were won by large ones. The Upper Tooting Band of Hope, a team born of the temperance movement, who would doubtless have some difficulty raising a side today and were not of the strongest then, recorded 30 and 25 against the Institute Junior's 79.[30] The following Saturday, Stanley were dismissed for 7, did rather better in their second innings with 28, but still failed to come anywhere near Institute Junior's single innings 55.[31]

On this occasion, George's contribution seems to have been just one catch in the first innings and a wicket in the second, the destroyer being one of his teammates by the name of Heath.

He was, however, playing against boys and young men older than himself and far from being content with holding his own, was a match-winner on several occasions. His contributions with the bat, mostly at no 1, occasionally at 2 or 3 were 3, 6, 7, 13, 2, 14, 6, 11, 2, 7 and 2. In later years, he would have regarded such statistics as representing a run of poor form, but in the context of the match scores of the time, they were respectable enough and could be multiplied by a factor of five or six to arrive at a present-day equivalent. But his bowling continued to dominate and would do so the following seasons.

On one occasion he was joined by one of his half-brothers, but as the scorecard has no initials and reads just 'Pattle' there is no way of ascertaining which one. It looks as though he was making up the numbers as he batted at no 11, and made 2 in what seems to have been his only appearance.[32] It was possibly Frank Pattle, who in 1880, can be found playing for Avenue Cricket Club, against the Anchor Club whose results were reported frequently in the local press. In a match which his team lost by 44 runs to 39, he made 10 at no 5, having taken the wickets of Anchor's nos 9 and 10, one caught and one hit wicket.[33] However, George's elder brother, Stewart, was in the same team on more than one occasion, including that when George may have made his first senior team appearance. The match is reported as being played by 'Church Institute' rather than 'Church Institute Junior', but that may be misleading, as it was a nine-a-side match against the none too strong Band of Hope and the Institute side has the appearance of a scratch team masquerading under the banner of the senior side. Unfazed by the team title, however, George had seven of the eight wickets available, the other, to round off a family occasion, being caught by Stewart who also made 11 not out.[34]

There was clearly a family interest in cricket and no small amount of talent. Stewart and George's younger brother, Joshua, still a toddler at this time, were both to become professional cricketers in their own right (albeit not at first-class level), Joseph Pattle, as Charles Pond, was to be active in George's benefit and in 1884, a scorecard for a Laburnum House v Church Institute fixture has 'st G Lohman' [sic] and the following week the same team has a bowler named Lohmann,[35] unlikely to be George as by this time, he was on Surrey's books and there is no record of his ever having kept wicket, maybe Stewart with the wrong initial, but not impossible that it is their father, aged 50 and still capable of playing club cricket.

Alma Cricket Club

SISSONS HAS the family living at 2 Hafer Road from 1866 to 1886[36], a respectable brick-built end terrace two storey residence which still stands, and though the evidence is that they lived there from some time before 1885 to 1887,[37] they were certainly not there for a twenty year period, as the 1881 Census of Population shows the whole family of mother, father and five children, including the youngest child, Joshua, born in 1875, living at 24 Orbel Street, a two storey, semi-detached brick built house still standing in what was then and is now a quiet residential area. The Pattle family have now flown the nest; Henry has followed his step-father into the Stock Exchange and is lodging in Bolingbroke Road, Battersea. Frank does not appear. He may be overseas.[38]

It was quite possibly this change of address which led George to move on from the Church Institute and join the Alma Cricket Club. It is conceivable that it might have been connected with the Alma Tavern on York Road, built in 1854 and called after the battle of that name in the Crimean War. There is also an Alma Road near Wandsworth Town station, but there is a reference in the *Wandsworth and Battersea District Times* to a match between Will o'the Wisp of Battersea against the Alma Club of Pimlico in Battersea Park.[39]

In a feature in *Cricket*,[40] when he had become established as a regular Surrey player, the connection with the Club is mentioned, specifically that he spent the 1881, 1882 and 1883 seasons with them after playing little cricket in 1879 and 1880. On the assumption that the information was provided by Lohmann himself, there seems little reason to doubt the truth of it, but no concrete evidence in contemporary newspapers of his participation has been unearthed.

Private grounds apart, the three major public areas in Lohmann's south London were Wandsworth Common, where he had played for the Church Institute, Clapham Common and Battersea Park which was a more convenient venue from Orbel Street than either of the others and was possibly the venue for the Alma's home matches. Pimlico is on the other side of the river, but Battersea Park is easily accessible via Chelsea Bridge. There is also evidence, however, that Regent's Park was used.[41]

Towards the end of 1883, Stewart and George turned out for the Liberal Club against the Conservative Club. They totally spoiled what would might otherwise have been a well-balanced match and produced a result which Mr Gladstone would doubtless have wished to replicate at the next general election.

> Laburnham House [sic] v Beaconsfield Club
> A match between the above clubs (representatives of the Liberal and

> Conservative parties) took place on Saturday afternoon (8th Sept) on the match ground, Battersea Park. The Beaconsfield who were the first to bat were all disposed of for 12, G Lowman [sic] taking seven wickets for five runs. The Liberals obtained 235 runs, S Lowman scored 101, G Lowman 55, extras amounting to 29.[42]

From the 1850s onwards, cricket clubs had been mushrooming all over London, the local Battersea Club being founded in 1859 and celebrating its 'silver wedding' in some style in 1884. From local press reports that was a major club in the area, certainly featuring more than the Alma. Clubs were required to pay to have their scorecards included in *Cricket* which had national, indeed international, coverage of the game and the larger better-known ones did so, along with numerous 'fancy-hat' teams and those with public school and university associations. However, at local level, smaller concerns could pay to have their scores inserted in the columns of a local newspaper, in this case the *South London Press* and the *Wandsworth and Battersea District News*, and dozens did so. Even those who chose not to pay for the publicity of press coverage could expect to receive some mention when their fixture list matched them with one of the teams who paid their 5/- to have their deeds recorded for posterity. Consequently, the only reports and results available are those submitted by their opponents.

Battersea was the largest and best-known club in the area, certainly the one which received most press coverage and good enough to merit fixtures with Dorking, Surrey Club and Ground and MCC. It seems unusual that a cricketer with Lohmann's talent did not gravitate in that direction from where there may have been more of a natural progression towards the county club. In 1888 Stewart played for Battersea against Surrey Club and Ground, but there is no evidence that George ever represented them. It is virtually certain that he would have arrived on the first-class scene somehow, but the way in which he did so owes more to serendipity than conscious cricket career planning on his part or active recruiting by the club.

Surrey

HIS INTRODUCTION to Surrey cricket was accidental, like many life-changing events, a question of being in the right place at the right time. Although later obituaries and personal profiles place his introduction to The Oval as the beginning of the 1884 season, in his 'chat' with W A Bettesworth, who conducted a number of interviews with players and personalities and reproduced them in book form some years later, George recalls that he was there at the end of the 1883 season.

> A friend of mine was chosen for a Colts' match at the Oval… When he was batting in the nets I bowled to him, and afterwards he asked me to bat. I had only been batting a few minutes when the then head groundsman at the Oval came up to me and said, 'You are not playing in this match and so you have no business to be batting.' …I was dreadfully disappointed; so I walked disconsolately away. In a few minutes Dick Humphrey came up to me and asked …'Will you kindly go to the nets again – the Hon. Robert Grimston wants to see you bat.' I did as I was asked and went through a sort of test performance… and it was through this that I afterwards played for Surrey, for I was asked to play in the Colts' match in 1884.[43]

Mr Grimston, says Bettesworth, in a footnote to the interview, was always greatly interested in young cricketers and for several years, he and Mr Fred Burbridge coached the Colts early mornings before the matches started.

There is a variation on this story in an interview with the *Clarion*[44] in that it was W W Read who was impressed by Lohmann's bowling rather than Grimston by his batting. Almost a decade had elapsed between the events and the interview and there is a four year gap between the *Clarion* interview and the Bettesworth one, so perhaps Lohmann's memory is blurred or perhaps both versions are true. It is at least possible that they took place on separate occasions, but the stories are consistent in that it was Lohmann's being fortuitously present at The Oval which led to his eventual selection for the Colts, rather than his being caught by the county's comprehensive scouting network. It suggests that perhaps he did not play very much cricket after his teenage and pre-teen successes with the Church Institute. The sparse references in the local press would certainly point in that direction and although the Church Institute receives a mention in the *Clarion* interview, the Alma Club does not feature.

Later Residences

BY 1884, the family had moved to 47 Kersley Street[45] opposite St Stephen's Church, now re-evangelised as the 'Church of the First-Born'. They were not there long, moving first to Hafer Road and then to 449 Battersea Park Road where Frances died in January 1887[46] while George was on his first tour of Australia. At the end of the decade, George wrote to the Committee from Salcott House, Wandsworth Common[47] and for the first part of the 1890s was giving his address as 5 Sainsbury Road, Upper Norwood.[48] The road runs parallel to the railway line at Gipsy Hill station, but the area has been redeveloped and the house no longer exists. The

1891 Census of Population lists George's father as a resident there, now a fifty-seven-year-old widower 'living on his own means'. With him are George's elder brother, Stewart aged 27 and a commercial traveller and Joshua aged 15, still at school. The area is respectable lower middle class, the neighbours being a gardener, dressmaker,[49] shop assistant, printer/compositor, traveller in wines and spirits and a bricklayer. The daughters are either no longer living there or were absent on the night of the census, 5 April 1891. George was definitely absent that night (he was in Bristol) and possibly using the house as a mailing address or occasional residence for home fixtures. It was not quite the empty nest syndrome, but a lot emptier than 2 Hope Villas twenty years previously.

1 He died on 13 October 1861
2 Post Office Directory 1858
3 Economic and Social Research Council: *The Seven Ages of Man and Woman*, reported in *The Times* 21 June 2004
4 Census of Population 1851
5 Weinribb and Hibbert *The London Encyclopaedia* p 120
6 p 11
7 p 26
8 On George Lohmann's birth certificate where his mother is the informant, his father is described as a Stockbroker, but almost four years later Stock Exchange records of applications for membership and re-election have him as Clerk to stockbroker Edward Bland (MS 17957/68). He applied successfully for membership for the year beginning 25 March 1869
9 Marriage certificate 20 February 1863
10 Stewart's birth certificate 13 October 1863
11 Reproduced in Edmonds *100 Greatest Bowlers* p 26
12 Julia's birth certificate, though the application for Stock Exchange membership two years later gives the address as Mayfair Villa, Falcon Road
13 Death certificate, which gives the address as Mayfair Villas
14 Press-cuttings file in Wandsworth Local History Centre
15 The reference to George Lohmann's schooling is in Robert Toms' *Logan's Way*, a publication based partly on James Logan's scrapbooks. No records of the school appear to have survived other than Trade Directory listings. It is assumed that the reference to Louvain School in the Lohmann entry by Ric Sissons in the *Dictionary of National Biography* is based on the information in Toms' book, as it repeats the same spelling error, omitting the final 'e' of Louvaine
16 Census of Population 1871
17 *Post Office Directory* 1876
18 The 1881 Census of Population has the family here, though Frances Lohmann's death certificate (1887) has 449 Battersea Park Road as the address, so it appears that once the Pattle family had flown the nest, there were frequent changes of residence.
19 Frances Lohmann's death certificate, 20 January 1887
20 Census of Population 1871
21 There is no mention of any clerk in Stewart Lohmann's annual applications for Stock Exchange membership
22 *Surrey County Observer* 21 May 1881
23 Bettesworth *Chats on the Cricket Field – Cricket* 30 July 1896
24 *Wandsworth Borough News* 1 February 1935
25 5 June 1880, reported in *Wandsworth and Battersea District Times* 12 June 1880
26 The *Wandsworth and Battersea District Times* for 1876, 1878, 1879 and 1881 in the

British Newspaper Library require some conservation work, are not available for public consultation until some unspecified date in the future. Nor are they held by the Wandsworth Local Studies Library. Consequently, much information on Lohmann's pre-first-class career is currently untraceable, but it may be assumed the successes of 1877 are not unrepresentative

27 2 June 1877, reported in *Wandsworth and Battersea District Times* 9 June 1877
28 9 June 1877, reported in *Wandsworth and Battersea District Times* 16 June 1877
29 16 June 1877, reported in *Wandsworth and Battersea District Times* 23 June 1877
30 28 July 1877, reported in *Wandsworth and Battersea District Times* 4 August 1877
31 4 August 1877, reported in *Wandsworth and Battersea District Times* 11 August 1877
32 30 June 1877, Church Institute Junior v St Barnabas Junior, reported in *Wandsworth and Battersea District Times* 7 July 1877
33 18 September 1880 reported in *Wandsworth and Battersea District Times* 25 September 1880
34 25 August 1877 reported in *Wandsworth and Battersea District Times* 1 September 1877
35 *South London Press* 17 and 24 May 1884
36 Sissons *George Lohmann:The beau ideal* p 11
37 *James Lillywhite's Cricketers' Annual* 1886-88
38 Census of Population 1881
39 30 June 1877
40 27 August 1885
41 Fixture versus One and All 8 July 1876, announced in *South London Press* 3 June 1876.
42 *Wandsworth & Battersea District Times* 15 September 1883
43 Bettesworth op cit
44 23 July 1892.
45 *Kelly's London Suburban Directory* 1884
46 Frances Lohmann's Death Certificate
47 Letter to Surrey Committee dated 17 January 1890
48 *James Lillywhite's Cricketers' Annual* 1891-96
49 This may be misleading. In 19th century Censuses, 'dressmaker' is often used as a euphemism for prostitute

CHAPTER 2

ON THE FIRST-CLASS SCENE (1884-85)

A new colt who seems likely to strengthen
Surrey's bowling materially
Cricket 1884

1884

THE LATE season casual and unscheduled visit to The Oval nets and the invitation from Robert Grimston conveyed by Dick Humphrey resulted in the eighteen-year-old George's selection for a few matches for the Colts and Club and Ground sides at the beginning of the 1884 season. It was the custom at the time to begin the season with such matches which were played almost daily, giving the junior players the opportunity to play alongside established players and the club the opportunity to assess the promise of the youngsters.

Surrey at the time were going through a transitional stage. (When were they not?) They had dominated the haphazard, semi-organised and casual county cricket scene of the 1860s, then, following a relatively fallow period in the '70s, were beginning to put together the team that would, under the captaincy of John Shuter, dominate the early years of the re-organised and more streamlined county championship of the '90s. The 'big names' of the '80s were, in addition to Shuter himself, the amateurs W E Roller and W W Read and the latter's namesake, the professional Maurice Read; Bobby Abel had made his début three years earlier and was now beginning to establish himself.

R H Lyttelton was to write that the county was showing the first signs of convalescence after a long period of grievous sickness. It was an appropriate analogy and would also apply to Lohmann in later years, though in a literal rather than metaphorical sense.

Under the sagacious secretaryship of Charles Alcock, The Oval was becoming a more commercially viable operation and already there were debates in committee on the potential conflict between using The Oval to develop Surrey cricket and marketing it for other, potentially more lucrative purposes. At the Annual General Meeting of that year, Frederick Gale had,

> offered some remarks on the advisability of devoting the whole use of the Oval to the development of cricket rather than allowing it to be used by different clubs

and,

> urged that the Oval should not be used as a playground for those in the immediate vicinity of Kennington, but that it should be used exclusively as a nursery for the County team. He suggested that there should be a match every Saturday at the Oval with the object of improving the cricket.[1]

Lohmann had little interest in club politics and finances at the time (Not many professionals do unless they are directly affected) but with the objective of improving the standard of cricket he was undoubtedly associated.

The eight matches in which he played provided evidence of much youthful promise, though his performances with the bat were as impressive as those with the ball and it could scarcely have been predicted at this early stage of his career that he would make an almost unimpeded progression from Surrey's junior ranks to become a more than competent batsman, outstanding fielder and Test match-winning bowler.

In an inauspicious start on Thursday 1 May, in a match against Broadwater, which the Club and Ground side won comfortably by an innings and 62 runs, Lohmann took a catch in the second innings, but, batting at no 9, had been bowled for a duck by C T Studd, who was later to abandon cricket and distinguish himself in the field of Christian missionary work overseas.[2] Two days later Lohmann managed 6 not out at no 4 in a dead situation against Richmond at Old Deer Park, as, at a time before declarations became part of the cricket scene, the Club and Ground side eased to 180 for 2 in reply to the home side's 57 all out.[3]

Given the opportunity to open the innings the following Monday for the Colts against Southwark Park at The Oval, he made 9 in the first innings, 27 in the second, to cause *Cricket* to comment that Lohman [sic], Osborn, Copinger and G Harris all batted in promising form.[4] In the case of Osborn, Copinger and G Harris, the promise remained unfulfilled and in the case of the remaining Colt deemed worthy of mention it was to develop in a rather different direction.

The following fixture against Clapham on Tuesday 6 May brought another innings victory and an acknowledgement in *Cricket* that Lohmann, Osborn, Forsyth and Harrison all played good cricket.[5] Again, Forsyth and Harrison do not feature in Surrey's first-class records, but a further 21 runs as opening batsman, 24 at no 3 against Richmond Town the following day, 24 against Surbiton and District on Thursday and, more spectacularly, bowling figures of 20.2-5-40-8[6] meant that by the time of Lohmann's appearance the following Monday for the Club and Ground against Eighteen Colts of Reigate and District, *Cricket* was spelling his name correctly[7], but more significantly, he was now on the margins of the full Surrey Eleven.

An outstanding all round contribution against Mitcham and District on Saturday 17 May further consolidated his position. Opening the innings, he made 50 out of 139, the next highest score being 27 not out, then proceeded to take five wickets (Not unusually for the time, 'the bowling analysis was not kept'[8]) including nos 1, 3 and 4 in the order, out of nine, one Mitcham player being absent.

It was this performance, following on the Surbiton match, which encouraged the selectors to give Lohmann an opportunity in the first eleven against second-class Leicestershire. Although he was later to occupy a regular spot at no 7 or 8, on the Surrey and England card, on this occasion, he was invited to open the batting with captain John Shuter. He was to recall later being selected.

> I played in one or two Colts' matches and did pretty well and in a match at Mitcham I made a few runs and took a few wickets. On the first morning of the Leicestershire match that year Mr Burbridge came to me and to my intense astonishment said, 'Will you go and have some practice? We want you to play today.' As it was my first match I remember exactly what I did. I made 12 and 0, took two wickets, and made two catches in the longfield. It has always seemed to me to be a curious thing that most young players, when they make their appearances in a big match are put in the longfield, where they feel all alone, and are, foolishly enough, no doubt, under the impression that everyone is watching them carefully. I think that they would gain much more confidence if they were placed close to the wicket at first, where they would be far less shy. I know that in my first two or three matches I used to walk backwards for twenty or thirty yards when I had to go to my place in the longfield, for I could not muster up enough courage to face the crowd.[9]

His wishes were to be fulfilled over a century later. The practice has now developed that young players are introduced to fielding in county cricket by being placed close to the bat under the helmet.

His first-class début followed in the next match at Derby on Thursday

29 and Friday 30 May. There were a couple of vacancies to fill because Walter Read and Diver were not able to play. He was a few days short of his nineteenth birthday. Derbyshire were not at their strongest. In their next match, they were to lose to the Australians by an innings and 40 runs and after following on, lost to Surrey in two days by five wickets. Barratt and Horner did the damage, taking seventeen wickets between them.

Batting at no 8, Lohmann made 20 and bowled 3-2-3-0 in the first innings and did not bowl in the second. Eighty-three to win in the last innings seemed something more than a formality at 14-3 with captain John Shuter retired hurt, but although Roller left at 41-4, Maurice Read and Jones took the innings to within nine of the required total and Lohmann came in to score the winning runs. It was useful experience of playing at a higher standard to which he would not take long to adjust.

He was omitted from the team for the next fixture at Trent Bridge which began on his nineteenth birthday, Walter Read and Diver returning. Nottinghamshire won the fixture between the nineteenth century rivals by seven wickets. Lohmann returned the following week for the match against Middlesex at The Oval, scored a few runs, 21 and 5, but failed to take a wicket, as Surrey went down by eight wickets and he found himself back in the Club and Ground side on the following Friday. But he missed no first-class cricket, playing against Gloucestershire on Monday 16 June. Abel was ill, so Surrey were not at full strength. Neither were Gloucestershire, *Cricket* reporting that,

> W G Grace was so lame that he was practically of little use in the field and his bowling was greatly missed.[10]

The visitors were demolished by an innings and 33 runs, mustering 240 and 115 against Surrey's 388. Lohmann made 24 not out at no 8, took 0-10 and 1-17. It was the first of his 1841 first-class wickets and it was an important one – W G Grace caught by Diver in the gully for 30: lame or not, it was a significant and memorable moment for the young professional.

The match was followed by the annual encounter with Cambridge University and on this occasion the emerging all-rounder showed his prowess with the bat, scoring the first of his 29 first-class fifties. Lohmann's obituary in *Wisden* was to suggest that even if he had never bowled a ball, he would still have made an impact on the first-class scene. It is all too easy to forget that he began his county career as an opening batsman and to disregard his contributions in that department of the game. *Cricket* reports,

> A plucky stand by the colt Lohmann and Wood, who put on 95 while together, entirely altered the aspect of the game. Wood's hitting was very clean and Lohmann's 69, though not faultless, was a highly promising display for a youngster.[11]

However, the cliché of cricket being a great leveller – and not only that played at first-class level – was amply demonstrated in the following match against the other university (at least, the only other one recognised in nineteenth century cricket) when the Lohmann contribution was no wickets in either innings and a 'pair' to boot.

So the young Lohmann was beginning to absorb the atmosphere of professional cricket, an atmosphere that further north was being slightly soured. The repercussions of a dispute between seven Nottinghamshire professionals and their committee still lingered on and three players – Barnes, Flowers and Shrewsbury – had staged a mini-strike and declined to play for the Players against the Australians at Sheffield unless their pay were increased beyond the normal £10 per match. The attitude of *Cricket* was perhaps predictable.

> The absence of Barnes, Flowers and Shrewsbury from the eleven which represented the Players against the Australians has evoked much comment, and certainly not of a kind favourable to the three professors. Under any circumstances their action would have been ill advised, but in this particular case, always assuming that the statement that they refused to play for the ordinary pay of the professionals in the match between the Gentlemen and the Players – ten pounds, to wit – to be correct, the course they have taken will be universally recognised as being singularly ill-timed. Cricket is not a source of personal benefit to those who guide the destinies of the leading clubs, and it is altogether unlike business where capital is mostly dependent on paid skill and labour. Cricketers of all kinds have been hitherto united by the common link of good fellowship, and it will be a bad day for the game when the tie between the clubs and those they employ is loosened, as is sure to be the case by any combination such as that of the Nottingham players. Every well-wisher of the sport will regret the attitude they have sought fit to take, and it is to be hoped that some explanation will ease the tension sure to be created.[12]

That of the MCC certainly was:

> The Committee of the Marylebone Club at their meeting on Monday last passed the following resolution: That the Committee of the MCC, having learnt with regret that Barnes and Flowers, the professional cricketers engaged on their staff refused to play for the Players of England v The

> Australian Eleven, at Sheffield on June 30 – one of the representatives – do by this resolution express their strong disapproval of their want of public spirit.[13]

Representatives of the establishment in the nineteenth century were generally more articulate and literate than those on the other side of the master-servant equation and were in a financial position to speak of good fellowship and public spirit while their employees were perhaps more concerned with earning sufficient to keep them in daily bread. The other side of the coin, of which *Cricket* and the MCC were aware, but chose to disregard, was the amounts being paid to the notionally amateur Australians and the excessive 'expenses' paid to the similarly notional English amateurs. It may well have been true that the committees which ran the county clubs did not benefit in personal terms, but a three day 'gate' of 40,000 upwards paying 1/- per head would generate sufficient revenue to enable even doubling the professionals' pay to be lost in the arithmetic.

The action of the Nottinghamshire men would have been part of the conversation of professional dressing rooms, separate from and out of eavesdropping distance of the less Spartan changing quarters of the amateurs, and would have formed part of the cricketing education of young Lohmann.

The standard pay of professionals was to remain £10 per match for a decade and more, though there had been no hesitation in increasing it when the occasion demanded, for instance the first home Test Match against Australia in 1880 when the Surrey committee were anxious to have no drop-outs; and though the nineteen-year-old would have neither the experience to form an opinion, nor the self-confidence to express it, he would later become acutely conscious of his professional worth and be instrumental in bringing to the professional a new respectability and – not insignificantly – more cash.

Omitted from the team for a while after the Oxford University match, Lohmann returned for the encounter with Lancashire at The Oval and in a match which Surrey lost by eight wickets, scored 32 and 17 and had a couple of wickets; then scored 25 but took no wickets in a high-scoring draw in the return match against Gloucestershire at Clifton, but against Kent at The Oval added a few victims to W G Grace and the two Lancastrians. Two economical bowling spells of 8-7-4-2 and 44-29-24-3 almost saw Surrey to victory, Kent finishing well short with only two wickets standing and Lohmann's eight first-class victims now included Grace and England captain and de facto king of Kentish cricket, Lord Harris.

A rain-ruined, low-scoring draw against Yorkshire at The Oval followed, Lohmann's innings of 19 being bracketed by *Cricket* with that of the two Reads, 'amateur' Walter and professional Maurice.

> The wicket had of course suffered from the heavy downpour and the scoring was below the average. Surrey, who won the toss, went in first and they were mainly indebted for their total of 110 to Mr Read, his namesake the professional and the Colt, Lohmann, who contributed 81 of the 100 from the bat.[14]

It was, however, in the next match, the last of the season, against Sussex at The Oval that Lohmann came of age as a bowler, his figures of 19-11-23-4 and 37-21-35-5 presaging things to come and causing *Cricket* to comment that 'Lohmann bowled exceptionally well as his figures will show'. Additionally, his second innings 4 not out may not seem especially significant, but as it was made in the context of Surrey losing six wickets while chasing a victory target of 32, it is evidence of the young professional's ability to keep a clear head under pressure and steady a sometimes unstable ship.

Reminiscing a quarter of a century later, Bobby Abel recognised the significance of the match in the context of Lohmann's early career.

> Our 'curtain' match at the Oval in September with Sussex, was chock-full of incident, and although we only had to get 30 to win in the fourth innings, the game was so fiercely fought that it provided the greatest and closest finish of that season.
>
> W W hit out to the tune of 83 for us, while Lohmann gave a glimpse of the form which made him the greatest bowler Surrey has ever possessed.[15]

In his first first-class season, Lohmann had scored 271 runs at 19.35 and taken 18 wickets at 17.38. He had let no one down and if his performances in his ten matches were less spectacular than those of subsequent years, there was already evidence of an ability to produce the goods when it really mattered. The game is littered with careers of players with half-decent batting and bowling averages who have not had the mental strength to perform when the pressure was really on. Lohmann was the converse of that.

In its end of season review *Cricket* commented:

> A new colt who seems likely to strengthen Surrey's bowling materially was introduced this year in Lohmann. He makes the ball do a great deal, and as he uses his head well, bids fair to be a great help to the county.[16]

Lillywhite's too was cautiously optimistic. Under *The Leading Professionals*:

> LOHMANN G Came out for Surrey last year, and with considerable success; very promising round-arm bowler, with plenty of work, varies his pace and pitch with judgment; ought with pains to be a good bat; fair field.[17]

and, in summarising the season:

> In Lohmann, Surrey has a very promising young cricketer, and his form all round last season was good enough to justify the hope that he will be a very valuable acquisition to the old County. His bowling in the latter matches was very effective, and as he is very fond of the game, and ready to learn, in addition to being a brilliant field, he should not only improve greatly in this department, but also in his batting in which he should also be very useful, having proved himself of no small abilities as a hitter.[18]

Surrey's Annual Report mentioned that,

> Two very promising professionals were introduced into the eleven in Wood and Lohmann, and it is hoped that both will be of permanent value to Surrey.[19]

The forecasts were not inaccurate but, with the benefit of hindsight, erred on the side of caution and underestimated Lohmann's future contribution to his county and the game. Partnered first by Yorkshire-born Beaumont, then Nottinghamshire-born Sharpe and Lockwood and finally, local boy Tom Richardson, he was to bestride the narrow Surrey world like a colossus and spearhead what was – with the possible exception of the 1950s – the greatest period of Surrey history.

1885

NOW ESTABLISHED as a crucial member of the 1st XI, Lohmann was not to be omitted from the team on the grounds of form for a decade. 1885 began with a flourish and some spectacular bowling figures which were to become a feature of Surrey's scorecards for the next eight seasons in each of which he was to take more than 100 first-class wickets – more than 200 in three of them.

He had played in a trial match for Mr W W Read's side against captain Mr J Shuter's side. He retired hurt for 11, but the injury was insufficiently serious to prevent him playing for the Club and Ground side against Broadwater at Godalming where Read made 100 not out and Lohmann 20 in a total of 265. The match was then rained off before the hosts had an opportunity to bat. Selected to play against second-class Essex at The Oval, he demolished the visitors with a phenomenal 39-25-33-7. 'Lohmann's bowling in the second innings was the best in the match' reported *Cricket*[20] and *Wisden* referred to 'the admirable bowling of Lohmann.'[21] Later the same week in the first first-class match of the season on a fast wicket against Hampshire, he had an even more impressive 13.3-9-13-7 and 18-10-16-5.

In the first innings, Hampshire collapsed from 20 for 2 to 23 for 9, recording five 'ducks' in the process, before recovering slightly to be 32 all out. Surrey replied with an impressive 461, captain John Shuter leading the way with 135 and Lohmann, batting at no 5 being run out for 28. The visitors did a little better in their second innings, but not well enough to avoid a defeat by an innings and 280 runs with more than a day to spare.

Again, *Cricket* enthused,

> Lohmann again bowled with extraordinary success for Surrey. In all he was credited with twelve Hampshire wickets at a cost of twenty-nine runs. These are remarkable figures.[22]

Wisden reported,

> ...some curious cricket was witnessed on the opening day. Hampshire were got rid of in an hour for a total of 32, and then Surrey made 404 for the loss of six wickets. The only excuse offered for the Hampshire batsmen was that they had been playing on heavy wickets, and therefore found the going too fast for them.
> Not one of them seemed to be able to offer resistance to Lohmann's bowling... Lohmann at one stage took four wickets in seven balls.[23]

The third day was not, as it would be nowadays, a day off. The Club and Ground side at Richmond was strengthened by Lohmann's presence, and, though his return was a more modest 11-4-32-2, his victims were the opening batsmen. He contributed 25 with the bat as the county side went down by 79 runs.

The 1st XI steamroller, however, moved on, crushing Leicestershire by an innings and 153 runs, then performing a similar demolition job on Middlesex who, in reply to Surrey's 166 were summarily dismissed for 25, their lowest total against Surrey and their second lowest in all first-class cricket, and 77. On this occasion, however, Lohmann with 3-9 and 2-28, played a supporting role to Yorkshire-born John Beaumont, enjoying his first and best season with Surrey, who had 16-12-11-6 and 37-21-37-6. Apart from half-a-dozen overs by Horner and Mr Roller, the pair had bowled unchanged throughout the match.

The Whitsuntide fixture against Nottinghamshire at Trent Bridge, Lohmann's first with Surrey's traditional rivals, ended in a hard fought draw with honours even, bringing to an end Surrey's run of victories by an innings. *Cricket* referred to 'the good play of Lohmann and Mr Roller'.[24] Lohmann and Beaumont again dominated the bowling, taking ten of the fifteen wickets to fall, but were unable on this occasion to bowl their team to victory.

Then it was down the road to Derby for the match which marked the anniversary of his first-class début. The bandwagon began rolling again as he took six more wickets, Beaumont had eight and Barratt chipped in with three to remove the Derbyshire tail in the second innings as Surrey claimed yet another two day victory by an innings and 62 runs.

Twelve months earlier, following his début, Lohmann had been omitted from the side which played at Trent Bridge. By contrast and in recognition of his match winning-contributions, he was selected for his first representative match, the Players of the South against the Gentlemen of the South at The Oval. Again, he was a member of a team which won by an innings (and 20 runs) in under two days. The Professionals' star was William Tester of Sussex who scored one of his two first-class centuries and took a career best 7 for 40. He was to die, aged 33 just four years later. Lohmann did not set the Thames on fire, taking 3-60 in the first innings and 1-19 in the second and was bowled by his Surrey colleague Walter Read for 13. It probably did not concern him much. He had cemented his place in the Surrey side and earned representative honours. He was just twenty years old, celebrating his birthday on the second and what turned out to be the final day of the match.

His head could have been in the clouds; instead, his feet remained firmly on the ground and despite his impending celebrity, he was still more than happy to join in informal games on Clapham Common. Anthony Meredith relates one such instance involving future Surrey captain, Digby Jephson.

> Clapham Common was, of course, a marvellous place for the boys to play casual cricket. Digby always treasured one occasion when he was there as a 14-year-old. 'Three of us were playing cricket on the wilderness of Clapham Common. A young man watched the game for a little and eventually took a hand. He bowled to us and he batted for us and we learnt something. At the end of half an hour he left. We asked his name. "Lohmann," came the reply. We said, "Good morning and thank you.'

> George Lohmann, 20 years of age when Digby met him, went on to be one of England's greatest medium-pace bowlers.[25]

A drawn match against Oxford University at The Parks followed. The students followed on after replying with 282 to Surrey's total of 424 in which Lohmann supported Diver's 143 with a rapid 86 as the scoring rate hit 100 per hour and they 'hit the worn out bowling with the utmost freedom'.[26]

Then to Lord's where, despite the start being delayed until 3pm on the second day, the London rivals managed to complete all four innings on a rain-affected pitch, Surrey's comparatively huge 120, supplemented by 61 in the second innings allowing them to scrape home by 12 runs against Middlesex's 88 and 81. Lohmann and Beaumont shared 16 wickets equally.

The lot of the professional cricketer and the need to take every opportunity to maximise income is indicated by the following announcement which appeared in *Cricket* the same week.

> The SOUTH OF ENGLAND PLAYERS' ELEVEN which defeated the Gentlemen at the Oval, on June 1 and 2, and which includes G G and F Hearne, Abel, Maurice Read, J Hide, Humphreys, Tester, J Jones, Lohmann, Wood and Bowley will be at liberty to play two-day or three-day matches through September against eighteens or twenty-twos. For terms etc apply to G G Hearne, Fern Villa, Brownhill Road, Catford SE. Alec Hearne will also be at liberty to join the team.[27]

The visit of Gloucestershire to The Oval saw Surrey's first defeat of the season, albeit by the narrow margin of two wickets. The home side had batted badly in the second innings and been all out for 91, leaving Gloucestershire 129 to win. At 103 for 2 only one result seemed possible. Then wickets started falling. W G Grace had delayed his appearance until no 7 and when he was caught behind for a duck by Wood off Lohmann, it was 110 for 6 and the pendulum seemed to be swinging in the other direction. However, Gloucestershire rallied. For once, Lohmann was unable to produce a match-winning performance, though his 19-10-32-4 was respectable enough, as was Beaumont's 3-40 and both ensured that the visitors had to fight all the way. Had there been a Man of the Match, it would surely have gone to Gloucestershire's professional, William Woof who, having already taken twelve wickets in the match, kept his head to steer his county home.[28]

Against Essex at Leyton the following week Mr Read enjoyed himself with 214 not out. Back at The Oval there were fixtures against the universities. Both were won easily. Against Cambridge, Lohmann bowled a couple of wides, so rare that it is worth remarking on, and Oxford were beaten by an innings, Lohmann and Beaumont dividing eighteen wickets equally between them, the other two being run out.

> Though Surrey had not its full strength the bowling of Beaumont and Lohmann was so effective that the game was over on the second afternoon.[29]

The county team that was to dominate English cricket over the next decade was beginning to take shape as was amply demonstrated in the match against Sussex at the end of June when they amassed a total of 631. In days of shirt-front pitches and four-day cricket, totals over 600 are not uncommon. In the 1880s they were not unknown, but rare, and to put this total in context, it was at the time the second highest by Surrey (650 had been registered against Hampshire two years previously), the fourth highest in all first-class cricket and the highest by a county in a first-class fixture. Mr Roller had 204, Mr Read 163; ten Surrey batsmen reached double figures. Sussex had no reply, capitulating by an innings and 221 runs.

It was a tribute to the quality of the groundsmanship at The Oval that there was similar big scoring in the Gentlemen v Players match which followed immediately afterwards. *Cricket* commented enthusiastically

> I do not fancy that any ground can claim such a record as was achieved at the Oval last week. In all 2,085 runs were totalled for the loss of 65 wickets, an average of over 32 runs. Surrey and Sussex produced 1,041 for thirty, the Gentlemen and Players 1,044 for thirty-five wickets. For a week of first-class cricket, this has, I should think, never been equalled.[30]

It was then on to Southampton for another demolition job on Hampshire. Surrey won in under two days by an innings and 252 runs, the hosts replying to 390 with a somewhat less convincing 104 and 34. Not for the only time did *Cricket* describe Lohmann's match figures as 'remarkable'. They were 12 for 34 – 18.2-13-18-8 at second change in the first innings, his best figures to date, and 17-10-16-4 bowling through the innings in the second – remarkable, indeed, but by the standards Lohmann was to set over the next seven years, almost the norm.

Then, the following week, along the coast at Hove, Sussex were brushed aside as Surrey topped 500 and won by an innings and 124 runs, Lohmann bagging five in each innings – not 'remarkable' this time but 'very effective'. That match finished on Wednesday 15 July. The following day, Surrey began another three-day match in Liverpool, and that unfortunate juxtaposition of fixtures (ill-planned travelling schedules are not peculiar to the twentieth and twenty-first centuries) was perhaps partly responsible for Lancashire piling up 364 in their first innings. A major contributor was one of George's future international bowling partners, Johnny Briggs, selected for his batting and fielding rather than his bowling at this time. He hit a career-best 186 and with Richard Pilling, added 173 for the tenth wicket, still a Lancashire record. Third day rain came to the assistance of a Surrey team on the brink of almost certain defeat.

Surrey then crossed the Pennines to Bramall Lane. No rain to help now and, despite John Beaumont's nine wickets against his native county, Surrey's batting let them down and they slumped to defeat by 188 runs. They moved on, a short trip down the road from Sheffield to Gravesend. If victory and the occasional defeat by a large margin had characterised the season, that was all to change here as the young Lohmann on this occasion demonstrated his prowess as a batsman.

Against Kent, Beaumont continued the form he had shown against Yorkshire and took the bowling honours with twelve wickets in the match, leaving Surrey a modest 154 to win in the fourth innings. Let *Cricket* take up the story.

> Eight wickets were down for 98 when Beaumont joined Lohmann. There were still wanting 58 to win and the game seemed a certainty for Kent. Though Beaumont escaped the chance of a stumping, Lohmann and he, however, gave no other chance and thirty-four had been[31] added when the former was caught at the wicket. Mr Horner, the last man, came in to Lohmann with 32 runs still required, and soon after his arrival a general appeal for a catch by the wicket keeper was given in his favour. After that the two batsmen continued to put on runs steadily, and there was intense excitement as the scores rose. In consequence of an agreement between the captains it was decided to play the match out and it was twenty-five minutes to eight, before Mr Horner, who might have been run out in scoring it, made the winning hit. Lohmann carried out his bat for 34, a most creditable display of batting under the circumstances. Mr Horner also deserves the highest praise for his judicious play at the crisis. To this pair Surrey owed a well-earned and most exciting victory. In their second innings five batsmen failed to get a run.[32]

This was an innings contrary to Lohmann's usual swashbuckling, fast-scoring style, but one which none the less demonstrated a maturity not always found in one of his years and underlined his ability to adapt to the circumstances, to 'step up to the plate' in the modern idiom and produce the goods when it mattered.

A hard fought draw against Nottinghamshire at The Oval followed. Derbyshire were beaten by an innings and 50 runs, Somerset even more comprehensively by an innings and 301 runs, Lohmann chipping in 30 at no 10 in an all out total of 635. Not required to bowl in the visitors' first innings of 86 all out (once again, Beaumont had five), he bowled more overs than anyone else in the second, finishing with figures of 43.1-20-76-4 to complement Beaumont's 5-86, as Somerset offered a little more resistance, but were still comprehensively beaten.

Lohmann's rich vein of batting form continued in the following match against Kent at The Oval, his second innings 92 not out in a drawn match being his highest to date.

Less than a month after their narrow win at Gravesend, Surrey had a similar one wicket victory over Lancashire at The Oval, although on this occasion, Lohmann had been part of a late innings collapse which had resulted in Beaumont having to hold up an end at no 11 while Diver (Mr Diver at this stage – he was to downgrade socially by turning professional the following season) knocked off the runs.

Towards the end of the season, neither Surrey nor Lohmann enjoyed quite the same success as they had earlier. They lost again to Gloucestershire in Cheltenham Week and, although they then beat Somerset by an innings and five runs in two days, later the same week they went down to Yorkshire by three wickets. The Lohmann 'decline', however, was only relative. In his last two first-class matches of the season, he had match figures of 8-57 and 8-124.

In his first full season in first-class cricket he had taken 142 wickets at 14.34 in 1267.1 four-ball overs, as well as scoring 571 runs at 17.84. If the test of an all-rounder is to keep the batting average above the bowling average, he had certainly done that and throughout his career was to continue to do so in most seasons, both at home and overseas. On the bowling front the extent of his and Beaumont's contribution and the transformation of Surrey's attack from the previous year was commented on in the following year's *Wisden*.

> Only a comparatively small part of the bowling fell to those who bore the bulk of it in 1884. In that year Barratt and Mr Horner took 245 of 404 wickets credited to the bowlers, but in 1885, they only obtained 60 between them, Mr Horner bowling in 17 matches and Barratt in 10. Their places as the two principal bowlers were taken by Lohmann and Beaumont, the latter being a new hand in the eleven, and a Yorkshireman by birth but qualified to play for Surrey by residence. Out of 462 wickets which fell to the bowlers, Lohmann and Beaumont took the large proportion of 275. Lohmann who was tried a little in the previous year with moderate success took 152 at the comparatively small cost of 13-85 runs per wicket.[33]

They had certainly contributed to a successful season for their adopted county – neither having a birth qualification to play for Surrey – as the record of twelve wins from 20 matches contributing to the Champion County title would demonstrate. It was not enough to win it, but better than ever before. Until late July, they had suffered but one defeat and over the season the difference in the strength of Surrey and the opposition of 9639 runs for 368 wickets against 7936 for 491 was described by the Almanack as 'extraordinary'. Four times they had topped 400, going on beyond 500 once and 600 twice.

On 27 August the impact Lohmann had had on the game in his first full first-class season was duly acknowledged with a profile in *Cricket* which, having outlined his achievements to date, opined, perhaps a little over-cautiously in an age given to hyperbole rather than understatement, that 'with care Lohmann ought to make a first-class cricketer'. The feature went on,

> He bowls fast round with a high delivery, and when the wicket helps him he gets a lot of work from the off. He is not afraid of pitching the ball up as many bowlers are, and varies his pitch and pace with judgment, his slow ball being particularly dangerous. He is likely, too, to train on into a good batsman. He plays the ball hard and can hit freely, although a little more discretion in his hitting, which will come with experience, will improve his play materially. Lohmann is also a capital field anywhere.

On 6 August his bowling partner, John Beaumont, had been similarly profiled. Lohmann's senior by more than a decade, he contributed little to Surrey's subsequent successes and finally retired from the first-class game in 1890. But, constant throughout cricket history, great bowlers have generally operated in pairs, ensuring no escape at the 'other' end and in that season of 1885, by operating in tandem with Lohmann, Beaumont had contributed perhaps more than he realised to the future success of Surrey – and England.

Abel summarised the season in the following terms

> The Surrey Team of 1885 had in it the makings of a Champion side, and but for a narrow defeat by Gloucestershire at the Oval by 2 wickets followed by a severe thrashing by Yorkshire could have taken first place among the counties instead of having to wait two more seasons for that honour. In batting we were stronger than ever, while our attack presented an entirely new face with Lohmann, J T Beaumont and T Bowley as bowlers. Lohmann blossomed out as a great bowler, and Beaumont (a Yorkshireman) and Bowley (like Arthur Mold, a Northamptonshire player) stepped into the county at the precise moment when the powers of Barratt, Mr Horner and Jones were on the wane. Never was a side more fortunate than Surrey in 1885 in having three great bowlers to step into the shoes of those of previous seasons.[34]

1 *Cricket* 8 May 1884
2 Ib
3 Ib
4 Ib
5 Ib
6 Surrey CCC Yearbook 1884 p 35
7 15 May 1884
8 Surrey CCC Yearbook 1884 p 39
9 Bettesworth
10 *Cricket* 19 June 1884
11 26 June 1884
12 3 July 1884
13 10 July 1884
14 11 September 1884
15 Abel *Life and Reminiscences* p 43
16 25 September 1884
17 p 243
18 1885 p 243
19 24 April 1885
20 14 May 1885
21 1886 p 199
22 21 May 1885
23 1886 p 200
24 28 May 1885
25 Meredith *The Demon and the Lobster* pp14-15
26 *Wisden* 1886 p 66
27 *Cricket* 11 June 1885
28 *Cricket* 18 June 1885
29 *Lillywhite's* 1886 p 92
30 *Cricket* 9 July 1885
31 actually 56
32 *Cricket* 30 July 1885
33 p 198. The figures are as given by Wisden at the time and here and elsewhere do not coincide with those as revised by the Association of Cricket Statisticians and Historians, partly because the division between first-class and other cricket was less clearly defined than it has subsequently become. Further, averages were at this time expressed as an integer and 'number over' rather than a decimal fraction. The bowling average of 13.85 (miscalculated, in any case, 2051/152 being 13.75) would in decimal notation be 13.49
34 Abel op cit p 44

CHAPTER 3

ENGLAND CRICKETER (1886)

The Coming Man
Albert Craig

Promise Fulfilled

A LATE Easter saw the start of what for Lohmann was to be a significant season which twelve months later *Wisden* summed up as follows:

> Lohmann more than bore out the promise given by him in 1885 and his right to a place in the England Eleven in the three representative matches against Australia was scarcely questioned.[1]

Gloucestershire were comfortably beaten by five wickets, Lohmann and Beaumont's first innings 5-57 and 4-64 respectively being too much for W G and his colleagues. The match was significant for producing the first of Bobby Abel's 74 first-class centuries.

Lohmann then played for Twelve of Surrey against Eighteen Colts,[2] but he was soon climbing a steep ladder to the pinnacle of the game and international honours. The way to Test cricket was paved by his performance for Surrey in the match against the Australians on 20, 21 and 22 May. It was the first of numerous encounters with what were at the time England's only serious international rivals. There were seven that year – two for Surrey, three for England, one for the Players and one for the South of England. In later seasons, 1888 and 1890, there would be ten and a dozen, as various privately raised sides played full first-class fixtures against the tourists.

The touring side may have lacked the strength of its predecessors of 1880, 1882 and 1884 and the sidelining of Spofforth because of illness was to the county's advantage, but the match was nevertheless a significant milestone in the history of the game, being the first time the

Australians had been beaten by a county side. Lohmann's contribution was paramount. Having compelled the Australians to follow on, Surrey struggled in the fourth innings, but eventually won by three wickets. The Australians and the amateurs of Surrey were presented to the Prince of Wales, whose first visit it was to the ground of which he was landlord, and his eldest son, Albert Victor. The latter was to die six years later and the succession passed to his younger brother who subsequently became George V. The professionals were not so presented, but were to demonstrate their cricketing skills on the field of play rather than their social skills off it.

> ...the honours were fairly carried off by Lohmann who was in excellent form throughout. Going in with the sixth wicket down at 110, he played with great confidence and carried out his bat, scoring 46 of 61 while he was in...
> Lohmann too was as successful with the ball as he had been with the bat and it was mainly due to him that the Australians had to follow on in a minority of 89 runs. Lohmann was credited with six wickets at a cost of 33 runs.

He took them with no assistance from the field, five bowled and one LBW. The Australians did rather better in the second innings, but a thunderstorm on the third morning produced conditions in which Lohmann would rather have bowled than batted and made the eventual target of 84 more than notional.

> Lohmann came in with sixteen still wanting to win and four wickets to fall, and great credit is due to him to the judgment he showed at the crisis. Wood was out at 78, but Lohmann soon made the game a tie and Jones, running out to Evans with a boundary hit, left the County in possession of a well-earned victory with three wickets to spare.
> It was Lohmann's match in every way. In addition to his great success with the ball, he made 51 runs without being once out, and he has undoubtedly added materially to his reputation by the excellent all-round cricket he showed on the occasion of his first meeting with an Australian team.[3]

> The principal feature of the game was the splendid all-round play of Lohmann.[4]

Wisden drew a comparison between events on and off the pitch

> The [Australian] team had the honour of being presented to the Prince, as did the leading officials of the Surrey Club and the amateurs of the side. The honours however distinctly rested with the young professional George Lohmann...

The contrast was one which was doubtless not lost on the impressionable twenty-year-old. He was beginning to experience what Lincoln Allison has called 'a feudal symbiosis on and off the field'.

Growing in confidence, the young professional now began to produce a number of match-winning bowling performances which put him in the frame for international honours. They included match figures of 9-69 against Essex (6-29 in the second innings), 10-74 against Middlesex (8-43 in the first innings), 9-51 of 16 to fall against Oxford University, 13-98 against Lancashire on a batsman-friendly surface at The Oval. Innings figures of 6-14 and 6-69 against Essex and Notts respectively failed to result in his being selected for the Players against the Australians at Trent Bridge, but he continued to shine against Middlesex. Second innings figures of 7-86 told their own story and together with an outstanding all-round performance in the following match against Cambridge University at The Oval secured his selection for the first Test Match at Old Trafford.

Beaumont and Bowley had provided valuable support to Lohmann all season and at times took the lead, bowling out Cambridge University for 85, leaving George to contribute 86 with the bat in a partnership of 162 with W W Read, still the seventh wicket record for Surrey against Cambridge University. Despite that and 27 overs in the first innings, he was still fresh enough, however, to play a major role in finishing the match, bowling five and catching two at slip as Surrey won by an innings and 59 runs. 'Capital cricket' was *Wisden*'s comment on Lohmann's batting, adding that he 'bowled very effectively when Cambridge went in a second time'.

Surrey were 'on a roll' and put together a sequence of results that led to 15 wins in their 20 first-class matches that season.

Cricket's reports became inevitably repetitive.

> Lohmann's bowling proved very effective.
> Lohmann's bowling was the most noteworthy feature of the Surrey side
> The victory of Surrey was in a very great measure due to the bowling of Lohmann.[5]

However, Surrey's fixture against Lancashire at Aigburth, was perhaps not the best preparation for a Test début, as the visitors suffered one of their four first-class defeats that season and a heavy one at that – by an innings and 27 runs. Lohmann had 3-94 in 42 overs, falling twice to the amateur and Cambridge blue, A G Steel, who bowled almost a hundred overs in the match for 4-101 and 5-97. In days of central contracts, neither would have featured in the match.

First Test Match

LOHMANN'S PERFORMANCES in his early Test matches were similar to those in his first matches with Surrey in that he took a while to make an impact with the ball but made significant contributions with the bat and in the field. At Old Trafford he opened the bowling with Edmund Peate of Yorkshire, but took only one wicket in the match, that of Thomas Garratt, caught behind the wicket by Richard Pilling. However, he did take three catches and, coming to the wicket at 160 for 7, still 45 behind Australia's first innings total, produced a mature innings of 32 which saw England to an invaluable first innings lead of 18 paving the way for local man Richard Barlow to demolish Australia with 7-44 in 52 overs and leave England with a modest target of 106. They achieved it with four wickets to spare and without requiring Lohmann's services.

Wisden enthused about his batting, which complemented Barlow's more defensive style,

> Then, when it seemed most probable that the Australians would lead on the first innings, Lohmann and Barlow made an invaluable stand, and quite altered the aspect of affairs. When he scored only a single, however, Lohmann was badly missed from an easy chance by Palmer at long-on, and for this mistake the Australians had to pay very dearly. Lohmann hit with great verve and judgment while Barlow played his usual sound and steady game.[6]

Lohmann returned to the capital for his first appearances in the Gentlemen v Players matches, played back-to-back at Lord's and The Oval. He had played the previous year in the Gentlemen of the South v Players of the South match, but the 1886 fixtures were his first experience of the encounter which reflected the class divisions of Victorian England and continued to do so until the abolition of the amateur–professional divide almost eighty years later. He acquitted himself well enough in a five-wicket win and a draw taking seven wickets in each match including W G Grace and A N Hornby in the first and E M Grace and, a particularly satisfying scoreline, his county colleague W W Read, c Abel b Lohmann 0.

Second Test Match

THE SECOND Test at Lord's was another success for England, but something of a non-event for Lohmann. Australia failed to respond to England's 353 and lost by an innings and 106 runs. Arthur Shrewsbury recorded the highest individual innings for England (164) in 23 Test matches to date (though W G Grace was to pass it in the next Test with 170), but George, demoted to no 11 despite his innings at Old Trafford, recorded 7 not out, bowled only seven overs in the first innings, 21 in the match and ended wicketless as Lancashire's Johnny Briggs turned out to be the match winner with 5-29 and 6-45.

On 15 July, the Surrey Committee granted Lohmann leave of absence. No reason is given and he does not appear to have missed any matches. It may have been to play in two Test matches and the Gentlemen v Players matches at Lord's and The Oval which occupied the first half of July.

His hour was not yet come (at least at Test level) but was not far away and the matches between the second and third Tests brought more success with both bat and ball. At Beckenham against Kent, batting at no 7, he recorded the first of his three first-class centuries.

> The two Reads made the first stand, and 125 runs, the result of admirable cricket, were added while they were together. Even this performance, though, was beaten for the sixth wicket by Mr Roller and Lohmann. The professional hit with great determination, and he was credited with 107 (the first innings of three figures he has made) of the 144 runs. [7]

Wisden summarised,

> After [Walter Read's] dismissal Lohmann went in and actually made 80 runs out of 103 before the call of time. He made some fluky strokes, it is true, but his hitting was of wonderful power.
> On the second morning Lohmann increased his score to 107 – the first hundred he has ever made in his life... Lohmann hitting fifteen 4's, two 3's, ten 2's and twenty-one singles.[8]

He followed up with seven wickets as Kent narrowly avoided an innings defeat, then for good measure opened the second innings with his friend, Maurice Read, to knock off the handful of runs required to win the match. From no 11 via no 7 to opening bat in three innings in two matches is a meteoric rise, indicating that, Surrey, if not England, were alive to Lohmann's capabilities as an all-rounder.

For the next match it was back to The Oval for a second contest between the tenants and the Australians and a second defeat, this time far heavier, for the beleaguered tourists.

Bowley destroyed the visitors in the first innings with 7-64 and the batsmen rubbed it in, racking up a massive 501 – Maurice Read 186, Abel, at the crease on all three days of the match 144, Walter Read 80 and

Lohmann in his no 7 slot, 31 not out. Bowley's first innings performance was supplemented by Lohmann's 6-58 in the second as the Australians went down by a decisive margin. Spofforth finished with 1-102, figures comparing none too favourably with those of the Surrey professionals. Surrey's total and the margin of an innings and 209 runs were the highest scores and heaviest defeat suffered by an Australian team in England

The Committee responded appropriately to the achievement.

> It was decided that a framed photograph of the eleven which beat the Australians at the Oval on July 31 be given to each of the three amateurs who played, an unframed to each of the professionals. It was decided that £5 each be given to Abel, Read, Lohmann and Bowley, £2 each to Jones, Diver, Beaumont and Wood.[9]

Whether it was symbolised in a royal handshake or a photograph frame, the contrast between the treatment of amateurs and professionals was stark. It was the rich man in his castle and the poor man at his gate, social distinctions pre-ordained by a deity who presided over an empire on which the sun would never set. Horizontal division might have been acceptable, but it was vertical. It was upper and lower, superior and inferior and, though the upper salved their consciences with charitable works and benevolent despotism, there was little significant inter-class movement. Even after the Second World War amateurs travelling to Test matches were entitled to a first-class railway fare, professionals to a third-class one.

The press, both at home and overseas, were alive to the inequities and iniquities.

> If a man be paid for batting or bowling he can surely retain his front name, and surely he can walk out of the same door as another man when they have to play on the same field. There are no distinctions in Australia between the cricketers. They are either all amateurs or all professionals whichever you like. Is not such a system possible in the mother country? Nay, is it not better than ours for its honesty?[10]

It would take the effects of the 1870 Education Act and the gradual erosion of the class system in the following century to make a difference, but there were movements for change, in British and European society and on a smaller scale in cricket and George Lohmann was to be a part of that.

Meanwhile, he continued to do an enormous amount of bowling – 84.2-52-73-4 in a seven wicket defeat by Nottinghamshire, then 30-8-55-1 and 41.2-24-50-5 in an innings defeat of Derbyshire – albeit four ball overs, but still enough to make a modern day medium pacer resting between Test matches blench at the thought. It played him into form for his first significant Test match performance.

Earlier in the season, *Cricket* had commented on Lohmann's batting,

> LOHMANN's batting figures against the Australians are so curious that I think they deserve the distinction of a paragraph to themselves. This is the young cricketer's record so far in Australian matches
>
> | | First Inns | Second Inns | Total |
> |---|---|---|---|
> | May 20 Oval Surrey v Australians | 43 (no) | 8 (no) | 51 |
> | July 5 Manchester England v Australians | 32 (b) | | 32 |
> | 19 Lord's England v Australians | 7 (no) | | 7 |
> | 29 Oval Surrey v Australians | 31 (no) | | 31 |
>
> In five innings, it will be seen, he has scored 121 for only once out, average 121.[11]

The Third Test was to bring that average down to 64, but it was still a respectable performance for a 'number 11'.

Third Test Match

TWO WEEKS after their encounter with Surrey, the Australians returned to The Oval, this time for the third and final Test and their third and final defeat – as in the Lord's Test and as against Surrey, by an innings.

It was in this match on his home ground that Lohmann first made an impact as a Test match bowler. One lower order wicket in 57 overs in two matches had not set the international scene alight, but now he was to demolish Australia almost single-handedly with figures of 30.2-17-36-7 as the tourists collapsed to 68 all out against England's formidable 434. Following on, they did slightly better, mustering 149. Lohmann had 5-68 in 37 overs, bowling his team to a victory by an innings and 217 runs, their largest so far, in 24 Test matches. On only three occasions subsequently have England beaten their oldest adversaries by a larger margin.

W G Grace made 170, at the time the highest individual score in Test cricket, and shared a first-wicket partnership of the same number of runs with William Scotton of Nottinghamshire. Renowned for his defensive technique, this was one of two occasions on which the latter batted for more than an hour without adding to his score. He contributed 34 to what was then the highest opening partnership in matches between the two countries. It provided the foundation for Grace to continue, for Shrewsbury's 44 and Walter Read's 94.

Johnny Briggs contributed 53 at no 9 and then provided the main support in Lohmann's demolition job. The pair bowled throughout the first innings and more than two-thirds of the overs in the second. He had six wickets for 58. This was the beginning of a combination that was to win England a number of Test matches over the next decade. They were later to be joined by Yorkshire's Bobby Peel and the two left-arm spinners were to prove the ideal foil to Lohmann's medium pace, the trio spearheading England's attack. In practice, however, there was probably less difference between the two styles of bowling than would be assumed today. In a contemporary appreciation, Briggs is described as 'fast, round-arm, left, with a slight break from leg'.[12]

Briggs was Lohmann's senior by three years and his career followed a similar pattern in that he began his first-class cricket as a batsman and outstanding fielder and his bowling was later to eclipse his batting. He was to die all too young, just a few weeks after Lohmann, in January 1902. He never recovered fully from what is now known to be epilepsy, suffered a serious fit during the Headingley Test match in 1899 and though he made a comeback with Lancashire in 1900, he had another breakdown and was to die in the Cheadle Lunatic Asylum.

Cricket summarised:

> When the Australians went in to bat the wicket was drying and altogether in favour of the bowlers, Lohmann and Briggs took full advantage too of their opportunities, and in a little over an hour the innings was over for the small total of 68. Lohmann, helped by the ground, got a lot of work on the ball and his figures were remarkable. This is the most decisive victory ever recorded over an Australian team in this country.[13]

Wisden, with more time to reflect, concluded:

> ...the terror had to a large extent gone – the encounter between England and Australia was not the unique and nervous thing it was in 1880, or the battle of the giants of 1882. We were far more familiar with what the Australians could do with the bat and with the ball. Moreover – and this is a very important factor in the case – our own professional batting and bowling had greatly improved since the last visit, and the Australians were meeting with men who bowled more after their own fashion, and who batted with a determination and fertility of resource which at the most they could only hope to equal.[14]

The margin of victory exceeded that in the Surrey match a couple of weeks earlier by eight runs. Lohmann had played a decisive part in both. The morale of the tourists was at a low ebb.

Lohmann returned to county cricket and a victory against Kent, again with some assistance from the pitch.

> The wicket was drying fast as Kent began to bat, and Lohmann's bowling proved so effective that F & G Hearne and Mr Patterson were all out to him without a run...
> Lohmann, Jones and Beaumont all bowled well at the finish.[15]

Following his outstanding performance in The Oval Test match, Lohmann's services were now in demand. Lord Londesborough had asked if he could be released to play in the Scarborough Festival match against the Australians. The Surrey Committee 'could not see their way to spare Lohmann from the Hampshire match.'[16] In the event he did not play in either, but at a time when modern-day international bowlers would be putting their feet up, he concluded his season for Surrey with figures of 55-33-39-5 against Kent, 50-20-65-5 against Gloucestershire, then played no fewer than three representative matches against the tourists, for the South of England at Gravesend, the Players at Bradford and the South of England again at Hove, turning in figures of 49-21-84-4, 55-20-111-2, 45-25-64-1 and 52-27-66-4. A week after the end of the last match, he was on his way to Australia.

There was no County Championship in anything like its present form at the time, but a 'Champion County' by popular acclaim of the press and general agreement among the participants. In 1886, as had been the case in most previous seasons, the honours had gone to Nottinghamshire. Surrey had not featured since 1864. It was all to change.

With perhaps more than a slight Surrey bias, Abel summarised the season as follows.

> Surrey were acclaimed on all hands as the finest County side in 1886, although by a paper reckoning we only took second place in the Championship. Notts went through their programme of 16 matches undefeated, winning 7 and drawing 9. We won 12 out of 16 games, losing 3 and drawing one.[17]

His view had some validity. Under most systems, twelve wins and a draw would have gained more points than seven wins and nine draws.

In first-class cricket, in 1715 overs, 809 of which were maidens, Lohmann had taken 160 wickets at a cost of just over 15 each. On fifteen occasions, he had taken five in an innings and on three, ten in a match. On top of that, he had scored 728 runs at 23.48 and taken 32 catches. He had also played some non-first class matches and there were to be seasons in which the workload was heavier.

1 1887 p 126
2 Surrey CCC Yearbook 1886 p 36
3 *Cricket* 27 May 1886
4 *Athletic Record* 25 May 1886
5 3 & 10 June 1886
6 *Wisden* 1887 p 29
7 *Cricket* 29 July 1886
8 1887 p 188
9 *Cricket* 10 August 1886
10 *Diamond Fields Advertiser* 19 May 1894
11 5 August 1886
12 *Sporting Snatches for 1890. Portraits and Biographies of Sporting and Dramatic celebrities.*
13 19 August 1886
14 1887 p 4
15 *Cricket* 26 August 1886
16 Surrey CCC minutes 20 August 1886
17 Abel *op cit* p 50

CHAPTER 4

TO AUSTRALIA WITH SHAW AND SHREWSBURY (1886-87)

I love a sunburnt country,
A land of sweeping plains,
Of ragged mountain ranges,
Of droughts and flooding rains
Dorothea McKeller

Australian Tours: The Context

FOR MORE than twenty years, tours to and from Australia had been a significant part of the professional cricket scene, but until 1903/04 when MCC, having established the Board of Control for 'Test' Matches at Home in 1898, then took over the responsibility of selecting teams for overseas tours, these were privately arranged affairs. As early as 1861/62, H H Stephenson had led a team composed largely of Surrey players to the southern hemisphere. His nephew, Maurice Read, was later to tour Australia on four occasions, the last three with Lohmann. After the 1861/62 tour, Charles Lawrence settled in Australia and in 1868 brought a team of Aboriginal players to England. 1876 saw the first white Australian team in England and the following winter, James Lillywhite's touring side met a combined Melbourne and Sydney XI on equal terms – Eleven v Eleven – rather than against odds, a fixture subsequently regarded as the inaugural Test Match. It was not, however, until 1880 that a similar fixture was arranged in England. Two years later, Australia had their first victory against a full-strength England team on English soil. A famous mock obituary appeared in the *Sporting Times* and the Ashes were born.

These tours, however, were unashamed commercial ventures, the main objective being not to regain or retain the Ashes, but to maximise the profits for the organisers. Five Test matches had been played on the

1884/85 tour, but in 1886/87, Lohmann's first venture overseas, there were only two, both in Sydney, against 'Combined Australia' the time which could have been used for similar matches in Melbourne being employed for three fixtures against the Melbourne Cricket Club's Australian Eleven, less attractive than they might have been on account of that team's poor performance against England the previous summer. In addition to those there were three matches against New South Wales, two against Victoria and an end-of-term Smokers v Non-Smokers, as well as numerous up-country non-first-class matches against Fifteens, Eighteens, Twenties and Twenty-Twos in between.

The matches provided a winter earnings opportunity for professional cricketers who would otherwise be compelled to look for employment outside the game to supplement their summer match fees. But it was not only the professionals who sought pecuniary advantage in such enterprises. The *soi-disant* amateurs were in on the act too. To distinguish between amateurs and professional by saying the latter were paid and the former were not is naïve and over-simplistic. Both were paid, but the professionals called their income 'wages' and the amateurs 'expenses' and in many cases, particularly those of W G Grace and W W Read, expenses were several times greater than their playing colleagues' wages. Cricketers were paid on the criterion of how good they were. Whether they played as amateurs or professionals reflected their social status and the class divisions of Victorian England. The convict colonies of Australia were different, albeit with an artificial class structure imposed by state governors and other dignitaries sent from the 'mother country'.

The Australian press were alive to the hypocrisy of the amateur/professional divide and though W G Grace had not toured Australia since 1873/74 and would not do so again until 1891/92, the anomaly of his position was keenly perceived.

> The expenses incurred by the runners of the amateurs will be in excess of those of the professionals, while the quality of the cricket will be superior among the latter. Take W G Grace's little fee; if it is anything approaching his last demand for £1500, the MCC had better transfer their affections to the professional players, four of whom could be retained for the same fee. Then again they are compelled to enlist in the services of four professional bowlers because the amateurs are somewhat deficient in that department of the game.[1]

The Journey

A WINTER tour to Australia in the nineteenth century was not a question of sitting on a jumbo jet for twenty-odd hours with a brief stopover somewhere in the far east, then being whisked between state capitals by efficient internal air services, but rather a sea journey in often none too pleasant conditions of about six weeks, travelling by coastal ferry or overland – often overnight – for four or five months of cricket. Tourists could expect to be away from home for eight or nine months, leaving immediately after the end of an English season and not returning until the following one was into its third or fourth week.

The 1886/87 tour of Australia was organised by Alfred Shaw and Arthur Shrewsbury of Nottinghamshire and James Lillywhite of Sussex. Nottinghamshire fielded an almost entirely professional side and Surrey had only just begun to challenge them for supremacy on the county circuit. Shrewsbury was to captain the side. Lohmann was to say later that he regarded him as the best batsman in England, perhaps in the world, but, preferring a bit of excitement to the concept of 'batting time', he would not cross the street to see him play.[2] Shaw and Lillywhite played no first-class cricket on the tour. As a result of Lohmann's performances for both Surrey and England in the summer of 1886, he was virtually an automatic choice and was one of the party which left Plymouth on the *S S Cuzco* on 18 September.

Regular reports were filed in the columns of the *Sporting Times*, some by 'a member of the team'. Some of Arthur Shrewsbury's correspondence has survived and although Lohmann is not mentioned in it, he would inevitably have suffered with the rest of the party seasickness in the Bay of Biscay, quarantine in the Mediterranean, the excessive heat of the Gulf and the general boredom of the voyage, alleviated to an extent by the fancy dress parties, sing-songs and minstrel entertainment that were an integral part of long sea voyages in the nineteenth century and beyond. In a letter to his sister, dated 24 September from the 'Mediterranean Ocean', Shrewsbury writes,

> We have been favoured with pretty fair weather from the time we left Plymouth, although at the present time and in fact for the three previous days, we have had glorious weather with a very calm sea. As was to be expected several of our team was very unwell for two or three days at first. Among the very worst by a long way being Gunn, although Barlow, Lillywhite, Briggs, Bates, Read and myself have been far from well and consequently have been absent from the dinner table on more than one occasion. Gunn talked about leaving the ship at Naples, as he said he could not stand the journey, but of course now that he is all right he don't think anything of the kind. It was a transformation scene, seeing him being led about one day and the following day dancing, singing and romping about the deck, having forgotten about being ill.

Sea-sickness behind them, the next health issue was the avoidance of cholera. From Port Said, Shrewsbury wrote to 'L' on 29 September,

> We are now in Quarantine on account of our hitching at Naples where cholera prevailes [sic]. We have not the slightest illness on board, and it is very strange to see the Yellow Flag flying at the mast head to denote that no one is allowed to board us.

Meanwhile, 600–800 tons of coal had been taken on board, as well as 450 tons of dried fruit for the 'Colonials Christmas Plum Puddings' and other 'neccessaries' for Christmas festivities, such as Maltese lace, cigars, cigarettes and Turkish Delights. However, the boredom of the routine of life at sea is never far from the surface of the correspondence.

> Bath every morning at eleven, with a little gentle exercise afterwards. Board ship life is not very pleasant, you have a great deal to [sic] much spare time on your hands you don't know what to do with.

The heat as the vessel moved further south could not have helped and was too much even for the crew. From the Red Sea on 6 October where his cabin temperature was 96° F and the sun temperature 160° F he wrote,

> The Chief Steward and many of his men could not stand the excessive heat and consequently could not attend to their duties… For two days and nights it has been a continual Turkish bath, persperation [sic] coming out from every pore in your body and under clothing being always wet through.
>
> Their [sic] has been two deaths, a child yesterday and an old woman of over eighty this morning, both of which have been duly consigned to the deep.

From Aden to Adelaide was another 6135 miles and took around 22 days. Head winds for eight or nine days, however, delayed the arrival. Thoughts were beginning to turn towards the cricket and the preparation for it.

> Oct 24th Sunday afternoon
>
> Cannot say at present whether we stop to play at Adelaide, but if so am certain have to go direct from board to ground, as the match is sure to commence on Saturday the 30th. We have had plenty of cricket on Board, but this is not the same as playing on turf.

They were not to arrive in Adelaide until the evening of Friday 29 October, so late that the planned formal welcome was abandoned. They were, however, practising by 10 am the following day in preparation for a fixture against Fifteen of South Australia.

The Cricket

AT THE beginning of the 1886/87 season, just four years after the Ashes triumph at The Oval, Australian cricket was at a low ebb. The 3-0 defeat in England in the previous northern hemisphere summer was keenly felt in the colonies and J C Davis, writing as 'Not Out' in the *Sydney Referee,* was not alone in finding no kindly light amid the encircling gloom.

> Surrey succeeded in beating the Australians in both the matches which took place; and this is the first time that the latter have been beaten twice by a county eleven. Many explanations of these disasters have been offered, but the truth has to be acknowledged that the team has proved itself distinctly inferior to any yet sent to England. Neither batting nor bowling is at all up to the mark and the injury which Spofforth sustained early in the season made the bowling weaker than ever.[3]

Comments in the *Australasian* and other Australian newspapers were not dissimilar.

Conversely, *Cricket* had been optimistic about English prospects.

> The twelve who will form the playing strength are a strong combination and are sure to give a good account of themselves. Everyone will wish them a pleasant as well as successful trip.[4]

Now, however, Lohmann had to use his cricketing brain to learn how to adjust his bowling to the more batsmen-friendly pitches. He commented,

> When there was no rain they were so good that it was impossible to get any work on the ball and so all one could do was to vary the pace and the positions of the field. Of course, there is much in knowing a batsman's strokes.[5]

In his first match in Australia, Lohmann was clean bowled for 0. He bowled well, but Barlow was the chief wicket-taker. However, it was early days yet. The team went on to Melbourne for the first first-class match against Victoria starting the following Wednesday, 6 November. The party travelled overland the whole way, the first English touring party to have been able to do so. Australian railway services were improving.

> This is the first time any English cricketers have been able to travel overland from the capital of South Australia to Melbourne, and after January 1st 1887, trains will run through with sleeping cars attached, in about eighteen hours, while before many months have passed, there will be an unbroken railway service from Adelaide to Brisbane, via Melbourne and Sydney.[6]

Lohmann dominated the Victoria fixture from the first ball when Lewis was caught behind the wicket. His opening colleague, Trinnick made two before Lohmann removed his leg bail. The openers were back in the pavilion before double figures were on the board. The feature of the game said *Wisden*[7] was Lohmann's bowling. His first innings figures were 86.1-34-115-6 and in the second he had 62-24-80-8. He had arrived. The match was drawn. But is there any recent example of a bowler of any kind bowling the equivalent of almost one hundred six ball overs on the first first-class match of an overseas tour?

Twenty-first century physiotherapists and fitness advisers would have had something to say about 'burn-out'. They might have been half-a-dozen years or so early, but they would not have been wrong.

The Melbourne Club had been responsible for the Australian team which had performed less well than its predecessors on the 1886 tour of England and Victorian cricket was suffering from a massive inferiority complex. Then, as now, Victoria was a sports-loving state, but while Australian Rules Football was drawing large crowds (37,000 is mentioned for matches for the premiership between 'football mad' Ballarat and South Melbourne),[8] cricket was not and the colonials were seeking 'new blood'.

With rare exceptions, sporting icons have but short reigns, and Spofforth, hero of the seventies and early eighties, was being replaced as a rôle model by a twenty-one-year-old Englishman. Following the Victoria match, he demolished Eighteen of Parramatta. In a low-scoring game, the locals responded to the Englishmen's 67 and 78 with 73 and 49. The press referred to 'awful slaughter', as eight wickets fell for seventeen runs, one run out and seven to Lohmann. He had already taken 8-34 in the first innings, but surpassed even that in the second.

> Lohmann was the best of the match, taking twelve wickets for 21 runs in the second innings of the Eighteen. His name is indeed already famed throughout Australia, the boys shouting "Now then, one from Lohmann!" in the same style that Spofforth was lionised a little time ago. Public idols in any sport here are soon made, and as soon lost.[9]

As on the boat, Australia also had its discomforts. From the Oxford Hotel in Sydney, Shrewsbury wrote to his sister on November 17,

> ...there are thousands of Flies out here, which settle on your face and hands and other parts of your body and wont be driven of

and from the same venue a month later,

> The weather here is extremely hot and it is impossible to walk around during the daytime without being in a profuse persperation. We have been playing some matches upcountry and to put it mildly was literally eaten by flies.
> Australians seem to feel greatly the terrible thrashing their champions recently received in England, and are eager to see some good new men come to the front. No one here speaks of the team who have represented them at home except to reproach them for their want of success, and any new form by new men is greeted by them with the greatest of pleasure.[10]

But if interest in cricket was waning in Victoria, there was no similar trend in New South Wales. The fact that the colony beat the tourists twice in three matches and some of the local gamblers consequently made a killing certainly helped, but there did seem to be an interest in the game for its own sake which extended from the betting fraternity through large numbers of ladies to the Governor and his wife.

> Lord and Lady Carrington were again present and watched the game till its close with keen interest. Upwards of 14000 people were on the ground, the Grand Stand being filled principally by ladies. The crowd was a most orderly one, and the roar of satisfaction which followed the winning hit was a thing long to be remembered. The result of the match was the biggest surprise over cricket for a long time. 5 to 1 was always on offer and in many cases 10 to 1 was laid on the losers. Even money, too, was offered that they won in an innings. Still I am pleased to say that betting on cricket is on the down line in Sydney, though with such a betting loving people it can hardly be expected that it will cease altogether.[11]

The tourists lost by six wickets at Sydney, Turner and Ferris foreshadowing the next few years by taking all twenty wickets between them and all eleven to fall in the second fixture a month later when the Englishmen won by 9 wickets.

Socially, the tour was hugely successful. Everywhere they went they were fêted at stations, accompanied by bands and hosted at civic receptions, as the Australians, particularly those in the country towns, spared no effort to compensate their guests for harsh travelling conditions at inconvenient times. Following the fixture against Eighteen of Goulbourn, the tourists moved on to Cootamundra, later to become better known as the birthplace of Sir Donald Bradman. There were no trains out of Sydney on Sundays, so they were obliged to take the Saturday night mail which reached Goulbourn at 3 am and arrived in Cootamundra at 8.15 am. Nevertheless,

> There we were welcomed with bumpers of champagne, and in the afternoon buggies galore were at our disposal, the whole team driving out about six miles to a well-managed farm owned by a Mr Coker. The proprietors received us with great hospitality, and wine, whisky, tea, coffee and cake were freely passed around to the visitors who numbered over thirty. Some splendid fields of wheat were seen, some of them over 200 acres, standing perfectly upright and at least six feet high. This district is considered the best for wheat growing throughout New South Wales, or even all Australia.[12]

This seemingly boundless hospitality and idyllic scenery were partially counterbalanced by natural phenomena which must have made the tourists believe that they were experiencing a resurrected Exodus as excessive heat, a plague of flies, thunderstorms and even an earthquake combined to enliven small town New South Wales. It is a fair assumption that none of this served to improve the pitch as the following morning, the Twenty-two of Cootamundra lost their last ten wickets for one run and failed to avoid the follow on.

Against Eighteen Sydney Juniors, 'Lohmann again distinguished himself at slip' but while the non-first class matches were doubtless financially advantageous, their value in cricket terms was limited.

> It would be useless to describe the play, as it was merely a procession from the Pavilion to the wicket and back again.[13]

Despite some appalling weather, the tourists continued to play in circumstances where all logic dictated a match should be abandoned without a ball bowled. They arrived in Lithgow, a small coal-mining town, unable to compete with Newcastle and Wollongong for the lucrative Sydney market. It had rained for four days continuously and water was several inches deep in the middle of the ground: but ingenuity prevailed. One part of the ground was much higher; some "cocoa matting" was obtained and laid on the rough outfield. A hit to the resulting shortened boundary on one side was deemed to be worth two, rather than the traditional four; the bounce was variable, the uneven surface producing bouncers and shooters indiscriminately. The scene was not without amusement for the spectators, as fielders were obliged to run through large puddles of water, producing a climax of fun and laughter when they fell down in it.

The Twenty-two of Lithgow were dismissed for 18 and 27. There had been lower single innings totals, but, though many records of the cricket of the time are incomplete, inaccurate or both, this is thought to be the lowest aggregate total across two completed innings by a team of Twenty-two.

In the rather more serious cricket of the second match against New South Wales, when Shaw's XI avenged their earlier defeat with a nine wicket win, Lohmann displayed his not inconsiderable batting talents, top scoring at no 10 with a vigorous and entertaining 40 not out. He took a particular liking to Australia's new *wunderkind*, Charles Turner, striking him for a leg-side four and, in the same over, depositing him 'clean out of bounds into the Ladies Reserve'.

After that, it was back to Melbourne for a 'timeless match' against the Melbourne Club's Australian XI. The timelessness was doubtless not lost on Lohmann as he returned figures of 94-48-105-2. At the time, the follow on was compulsory if the first innings deficit were 80 or more, so having replied to the Australian XI's 294 with 201, the tourists found themselves batting again. They did rather better second time round with 264, anchored by Shrewsbury's 62. Lohmann's 32 not out was the bonus which ensured an adequate margin and eventual victory by 57 runs. After his efforts, he was excused the bulk of the bowling in the second innings, sending down only eleven overs. Briggs, who had bowled a modest 83 overs in the first innings, followed up with a match-winning 62-42-42-5.

Christmas was spent in Ballarat, though getting there in time for Christmas Day was not without its difficulties.

> Crowded trains were running from Melbourne and the Englishmen wanting to reach Ballarat to spend Christmas Day travelled in the luggage van with the baggage. They arrived at Ballarat a little before midnight, when songs and carols began, and were continued till nearly daylight.
>
> Christmas Day was exceedingly hot, and most of the team spent their time in the hotel till the evening. Altogether, the day was quite enjoyed. Sunday, December 26 was still hotter, and a hot northerly wind prevailed on the following day, blinding clouds of dust filling the streets and penetrating every crevice.[14]

A draw in the second of the matches against the Melbourne Club's Australian XI, this time scheduled for four days, was followed by a nine wicket win over the same team in Sydney in the last match before the match against 'Combined Australia', otherwise known as the First Test Match.

The Test Matches and New South Wales Again

IT WAS not the strongest side Australia could field, but two of them were strong enough to bowl out England for what remains their lowest ever Test score of 45 (though they came mighty close to beating it with 46 in Trinidad in 1994). They were invited to bat on a wet pitch – the first instance in a Test match of a team winning the toss and deciding not to bat – and decimated by a couple of débutants, but not ones with which they were unfamiliar, John Ferris and Charles Turner. Almost incredibly, Shaw's team came back to win the match by 13 runs.

Shrewsbury's reputation is not that of a man prone to excessive emotion, so the following extract from a letter to his sister written after the match on 1 February 1887 is some indication of the pride he felt in his team's performance, particularly that of his newest protégé.

> We have just finished a match against the Combined Team of Australia and I don't think that during the time I have played Cricket, I have ever played in a match that was literally pulled out of the fire as this one was. It was so entirely unexpected that the people out here could scarcely realise that we had won. It was a glorious victory and I am sure the Cricket Public at home will be more than pleased with the result considering the up-hill game we had to fight. All our players during the Combined last innings worked and fielded like a huge machine, every man thinking that it was on their individual efforts the match might depend. I shall never forget the shout our players gave when Lohmann bowled the last man (Spofforth) out and the groans of disappointment that arose from the spectators. I am sorry that some of the players did not take their defeat as graciously as we should have liked, saying that our Umpire (Rawlinson of Yorks, an old experienced umpire) had given two bad decisions. I won't enter further into what was said, but should wish that the Colonial Team could bear a licking with the same graceful manner as they can a win.

It was Spofforth's last Test match. He had now given way to Turner and Ferris. No batsman, he was bowled in both innings by Lohmann, as he had been in the first innings in the final Test at The Oval the previous summer. It was a significant and symbolic eclipse.

Between the two Test matches, there was yet another defeat by the New South Wales team. Again, Ferris and Turner dominated the bowling taking 18 wickets between them.

The Second Test also saw the Englishmen emerge victorious. It was perhaps no surprise that they should do so. The game was billed as The International Match: All Australia v All England in the *Sydney Morning Herald* which expressed the view that this was a 'mongrel All-Australian Eleven' and the New South Wales team was far stronger.[15] Even allowing for a little local bias, the opinion had some validity as was demonstrated by the results against the colony and against the team selected for this match.

Having commented on the fine weather and attendance of around 9000, the newspaper dealt with a domestic quibble,

> Despite the protest made against the band being stationed close to the press-box on a former occasion it was again located in the same place

before passing to the quality of the play,

> Lohmann shone out as a bowler for the first time on the Association Ground. He got the magnificent average of eight wickets for 35 runs… Three times did Lohmann take the middle stump and he captured nearly every wicket by enticing the batsmen to play forward, the ball always rising over the bat as they did so.[16]

It was the first instance of a bowler's taking eight wickets in a Test innings. The figures remain the best in a Test match at the SCG and the best for England in a Test in Australia.[17] The happiness of the occasion was, however, overshadowed by sad news from home.

> During the day Lohmann whose bowling was such a feature in the game on Saturday learned by a mail letter of the death of his mother.[18]

She had died, aged 56, on 20 January, of heart disease occasioned by asthma and angina. Unsurprisingly, his second innings performance was less effective, the *Sporting Life* reporting that 'he was naturally a bit cut up, and off colour with the ball'.[19]

The fourth innings target of 222 was beyond the Australians and England wrapped up the match on the fourth day, winning by 71 runs albeit with a little help from their opponents in the field.

> Lohmann played with a crape band on his arm in memory of the death of his mother; and Read, who hails from the same county – Surrey – wore a similar band of mourning. Mr Swift, one of the umpires, being absent, Gunn performed his duties and Ferris fielded in his place. Shortly before Ferris went in to bat Turner relieved him and, as will subsequently be seen, played a very important and not altogether welcome part in the field… Allen hit Bates to mid off and Turner made a very smart catch.[20]

Player-umpires and substitutes fielding for the opposition are generally associated with lower-grade club cricket than internationals.

In the nineteenth century matters were more informal but it does reflect the status of bowlers as the game's dogsbodies and gofers that, when five batsmen were out overnight and would take no further part, the substitute fielders were Ferris and Turner each of whom had bowled more than a hundred overs in the match.

Home Straight

ANOTHER 'TIMELESS' match against Victoria followed, Shaw's XI winning by nine wickets, thanks in no small part to the captain's 144 and Lohmann's 5-44 in the second innings.

One of Lohmann's less spectacular performances was in the Smokers v Non-Smokers match, comprising mixed Anglo-Australian sides in Melbourne. As the presumably fitter Non-Smokers continued their first innings into the third day of four (the Laws still had no provision for declarations) and ran up what was at the time a world record innings of 803, Lohmann returned a none too impressive 48-18-113-0.

Overall, however, Lohmann's first overseas tour was a success for him and for the team. In its analysis of the tour *Cricket* summed up his contribution in complimentary terms. Analysing the players in the order of their batting averages, it offers the following assessment.

> Lohmann, with an average of 17, did fairly well and at times played brilliantly. His century against the East Melbourne Club was a very dashing performance, and on several occasions, he did great service by staying the latter part of the innings when runs were much wanted. In bowling he was somewhat disappointing, but several times proved very destructive, and his fifty-nine wickets for an average of little more than 15 runs per wicket is very good, although not to be compared with the analysis of their opponent (Turner). With Briggs he bowled considerably over 5,000 balls and comes next to him with 154 wickets. He fielded magnificently at all parts of the field.[21]

Richard Barlow followed a week later by commenting that 'Lohmann on his day could not have been improved upon'.[22]

Following upon Australia's below par performances in England the previous summer, English domination continued. 'Felix' of the *Australasian* was impressed by the tourists, especially their fielding, but regretted that, because of internal Australian politics, namely the antagonism between Sydney and Melbourne, on no occasion did the tourists meet a full-strength Australian side.

However, on the positive side for Australia, the tour saw the beginning of the rise of Charles Turner and John Ferris. Turner was to remain at the top of his profession rather longer, but their pre-eminence in the Australian attack is demonstrated by their taking between them 36 of the 40 England wickets to fall in the two Test matches on top of 49 out of 51 in the state matches. They had now taken over the rôle of Spofforth who had bowled just a dozen overs for one wicket.

Financially, the tour had just about broken even, but, despite the heat, the flies and the travelling, there was little doubt that the party had enjoyed the social experience. Mordecai Sherwin commented

> I came out to enjoy myself and I have done so. I like the climate – Victoria especially, and I like the free-and-easy style of the colonists. In the country towns we had a particularly pleasant time. In the evenings we would... sing our favourite songs and glees... Everywhere we went we were treated most hospitably and during our travels we saw some very beautiful scenery. But the rain! I shall never forget it. It seemed to rain in every town we visited... At Bowral, we were above our ankles in water in our tent, and cricket bags and boots were floating around in a manner quite novel to us.[23]

In playing terms too, the tour was a huge success. The two defeats by New South Wales apart, the tourists were undefeated in the other eight first-class matches, winning six, including the two matches against 'Combined Australia', subsequently deemed to be Test matches, and drawing two. Of the nineteen matches against odds, they won six and drew the remainder.

Indeed, so successful had the tour been from the tourists' perspective that the Melbourne Club invited their colleagues in New South Wales to join them in a venture to offer contracts to some of the English amateurs. The Sydneysiders, however, were having none of it. At the end of the summer, press reports suggested that Lohmann was in negotiation for a coaching position with a Melbourne club.

> It was rumoured that Briggs' services were to be enlisted on behalf of one of the Metropolitan clubs and that Lohmann was in treaty with another club as tutor, but nothing has been made public as yet.[24]

The Editor of *Cricket* had also gathered from a Melbourne newspaper,

> The South Melbourne Executive also are recommended to consider the advisability of importing a man, and it is thought that the presence of two such fine all-round cricketers as Briggs and Lohmann would instil [sic] new life into the much-neglected club practice in Melbourne, as well as by their play and instruction improve the form of rising cricketers.[25]

The return journey saw them arrive in Colombo for a 40-hour stop-over on Monday 10 April. As on the outward trip, the time was partly filled by minstrel entertainment, whist tournaments, tugs of war, trial by jury and dances. The party arrived in Aden a week later and landed at Plymouth on 8 May. The 1887 season had already started.

1 *Sydney Referee* 20 October 1886. MCC here is the Melbourne Cricket Club
2 *Cricket* 26 November 1891
3 20 October 1886
4 *Cricket* 17 September 1886.
5 Bettesworth *op cit*
6 *Cricket* 30 December 1886, reproduced from *Sporting Life*
7 1888 p 323
8 *Cricket* 24 August 1887
9 *Cricket* 30 December 1886, reproduced from *Sporting Life*
10 *Cricket* 30 December 1885
11 *Cricket* 27 January 1887 reproduced from *Sporting Life*
12 Ib
13 *Cricket* 27 January 1887
14 *Cricket* 24 February 1887
15 3 March 1887
16 *Sydney Morning Herald* 28 February 1887
17 There is a discrepancy between *The Wisden Book of Test Cricket* and *Cricket Archive* on the bowling figures. Both are agreed on maidens, runs and wickets, but *Wisden* has 25 overs, *Cricket Archive* 27.1. Press reports confirm the accuracy of the latter, the *Sydney Morning Herald* describing the end of the Australian first innings as follows: Ferris hit Flowers to square leg for a single, but the first ball of Lohmann's next over beat his defence. Bowling figures were usually expressed in balls rather than overs at the time and the likelihood is that in a scorebook or press report 109 has been misread as 100
18 *Sydney Morning Herald* 1 March 1887
19 *Cricket* 14 April 1887
20 *Sydney Morning Herald* 2 March 1887
21 5 May 1887
22 *Cricket* 12 May 1887
23 *Cricket* 5 May 1887
24 *Sydney Referee* 31 March 1887
25 *Cricket* 5 May 1887

CHAPTER 5

CHAMPION COUNTY (1887)

...success seems powerless to spoil him
The Surrey Team in 1888

BY THE standards of the following three years, 1887 was not Lohmann's most spectacular or successful season, but it was still good enough for Surrey to replace Nottinghamshire as the nominated Champion County for the first time since 1864. *Wisden* commented,

> Lohmann did even better all round work than in 1886 and he was indeed a tower of strength on the side ...the honours of the side were divided between Lohmann, Mr Key and Mr Walter Read.[1]

Cricket had said,

> Lohmann's performance in particular was worthy of the highest praise. He bowled altogether 1,634 overs, and considering the grounds were all against the bowlers, this was a remarkable performance.[2]

Subsequent statistical refinement has reduced the number of overs to 1631.2, but, in a batsman-friendly summer, his final tally of 154 wickets is way ahead of anyone else. Only four other bowlers reached a hundred, the nearest to Lohmann being Briggs with 114 in slightly fewer overs. Strike rates and economy rates as indicators of bowling performance belong to later generations, but if they are to be applied retrospectively, then Lohmann has 45.31 and 1.47 per four-ball over against Briggs' 55.86 and 1.26, giving some support to later appreciations of Lohmann that he bowled for wickets, not for maidens.

The Surrey Team in 1888, a publication of the *Cricket* office with biographical sketches churned out the statistics sausage machine-style, concluding with a mini-character study.

> At Trent Bridge, in Surrey's first match with Notts, his bowling was the principal factor in the success of the former, taking in the match ten wickets for 105 runs. Against Yorkshire he took six wickets for 48 runs in the first innings besides scoring 54. Other performances included eleven Leicestershire wickets for 74; 13 Lancashire wickets (in the return at the Oval) for 111, in addition to scoring 60 in the second innings; 11 Yorkshire wickets for 69; 13 Sussex wickets for 97; 13 Hampshire wickets for 62; and five Essex wickets for 30 runs... Well conducted and gentlemanly, he is generally liked, for success seems powerless to spoil him.[3]

In the Bank Holiday fixture at The Oval, Lohmann and Maurice Read led Surrey to a four wicket victory and double over the former champions. Their deeds were recorded in verse by Albert Craig, the 'Surrey poet'. Yorkshire-born, he wrote about two hundred poems on cricket which he reproduced and sold to The Oval crowds,

> But when Maurice and Lohmann, with willow in hand,
> Sound judgment and courage displayed,
> They made a most timely and capital stand –
> Faint hearts were no longer dismayed.
> They soon set to business and altered the score;
> And it's not the first time, for they've done it before.

On the batting front, Lohmann's career-best 115 at Hove held the first innings together in a match which, despite his second innings duck, Surrey went on to win by the narrow margin of one wicket.

Wisden waxed lyrical,

> Lohmann, who had gone in at the fall of the fourth wicket, displayed some of the best cricket of his career. He received some little help from all his partners, but the run-getting was largely his business. He made no mistakes, and yet in two hours and forty minutes, by confident, clean, hard hitting, he scored 115, and altogether changed the position of the game...
> Lohmann's eight wickets in the match cost 128 runs, but the famous young Surrey cricketer bowled, as he batted, far better than any of his colleagues.[4]

In addition, he had five other half-centuries to finish with the highest aggregate of runs, 843, and average, 25.54, of his first-class career.

If Nottinghamshire had become champion county the previous year by dint of their higher number of drawn matches, Surrey's captain John Shuter was determined to win. At that time declarations were not permitted and, to allow his team more bowling time, he instructed his batsmen to deliberately sacrifice their wickets. Hence, the 'hit wicket' and two stumpings towards the end of the second innings card.

Bobby Abel remembered it well,

> Surrey v Notts were the great matches of that season. The first game at Trent Bridge was the epoch-making one – which eventually led to the institution of the closure rule.
> Lohmann had a giant's share in winning the remarkable game for us by 157 runs. He bowled nearly all the afternoon, sending down 60 overs for 66 runs and 5 wickets, always keeping a perfect length and breaking both ways.[5]

Against Hampshire at Southampton, Lohmann took a wicket with his first ball in both innings. The significance of his contribution to a Championship-winning season was not lost on Abel.

> Jubilee Year of 1887 will be remembered by cricketers as one of the finest seasons within living memory. Hard wickets predominated from start to finish and the national game was played under ideal conditions...
> This was a great year for Surrey cricket. Lohmann was recognised as the finest all-round cricketer – and greatest bowler – in England, while eight of the eleven had batting averages of 20 and over.[6]

In later years, Sir Pelham Warner was to recall, as a boy of thirteen, seeing Lohmann for the first time in a match commemorating the MCC's centenary.

> The first time we ever saw him play was at Lord's, in June 1887, for England against the MCC, when A E Stoddart and Arthur Shrewsbury played innings of over 100 for England...[7]

Performances with the bat tend to be more memorable for spectators than those with the ball and it is perhaps inevitable that the opening partnership of around 300[8] by Stoddart and Shrewsbury should have stuck in the mind rather than Lohmann's performance of 57-29-62-6 (including the wickets of W G Grace, William Gunn and Lord Hawke – all bowled) in the dismissal of MCC for 175. Stoddart and Shrewsbury had laid the foundations for a total of 514 before MCC were bowled out again for 222.

Also recalled in Warner's feature is a 'wonderful catch' by Lohmann off Tom Bowley in the Bank Holiday fixture against Notts at The Oval.

In more formal, but no less laudatory terms *Wisden* recorded:

Against Lancashire,

> After luncheon, however, Lohmann sent down 11 overs and a ball for 11 runs and 5 wickets, the famous Surrey professional getting rid of eight of the ten Lancashire batsmen.

and, in the second innings,

> The light was very defective, but Lohmann cut with great power and judgment, and although he had no chance of victory, it was not until just before time that he put up a ball to cover-point and was out for 60. This innings was one of the best Lohmann ever played and included nine 4s, two 3s and five 2s.[9]

Against Yorkshire,

> It is seldom that a good victory to Surrey has to be mentioned without special praise being said about him, for he took in the two innings eleven wickets for 69 runs, getting a lot of work on the ball and at times seeming almost unplayable.[10]

Against Sussex,

> The wicket, however, was so bad and the light so treacherous that it seemed at one time that Sussex would not save the game after all. Lohmann made the fullest use of the advantage afforded him by the ground, and got rid of batsman until seven were out for 61. When time was called and the match was left drawn, Lohmann had secured all the wickets that had fallen at a cost of but 34 runs.[11]

and earlier in the Trent Bridge Whitsuntide Bank Holiday fixture,

> Too much praise cannot be afforded to George Lohmann who thoroughly kept up what is now almost a tradition, that Surrey seldom gain an exceptional victory without he has a large share in obtaining it. He bowled with great determination from the first, kept a beautiful length and got a lot of work on the ball from both sides.[12]

The County Championship was not formalised until 1890 and press opinion, which determined the winner, was not always unanimous. *Wisden* has compiled a list of "most generally selected" champions, based on the research of the late Major Rowland Bowen.[13] There were no quibbles with Surrey's claim to the title in 1887. Their record of twelve wins, two defeats and two draws against other first-class counties spoke for itself. The last time it had been theirs was in 1864 when matters were even more informal and it was possible for players to turn out for more than one county during the course of the season. The year had been a golden one, both for the Queen and the tenants of her nearest first-class county ground, owned by and bearing the coat-of-arms of her eldest son.

Lohmann was rewarded with a special gratuity of £25, in comparison to the £5 awarded to the other regular professional members of the eleven, firm positive discrimination and a recognition of his worth and value to the club.[14] Along with Beaumont and Bowley he was awarded his county cap. They became the thirteenth to fifteenth names on a list now stretching to around two hundred.

1 *Wisden* 1888 p 2
2 *Cricket* 15 September 1887
3 p 31
4 *Wisden* 1888 p 121
5 Abel *op cit* pp 54-55
6 Ib p 57
7 *The Cricketer* 25 August 1925
8 The scorecard is incomplete: Shrewsbury made 152; Stoddart 151
9 *Wisden* 1888 p 24
10 Ib p 29
11 Ib p 33
12 Ib p 59
13 p 550 of 2005 edition
14 Surrey CCC minutes 20 October 1887

CHAPTER 6

AUSTRALIA AGAIN (1887-88)

Sydney is the very finest cricket ground I have ever played on,
both for general appointment and turf
George Lohmann 1895

ALL COMMON sense pointed to one governing body for Australian cricket, but that was not to happen until 1905. The politicians had sunk their differences four years earlier, embracing federation in the Commonwealth of Australia. At this stage, however, the rival interests of Sydney and Melbourne, with acrimony never far below the surface, resulted in there being two tours competing for attention – and more importantly, cash – in the winter of 1887/88. One was led by George Vernon of Middlesex, the other, again, by Shaw, Shrewsbury and Lillywhite. It was the third occasion the latter trio had organised an Australian tour. Overall, there had been nine previous ones. Sensibly, the two parties joined forces for the only Test match of the tour, having sailed together from Plymouth on the *Iberia* on Saturday 17 September.

Twelve months after their return *Wisden* made the following judgment,

> Two English teams visited Australia in the season of 1887-88 but it is certain that such a piece of folly will never be perpetrated again. Having regard to the fact that eleven-a-side matches are only practicable at Melbourne, Sydney and Adelaide, it was clear from the first that two combinations would not be able to pay their way...[1]

Lohmann was in the Sydney-based Shrewsbury tour. Six of the seven first-class matches were played at the SCG in addition to the Test, the other against Victoria at Melbourne. Vernon's team supplied something close to a distorted mirror-image of that, playing four at Melbourne, two at Adelaide and two at Sydney.

The tour did not get away to the best of starts. There was no play on the first scheduled day in the first of their three matches against New

South Wales and although the match was deemed to be 'timeless', in under seven hours' playing time it was all over. Percy McDonnell won the toss and invited the tourists to make use of a rain-affected pitch: 49 all out suggested that he had made the right decision. New South Wales replied with 94. Shrewsbury's team managed 66 in their second innings and the locals sewed up the match with a ten wicket win. *Cricket*, which had received only the totals, made an intelligent guess.

> No details have arrived yet as to how the England players got out, and in the absence of any further information, we must assume that Turner played an important part in their dismissal.[2]

The assumption was not far wide of the mark. Turner had 4-22 and 6-23, Ferris 6-24 and 3-35. For Shrewsbury's team, Lohmann had 5-26 and Briggs 3-35. Shrewsbury had 20 in the first innings, Lohmann, opening the batting, the same score in the second. No one else in the visiting side reached double figures.

A month later, the tables were turned as Shrewsbury's team recorded a victory by the same margin. Then, just before Christmas, the tourists played their only match away from Sydney, travelling to Melbourne where the state side were beaten by an innings and 456 runs. Had the declaration been legalised, Shrewsbury might well have closed the innings before it reached 624 in reply to 68 all out, but he doubtless felt satisfied with his own 232.

It was a different story back in Sydney in the New Year when New South Wales won the third of their three fixtures with the tourists by 153 runs. Lohmann bowled almost 150 overs in the match with marathon efforts of 78-47-68-7 and 70.3-34-97-7, figures bettered only by Turner who returned 8-39 in the first innings and 8-40 in the second.

In the match against 'Combined Australia', a team not very different from that which was to turn out a week later in the Test match, Shrewsbury's Team won by 5 wickets, thanks mainly to Lohmann who had figures of 5-83 and 7-43.

The Test Match

ALTHOUGH *CRICKET* reported the match as Combined English Teams v New South Wales and Victoria, it was subsequently deemed to be a Test Match, though 'Australia' were far from being at full strength.

> ...the Englishmen sank all rivalry for the glory of Old England, some of Australia's leading cricketers drew back when the pinch came, and could

> not or would not get away from business. Giffen, Horan, Jarvis, Bruce, Lyons and Trumble could not get away, so that the team was miserably weak.

Of the half-dozen unavailable, three were from Victoria and three from South Australia, reflecting the rift in Australian cricket.

This was the first time Lohmann and Peel had bowled together in Test cricket. The effect was devastating. England, again invited to bat by McDonnell, had crawled to 113 all out in 100 overs, their innings anchored by Arthur Shrewsbury's 44. He was seventh out at 102, having faced 150 balls. Then Lohmann and Peel got to work.

> The combined team only had an hour to bat. During that short time, Lohmann and Peel held complete sway... Lohmann, taking full advantage of the wicket, bowled with rare effect and was well nigh unplayable, as also was Peel, whose balls cut about in all directions.[3]

At the close, they were 35 for 8. Their final total of 42 all out remains their lowest at home. England eventually won by 126 runs – 'in the most hollow fashion', said *Cricket* – and the match aggregate of 374 exceeded by just 11 that of The Oval Test in 1882 which gave rise to the Ashes. Lohmann had 5-17 and 4-35, Peel 5-18 and 5-50, eclipsing Turner's 5-44 and 7-43 and Ferris's 4-60 and 2-43.

Bobby Peel was Yorkshire's equivalent of Johnny Briggs. He had come relatively late to Test cricket at the age of 27. He was to play twenty Test matches, and along with Lohmann and Briggs, dominated England's bowling for a decade. It was an era characterised by low scores. Certainly the art of groundsmanship was less sophisticated than in later years and, although there was limited pitch covering, from 1884 it had been illegal to cover once the match had begun.[4] Inevitably conditions were bowler-friendly, at least to those bowlers able to exploit them as this trio undoubtedly were, but so, of course, were Ferris and Turner. When the five played in the same match on a rain-affected pitch, it was almost pre-ordained that it would be low-scoring. And so it was on this occasion when Lohmann and Peel demonstrated such mastery of their craft that Briggs, arch-destroyer at Lord's a little over eighteen months earlier, was not called upon to bowl. Between them, the quartet of Ferris, Turner, Lohmann and Peel took 37 of the 39 wickets to fall to bowlers at a combined cost of just 300 runs. Actual playing time was not much over two days, but two days washed out completely and an intervening Sunday meant that the match was spread out over almost a week.

Peel's career was to end in disgrace, his fondness for the bottle causing him to be dismissed by Lord Hawke in 1897, though the story of his urinating on the pitch is probably apocryphal. According to A A Thompson in his book *Hirst and Rhodes*, Peel was dismissed after a match at Chesterfield. The evidence is anecdotal and based on an interview with Hirst. It was a ground on which Peel never played a first-class match. In 1897, the Derbyshire–Yorkshire match was played at Derby. Peel had five wickets in the second innings and continued to play after that, his last match for Yorkshire being against Middlesex at Bramall Lane.[5]

The tour was rounded off with two matches against the Australian XI selected to tour England in the summer of 1888. In the first of these, McDonnell once again chose to field first, but Shrewsbury's team's total of 173 was sufficient to win by an innings and 42 runs. Lohmann and Briggs bowled through both innings and shared the twenty wickets between them. The last match of the tour was won comfortably by 158 runs, the captain registering his second double-century of the trip.

So, other than the two matches against New South Wales which had been dominated by Turner's bowling, the tourists won five of their first-class matches in addition to the Test and, after a handful of non first-class matches in New Zealand, came back to England satisfied with the performances, if not with the profits.

> The Englishmen, after their defeat of the Australian team just starting for England, spent the remainder of their stay in Sydney bidding farewell to numerous friends.
>
> The Union Company's steam-ship 'Hantoro' was advertised to leave Sydney direct for Wellington on Saturday March 17, at 10 pm and punctually at that time she sailed away amidst hearty cheers from a large gathering of friends. On clearing the heads it was soon apparent that the bad sailors were in for a gruelling, and for about three days very little was seen of about three parts of the party, a strong southerly gale blowing the whole time. On Thursday, in passing through the Cook's Straits, a heavy westerly wind blew, but, being favourable, this assisted us in reaching our destination somewhat earlier, and we arrived at Wellington that afternoon about half-past four and were met and welcomed by many gentlemen of that city.[6]

Lohmann seems to have recovered from the voyage fairly quickly. His workload showed no signs of diminishing. On the other side of the Tasman Sea in a match beginning next day, he had 13-37 and 5-70. Against Eighteen of Wellington, he returned 23.3-13-37-3 and with Briggs bowled unchanged against a similar number of Canterbury. On the tour overall, he had taken 63 wickets at 11.98 in all first-class matches, 210 at 8.27 in all matches.

Vernon's team returned home. It seems to have been the more sensible option.

Wisden took the view that,

> Though we cannot help thinking the visit was mistaken it is only right to say that the team played in a style that did huge credit to English cricket. ...the batting of Shrewsbury and the bowling of Lohmann and Briggs may rank among the best achievements of our players in the colonies... These three players were the mainstay of the side and no praise can exceed their deserts.[7]

Similarly, *Cricket* said,

> Briggs, Lohmann, Mr Smith, Preston and Pougher bore the brunt of the bowling, and in this department the team was particularly strong. The first two named got over 200 wickets, and though Briggs took more wickets during the tour, Lohmann's figures were the best in all eleven-a-side matches.[8]

1 1889 p 286
2 24 November 1887
3 *Cricket* 29 March 1888
4 Rosenwater *Wisden* 1970 p 132
5 For a fuller description, see Sissons *The Players* pp180-182
6 *Cricket* 3 May 1888, from *Sporting Life*
7 1889 pp 306 & 322
8 *Cricket* 9 August 1888

CHAPTER 7

HALCYON DAYS: 200 x THREE (1888-90)

...a threefold cord is not quickly broken
Ecclesiastes 4.12

FOR EACH of the seven seasons from 1885 to 1891, Lohmann was Surrey's leading wicket-taker. In the graph of wickets taken, he reached a high plateau in the 1888, 1889 and 1890 seasons, achieving a rare hat-trick of 200 wickets in each of three consecutive years. He was the first bowler to do so. In the history of English first-class cricket, only half a dozen bowlers have taken 200 wickets in a season on three occasions and only three (Freeman, Parker and Goddard) on more occasions than that.

1888

Oh my Hornby and my Barlow long ago
Francis Thompson *At Lord's*

At the Annual General Meeting, the Surrey committee looked back to a successful season in 1887 and in a smug mood of self-congratulation, reported,

> In recognition of the successes of the eleven, your committee felt that they would only be carrying out the wishes of the members by presenting to each of the team some token in appreciation of an exceptional year. Messrs J Shuter, Read, Key and Roller of the amateurs, and of the professionals Lohmann, to whose all round cricket the County owed very much, all received special recognition and every one of the eleven was rewarded.[1]

They were not rewarded with the same amount, nor was the financial largesse distributed in proportion to each player's contribution. Mr Read received £100, Messrs Shuter, Key and Roller £82.7.6, Lohmann £25 and the rest £92 between them.

After the hot summer and parched, flat wickets of 1887, 1888 was one of the wettest on record, ideal conditions for the Surrey crowd's hero.

After half a dozen of the side had spent the winter in Australia, playing against teams of varying names, but containing many of the same players, Surrey's first fixture of the summer was against… the Australians. Although a clear case of overkill for the players, for spectators, a season's opener of County Champions v Australians was likely to have popular appeal. However, it was no contest; the county were unable to repeat the successes of 1886 as, with Turner and Ferris again on top form, the visitors ran out winners by an innings and 145 runs. Lohmann had to leave the field with an injured toe and Beaumont injured a finger. Eight bowlers were used in all, but only Bowley with 4-77 had any measure of success.

However, when it came to inter-county cricket, Surrey were virtually unstoppable, as they benefited from what was, in terms of wickets taken, the most purple of Lohmann's eight year purple passage. For eight consecutive seasons, he took well over a hundred first-class wickets, more than 150 in seven of them. Against Gloucestershire at The Oval, he had 6-45 and 6-21 as Surrey won by an innings and 37 runs, 'a fine performance considering he had only been a few days on shore'.[2]

Yet another marathon bowling performance followed, as at Trent Bridge he took ten wickets in the match (53.3-23-70-6 and 43-26-43-4) and held two slip catches in a nine wicket win.

> Lohmann was in his best form and he clean bowled Scotton, Mr Dixon and Gunn in succession.[3]

In the Players of England v Australia match at The Oval, the contest was once again Lohmann and Briggs v Turner and Ferris with walk-on parts for Peel and Trott. On this occasion, the Englishmen came out on top as Lohmann (3-45 and 4-41) and Briggs (3-8 and 6-54) bowled the Players to a ten-wicket victory.

First Test Match

THE LORD'S Test had an element of déjà vu about it. It was almost a repeat of Sydney five months earlier as 40 wickets fell in under two days for a match aggregate of 291, the lowest in any Test between the two countries. This time, however, the boot was on the other foot as Australia ended a run of seven consecutive defeats with a 61 run win. The same four bowlers were responsible, plus this time Briggs, the quintet accounting for all but four wickets – and two of those were run out. Lohmann's contribution was 20-9-28-2 and 14-4-43-4, and with the bat, 2 in the first innings, lbw b Turner and, in the second, 0 st Blackham b Ferris, one of his four stumpings in the match.

Cricket commented,

> ...the Australians found Peel and Lohmann as difficult when they went in again.
>
> Turner and Ferris, since their arrival in England, have so thoroughly upheld their reputation as two of the most effective bowlers of this or any other age on sticky wickets.[4]

Back to county cricket and Middlesex at The Oval where George Burton achieved a rare 'all ten' in Surrey's first innings restricting them to a lead of two. However, Lohmann's demolition of Middlesex for 53 with 42-11-32-7 in the second innings left Surrey with a target of 52 which they struggled to reach, losing seven wickets in the process.

Then to Beckenham where Surrey destroyed Kent in two days, Lohmann bowling them out, coincidentally for another 53 in the second innings with 31-22-23-8. The following week, Surrey met the Australians at The Oval in the second of three such fixtures and were on their way to avenging their earlier defeat but were foiled by the rain. Following on, the tourists were still behind at the close on the second day. Frustratingly, no play was possible on the third. Australia had been bowled out for 52, Lohmann 5-24, supported by Bowley, 2-21, and Beaumont, 2-6.

The match against Lancashire at Old Trafford, scheduled for 2, 3 and 4 August, was particularly memorable in that 3 and 4 August were not required. It has gone into Surrey's record books as only one of five first-class matches in the county's history (excluding contrived finishes) to be completed in a single day. It was the only one in Lohmann's time.

Lancashire won the toss and batted and were dispatched for 35. (Not their lowest; that was 27 on the same ground seventy years later.) Surrey replied with 123 and bowled out Lancashire again for 63 – even that represented a recovery from 38-9, after a collapse from 36-2, five wickets falling at 37 – before the close to win by an innings and 25 runs.

Lohmann bowled through both Lancashire innings, 23.1-18-13-8 in the first and 21-10-38-5 in the second, Beaumont claiming the other five for 19. My 'Hornby and my Barlow long ago'[5] were both bowled by Lohmann in the first innings (Beaumont was to have them in the second). At one stage, Lohmann had four wickets in five balls and his thirteen in the match were taken without assistance from his fielders, ten bowled, two LBW and one caught and bowled.

> The instances of first-class fixtures completed in one day are so rare, that if for no other reason the first match of the season between these counties, begun and ended at Old Trafford, Manchester on Thursday, would rank prominently amongst the curiosities of a remarkable season.[6]

> Even the Manchester folk, whose sympathies were naturally with the batting side, appreciated the greatness of this performance, and awarded the Surrey professional a hearty round of cheering.[7]

The *Manchester Guardian* saw the result as 'the most decisive and damaging defeat which Lancashire has ever sustained in the cricket field'. Surrey were at full strength, Lancashire, because of a number of injuries, some way below.

> On paper, the Surrey team ought to have played sixteen of Lancashire. The wicket was in a condition which gave Lohmann a great advantage. Soaked with recent and prolonged rain, the ground had not recovered when the sun came out yesterday, and in consequence it played rather rough and treacherous. Lohmann, bowling from the Stretford end, found a spot on the off side which exactly suited him, and he was for the greater part of the first innings absolutely unplayable. Mr Hornby showed unusual care but he was bowled by a very fast shooter. Then the wickets fell with almost ridiculous rapidity, Lohmann at one stage getting six men out for the same number of runs. Barlow exhibited admirable defence, but even his guard was broken through time after time, and at last he succumbed to a tremendous break-back.[8]

Years later, when G A Brooking was indulging in the perennial pastime of selecting an all-time England XI (to 1926), Lohmann was included and this match recalled,

> G A Lohmann was undoubtedly the best bowler of the eleven. As a youngster I recollect reading with consternation the fact that Surrey had dismissed Lancashire for 35 and George Lohmann's bag was 8 wickets for 13. Palatine stock slumped badly that day, for the match began at noon and, by close of play, the Red Rose were beaten by an innings!
> He was right arm, slightly over medium pace, with a beautiful action and varied his deliveries with great judgment. A magnificent fielder at short slip and a dashing batsman who was always at his best when runs were badly wanted. No occasion was too big for him; he was the idol of Kennington Oval and endeared himself to many who never had the privilege of knowing 'the best of Georges'.[9]

Also memorable, but for quite opposite reasons, was the following Saturday afternoon. An enterprising local club, Dukinfield, recruited Lohmann to play for them. His performance was not quite so impressive. Lohmann himself told the story some time later in his interview with W A Bettesworth.

> Lohmann was one of those men to whom curious and interesting experiences seem to come as a matter of course. Perhaps the most curious experience that he ever met with occurred when he was playing in a village match in Lancashire. 'We played Lancashire,' he said 'at Manchester in 1888 – a very wet summer – and the match was finished in one day. I received several telegrams asking me to play on the Saturday at Dukinfield in a very keen local match, and enquiring what were my terms: I asked what I thought were absolutely prohibitive terms, namely £10. The terms were accepted and I went. I changed in a tiny pavilion, and went out to field as we had lost the toss. I had to begin the bowling. My first ball was hit straight out of the ground for six, and in a short time 60 went up with no wicket down. I suggested to the local captain that he had better take me off, but he said that if he took me off, the spectators, who kept pouring into the ground, would want their money back, and would also see that they got it. So I continued to bowl. By-and-by I got one wicket for 92 and the score was about 190. Then the captain took me off, but I had to go on again and took another wicket. In the end I had 2 wickets for about 120 runs. Our side went in. I thought to myself, "Now you really must do something in batting. It will never do to make only a few." Unfortunately, I was promptly bowled first or second ball, and our side made only about 42. There must have been a crowd of about three or four thousand on the ground, chiefly miners, and the sort of remark that I heard as I passed through them on my way back to the station was, "That's 'im – 'e's no bloomin' Lohmann. 'E's a bloomin' fraud." There was a four-wheeled cab at the entrance to the ground, and I jumped in as quickly as I could. At the station I retired into the waiting room – the ladies' waiting room if you please, because I felt I should escape the crowd there – jumped into a first-class carriage the moment that the train came in, pulled the blinds down and still did not feel happy till I got back to my hotel. I shall never forget the sad and reproachful looks of that crowd, and I have never played in a match of that kind since then.'[10]

It is a good story, but whether the scores are as related or whether it actually happened at all is open to question. There is no mention of it in the following Monday's *Manchester Guardian*. Coverage of local cricket by that newspaper is spasmodic in nature, but there is some and in his Cricket Notes column, the Sports Editor, while continuing to bewail the weakness of the Lancashire team the previous week mentions that the Rev Mr Napier was unable to play although it was noticed that he was playing on Saturday. It seems almost impossible that if Lohmann had turned out for a local side in front of three or four thousand witnesses, news of it would not have got back to the local newspaper[11] and it would surely have merited a line or two. Furthermore, the match against Lancashire having been completed on Thursday, it seems unlikely there would have been much enthusiasm for still being in Manchester on Saturday evening when there was a fixture at The Oval the following Monday.

If it did happen, it was an experience he was able to put behind him as, in the Bank Holiday fixture, he helped Surrey beat Nottinghamshire by 78 runs.

> In the hour that was left on the second day, Beaumont and Lohmann bowled with startling effect and when play ceased six batsmen, five of whom had failed to score, were out for 39 runs.[12]

He then warmed up for the second Test match with 6-56 and 6-22 against Sussex at The Oval after Surrey had reached what was then their highest ever total of 698 (It has been passed on only six occasions since then.) Monty Bowden with 189 not out and W W Read with 171 were the main contributors. Shuter, Key and Abel all topped fifty, Lohmann a modest two dozen at no 3. Sussex used eleven bowlers before being bowled out for 114 and 99 to give Surrey victory by the margin of an innings and 485 runs. It remains their biggest ever win.

After their defeat at Lord's England turned the tables at The Oval to win the second Test by an innings and 137 runs. The wicket-takers on this occasion were Briggs, Peel and Barnes, but Lohmann could scarcely be kept out of the match. Batting at no 10, he had his highest Test innings and only half-century – of 62 not out: it contained just one single. His catch to dismiss Bannerman was to be described by Sir Pelham Warner as one of many that were 'historic'.[13]

Lancashire gained their revenge in the return match at The Oval two weeks later when they won by nine wickets, Surrey's only defeat that season in inter-county matches. Lohmann's contribution, however, was not untypical in that he batted at no 3 and bowled 94 overs in the match, including 75-22-135-6 in the first innings.

Of that match, Abel was to write,

> In the ordinary way that year our first innings of 294 would have placed us beyond fear of defeat, but through dropped catches we allowed the Lancastrians to exceed our score by 82. The credit of this was due to Mr J Eccles who went on first and was not dismissed until he had scored 184

> – by far the biggest thing he ever accomplished in the cricket field. He was missed twice before he had made 30, and eight times in all. We gave up all hopes of ever catching him, so George Lohmann simply bowled at his stumps over after over and at last broke through his defence with a ball which would have beaten almost any one.[14]

Later that month as Surrey beat Yorkshire at Park Avenue, Bradford, by an innings and 228 runs, Lohmann's performances made a huge impact.

> Lohmann's bowling was again one of the principal factors in Surrey's success. Altogether it will be seen he took 13 Yorkshire wickets for 119 runs. As in addition he scored 80, the value of his all round contribution to the side can be appreciated.[15]

Surrey had by far the better of a rain-ruined draw against Gloucestershire at Clifton College and were on top from the time Lohmann bowled W G Grace for a duck. The home side were all out for 39, still their lowest total against Surrey. No one reached double figures, as Lohmann mopped up with 13.2-4-17-7, Beaumont taking the other three. There was no play on the second day and scarcely any on the third as Surrey reached 267-8.

> In this success of Surrey, Lohmann, as he has done so often, played the leading part, and his performance was a most remarkable one, on a par with his great achievement against Lancashire at Manchester early in the month.[16]

The final Test of the series at Old Trafford was wrapped up before lunch on the second day – the shortest on record in which a result was obtained, England again winning by an innings. After his batting performance at The Oval, it was a case of 'after the Lord Mayor's show' for Lohmann. He was run out for 0, then had 1-31 and 3-20 as Australia replied to England's 172 with 81 and 70, Peel being responsible for the bulk of the damage.

September was continuous cricket against the tourists as the circus travelled to Scarborough, Holbeck, Old Trafford and Hastings. Lohmann turned out for Lord Londesborough's XI, Shrewsbury's Australian XI and the South of England. The general pattern was much the same with Ferris and Turner dominating for Australia, counterbalanced by Lohmann, Peel and Briggs doing likewise for the various home combinations. As if that were not enough, on 20 September, Surrey began a third match against the Australians. The latter won by 34 runs, Ferris and Turner taking most of the Surrey wickets, Lohmann, Beaumont and Bowley most of the Australian ones.

Cricket reported that Lohmann 'made two very fine catches at short slip' but 'strained his foot badly'.[17] It does not seem to have prevented his taking five wickets in the second innings or scoring a rapid 36. But strained foot or not, the strain of the season must have been catching up by this time.

It was the eleventh time Lohmann had appeared against the Australians on top of seven two years earlier and two tours down under in between. The goose surely needed to recharge its batteries or the supply of golden eggs would be discontinued. In November *Cricket* carried the following 'Report from Australia',

> We are all in Sydney inclined to oppose any further International cricket at all events for some years. I see that Lord Harris says England will require a comparatively early visit, but that can hardly take place in the face of our Association report which contains a clause to the effect that the Association will not grant patronage to any Australian team visiting England for four years or to any English team visiting Australia for three years.[18]

Perhaps that final Surrey fixture was a bridge too far for Lohmann. It may be that his injury was the cause of his declining a place on Major Warton's tour to South Africa. That may not have done him any harm. He had had two-and-a-half years non-stop cricket interspersed with two journeys to the other side of the world and back.

In recognition of his and Surrey's successful summer, he was rewarded 'for good cricket during the season' with £50, the other professionals sharing £120.[19] Mr Read again received £100 and Mr Key a wedding present costing £ 52 18s 7d.[20] Professionals did not feature when wedding presents were under consideration.

Abel summed up Lohmann's contribution to Surrey's championship season.

> Lohmann was then at his best, and on some of the bad wickets almost unplayable. He captured twice as many wickets in championship fixtures as all the remaining bowlers combined, 142 at something less than 9 runs apiece, Beaumont and Bowley following him with 59 and 34 while the remaining Surrey bowlers did not amount for 20 among them.[21]

In addition, Lohmann had taken 45 catches in first-class matches, a record at the time.

From the wider, national perspective, *Wisden* took a similar stance,

> Beyond everything else, the feature of the season was Lohmann's bowling. With the wickets to help him, the great bowler surpassed all he had done in previous years for his county, and obtained a truly phenomenal record.

> In the fourteen first class[22] matches he took 142 wickets at an average cost of under 9 each, and in the whole list of matches from only one of which he was absent, he took 207 wickets for less than 10 runs each.[23] Bowlers, of course, had very much their own way in 1888, but for all that it would be difficult to praise Lohmann beyond his deserts. Fortunately for him he was in perfect health all through the summer, and it really was a close thing between him and Turner, the Australian, as to which was more consistently excellent. It was only natural that while bowling in such an extraordinary way he should to some extent fall below his batting form of the previous year, but on many an occasion when runs were wanted, he proved himself exactly the right man in the right place, while his fielding in the slips was something quite exceptional. It was in 1885 that Lohmann first established his reputation, and so far each succeeding year has found him greater than he was before.[24]

Turner, on his first tour, had taken 283 wickets at 11.68. Lohmann and he were named in *Wisden* as two of the Six Great Bowlers of the Year, one of several precursors of the Five Cricketers of the Year. They were accompanied by Briggs, Ferris, Peel, and Woods.

Four years after *Lillywhite*'s lukewarm optimism about Lohmann's future in the game, the *Chief Cricketers of 1888* acknowledged the progress he had made.

> One of the very best all-round cricketers of the day; a reliable bowler on all wickets with plenty of work, varies his pace and pitch with judgment; a very dangerous bat at times, with plenty of hit, always reliable at a pinch; a brilliant field anywhere, particularly successful at short-slip where he made a number of wonderful catches.

1889

A bottle of wine and a biscuit
Johnny Briggs

REFRESHED BY a winter's rest, Lohmann embarked on what was to be another season of success for himself and his county. For the previous two Aprils he had been on his way back from Australia. Now his pre-season warm up had to be in England and he reeled off 103 for Leighton against Mr O G Radcliffe's team.[25] Once again, however, it was not for his batting that Lohmann would be remembered in future years.

> ...when I began to take an interest in county cricket, Sussex and Surrey were weak. Middlesex and Kent variable. By 1889, however, the tide had turned – in favour of Surrey. And the triumphal progress of the Ovalites was largely due to the prowess of one man – George Alfred Lohmann.
> Lohmann was just the cricketer Surrey needed. The attack depended almost entirely on Edward Barratt, a native of Stockton-on-Tees and a slow left-hander, and George Jones, medium pace.
> Every possible attempt was made to strengthen the Surrey eleven. Two new bowlers were introduced – John Beaumont, a Yorkshireman, and Thomas Bowley, a native of Notts. Both were fast and both were good. And then came Lohmann – right-hand medium pace with a very deadly faster ball and the power of turning it either way. He also knew about the value of flight and made full use of his knowledge. With his very high delivery, he was continually dropping short of what the batsman expected. Indeed, it has been said that he was the first English bowler to follow the example of Spofforth and make variety the chief weapon of his attack.[26]

The season brought with it a number of changes, including five-ball overs, provision for a captain to declare an innings closed – albeit only on the third day – and it was to be an Australian-free summer.

Lohmann's elder brother, Stewart, also made a bit of an impact, after playing a few games for the Colts in earlier seasons. He played for George's XI against L Hall's XI at Scarborough.

> S B Lohmann, an elder brother of the famous Surrey cricketer, who had played on a few occasions for the Surrey Colts was the chief scorer with a well got 35, and the two Lohmanns, as will be seen, were responsible for more than one half of the total got from the bat.[27]

He also played for his brother's XI against Streatham the following year and doubtless in other matches receiving no press coverage. He was later to play professional cricket in the USA for the Merion Club in Philadelphia.

In a non-first-class fixture with Essex, George Lohmann and his newly acquired bowling partner Sharpe, the successor to Beaumont and Bowley, began a successful partnership which was not restricted to bowling.

> The performance of Lohmann and Sharpe at the Oval on Monday, in putting on 149 for Surrey's last wicket is not, it will be useful to know, the best performance of its kind in Inter-County Cricket, at least in the matter of runs added. In the actual record Surrey was a participant, though in that instance, the sufferer, as Briggs and Pilling were able to increase the Lancashire total against the Surrey bowling in July 1885 at Liverpool, by

173 runs for the tenth wicket.[28] In one respect, Lohmann's achievement was, however, I should say, unique. Going in fifth wicket down, he only had, I believe, three balls to play before Sharpe the eleventh batsman came in and he got every run in his score of 105 after the ninth wicket had fallen. I question whether there is another instance in important matches of one of the last two batsmen in a side adding 100 after commencing the partnership without a run to his credit.[29]

Sharpe's career with Surrey was to be effective, but relatively brief, that of William Lockwood, another Nottinghamshire-born player rather longer. Both had qualified for Surrey by residence.

By this time it was virtually accepted that Lohmann would take wickets every match to the extent it was almost newsworthy if he did not. He averaged just under 7.5 wickets per match, including his innings and match best for Surrey, 9-65 and 15-98 against Sussex at Hove, where,

Lohmann who had taken nine of the ten Sussex wickets in the first innings again bowled with remarkable success and half the side were out with the total only 43.[30]

Accolades were so frequent they began to border on the tedious.

In James Lillywhite's benefit match, South v North at Priory Park, Chichester,

Lohmann bowled, as will be seen, with such success, that they were in a minority of 91 runs when the tenth wicket fell.[31]

Against Middlesex at Lord's,

Lohmann bowled with great judgment and discrimination. He kept up the Pavilion End throughout, and took eight of the wickets at an average cost of under 11 runs.[32]

His final figures were 47-21-86-8.

Against Yorkshire at Bramall Lane,

...no one but Peel offered any lengthy resistance to Lohmann's bowling.[33]

In the return match against Sussex at The Oval,

Lohmann proved too good for the remaining batsmen.[34]

Against Gloucestershire in the Cheltenham Festival when he took 6-68 and was twice responsible for the dismissal of W G Grace,

> Lohmann and Beaumont bowled with such success at the outset that six of Gloucestershire's best batsmen were down with the total 45.[35]

and at The Oval in an eight-wicket defeat by Lancashire,

> The only bowler who seemed to trouble the Lancashire men at all was Lohmann and he had, at times, very bad luck, time after time beating the batsmen, but without success. Still, his analysis of 51 overs for 65 runs and seven wickets was a very fine one.[36]

and in the return match against Yorkshire,

> When Lohmann... came on again the game underwent a great change.[37]

In the previous match with Kent, Lohmann and Beaumont had bowled Kent out for 48 and 53. Curiously, their analyses were almost identical; Beaumont bowled two more balls; Lohmann two more maidens; both had match figures of 10-49. In between, Martin and Wright had bowled Surrey out for 92, so only four bowlers were used in the match.

There were also some useful contributions with the bat.

Against Leicestershire at The Oval,

> ...the stand of Mr Read and Lohmann altered the game altogether and while they were together the score was increased by 122 runs.[38]

And in the second innings,

> another useful stand was made by Mr Key and Lohmann. The latter played carefully.

At The Oval against Sussex,

> Mr Read and Lohmann caused several changes of bowling.[39]

and against Lancashire,

> ...of the Surrey batsmen only Mr Key, and subsequently Lohmann, showed any competence and both played really good cricket... Lohmann joined Maurice Read, and then came the very best cricket of the match. The

ground was improving every minute, but from the first the two batsmen never seemed to be in the least puzzled by the bowlers and hit all round with composite confidence and judgment... Lohmann continued to hit with equal freedom and ultimately carried out his bat for 66, one of the very best innings he has played.[40]

Lohmann's batting made an impression on a youthful Pelham Warner,

We once saw him make 66 runs on a bad wicket against Lancashire at the Oval, an innings which we have never forgotten. Surrey had followed on and five wickets fell before Barlow and Briggs for 25 runs. Then Lohmann joined Maurice Read and we saw some superb cricket. The wicket was still difficult... and both batsmen were hit, but the batting was perfect and the Surrey crowd, always so keen and appreciative of any good thing, yelled with delight at any run-getting stroke. Lohmann is the finest all-round cricketer Surrey has ever possessed.[41]

Warner's recollection of the detail might be fallible. It was Watson and Briggs who had done the damage and the score when Lohmann joined Maurice Read was 84-6; but it is significant that Lohmann's batting, if not the statistics of the match, remain bright and vivid in the memory 35 years later.

Earlier in the season, in the Gentlemen v Players match at Lord's, Lohmann and Briggs had operated in tandem to dismiss the Gentlemen twice in a day and win the match for their side by ten wickets. Briggs was to recall,

George Lohmann and I started at a quarter to twelve, and bowled up to luncheon time on a boiling hot day, when we had our first rest. It may show you how bowling knocks up a man when I say that on reaching the pavilion, George said to me: 'Johnny, I can't eat any lunch.' 'No more can I,' I said. So we agreed to have a bottle of wine and a biscuit. This may seem to some people shocking extravagance for professionals, but after all we had to do the best for our side. After our lunch we bowled straight on (the Gentlemen had to follow) until 5.30 when Lohmann had to give up. I kept on until the match was finished and we were both dead beat. Sherwin, our captain, was anxious for us to do a record, and I would have given almost anything to have been able to say that I bowled through two innings with George Lohmann.[42]

In a total of 148, Lohmann had 33-7-81-4 and Briggs 33-14-57-5 and in the follow on total of 137, 29-10-58-4 and 35.1-17-41-4. Shacklock bowled the residue of 7-1-27-2. Given the dehydrating effects of alcohol, the pair's performance verged on the miraculous.

For the second consecutive season, Lohmann had taken more than 200 wickets, this time at 13.43, contributing to Surrey's again being county champions – or at least part-champions. On the informal rule-of-thumb of one point for a win and half a point for a draw, Surrey had 10.5 points, but so did Lancashire and Nottinghamshire, albeit with fewer wins. The situation led to correspondence and discussions about whether a draw really was worth half a win and whether the head-to-head between the counties involved should play a part. The result was that the championship was formalised for the following year, initially on an all-play-all basis home and away, with points determined by ignoring draws, and deducting the number of defeats from the number of wins. In most seasons, it would have produced the same county champions and placings very similar to those resulting from more complex methods of awarding bonus points either for a first innings lead, faster scoring or reaching fixed targets of runs and wickets.

In *Cricket* in 1889, *Lillywhite's* summarised,

> The chief honours in bowling were, it goes without saying monopolised by the professionals. Lohmann, Attewell, Briggs, Peel, Wright, Martin and Mold each took over a hundred wickets, and the first named had the distinction of being the only one able to take more than double that number… considering the amount of work that Lohmann had to do throughout, his success was remarkable.[43]

and later, when reviewing Surrey's season,

> Lohmann's batting more than once saved Surrey at a critical moment… Lohmann's bowling was as usual one of the most notable features of Surrey's cricket.[44]

The Committee was less generous to its professionals than it had been the previous season, possibly because the title of Champion County was shared rather than awarded outright, but more likely because of a cavalier, ill-considered decision of a committee with a patronising attitude towards its professionals. It resolved,

> that the sum of £100 be divided equally between the leading professionals Read, Lohmann, Beaumont, Bowley, Wood, Abel, Henderson, Lockwood and Sharpe.[45]

It could scarcely have been expected that Lohmann would not have noticed the difference between the 'bonus' and that for the previous season. His letter to the Surrey Secretary was direct and to the point.

> Salcott House, Wandsworth Common
> Jan 17, 1890
> Dear Sir
> Your cheque to hand for which I thank you. I fail to see why my services should be less worthy of recognition in 1889 than those rendered in previous years. Kindly place this before the Committee.
> Truly yours
> G A Lohmann
>
> Mr Roberts gave notice that he would move at the next meeting that a sum not exceeding forty pounds be given to Lohmann but that the Committee do not pledge themselves in any future year to grant any bonus to any of the Surrey players.[46]

It was part of a continuing power struggle between the committee and their professionals. The committee members owed their position as officials of a prestigious club mainly to the efforts of their paid employees, but they continued to view the relationship between them as one of benevolent despotism and the committee wished to make it clear that they reserved the right to withdraw the benevolence whenever they chose to do so. However the services of those on whom their position depended needed to be retained and on 17 April they received a report that Lohmann's bonus had been topped up by £38.17.9 to £50 and the others by £8.17.9 to £20.

1890

> ...the best all-round man among English cricketers
> *Wisden* 1891

THE RESOLUTION of the Australians to take a break from international cricket for a while did not last very long. In the Spring of 1890 they were back for a 38-match tour. Lohmann played against them in no fewer than twelve. It would have been thirteen had it not been for the Old Trafford Test scheduled for late August being completely washed out.

He resumed hostilities with them at Sheffield Park, the private ground of Lord Sheffield, set in lavish grounds near Uckfield, between East Grinstead and Lewes, in Sussex. The field is still there, but has not been used for cricket for some time and the elegant Victorian pavilion has long gone as have the facilities for the 25,000 spectators who were admitted free to what, except for 1888, was the traditional opening fixture of Australian touring teams between 1884 and 1896. In the last year, the match was attended by the Prince of Wales. It was the apogee of country house cricket.

As Henry Holroyd, the future 3rd Earl of Sheffield had joined the diplomatic service and been Member of Parliament for East Sussex. But it is as a patron of cricket that the bachelor aristocrat is best remembered. He had been a minor, but significant, player in the organisation of the first Test match in England in 1880, as President of Sussex, agreeing to Surrey's request to rearrange his county's fixture with the tourists to enable the match to be staged.

On inheriting the Sheffield Park estate, he arranged to have a cricket ground laid out, with facilities for first-class cricket. Situated on the south-east fringes of the estate, it commanded spectacular views of the house and gardens, designed by Capability Brown. It also had the beneficial side-effect of providing employment for agricultural labourers during a period of economic depression.

The 1890 fixture was one of two occasions on which Lohmann played there (the other was for Lord Sheffield's XI against the MCC in the following season) and from the point of view of his Lordship's team, it was not an auspicious one. The second day was washed out completely and the Australians completed their first innings for 191 early on the third. Whether it was the rain-affected pitch or the traditionally lavish hospitality is debatable, but Ferris and Turner ran through the hosts for 27, of which W G Grace contributed 20 and Lohmann was joint second highest run maker with two. They did slightly better in the follow-on, but not well enough to prevent the tourists completing a flying start to their visit with victory by an innings and 34 runs. There were, however, plenty of other opportunities for Lohmann and his colleagues.

For Surrey, Lohmann's regular strike partner was John Sharpe who had made a dozen first-class appearances the previous season. At a time when the responsibility for the selection of Test teams lay with the ground authority, he was selected for The Oval Test but not the other two. It was perhaps as ironic that Sharpe, a Nottinghamshire man, should make a significant contribution to the Surrey attack as it was in earlier years that John Beaumont, the Yorkshireman, now giving way to Sharpe, should have done so.

> In one or two directions some cheap satire was indulged in about Surrey owing so much to a Nottingham bowler, but the sneers were quite beside the mark. Sharpe as a colt was quite disregarded at Nottingham, and the Surrey committee having developed his talents at the Oval, had every right under the existing residential qualifications to profit by them.[47]

However, *Wisden* was in no doubt about the role of this new star in an otherwise not very sparkling Surrey bowling firmament,

> More remarkable than any of the batting for Surrey in 1890 was the bowling of Lohmann and Sharpe. Of the work done by these two players it would be impossible to say too much, and their achievements were certainly among the very best of the season. Their records are curiously alike, but both in the first class county matches and in all engagements Sharpe had the distinction of beating Lohmann in the averages.
>
> Lohmann, though beaten in the bowling averages by his younger colleague, proved himself just as great a cricketer as ever and was far and away the best man in the Surrey eleven. Not only did he have the splendid record of 113 wickets in first-class county matches and 154 wickets in all matches, but he came out second in one batting table with an average of 29 and seventh in the other with an average of nearly 26.
>
> When, moreover, we add to his skill with the bat and ball his surpassing excellence in the field, it is no exaggeration to pronounce him at the present time the best all-round man among English cricketers. The weakness of Surrey cricket in 1889 was the lack of change bowling. Everything depended on Lohmann and Sharpe, and had any accident happened to either of the two great bowlers there is no saying how the county would have fared. Beaumont and Bowley fell so far below their old excellence that they played only on rare occasions.

Again, there were some remarkable performances, as at Derby when he was unable to bowl in the first innings because of a strained shoulder, but came back in the second to take 4-29 in 20.1 overs. It was a non-championship match, the only occasion on which W E Roller captained Surrey and one which speaks volumes for Lohmann's commitment and professionalism.

> In the first innings, Lohmann said that he was unable to bowl on account of a sprained side. The consequence was that Derbyshire made a lot of runs and we eventually put them in for the fourth innings of the match to get about 120 on a plumb wicket. It seemed odds of a hundred to one that they made the runs. But I went up to Lohmann and said "You've got to bowl, whether it hurts you or not". He said "All right. I'll see what I can do." Seldom have I seen him bowl and field as he did on that day; he took four wickets and caught out three other men and we won by about twenty runs.'[48]

With Sharpe at a wet Old Trafford, he emulated his performance with Beaumont against Kent at The Oval the previous summer, as they bowled through both innings, dismissing Lancashire for 61 and 50, in reply to

Surrey's 69 and 103. Briggs and Watson had, apart from three overs by Barlow, bowled similarly unchanged for Lancashire. Twenty-nine wickets fell on the first day and all ten wickets in Lancashire's second innings were bowled.

Albert Craig, the 'Surrey poet', provided the requisite doggerel.

> The Southerners showed at the wicket,
> A strange exhibition of Cricket;
> Sixty-nine was their score,
> Not a blessed run more,
> Yet the Lancashire 'cracks' fail'd to beat it.
> Surrey's chances improved every minute,
> Though their rivals strove bravely to win it;
> It was easy to tell
> As the home wickets fell,
> Unapproachable Lohmann was in it.
> You note down the fact as narrated
> Our champion is not over-rated,
> For twenty-one runs
> He drove seven from their guns,
> Seven men their positions vacated.

Once again, Lohmann had more than 200 first-class wickets, the first instance of a bowler reaching this target in three consecutive seasons. Others would repeat the achievement, but like Sir Roger Bannister's four-minute mile, no one else can ever be first. In all in 1890 he had 220 in 32 first-class matches. A measure of his accuracy, and of Sharpe's, is that he bowled two wides and Sharpe one – all season. Once again, Surrey won the county championship, but this time under the new arrangements, with six points, having won nine, lost three and drawn two of their fourteen championship matches. For the fifth year in succession, Lohmann had bowled more overs in first-class cricket than anyone else in the country. He had also broken his own fielding record with 49 catches.

Fifty years later, his performance in the Bank Holiday fixture at Trent Bridge was recalled by Sydney Santall.

> In 1890, I again went to Nottingham on the Whit Monday and, seated in the pavilion, watched another fine day's cricket. Notts batted first and William Gunn, as usual, played another excellent innings. But George Lohmann's wonderful bowling fascinated me most on this occasion. The wicket, I should imagine, was perfect, yet the great Surrey bowler sent down 65 overs for 81 runs and dismissed six of the Notts players, five of whom were leading batsmen.

> Lohmann, about this time, was at his best. I can see him now in my mind's eye, running up to bowl with his fair hair fluttering in the breeze and that slight touch of labour in his otherwise beautiful action. To watch him was an education to all cricketers. He was a great artist, and the hero of many a schoolboy in those far off days.[49]

At a club dinner to celebrate the season's success, in 'the new dining pavilion at the Kennington Oval, specially furnished and decorated for the occasion', Club president Viscount Oxenbridge summed up the season smugly.

> It had been stated that other important teams had fallen away because the men could not keep themselves fit, but certainly such a thing could never be said about the present Surrey team. Arrangements had been made that day by which the professionals would not go away empty-handed. The question of remuneration was always one of great importance to the Committee and it was their wish to continue the most cordial relations with the players.[50]

What the Committee said to the members and what they had recorded in their minutes following the post-season bonus negotiations of 1889 did not quite coincide. The professionals received similar bonuses to those of the previous season, Lohmann again £50, Walter Read his usual £100.

On the Test scene, England had the series sewn up 2-0 before the Old Trafford abandonment, having won by a comfortable seven wickets at Lord's, a rather less comfortable two wickets at The Oval. Lohmann had 0-43, 3-28, 3-34 and 3-32, being eclipsed in the second Test by débutant Fred Martin, Kent's left arm medium-fast bowler, who had twelve wickets in the match. Despite this, he was not invited to play at Old Trafford and appeared in only one more Test – against South Africa in Cape Town on Walter Read's 1891/92 tour.

1 *Cricket* 3 May 1888
2 *Cricket* 24 May 1888
3 *Cricket* 24 May 1888
4 *Cricket* 19 July 1888
5 Francis Thompson *At Lord's.* He is better known for *The Hound of Heaven*
6 *Cricket* 9 August 1888
7 *Wisden* 1889 p 87
8 3 August 1888
9 *The Cricketer* Spring Annual 1926
10 Bettesworth *op cit*
11 There was a *Dukinfield Herald*, but the earliest run in the British Newspaper Library is from 1890
12 *Wisden* 1889 p 327
13 *The Cricketer* 25 August 1925

14 Abel *op cit* p 63
15 *Cricket* 23 August 1888
16 *Cricket* 23 August 1888
17 1 November 1888
18 29 November 1888
19 Surrey CCC minutes 20 September 1888
20 *Cricket* 2 May 1889
21 Abel *op cit* p 63
22 i.e. inter-county matches
23 actually 209 at 10.9
24 1889 p 4
25 *Lillywhite's* 1890 p 207
26 *Cricketer* Spring Annual 1942 – *Looking Back* by a Country Vicar
27 *Cricket* 5 September 1889
28 Briggs and Pilling took the score from 191 to 364. Lohmann had 3-104.
29 *Cricket* 23 May 1889
30 *Cricket* 18 June 1889
31 *Cricket* 6 June 1889
32 *Cricket* 20 June 1889
33 *Cricket* 4 July 1889
34 *Cricket* 1 August 1889
35 *Cricket* 22 August 1889
36 Ib
37 *Cricket* 29 August 1889
38 *Cricket* 6 June 1889
39 *Cricket* 1 August 1889
40 *Cricket* 22 August 1889
41 *The Cricketer* 25 August 1925
42 Bettesworth *Chats on the Cricket Field* – *Cricket Field* 12 May 1894
43 *Lillywhite's* 1890 p 8
44 *Lillywhite's* 1890 p 83
45 Surrey CCC minutes 5 December 1889
46 Surrey CCC minutes 20 February 1890
47 *Wisden* 1891 p 4
48 Bettesworth *Chats on the Cricket Field* – *Cricket* 28 June 1900
49 *The Cricketer* Spring Annual 1940
50 *Cricket* 27 November 1890

CHAPTER 8

CHAMPIONS AGAIN (1891)

When Surrey ladled out defeat,
Who did it?
Norman Gale *The Hope of Surrey*

ALONG WITH around 29 million others, the name of George Lohmann is recorded in the 1891 Census of Population return. The personal details are accurate: age 25, Cricketer (Surrey), born at Kensington, Middlesex; the description and location rather more surprising. He is a Visitor at the Full Moon public house, 26 North Street, Bristol. The date of the Census was Sunday 5 April and the purpose of his visit is not clear. He appears to be unaccompanied, the other residents being the Landlord, his wife, sister-in-law, two school-age sons and eight bar and domestic staff. Nor can it be known whether the visit was just for one night or part of an extended stay.

Six months later he would be joining W G Grace on a third and final tour of Australia and it is conceivable that some early negotiations might have been going on. There were a number of club fixtures the previous day, and the previous week, on Easter Monday, 30 March, the county side, including Grace and George's former and future adversary, John Ferris, had played Twenty-four Colts of the county. Cricket in March and early April – at least outdoors – is unusual in England; it is unlikely anything was happening in Surrey and it is possible that Lohmann was taking advantage of the earlier start in the west to get a bit of pre-season practice – all speculative. In any event, six weeks later, he was starting another first-class county season with Surrey.

Before that, however, he played for the South against the North at Lord's.

> With the one exception indeed of M Read no one else but Lohmann offered any resistance to the Northern bowlers. His 61 was an exceptional good display of free cricket.[1]

It was his highest score of the season, his best bowling figures that year coming against Nottinghamshire at The Oval, following a useful contribution with the bat.

> Lohmann hit with such confidence and resolution that when he was out 59 had been added, of which his own share was 45…
> …no one else offered any resistance to the bowling of Lockwood and Lohmann… Lohmann bowled, with remarkable success at the finish taking seven wickets for only 20 runs.[2]

The match against Somerset was won decisively – by an innings and 375 runs. Having accumulated 449, Surrey still had time to take two wickets before the close on the first day. The other eighteen followed rapidly on the second day, as Somerset were bowled out for 37 – twice, Lohmann 11-40, Sharpe 9-31. No other bowlers were required.

Against Kent, during Canterbury week,

> When Sharpe was put on, however, he proved almost as destructive as Lohmann, and backed up by fine fielding, Surrey succeeded in dismissing their opponents in an hour and a half for the small total of 69 – exactly 100 runs in arrears. Helped by the ground Lohmann did a remarkable performance. His analysis was indeed quite out of the common.[3]

It was 18.1-12-14-6 and, in the second innings, 24-14-28-4.

Surrey were runaway winners of the championship. Once again, Lohmann had made a major contribution.

Although he registered no first-class centuries in the season, he had 105 for H Phillip's XII against Mr Pigg's XII on 17 September.[4]

When the time for annual bonuses came around, 'certain communications Lohmann had had with reference to his playing for Middlesex' concentrated the mind of the committee. He had also made it known that he was qualified by residence to play for Hampshire.

> …I have been living there for some years… I find that it is possible to be qualified for three counties at the same time, for I have a birth qualification for Middlesex, my father lives in Surrey and has done so nearly all his life, while by residence I am qualified for Hampshire.[5]

What had now become his 'usual honorarium' became a 'fixed and absolute payment' and he was guaranteed at least £300 per annum irrespective of the number of appearances and of his performances.

> Viscount Oxenbridge reported the result of the interview he had had at the request of the Match Committee with G A Lohmann on the subject of certain communications Lohmann had had with reference to his playing for Middlesex.
>
> Resolved
>
> 1. That Lohmann have a retaining fee of £100 during the season of 1892 with a claim of Surrey for his first services over and above the usual payments connected with Surrey matches.
> 2. That the usual honorarium of £50 shall be made a fixed and absolute payment.
> 3. That the whole payments to Lohmann the one year of 1892 shall not be under £300.
> 4. That this arrangement be for the season of 1892 only.[6]

The contract was at the time unique, but the precedent was followed in later years by similar arrangements with Hayward and Richardson and blazed the trail for other counties and their professionals to follow. It was raw market place economics with price determined by supply, demand and competition. It was also a recognition of professional value, though for Lohmann, professionalism was never only a matter of money, but of approach to the game and attitude of mind.

1 *Cricket* 14 May 1891
2 *Cricket* 6 August 1891
3 *Cricket* 13 August 1891
4 *Lillywhite's* 1892 p 187
5 Bettesworth *op cit*
6 Surrey CCC minutes 29 September 1891- special meeting

CHAPTER 9

AUSTRALIA WITH LORD SHEFFIELD (1891-92)

...of the three great test matches
Those Australian 'duffers' won two!

Declining Interest

THE TEAM which toured Australia in 1891/92 was, according to the *Sportsman,*[1] the strongest to leave England. Similar sentiments were expressed by the press on both sides of the world, as they were of Peter May's 1958/59 Australian touring party. The wisdom of making and believing such statements is questionable and sometimes a candidate for humble pie eating awards, as Tony Greig's intention to make the 1976 West Indians 'grovel'.

By the end of the 1880s, interest in cricket, particularly in Anglo–Australian contests, was beginning to decline. There were a number of reasons for this, not least a perceived diminution in the quality of Australian cricket, caused in part by the defection of some leading players to England and a surfeit of tours to and from the 'mother country'. Australian teams had toured in alternate summers since 1876 and English teams had reciprocated at roughly similar intervals[2] culminating in the farce of the 1886/87 tour being followed by two simultaneous tours the following season. Familiarity was breeding contempt and a sensible halt was called. It has been estimated that during that season, the largely self-destructive rivalries, by no means confined to cricket and its politics, between the colonies of New South Wales and Victoria resulted in no fewer than six variations of an Australian Eleven meeting four English combinations,[3] only one of which was designated a Test match.

A players' strike in the 1884/85 season had soured relations. The side which had toured England the previous summer contested the first Test match in Adelaide, but were replaced en bloc for the Melbourne Test when they declined to play for less than fifty per cent of the gate money. A sceptical cricket-watching public was not over-interested in politics, nor in lending its support to international matches of diluted quality, the main purpose of which seemed to be to line the pockets of the organisers and players (including, and perhaps especially, those of the amateurs), rather than contribute to improving the standards of the game.

A letter to the *Sydney Morning Herald* analysed the reasons, some specific to Australia at the beginning of the 1890s, others of general application which continue to be addressed by administrators more than a hundred years later. A few solutions were proposed, some of which have been implemented in part in the guise of limited overs cricket and others, for example, the 'split innings' have been the subject of experiment and continue to be debated within the International Cricket Council.

THE DECLINE OF CRICKET

> To whatever cause it may be attributed, there can be little doubt that there is nothing like the interest manifested by the public here in this once popular pastime. Where thousands of people used to pay to see a first-class match, and it was no unusual thing to see the ground absolutely thronged with enthusiastic spectators during intercolonial or international games, we now find a comparatively sparse attendance and not nearly the enthusiasm of old. One thing has certainly contributed in no small degree to this defection and that is the migration of some of our foremost cricketers to the mother country. Little wonder that public interest in the game should fall. We have at present an exceptionally strong English team on our shores while such men as W L Murdoch, Spofforth and Ferris who would prove of such valuable assistance to us are playing in England. Then there are features in modern cricket which, I think, materially lessen the public interest in the game. One is the length of time it takes nowadays to complete a match (usually more than the average lover of the game can afford) and another is the large element of luck which the extension of the game introduces. For instance, while it might often happen in a two or three days match, the weather could be equally favourable to both sides, it could scarcely be hoped in a changeable climate like ours that fine weather would prevail throughout a match of longer duration. Could not some system of half-time be introduced whereby this element of chance might be largely diminished? – say, that each side be allowed to bat alternately for half the playing time each day. To my mind, this plan would have many advantages. It would in the first place put the players on more equal terms as regards condition of wickets, would be less tedious and tiresome to them than a whole day in the field, and would prove more interesting to the public who are unable to attend throughout, as they would have the opportunity of seeing both sides bat

> and field on the same day. One thing is certain and that is public interest in cricket is declining here, and will continue to do so until some steps are taken to again popularise the game.[4]
> THE SCUD

Similar sentiments were expressed in correspondence to the newspaper. Maybe the ailing patient was ready for an injection of something different in the form of the first visit by an English touring side for four seasons. Perhaps the time was again ripe for a resumption of hostilities at the highest level. As in the 1930s, the economy was at a low ebb and a successful national team would be an effective antidote to depression – both economic and psychological. Australia had changed in the eighteen years since Grace's last visit, but so had the approach of the England captain.

There were also doubts in England about the strength of Australian cricket and some hostility towards the prospect of an Australian tour. Seven of the nine first-class counties opposed the idea, though it did receive some support from the second-class counties and the universities. MCC, in not untypical fence-sitting mode, expressed no opinion. Eventually, it was agreed to invite the Australians for 1894, though that was later modified and the next tour to England took place in 1893.[5]

Lord Sheffield seems to have had no other motive beyond patriotic benevolence and a wish to revive interest in cricket in Australia. Although he drove a hard bargain with the professionals, with the result that Gunn and Shrewsbury declined to participate, the £3,000 paid to W G Grace, plus travel and accommodation and the expenses of taking his wife and two children, Bessie and Charles Butler, meant that whatever the 'gates', his Lordship was always likely to be backing a loser. The professionals were paid around ten per cent of Grace's fee. Tom Horan had persuaded Lord Sheffield of the likely revival in Australian cricket that would be occasioned by resurrecting the practice of taking a strong English touring side.

Shrewsbury had given the benefit of his experience of four earlier tours including some on budgeting and the debilitating cost of Grace's involvement. Weighing the pros and cons, the Earl decided to go ahead. There was the added bonus that his own health was not good and he felt that the weeks at sea and months in the southern sun away from the harsh climatic conditions of an English winter could only benefit him.

A strong team was assembled, in the absence of Shrewsbury and Gunn, probably the best that could be produced. On the bowling, Horan commented that it was,

> as near perfection as possible. Attewell, Lohmann, Briggs and Peel are well known to us as a formidable quartet. They are unsurpassed in precision…[6]

The Voyage

ON 2 OCTOBER the team left England on the *R M S Arcadia*, seen off by a crowd of well-wishers and dignitaries. As on previous journeys to the Antipodes, with nothing to see but sea, boredom was always possible, but there seem to have been sufficient organised activities to help pass the six weeks spent on board. The Bay of Biscay, as always, affected both experienced and inexperienced sailors. The *Sportsman* reported from Gibraltar on 13 October,

> The passage up to the present time had been lovely, notwithstanding a long swell in the Bay of Biscay, which affected Attewell, and induced benevolence to the fishes on the part of Briggs, who offered them sustenance.

A fellow passenger was the explorer of Africa, Henry Stanley, accompanied by his wife and mother-in-law. Reports commented on his lameness and his using a crutch.

A brief break in Malta allowed time for a little cricket and a match was played on the Naval Ground on coconut matting over asphalt. The team wore its colours of purple, crimson and gold (nothing new about coloured clothing) against Eighteen of that island, comprising nine soldiers and nine sailors. Once again, as on the 1886/87 tour there was a hold-up, this time at Brindisi, but occasioned not by cholera, but by an accident to the mail-train.

In addition to the Malta match, there was also a stop in Colombo where the *Arcadia* arrived on 31 October and a fixture was played against Twenty-Two of All Ceylon. The tourists were all out for 142, their hosts 72 for 10 when rain curtailed the reply.

Interviewed for *Cricket* in Colombo for a feature which appeared under the headline 'The Best All-Round Cricketer in the World', Lohmann's optimism reflected the general mood.

> ...we are a bit weaker in batting than a representative England team ought to be, but we are very strong in bowling. We have as fine a wicket-keeper as there is in England, and Grace is a really good captain. Of course, Gunn or Shrewsbury would have greatly strengthened us, but we all mean business, and ought to give a good account of ourselves. I'll bet any one that, before we leave Australia, we make 500 in one innings somewhere...[7]

He was not alone in overestimating the success of the tour, his opinion of Grace's captaincy would be subject to review and he would have lost his bet, but not by much. The highest team score of the tour was to be 499, the last wicket, Gregor MacGregor's, falling to a run out.

Lohmann's profile, however, was at its highest. Arthur Shrewsbury, now retailing cricket goods, wrote to Alfred Shaw who was managing the side,

> If you could get W G or Lohmann to give us a good testimonial about Cricket Balls, it would do us good.[8]

As well as the stopovers, some scheduled, some enforced, the inevitable boredom was relieved to an extent by the usual and perhaps some less usual deck games,

> We continue to have splendid weather. It is just like steaming on a lake. We had some sports yesterday afternoon. The 60 yards race was won by M Read, 'Slinging the Monkey' was won by a passenger named Wagner who beat Stoddart. Mr J S Robinson was runner up to Lohmann for putting potatoes in a basket. Cock-fighting and the High Jump standing fell respectively to the Williams's, two brothers from Jesus College Cambridge. Dr Grace's daughter, Miss Bessie Grace won the Ladies race (egg and spoon). MacGregor and B Grace took the Needle and Cigar Race, and R Peel the Whiskey and Soda Race.[9]

Contests rather more competitive than egg-and-spoon races and putting potatoes in a basket lay ahead. In preparation, a practice net was erected, but it had its limitations.

> The team have been busy each afternoon with practice on cocoanut matting on the deck, the other passengers showing very great interest in the proceedings. The play was not carried out without difficulties and Lohmann found the awning above interfered with his 'dropping ball'.[10]

Notwithstanding the pessimism and scepticism of some of its correspondents about the state of cricket in Australia, the *Sydney Morning Herald* adopted an up-beat stance, giving high profile coverage to the tour and providing full statistical analyses of all the tourists, of the 1886/87 and 1887/88 tours, as well as performances in the 1891 English season. The newspaper expressed the view, supported by both observation and numerical evidence that 'Lohmann may be looked upon as the best all round man in the team'[11] and saw no reason to modify that view when the playing side of the tour got under way.

After the usual welcomes, telegrams, receptions and practice, the tour proper began on 20 November with a fixture against South Australia at the Adelaide Oval. The *Herald* commented,

> The English fielding was perfect, Briggs, Sharpe, Lohmann and Stoddart doing brilliant work… Attewell was the best bowler, keeping an excellent length. Lohmann also bowled well but was not so deadly.[12]

Grace had won the toss and invited the locals to bat on a damp pitch. They counteracted by opening with two tail-enders to occupy the crease while the pitch improved. The plan worked to an extent, as the first wicket fell at 63, but the regular batsmen failed to capitalise and added only a hundred more. Attewell had done the bulk of the damage with 44.4-17-47-5 and Lohmann had played a supporting part with 44-20-74-2. Lord Sheffield's XI batted the whole of the second day to establish a lead of 160, then dismissed their hosts for 98, Attewell once again being the destroyer-in-chief with 39-20-34-6. George Giffen, Australia's leading all-rounder, who had recently won an inter-state match against Victoria virtually single-handedly with a double century and 16 wickets, bowled through most of the English team's innings to take 7-152. His style was not dissimilar from that of Lohmann, being a mixture of off-spin and medium pace. But it was nowhere near good enough on this occasion as the visitors triumphed by an innings and 62 runs, a highly satisfactory start to the tour.

The huge win at Adelaide was one of several before the first Test. They travelled on to Melbourne where they annihilated Victoria, a state side not without its own internal problems, by the even larger margin of an innings and 107 runs. Lohmann was not required to bowl in the first innings, but had 5-41 in the second (coincidentally, so did Attewell), after an innings dominated by W G Grace who carried his bat for 159 in a total of 284. Apart from Abel's 29 in a first wicket partnership of 91, the only other significant contribution was Lohmann's aggressive 39 in a second wicket partnership of 70.

> Lohmann began vigorously as he usually does, and his fine driving knocked off the medium pace bowlers… played a fine innings, his cutting and driving being capital.[13]

The difference in English and Australian pitches was something to which the tourists had to acclimatise, but they seem to have done so reasonably well at least in the first part of the tour. The press commented on W G Grace's changed approach to batting.

> He does not attempt to watch the ball as closely as he has had to on English wickets during the last year or two, and he is quite right, for he knows it will come on all right, and that is more than he can rely on on the average English ground.[14]

The final first-class match before the first Test, played almost a month in advance of it, was a low scoring affair against New South Wales on a bowler-friendly pitch at Sydney. Lohmann had Jones caught and bowled from the second ball of the match and ended with figures of 33-13-44-4 and an almost equally impressive 32.4-17-35-2 in the second innings. His fielding, however, had a rare lapse from his usual high standards.

> First of all Lohmann the prince of slips badly missed him [Gregory] and McGregor followed suit a moment later.[15]

But it was as a batsman on this occasion that he made his mark. Coming in at no 7 with 67 still required, he and Bobby Peel steered the tourists to a four wicket win, the closest of the encounters with the state sides but good enough to provide the confidence boost generated by three first-class victories off the reel.

The month between that victory and the first Test match was spent 'on the road' between Sydney and Melbourne and the cricket played had more to do with maximising commercial gains than with serious preparation for the Tests. Half a dozen fixtures against opposition, superior in numbers, but of a quality which was, in the Antipodean vernacular, 'pretty ordinary' did nothing to replicate Test match conditions. There were matches against Twenty of Cumberland District at Parramatta, Twenty-Two of Camden, Twenty-Four of Bowral (twenty-three long forgotten, one Richard Whatman – who made 1 in the first innings at no 15 and, demoted to no 20 in the second did not do quite as well as that, c Lohmann b Briggs – remembered as the uncle of Sir Donald Bradman), Twenty-Two of Goulbourn and, either side of Christmas, the rather stronger Sixteen of the Melbourne Club and then Twenty of Ballarat.

The Englishmen won four, three by an innings, and drew two of these encounters which produced some eccentric-looking bowling figures such as Lohmann's 27-18-17-12 at Camden, 21-10-22-8 at Bowral and Briggs' match figures of 24-87 in the same fixture. Lohmann then enhanced his reputation as a batsman by making 106 at no 8 in the Ballarat match between Christmas and New Year.

Maybe these matches boosted confidence, but the results were meaningless in the context of first-class cricket and, as a consequence, the fall from and by Grace in the first Test match seemed even more traumatic.

Despite the *Herald*'s pessimism, there was a keen interest in the first Test match which began at Melbourne on New Year's Day. The same newspaper reported,

> The first of the three test matches between the English team led by W G Grace and a representative team of Australians was commenced today at the Melbourne Cricket Ground. There was such a gathering of people to witness the play as has yet been seen at a cricket match for many years past. The gate takings for the day amounted to £1110. The total number who passed through the turnstiles was 20,110. The Governor gave the cricket preference over racing. On meeting to elect a captain, Moses proposed Blackham, and the suggestion was unanimously approved as a compliment to Victoria. Blackham won the toss and Lyons and Bannermann went in to bat. The Englishmen took their places as follows: Grace, point, McGregor wicket, Sharpe and Peel bowling, Abel slip, Lohmann extra slip... The 'bowlers' made a short third slip...[16]

Already well established was the Australian practice of selecting a team, then choosing a captain from those selected, although nowadays it is done rather earlier than the morning of the match.

The match fluctuated over five days, the first time that one of these 'timeless' tests had extended beyond four. England had a narrow first innings lead of 24, dismissed Australia again for 236, leaving 213 to win. As Grace and Abel put on sixty for the first wicket, they seemed well on the way, but not for the only time in England's cricketing history, a dramatic collapse followed and they were eventually all out 54 runs short. For once, Lohmann's contribution was negligible, 0-40 in the first innings, 2-53 in the second and 3 and 0 with the bat, lbw b Giffen and c Bannerman b Turner. The defeat was unexpected. Grace defied his surname and acted with ill humour. The *Bulletin* reported,

> W G's manners haven't improved. He went regularly amok over the Melbourne defeat and grossly insulted a newspaper-man who asked him in a civil way for information.[17]

The *Bulletin*'s stance was traditionally semi-scurrilous, anti-Royalist, anti-British and anti-Grace but the behaviour reported here is consistent with that at other times on the tour.

In London, *The Times* used the unanticipated defeat as the basis for a leading article which envisaged an expansion of international sport, especially within the Empire and can perhaps be seen as a foreshadowing of the Imperial Cricket Conference, the Triangular Tournament and Olympic and Empire Games.

> An indefinite vista of matches belonging potentially as much to the vanquished as to the victors of today, stretches across the tracks of the future. Perhaps the popularity of this competition in national sport

> between the different parts of the empire is worthy of the serious attention of statesmen... There is something fascinating in the idea of such a pan-Britannic gallery, recalling the pan-Athenian festivals of old. Its value might be only sentimental; but those who scan the field of politics, even colonial politics, see that sentiment is still a power in the field.[18]

The cricket aside, the Melbourne environment could have done neither Lohmann nor anyone else any good.

> The place has been dubbed Marvellous Smellbourne on account of the variety and strength of the odour emitted from badly-drained streets and backyards.[19]

It was doubtless a contributory factor to the health problems which would begin within the year and dog Lohmann to the end of his days. His relatively indifferent performance in the Test match may not be unconnected. The fielding brilliance was still there. The dismissal of Moses from Sharpe's bowling on the second day was described in the following terms,

> George Lohmann made the most brilliant of catches as easily and coolly as though taking such balls were a matter of everyday occurrence to him.

but, by contrast,

> Lohmann seemed to tire and did not bowl with his accustomed energy. Confining himself to off theory, he came in for a great deal of 'barracking' from the crowd, especially when Bannerman allowed one whole over to pass him.[20]

Although Lohmann was a long way from being written off, as his subsequent performances, particularly that in the next Test at Sydney were to demonstrate, the first clues to his declining health may perhaps be detected.

After the Test match, it was back to minor cricket where Lohmann continued to turn in some outstanding performances, for example his 36-14-57-13 and 43-21-67-7 in the drawn match against twenty Combined Juniors at Melbourne on 23, 25 and 26 January. In the second innings, as their opponents unsuccessfully chased a target of 141, he and Attewell were the only bowlers used, the Nottinghamshire man finishing with 43-25-30-9.

> Lohmann's 20 wickets for 124 runs was a fine exhibition of bowling form, better even than Attewell's 10 wickets for 48.[21]
> The last men made a very feeble resistance to Lohmann's bowling.[22]

A repeat of that kind of resistance in the second innings would have resulted in a win for Lord Sheffield's team. The Juniors were 106-16, when stumps and the match were drawn at 2 pm, an uncommonly early finishing time, but one occasioned by the railway timetable. The Englishmen had to catch the train to Sydney for the second Test match.

On 29 January in Sydney, under what might be termed 'English' conditions, the tourists spearheaded by Lohmann, began the match as though they would have no difficulty avenging the defeat at Melbourne. His inconsequential contribution to the first Test forgotten, in circumstances which could have been made for him, Lohmann, for the second time bagged eight wickets in an innings at the SCG.

> Lohmann's bowling was very deadly. He seemed to find a spot on the off and troubled all the batsmen. The Surrey crack, however, bowled a splendid length, and varied his pitch and pace with judgment, and may well be congratulated on a performance of such singular merit. It is worthy of remark that Lohmann was not tried first, his club colleague Sharpe having led off without success…[23]

In January 2004, Anil Kumble slipped into fourth place amongst a group of Englishmen who had monopolised the top positions on the leader board of best Test bowling performances on the ground. It was the last Test match for Steve Waugh, born one hundred years to the day after the man who still occupies the first two places.

> The weather was such as at times to cause apprehension of rain, and alternately the sky was darkened with heavy clouds under the influence of a strong south-easterly breeze, and again brightened up.
> Lohmann proved very successful with the ball taking eight wickets for 58 runs. His success was due in a large measure to the splendid manner in which he and the other trundlers were backed up by the fielders, who worked with untiring zeal, Sharpe in particular doing yeoman service.[24]

Looking back six years later, George Giffen, who was caught by Abel off Lohmann's bowling for six remembered Australia's first innings.

> The wicket, though not a bad one, would help the bowlers slightly, and unless more rain fell, it was bound to improve. However the only game was to go in first. This we did and our opponents got rid of us for 145, or rather George Lohmann did, for he secured eight wickets for 58 runs. The wicket assisted him a little, but really he bowled magnificently. He was at his best then, and on that day was unplayable. I had a great admiration for

> Lohmann's bowling. He was a bowler after my own heart. Seldom trying to weary batsmen with off-theory, he preferred to out-manœuvre them, and I doubt whether England has produced, in my time, a bowler of more resource and one who had greater command over the ball.[25]

Lohmann's performance, outstanding as it was, was still insufficient to bring England victory. Australia, after conceding a lead of 163 in the first innings, battled back in the second, Bannerman spending the whole of the third day scoring just 67. Overall, he was at the crease for seven hours[26] and faced 611 balls, a strike rate of just under 11 runs per hundred balls. Of the 204 balls bowled to him by Attewell, he scored from just five. Twenty20 it was not and, while it may have made for tedious watching for the non-connoisseur, coupled with Lyons' contrasting 134 in a 165-minute partnership of 174 with Bannerman, it had the desired effect. Briggs ended Australia's second innings with a hat-trick (Giffen, Callaway and Blackham) and figures of 4-69, but the victory target of 230 was out of reach. Australia won the Test and, against all pre-tour predictions, were 2-0 ahead in the three-match series.

The *Bulletin* gloated,

> The glorious uncertainty of cricket is exemplified by the fact that the admittedly strongest cricket team which has ever visited Australia has done worse than the weaker predecessors did in international matches.[27]

Cricket went for Shakespearean analogy,

> Do I wake, do I sleep or are visions about?

and followed it with doggerel of somewhat lesser quality.

> ENGLAND v AUSTRALIA
> If memory doesn't deceive us
> (As memory frequently will)
> Last Autumn saw estimate grievous,
> From many a pessimist's quill,
> Of cricket in o-er-the-sea Britain,
> How cricket was there on the wane;
> Some columns of cavil were written,
> We fancy, in that kind of strain.
> No Cornstalks are welcome this season,
> No Giffens are crossing 'the streak';
> And this, we're assured, is the reason –
> Colonial cricket is weak!

Yet the past winter's cable despatches
Scarce square with this critical view –
For it seems of the three great test matches
Those Australian 'duffers' won two![28]

New South Wales – a Century

AFTER MORE minor cricket, the tourists returned to Sydney and again met New South Wales. It was a significant match as, after the disappointment of the Test series defeat, it meant a return to winning ways for Lord Sheffield's team who won it by seven wickets. It was significant for Lohmann too who scored the third and final first-class century of his career to go with earlier ones at Beckenham and Hove and to add to that scored earlier in the innings by his friend and Surrey colleague, Maurice Read in a total of 414. Lohmann's innings lasted 155 minutes, containing eight fours and strokes all round the ground.[29] He was eventually caught on the boundary for 102.

> Lohmann was the only man on the side, until Attewell came in, to force the game at all. Ball after ball he lifted to the on while he lay back and made his drives equally well; in fact, his batting was brilliant all round the wicket. The catch which dismissed him was a fine one, made right on the boundary.[30]

The local press was not quite as complimentary,

> Lohmann too secured the highest distinction of making a century, but he hit with a kind of recklessness and must thank good luck more than good cricket for the score.[31]

and later was critical of Lohmann's approach to batting generally. In its summary of the tour, it concluded,

> The batting was at intervals a trifle uncertain and on one or two occasions a few of them – notably Lohmann – forced matters injudiciously when clear-headed coolness and determination were required.[32]

Lohmann was later to describe Sydney as the finest cricket ground he had played on.[33] Eight wickets on two occasions in Test matches and his only first-class century outside England might have helped him form that opinion.

It was then off to Tasmania for a bit of relaxation and more one-sided cricket. Eighteen of Southern Tasmania were beaten by an innings and 40 runs at Hobart. Apart from a handful of overs by Briggs and Sharpe in the second innings, Attewell and Lohmann bowled through both innings, Lohmann having the more impressive figures of 45-22-50-12 and 37-20-52-13. He was described by the *Hobart Mercury* as 'next to unplayable' and a 'revelation to Tasmanians'.

> Everybody, of course, has heard of Lohmann, but few imagined that he was so deadly with the ball as he turned out to be.[34]

At Launceston the following week, Northern Tasmania did rather better than their southern counterparts, following on, but managing to hang on for a draw. It was an occasion for the bowlers to enjoy themselves with the bat. Attewell and Briggs made half-centuries. Lohmann chipped in with 43.

> Lohmann was content with fours, while little Briggs banged one clean out of the ground for 6. Then came another spate of brilliant play. At 291, Lohmann was caught in the slips after a brilliant innings.[35]

Then it was back to more serious cricket, as the double was completed over Victoria with a nine wicket win, and to the concluding match of the tour, the Adelaide Test Match.

The strongest team ever to leave England would not have expected to have gone into the final test needing to avoid defeat to prevent a series whitewash. As it happened that was never on the cards. The weather was entirely in the tourists' favour, they had much the better of the batting conditions and ended up winning comfortably by an innings and 230 runs, the largest margin of victory in any Test so far. England's 499 was also their highest total (though Australia had made 551 at The Oval in 1884) and they fell tantalisingly short of 500 when wicket-keeper Gregor MacGregor was run out. Lohmann was the only Englishman to make no contribution to the score. From a personal point of view, it was not his best Test match. He dropped a catch on the boundary, not his regular fielding position but still uncharacteristic.

> Bruce went out to every ball of Briggs's next over, and having scored off two, put the next into Lohmann's hands on the boundary, but it did not stay there.[36]

Nevertheless, he played a valuable supporting role to Johnny Briggs in Australia's first innings of 100, bowling through with the Lancastrian and claiming 3-46 while his colleague took the honours with 6-49. He also took a crucial wicket in the second innings in the half dozen overs he bowled to break up the Briggs–Attewell monopoly.

> Lohmann was put on in the Lancashire man's place. The change had the desired effect, McLeod popping one softly into Grace's left hand at point... Blackham missed a straight one from Attewell and the game was over.

It was Lohmann's last match in Australia. Despite his 8 for 58 in Sydney in a losing cause and despite some outstanding performances against lower quality opposition in the up-country matches, the consensus of the critics was that, by his high standards, it was a slightly disappointing tour. Perhaps eight summers of professional cricket in England, the polluted atmosphere of London and three gruelling tours of Australia in six winters were beginning to have an effect on his performance and, although doubtless neither he nor any one else realised it at the time, on his long-term health.

There were reports that Lohmann had been offered a professional appointment with the East Melbourne Club at £300 per annum and that Attewell, Briggs and Peel had received similar offers.[37] All had declined, ostensibly on the grounds of the offers being insufficient, but perhaps there was an element of not wishing to spend every winter away from home.

Umpiring Controversy

RELATIONS BETWEEN players and umpires have been a bone of contention throughout the history of the game. Sportsmen playing at the top of their profession deserve a similar quality in officials and do not always get it. Today's system of neutral umpires, television replays and match referees, may eliminate accusations of home bias (though counter-bleats of racism are not unknown), but does not necessarily raise standards of on-field officiating. It does, however, represent a huge improvement on days when officials were locally appointed and required no qualification other than availability to take the field in first-class cricket.

However, the general convention over the years has been that the umpire's decision, however bad, is binding and the players are obliged to accept it. Officials in any sport change their minds in response to player pressure so rarely that when they do so it is a newsworthy event. The custom that the umpire's decision, like the editor's, is final is, however, one that was never accepted by Grace. The anecdote about his replacing the bails and continuing his innings on the grounds that the spectators had paid their admission money to see his batting rather than some nonentity's umpiring may well be apocryphal, but is not untypical of his approach and entirely consistent with other well authenticated tales of Grace's behaviour towards umpires on the field. Teresa McLean sees the relationship between cricketers and umpires as part of the deference of the nineteenth-century class system. Amateurs tended to receive more favourable verdicts than the professionals.[38] However, then, as now, deference was a somewhat less significant part of Australia's social scene than it was in the old country.

Lohmann was involved in two incidents which gave rise to questionable umpiring decisions, though there is no evidence that he was in sympathy with Grace's subsequent aggressive approach. The first was in the Second Test in Sydney where the *Morning Herald* reported,

> Giffen played a ball into the hands of Lohmann fast and low down. Lohmann threw the ball in the air in token of a catch and the umpire gave the fatal signal by raising his arm. Giffen kept in his crease for some time as if he doubted the catch. The umpire, however, signalled again, and he left.[39]

Smith and Williams, basing their description of the incident on the match report in the *Australasian*, have a different and rather more colourful version, suggesting that Lohmann shovelled the ball off the pitch and tossed it to Grace who threw it in the air.[40] Whichever version is correct (and in the absence of any living witnesses or recorded highlights, we shall never know), it was unfortunate for Giffen. This was not the better known George Giffen, but his younger brother, Walter. Nor was it, as Smith and Williams suggest, his Test début. That had been three years earlier on the same ground when he had opened the innings and, as on this occasion, been one of Lohmann's victims. He was the first of Briggs' hat-trick victims in the second innings and concluded an undistinguished Test career at Adelaide in the third Test, with a career best of 3 and an aggregate of 11 in six completed innings, on each occasion being dismissed by Lohmann in the first innings and Briggs in the second. There have been more fortunate Test cricketers.

The incident was relatively insignificant and perhaps the result of genuine uncertainty, but the second later in February lit the blue touch paper, giving rise to acrimonious correspondence, a special meeting of the committee of the New South Wales Cricket Association and damaged relationships between hosts and guests. The *Sydney Morning Herald* followed the story in some detail.

> A special meeting of the committee of the New South Wales Cricket Association was held last night at the Oxford Hotel to consider Dr Grace's reply to a letter from the association stating Mr Briscoe has complained of the use of offensive language towards him by Dr Grace in the return match between Lord Sheffield's team and New South Wales. Mr R Teece occupied the chair. It will be remembered that on the return of New South Wales

to the field on the ground that when he gave not out on an appeal for a catch off Lohmann's bowling, Dr Grace said to him: 'That is unpardonable; the sooner we go home the better: you must be blind: you will not give anyone out.' Dr Grace's reply as addressed to the secretary was as follows:

Launceston, 10th March 1892
Dear Sir –
I think it is a great pity that this was not gone into as I requested, before we left Sydney. Mr Briscoe's statement that he gave Charlton not out because Lohmann crossed him, is not at all satisfactory. My team is unanimous that Lohmann did not cross him; the ball was well to the off and ought to have been easily seen by the umpire. Again, if Mr Briscoe thought that Lohmann crossed him, why did he not say so at the time? Mr Briscoe's last assertion about the senseless appeals are [sic] quite unwarranted and uncalled for. I did not insult Mr Briscoe, nor did I think him a cheat. The umpiring question will have to be gone into thoroughly, and some new plan adopted or cricket will not be worth playing, as there is not the slightest bit of pleasure in playing under the present system of umpiring in Australia.
Believe me, yours truly
W G GRACE

The Chairman pointed out that Dr Grace had evaded the point at issue, viz as to whether he made use of objectionable statements to the umpire. Mr Briscoe recapitulated what had occurred, and stated that he informed Lohmann at the time that the reason he gave the batsman not out was because he (Lohmann) ran across after delivering the ball and so prevented him from seeing what the batsman did at the moment the ball reached him. With regard to Dr Grace's statement that the English team were unanimous that Lohmann did not cross over, he would point out the absurdity of it. How could the fielder at square-leg for instance, and the men at several other places in the field give any opinion on the matter? Attention was drawn to the fact in the ensuing discussion that the question was not as to the method of selecting umpires, or as to whether the umpire did or did not see a catch, but it was whether Dr Grace addressed certain offensive remarks to the umpire on the field of play. It was ultimately decided that the secretary should write to Dr Grace asking him specifically if he had made use of the statements complained of, and in the meantime the secretary should collect further evidence to what occurred. The meeting was then adjourned.[41]

Whatever the rights and wrongs of the affair, if Briscoe's evidence is to be believed, there seems to have been an absence of communication between the bowler and his captain, both during the match and afterwards. That is at least consistent with other stories of antagonism between the two. Similarly, the incident, although the one receiving the most publicity, is in the same vein as Grace's objection to substitutes, runners, umpiring appointments, the timing of the tea interval and officials' views on the fitness of the pitch for play.

The Conflict with Grace

O Captain! my Captain! our fearful trip is done
Walt Whitman

THE UMPIRING controversy was part of a larger picture giving an insight into Grace's character and approach to the game at the time when his career was entering its long twilight. The fact that he was to captain the side was originally thought to have been an attraction. He had last toured Australia eighteen years before and a whole generation had grown up there who knew him by reputation alone. They were to be disappointed. Though still scoring prolifically and with more than twenty years of cricket still ahead of him, he was no longer the athlete of his youth, and his approach to the game was occasionally jaundiced and at times dishonest.

The attitude of the Australian press to W G was at best ambivalent, at worst positively hostile. As a cricketing legend and an influence on nineteenth century cricket he is unrivalled. However, by 1891, he was 43 years of age, overweight, and while he still had some outstanding contributions ahead of him, particularly in the English summer of 1895, he was quite clearly past his best. However, what he lacked in skill and fitness was compensated by arrogance, sharp practice and downright cheating and he did little to endear himself to the manager, his fellow cricketers or his opponents.

The *Bulletin* had scarcely anything complimentary to say about the 'burly and surly W G Grace'[42] and was not tardy in including any anecdote showing him in an unfavourable light. Whether it was true or not was a secondary consideration.

> Grace, it would appear, expects the 'colonials' to treat him as Hodge the umpire did in a match against some English bumpkins. Chawbacon, the bowler, sent the champion's bails into the air and the whole field of clodhoppers grunted and squealed. 'Not out!' blurted Hodge readjusting the wicket and then (aside): 'You were clean bowled, sir, and if it happens again I'll have to say out.'[43]

There was no doubt that, despite his designation as an amateur, Grace was a professional, not only in the sense of being paid to play the game, but in his whole approach to it and his kind of professionalism associated less with professional pride than with the professional foul.

> All cricketers who have met W G Grace hold the same opinion. Off the field an endurable personage. On the field he plays the game like a professional card expert; the veteran is master of every form of 'bluff' and appeals on the slightest pretext.[44]

Robert Low in his biography of Grace has suggested that the antagonism of the press was in part occasioned by Australians objecting to an Englishman playing the game in the Australian way – hard and to win – and mentions Jardine, Larwood, Greig and Botham, as being similarly singled out for special rough treatment.[45] That may be part of the story, but it disregards the fact that Grace was equally, if not more unpopular with the manager and the team.

Lord Sheffield on the other hand seems to have been a genuine public-spirited cricketing philanthropist, but the likelihood of his making any financial gain from the tour was always likely to be severely reduced by Grace's unreasonable conditions. Australians never have been over-impressed by the class divisions of English society and the good press received by Lord Sheffield was a result of what he did for cricket rather than the handle in front of his name. The dilettante amateur was an object of lightly mocking scorn.

> MacGregor, the English wicket-keeper, flies around Melbourne theatres while his team are playing a local substitute in the far North. Is the Australian climate too trying for the Cambridge boy?[46]

They were not to defer to Grace because of his amateur status and alleged social superiority. Neither was Lohmann. If he disagreed with his captain's tactics, he had ways of showing it.

> W G Grace and another bowler were being well knocked about in a match much to the disgust of the regular bowlers, when Lohmann let one go past him in the slips and did not go after it. 'Run after it, Jarge,' shouted the Doctor. 'We have to run after 'em when you're bowling.' This sally put the field in good temper and Lohmann smartly stopped a short cut in the slips. 'Well done, Jarge,' cried W G. 'You can field as well as any of us when you try.'[47]

Lohmann's comments, if any, are not recorded, his thoughts a matter of guess-work. Although the anecdote is related for amusement, it reveals a certain frostiness between the captain and his professionals. The sympathies of the press were entirely with the latter and the hypocritical social distinctions of England were the subject of acid comment.

> In England, the pavilion is, during intervals, the sanctuary of the gentleman, against that social outcast, the professional. In county matches the gentleman receives £25 as expenses – the pro. gets £5 as wages. The Brahmin cannot sup or sit down with the Sudra: yet the conduct of gentleman W G Grace – that champion exponent of British cricket and British bad manners – so disgusted Lohmann that when the team was bidding Sydney adieu, he told Grace straight: 'Not for £1,000 per week would I again join a team captained by you.'[48]

Stoddart and Grace came to blows. There is no evidence that Grace and Lohmann did anything similar (and Smith and Williams point out that there is no corroborating evidence to support the story of Grace–Stoddart fisticuffs) but it is clear that the hostility between the game's leading (sh)amateur and the senior professional was never far below the surface and frequently above it. Lord Sheffield was left to pick up the pieces and play the role of diplomat and conciliator, as the lack of success on the field was paralleled by behaviour off it which as a public relations exercise would have scored little above *nul points*.

> It is reported that English cricketers Grace and Lohmann had a little serious mill in Adelaide a couple of weeks ago. Later on Grace insulted Stoddart and was promptly 'plugged'. An exchange of blows again took place between the two on the morning of the embarkation per *Valetta* for London. It is known that one of the Englishmen was served with a writ for assault in a row at the bottom of which was a barmaid. Lord Sheffield 'squared' the writ for £90.[49]

The hostility does not seem to have been reciprocated, however and Grace was subsequently complimentary about Lohmann's enthusiasm for the game and also his social skills.

> ...when I was his captain out in Australia, 'George,' I used to say, 'it's time for a change isn't it?' 'Yes,' he would reply readily, 'don't you think I'd better go on at the other end?' It was not selfishness that prompted the reply, but simple keenness for the game and a sanguine feeling that he was going to get the wicket in a minute or two.
>
> I never knew anyone rise to an occasion better than Lohmann. He was generally most dangerous as a batsman when runs were most needed, and his bowling, as a rule, most deadly when the odds were against his side.

> ...Lohmann was as popular among cricketers as with the public, for though he was made so much of he was unspoilt by his success and was a gentleman to his fingertips. I remember how delighted everyone was with Lohmann when we were in Australia together in 1891/92. At one place a picnic was arranged and George who was always at everybody's service on a social occasion undertook responsibility for the luncheon. Provision was made for thirty people and about fifty turned up... But George got over the difficulty. How he did it I don't know, but the provisions for thirty did duty for fifty... The ladies were all in love with George for the attentive care with which he saw that everybody had what they wanted.[50]

While the team returned on the *Valetta*, again via Colombo, Aden and Brindisi, finally arriving in Plymouth on 8 May, Lord Sheffield left aboard the *Arcadia*, some time later. Doubtless he had enough of the minutiae of team management for a while and valued some time on his own.

Australian attitudes

WHILE THE reported gossip may be seen as part of the beginning of tabloid journalism when activities of sportsmen off the field begin to assume similar or more significance as those on it, there does seem to be a pattern of providing material for the *Bulletin* which rarely missed an opportunity to cock a snook at English behaviour and traditions, the more so when they were slavishly imitated in the rival state of Victoria.

> THE BULLETIN lately remarked on the fact that on a certain occasion during the tour of Sheffield's team the English professionals did not come out of the same gate as the amateurs. This unspeakably odious, not to say contemptible custom is maintained down South where a well known local professional (Jim Phillips of the MCC) comes out of the stand gate while the – haw – gentlemen come out by the members' pavilion. 'I hate fashionable Victorians,' wrote Francis Adams lately – 'they are such snobs. They are very little better than English people.'[51]

The imitation of Englishness and its imposition on Australian society was not a lifestyle that found empathy in the *Bulletin*.

> The season in Sydney is dawning again,
> So maidens in quest of a bean,
> Are curling their lips in a 'tongey' disdain
> An putting on airs from over the main –
> For 'tis O! to be English, you know.

They'll mourn for the Duke at the forthcoming ball[52]
And sport a black ribbon of woe
The names of the nobles who carried the pall
They will probably lisp with a thoroughbred drawl –
That's awfully English, you know.

The fashion has spread since the cricketers came,
Of hating 'colonial blow'
And the new season angst will 'think it a shame
That Australia played such a wearisome game' –
And beat the poor English, you know.

The dresses, my dear! Well we mustn't collapse
If we find them exceedingly low,
Nor blush to discover young Phyllis perhaps
Reduced to a skirt and a couple of straps –
The latest in English, you know.

And fellers from 'home' are delicious this year,
Our natives will not have a show;
I mean to get ready my bow and my spear
And capture the Johnnie who ventures too near
For 'tis O! to be English, you know.

As the tour drew to its close, Mr Sparks, Chairman of the Australian Cricket Conference wrote to Lord Sheffield,

> …saying how gratifying it was that the international contests had been characterised by the kindest social amenities which, it is hoped, may have an enduring influence for good. So far as Australia was concerned, it would not stop upon the steps of the pavilions, nor fade away at the gates of the cricket grounds.[53]

The diplomacy, though doubtless well-intentioned, camouflaged a deal of antagonism and ill-feeling that had arisen during the tour, both Anglo–Australian and within the English camp. However, while the Englishmen departed a less harmonious group than when they had arrived in Adelaide almost five months earlier, the negatives of the tour were more than counterbalanced by a revival of interest in the game in Australia and the more permanent legacy of a trophy valued at 150 guineas donated by his Lordship to stimulate inter-state competition between New South Wales, Victoria and South Australia. It 'caused the liveliest satisfaction amongst Australian cricketers'[54] and was to survive for more than a century before being replaced by the Pura Milk Cup – doubtless more commercially attractive to the Australian cricket authorities and fought for no less competitively by the states, but a title with less gravitas than the Sheffield Shield.

Despite losing about £3,000 on the tour, thanks in the main to the avarice of Grace, Lord Sheffield was keen to take a team to Australia the following year to focus on quality rather than quantity, eliminating the up-country jaunts and concentrating on the Test matches. It did not happen, but the suggestion was a hundred years ahead of its time, today's tours leaving little space for anything but Test matches and Limited Overs Internationals.

The *Australasian* picked up the theme, criticising the poor planning and overcrowded fixture lists that characterised overseas tours.

> Australian teams play far too many matches in England to permit of their doing justice to themselves in test matches in the old country, and it is to be noted that these test matches are invariably fixed late in the programme when the wear and tear of two matches each week, combined with frequent long rides by rail, have produced a staleness incompatible with a first-class exposition of cricket.
>
> We have an English gentleman willing to spend thousands of pounds in bringing the best team in England to play three cricket matches in Australia and that, too, after losing about £3,000 by the tour that has just closed.[55]

There was also a possibility that Lord Sheffield might take a team to Australia for 1894/95 for a similar arrangement of three international matches. According to a somewhat jaundiced Arthur Shrewsbury, the authorities in Sydney and Melbourne were reluctant to countenance the arrangement on financial grounds and a more traditional tour, organised by Stoddart, appeared more lucrative.

> Stoddart is taking a trip to the Colonies as an amateur of course with an English team, and by so doing has robbed Gunn and myself from taking a trip there with Lord Sheffield Team, who intended going out this fall – he only intended playing 3 international matches and then coming home, but this course wouldn't suit the Melbourne and Sydney authorities as enough new members could not be enrolled – so they boycotted Lord Sheffield's trip and for the good of Cricket and their own pockets invited Stoddart to take a team out on similar lines, as many Amateurs who are hard up and yet who continue to get a nice round cheque each season out of cricket.[56]

Postmortem

AS THE *Valetta* left Adelaide, the *Bulletin* reported,

> George Lohmann, whose father is a clergyman, has been captured by a Melbourne girl. She goes to England with him.[57]

It appears to be the only reference to such a relationship and no subsequent mention in either the English or Australian press has been traced. Had the *Bulletin* dignified the young lady with a name, it might have been possible to check against passenger lists. It is impossible to be categorical and it may well be that Lohmann's contemplation of taking a professional/coaching job at East Melbourne, had elements other than cricket associated with it. However, if the *Bulletin*'s factual accuracy about the 'Melbourne girl' is as accurate as that about Lohmann's father's profession, the service of which was towards Mammon rather than God, then the story may safely be disregarded.

Internal dissensions characterise losing teams and this one was no exception. There was clearly hostility between Grace and several of his players, and in what was, at least as far as the Test matches were concerned, an unsuccessful tour, the decline in England's fortunes is perhaps epitomised by the beginnings of a decline in Lohmann's abilities. His 40 first-class wickets at 16 represent, by his standards, a no more than satisfactory return, compared with the arbitrary benchmark of his career average of 13.73 or more relevantly on this tour, the averages of Attewell and Briggs both of whom returned just over 13.

Rev R S Holmes in his analysis of the tour in *Cricket* took the view that,

> …bowling was our vulnerable point, spite of the inclusion of such trundlers as Attewell, Peel, Briggs, Sharpe and Lohmann. And for this reason: with the exception of Sharpe none of the bowlers are fast; and on the perfect Australian wickets slow medium bowling loses all its 'devil'… Sharpe is very fast, I know, and on his day most deadly. But he has always seemed to have one characteristic in common with poor Fred Morley; he must get a wicket to bowl his best.[58]

In 'Some Remarks on the Tour' a month later *Cricket* concluded,

> Lohmann took the greatest number of wickets on the tour, and some of his performances against odds were remarkable. In eleven-a-side matches though, he did not quite come up to expectations, having the worst of a comparison with both Attewell and Briggs.

Read and Lohmann made runs freely on occasions and the latter was the only one of the team to get over a hundred twice.[59]

Smith and Williams, analysing each player, said of Lohmann,

Although Lohmann took 40 first class wickets at 16.07[60] on the tour he did not perform as well as many believed he could. In the lesser matches he was devastating, but he struggled when confronted by the better batsmen on true wickets. He did not play for England again until the 1895-96 tour of South Africa.[61]

Lohmann himself was impressed by the quality of their hosts' fielding in up-country matches.

The way some of the up-country teams in Australia fielded against Lord Sheffield's side was particularly smart; they never seemed to fear anything, but dashed in and got the ball. Some times, of course, it would bump over their heads – for the grounds were fearfully rough when we played on cocoa-nut matting. They also brought off a number of good catches being more used to the glaring light than we were. Fielding is the best part of country cricket in Australia.[62]

Arthur Shrewsbury, however, whose business interests and memories of losses sustained on the 1887/88 tour had kept him at home was surprised by neither the financial position, nor the result and the hard-headed professional realism comes through in a letter to Alfred Shaw,

I didn't know that Lord Sheffield had to pay for Grace's wife and family expenses in Australia. I thought he repudiated that before leaving England. If he hadn't taken Grace, Lord Sheffield would have been £3,000 better of [sic] at the end of the Tour. I told you what wine would be drunk by the Amateurs. Grace himself would drink enough to swim a ship.[63]

...and one to Bob Lewis in Australia,

...was not at all surprised at the results of the two test matches (you would have won the third as easily as you lost it had you won the toss) as I never considered the Lord Sheffield team a good one, being very far from it.
In today [sic] paper a cable is sent from Adelaide saying that Lord Sheffield is taking out another team over to Australia – a stronger one – next year and including self and I don't think Australia will ever see me again unless the inducement is much greater than the previous offer.[64]

The *Sydney Referee* with 'a plague on both your houses' approach had earlier castigated both sides for their mercenary approach to the game and implied that a pause in the hostilities might do no harm to either.

> The cablegram which appeared in the daily press last week announcing that the county clubs had decided to oppose the visit of an Australian Eleven to England before the year 1894 was received in Australia with very little concern... Lord Hawke has told Australians what they unfortunately already know to be an incontrovertible fact. It has been manifestly demonstrated that the chief object of the Australian team has been the raking in of shekels, the upholding of the honor and glory of Australian cricket a subordinate and secondary aim. Australia should feel the crimson blood of shame mantle to their cheeks on reading such a candid denunciation.
>
> This, however, is as discreditable to English as it is to Australian cricket. Lord Hawke styling the Australian team as speculators... We cannot deny the impeachment. By the same line of reasoning W G Grace and W W Read are no longer entitled to the designation amateur than George Lohmann.
>
> W G Grace receives £3,000 expenses to compensate for the loss of his professional services. If Lohmann were not engaged in the field, I dare say he would be at the desk and why make such an inconsistent distinction? Again W W Read is in receipt of a salary as Assistant Secretary of Surrey County Club, but the position is an absolute sinecure. He is also made the recipient of a bonus for the services he renders to the eleven. Lohmann too receives a bonus for his services and the authorities designate one an amateur and the other a professional, this kind of amateurism is wholly farcical, absurdly illogical and doing in a quiet way no small harm to the game in England as well as in Australia.[65]

Several years earlier the *Bulletin* had taken a pragmatic view, not objecting to Australians being regarded as professionals, but deprecating the social prejudice which the cricket scene reflected.

> We don't object to our men being regarded as professionals; but we do most strongly object... that the Australian, merely because he gets paid for an accomplishment he happens to possess, must grovel and lose his self-respect, and abuse and prostrate himself before every creature who puts an eye glass in his head to magnify his brains and wears white 'spats' to make his feet look small.[66]

Lohmann had been at the top of his profession for six years. Professional cricketers were expected to play cricket whenever and wherever required and most had no option but to do so, as the alternative was to lose income. The concept of 'resting' as part of preparation for the more important matches had yet to be invented. Thus, this tour gave fairly clear indications of incipient 'burn-out' caused by the effects on the body of non-stop cricket and on the lungs of the polluted atmosphere of Melbourne and, to a greater extent, London.

1 Smith and Williams *W G Down Under* p78
2 David Montefiore *Cricket in the Doldrums, the Struggle between Private and Public Control of Australian Cricket in the 1880s* suggests that 1889/90 was the first season for a decade in which no English team had played on Australian soil, p 72
3 Montefiore *op cit* p 70
4 24 November 1891.
5 *Cricket* 26 November & 31 December 1891
6 Smith and Williams *op cit* p 83
7 *Cricket* 26 November 1891
8 Letter dated 22 October 1891
9 *Cricket* 29 October 1891
10 *Sporting Life* 15 October 1891
11 9 November 1891.
12 21 November 1891.
13 *Cricket* 28 January 1892, reproduced from *Sporting Life*
14 Ib
15 Ib
16 2 January 1892
17 16 January 1892
18 7 January 1892
19 *Cricket* 28 January 1892, reproduced from *Sporting Life*
20 *Cricket* 25 February 1892
21 *Bulletin* 6 February 1892
22 *Cricket* 24 March 1892
23 *Sydney Referee* 3 February 1892
24 *Sydney Morning Herald* 30 January 1892
25 Giffen *With Bat and Ball* p 124
26 Smith and Williams *op cit p* 141. The *Cricket Archive* figure is nearer 7½ hours. At this distance, the difference is not significant. It was a long time!
27 27 February 1892
28 24 March 1892
29 Smith and Williams *op cit* pp 156-157
30 *Cricket* 14 April 1892
31 *Sydney Referee* 2 March 1892
32 *Sydney Referee* 6 April 1892
33 *Cricket* 4 July 1895
34 Sissons *George Lohmann:The beau ideal* p 40
35 *Cricket* 14 April 1892
36 *Sydney Morning Herald* 28 March 1892
37 *Cricket* 19 May 1892
38 *The Men in White Coats* pp 94-107
39 30 January 1892
40 *op cit* p 136
41 19 March 1892
42 30 January 1892
43 12 March 1892
44 *Bulletin* 6 February 1892
45 *W G* p 218
46 *Bulletin* 5 March 1892

47 *The Cricket Field* 9 July 1892
48 *Bulletin* 12 March 1892
49 *Bulletin* 9 April 1892
50 Grace *Cricketing Reminiscences* p 358
51 *Bulletin* 19 March 1892
52 Prince Albert Victor, Duke of Clarence, eldest son of the Prince of Wales and Princess Alexandra. He had died on 14 January, officially of pneumonia, but according to rumour of syphilis. He was one of the candidates for the role of Jack the Ripper
53 *Sydney Morning Herald* 29 March 1892
54 *Cricket* 31 December 1891
55 2 April 1892
56 Letter to Lohmann dated 21 August 1894
57 2 April 1892
58 14 April 1892
59 5 May 1892
60 actually 16.00
61 p 186
62 *Wisden* 1893 p xlix
63 20 January 1892
64 29 March 1892
65 *Sydney Referee* 16 December 1892
66 *Bulletin* 22 November 1884

CHAPTER 10

BEGINNINGS OF BURN-OUT (1892)

hardly as full of dash as usual
Cricket 1892

IN MODERN terms, Lohmann suffered from 'burn-out', but the decline in his health turned out to be far more serious. At the end of the 1892 season it would never have occurred to him or any one else that he had played his last first-class cricket for two-and-a-half years. The years between 27 and 30 are when fast and medium-pace bowlers would expect to reach their peak. But that assumes a training regime which intersperses periods of rest in between periods of intense physical activity. Twenty-first century international bowlers are cotton-wool wrapped, largely protected from the rigours of county cricket between Test Matches and Limited Overs Internationals and can expect to bowl perhaps 400-500 overs a year. The norm for regular fast bowlers and fast-medium bowlers in English first-class cricket in 2006 was around 500, slightly higher for spinners.

A hundred years ago and more the scene could scarcely have been more different. Occasionally, the boot was on the other foot. Power and influence in cricket lay not with corporate bodies like the ECB, but affluent and strong personalities like W G Grace, Lord Harris and Lord Hawke, the latter having no inhibitions about forbidding Hirst and Rhodes from playing international cricket to preserve their freshness for their native Yorkshire.

That, however, was probably exceptional; the more usual pattern for professionals like Lohmann was to play every possible match. In the six years from the beginning of the 1886 season to the end of the 1891/92 tour of Australia, he had bowled almost 12,000 overs, the equivalent of 1,500 six-ball overs a year in first-class cricket alone to say nothing of his contribution to non-first-class matches both in England and Australia. Professional bowlers were not exempt from performing in the up-country non-first-class matches against Fifteens, Eighteens, Twenties and Twenty-twos of here, there and everywhere. It was the expectation and, for many, paid as they were on a match by match basis, to decline to play would have a direct and immediate effect on their income.

It would, nevertheless, be incorrect to conclude that Lohmann was an unwilling party in undertaking such a massive workload. His idea of a rest was to change ends. He loved the game and, whatever the long-term effects on his health and fitness, was determined to play as much as possible, even to the extent of turning out in village cricket in Hampshire when not required on the first-class scene. Like the matches against odds in Australia against inexperienced opponents and officials, it provided him with a wealth of anecdote with which he kept his friends and interviewers entertained.

> I heard a funny remark made by an umpire when I was playing in Hampshire for Under Wallop against Upper Wallop. An old fellow who came into bat took his guard and said to the umpire, 'Be my toes in front of the wicket?' The umpire replied, 'Thee keep 'em out, I shan't tell 'ee whether they be or not.'[1]

Before resuming Championship cricket in June, Lohmann appeared for Lord Sheffield's team against the Rest of England at Trent Bridge, then in the resurrected Married v Single fixture at Lord's where his 58, 7-121 and 5-58 contributed to a five wicket victory and finally for Surrey at The Parks against Oxford University.

The first indication of an imminent breakdown in health came in early June when his limited contribution in the Nottinghamshire match and subsequent omission from the Cambridge University fixture was attributed to 'a touch of pleurisy'.[2]

Relentless non-stop cricket had taken its toll. Combined with the polluted atmosphere of London into which 200 tons of soot per day were poured over a river that resembled an open sewer, it ruined the health of a young man who, in other circumstances, would have been at the peak of physical fitness.

He was, however, back the following week for the match against Middlesex at The Oval. Although Lockwood was on this occasion the principal wicket-taker, Lohmann made an all-rounder's contribution to an eight wicket victory, opening the bowling and batting at no 3 in both innings, taking 4-29 in Middlesex's first innings 75, catching Stoddart and being at the wicket with his friend, Maurice Read, when the winning runs were hit. It was perhaps not Lohmann at his spectacular best, but it was a performance which epitomised his contribution to county and country over the years. There were very few matches in which his contribution was insignificant.

However, despite the imminent failure in his health, his bowling continued to be, in the vernacular of the game a century later, 'top drawer'. Against Yorkshire, in their first season at Headingley, when play eventually began after lunch on the second day, he took advantage of bowler-friendly conditions.

> Lohmann bowled with such success that the score was only thirty with half the side out...
> ...a hard earned victory by seventeen runs within three minutes of time. For their success Surrey were mainly indebted to Lohmann. In utilising any help the wicket can give he has no superior and on this occasion he was seen at his very best. In the match altogether he got fourteen wickets for 107 runs, and at the finish in particular he bowled with consummate skill and judgment.[3]

It was the third first-class match on the ground and one of only two played that season. His 8-70 in the second innings won the match for Surrey after Shuter had exercised the still novel tactic of declaring the second innings closed at 81 for 7, leaving Yorkshire to score 146 in 2 hours 5 minutes. Rev R S Holmes drew a not untypical nineteenth century parallel between performance as a cricketer and character.

> Great cricketers are invariably fine men; it's your fifth-rate club professional who thinks himself first-rate that hasn't a generous word to say for his more fortunate and capable chums. I have no secrets to disclose here but shall content myself with remarking that a Yorkshireman confidentially whispered that Lohmann would 'just make the ball talk on that wicket'. And so he did, sure enough, and 'talk' eloquently too – by deeds, not words – fourteen wickets altogether. Tuesday was glorious and never before have I seen such a crowd on a Yorkshire cricket ground; too big perhaps for current enjoyment, but scarcely big enough for the County treasurer... More rain on Tuesday night reduced the wicket to the condition of a 'batter pudding'. Surrey just won on the stroke of 'time'. They won the toss and they won the match. I don't deal with might-have-beens but with hard facts. The scoring reigned low, and the bowlers were happy ...Peel had a hand in the fall of seven wickets in the first hands; but Lohmann carried off all the honours of the match. Where he got that off break from on the Tuesday, goodness knows! Fletcher's wicket fell to a ball that came back at least fifteen inches. John Shuter's generalship was unstinted admiration. A stand was being made, so Abel was tried for an over; he got a wicket and then Lohmann was at once put on again, and bowled two more with successive balls. And what judgment in applying the closure. Ten minutes earlier and Yorkshire might have run home first, ten minutes later and a draw would have been certain.[4]

Lohmann's best batting performance of the season was his 73 against Somerset at The Oval. *Cricket* referred to 'the vigorous hitting of Lohmann' and reported that 'Lohmann continued to treat the Somersetshire bowlers with scant courtesy'.[5] Nor had there been any decline in the quality of his fielding. Against Leicestershire, 'Pougher was splendidly caught by Lohmann at slip off Sharpe'[6] in a match in which Lohmann had ten wickets for under a hundred.

However, his illness in June had been followed by injury a month later when he damaged a hand attempting a caught and bowled against Scotland at the Grange Club in Edinburgh.

Surrey won by an innings and 147 runs and there was subsequent debate on whether the fixture merited first-class status.[7]

He was doubtful for the Gentlemen v Players match at The Oval. In the event he did play, taking five wickets in a ten wicket win in which Shrewsbury's 151 not out was the difference between the sides.

John Ferris was now qualified for Gloucestershire. His début was against Surrey and was not the most auspicious: he was bowled by Lohmann with the first ball of the match. Rev Holmes, hypothesising that bowlers hunt in pairs, wondered how he would fare without Turner and suggested that Lohmann had not done as well without Sharpe's support who, like Beaumont before him, was never to prove quite so effective after a draining tour of Australia.

> It may just happen that he will miss his old chum, Turner. Great bowlers need support to do themselves ample justice. It has rarely happened in the history of cricket that a bowler has made a big name unless well backed up at the other wicket. Famous bowlers have invariably run in couples. We shall see whether Ferris is an exception to this rule. So far Lohmann seems to be missing the services of Sharpe, whose trip to Australia, has apparently done his bowling no more good than Bean's batting.[8]

Summing up the season, *Lillywhite*'s said,

> Sharpe's bowling lacked the devil which contributed so much to his success in the past and though never quite fit, Lohmann bowled with all his skill and judgment[9]
> ...Lohmann was never in quite the best of his health during the season and he was, in consequence, hardly at his very best. On the other hand, Lockwood was remarkably successful throughout and he was, beyond doubt, the best fast bowler of his day.[10]

Sharpe's lack of form was perhaps one reason Lohmann was not quite so effective.

His impending illness was doubtless another, as was the finger injury which seems to have caused him to desert his usual 'short slip' position.

In the return match against Yorkshire at The Oval, 'Mr Smith was finely caught by Lohmann in front of the pavilion',[11] but any decline in Lohmann's performance was relative and to be seen in the context of the remarkable standards set in earlier seasons. He still produced some very commendable performances. In that same Yorkshire match,

> Lohmann kept such a perfect length... Lohmann's performance was a remarkable one. On Saturday he bowled 19 overs for 26 runs and took six of the last eight wickets, five of them bowled. After he went on eight wickets fell for 66 runs and he fairly won the match for his side...

Lockwood's 6-51 in the first innings, when an injured Lohmann had been restricted to half a dozen overs, had helped, as had the earlier century opening partnership by Abel and Walter Read, but 7-50 by a less than fully fit Lohmann in the second innings was a significant factor in recording a double over their northern rivals for the sixth time in seven seasons. A week later, the popularity of the game, the August Bank Holiday, the attraction of a visiting side leading the Championship table and the traditional Surrey–Notts rivalry conspired to produce record attendances at The Oval. Just over 30,000 paying spectators on the first day, just under on the second and more than 3,000 on the third when, whatever happened, there was unlikely to be more than one session of play, were testimony to the popularity of a sport which had not yet been overtaken by football as a major attraction.

The match itself was worthy of the occasion. In a low-scoring encounter, Surrey led by five runs on the first innings, Shacklock's eight wickets for the visitors being equalled by Lockwood's for Surrey. Left with a none too easy 165 to win, Nottinghamshire reached their target with four wickets to spare, William Gunn scoring the only fifty of the match. Lockwood and Lohmann shared most of the bowling, but with three wickets each, were unable to force a victory on this occasion.

> The game was in every sense worthy of the high reputation of the two Counties, and it was played throughout in a sportsmanlike spirit which reflected the highest credit on all concerned.[12]

Again, Lohmann was complimented on his out-fielding.

> The catch in the outfield by Lohmann which dismissed Barnes was a fine piece of fielding.

As were the crowd on their behaviour.

> The Surrey crowd which has been so grossly libelled at one time or another, that it is only justice to call attention to what was after all, perhaps, the most remarkable feature of the match between Surrey and Notts, which caused such universal excitement in cricket circles during the week. It says much indeed for the sporting instincts of the thousands who stood to their places throughout Monday and Tuesday, in spite of every discomfort, that there was not the smallest hitch at any period of the match. It would be well indeed for the sport if the admirable behaviour of the Surrey crowd under the trying circumstances of the week, and with all the keen excitement of a close and stubbornly fought match, could be reproduced on all occasions and in all places.

However, in mid-August the Championship looked over. Nottinghamshire had won ten and drawn two out of twelve to give them ten points, Surrey eight out of eleven, losing two to give them six. For Rev Holmes, not happy at the discomfort at the Nottinghamshire match – "To be packed like herrings is not my idea of bliss" – that result was conclusive. Notts were the better team on the day and on the season.

> Say what we will, Surrey are not quite as strong this year; Walter Read and Lockwood are the exception. When I learned that Lohmann was encased in plaisters [sic] last week and that Wood's hands prevented him from playing, I said 'It's all up with Surrey'.[13]

He could scarcely have been more wrong. Nottinghamshire's players had been presented with medals and cheques for their victory at The Oval,[14] but faltered in the final straight, failing to win another match. Surrey galloped by, winning all their five last matches by comfortable margins, three of them in two days. Wood played in all of those, so did Lohmann, as he had in the preceding non-Championship matches against Derbyshire and Leicestershire. Reports of their ailments seem to have been grossly exaggerated. Lockwood took the limelight with 6-42 against Middlesex; 6-47 and 4-31 at Taunton, Lohmann with a supportive 4-31, as Somerset were decimated for 49 in 20 overs on a pitch affected by heavy rain; 7-42 and 5-37 against Gloucestershire, Lohmann twice dismissing W G Grace, Surrey's twin spearhead taking the last six wickets for twelve runs with Ferris relatively ineffective for the opposition; then 7-60 and 5-85 against Lancashire, with Lohmann again in a supporting role. In the final Championship match against Kent, Lohmann had the lion's share of the wickets. The clergyman's pessimism had been without foundation.

Against Lancashire, Lockwood sought to demonstrate, like most bowlers from time to time, that he could use a bat as well. A ball from Briggs was hit through a window, but Lohmann and his captain were not to be outdone.

> ...there was a double performance of Mr Shuter and Lohmann, which even outdid this. In quick succession the two batsmen each landed a ball from Briggs over the seats in front of the football pavilion. Both hits were measured, with the result that Lohmann's came to 120 yards and Mr Shuter's 115 yards at the pitch. The latter though was much the harder crack of the two and indeed the ball was travelling at a tremendous pace.[15]

Against Kent,

> ...so well did Lohmann and Lockwood, particularly the former, bowl, that in less than an hour and a half the innings was over, the last seven wickets having added 65 runs. Lohmann's bowling for Surrey was one of the best features of the match.[16]

The tail-end of the season for Lohmann involved the Scarborough and Hastings Festivals and a few more wickets, including 4-79 and 5-69 against C I Thornton's XI in the former – effectively the Champion County v Rest of England match which has appeared in various forms over the years.

> Barnes and Murdoch began the batting for the England eleven to the bowling of Lohmann and Lockwood, at the outset a series of disasters overtook the combined side.[17]

The match was abandoned as a well-balanced draw after rain washed out the third day. In the previous match, Lockwood had enjoyed himself with eight first innings wickets for the Players against the Gentlemen.

At Hastings in another era, Lohmann would have been man of the match for his half-century and nine wickets in the South's victory over the North by an innings and ten runs. Victory inside two days would in later years have meant a day off on the Saturday before the Gentlemen v Players match scheduled to start on the following Monday. It had been a long hard season. Lohmann had bowled well over a thousand overs, the other leading bowlers something similar, but a day off was not part of the thinking of the festival organisers who, doubtless with the potential loss of Saturday revenue uppermost in their minds, decreed another day's cricket – of sorts.

> On Saturday, the Players, instead of being allowed to bask in the sun on the promenade or pier, were called upon to take part in a North v South match with broomsticks. As this was not first-class cricket, it was perhaps more interesting to watch. Fast bowling was objected to, and slow bowlers, like Attewell and Peel, were considered unable to do justice to the occasion. Consequently, Kemble, Wood (the wicket-keeper), Wright, Gunn and Hewett had an opportunity of immortalising themselves. The North men played very good cricket… The batting of the South was feeble compared to that of their opponents… and only O'Brien, Lohmann, Abel and W W were able to convince the spectators that they were good enough to play in the team… In the follow-on Lohmann again proved that great judgment had been used in selecting him…[18]

It was doubtless all highly entertaining for spectators taking a holiday on the south coast. What the cricketers thought of it all is not recorded. For the Players against the Gentlemen, Lohmann supplemented 4-90 and 2-53 with a half-century in the follow on which rescued his team from a losing position and secured an eventual draw.

> Lohmann had from the first scored freely and with Peel runs came fast till the Surrey bowler was caught for a well hit, if not faultless, score of 68.[19]

Then, back to Surrey for the end-of-season warm-downs against Eighteen of Mid-Surrey and for Mr W W Read's Eleven against Sixteen of Reigate and District and the close season could begin.

In terms of wickets taken and bowling average, the season had not been Lohmann's most successful and the rise of Lockwood meant that for the first time in eight seasons, Lohmann was not Surrey's leading wicket-taker, but despite the effects of the preceding winter in Australia, despite injury and despite illness, the seriousness of which was not appreciated at the time, for the sixth consecutive season he had played a major role in a Championship winning team. During those six years, Surrey had won around seventy-five per cent of their matches, their nearest challengers, Nottinghamshire and Lancashire about fifty per cent each. It was a significant difference and no coincidence that Lohmann was at his peak during that period.

A constant factor throughout Lohmann's seasons at Surrey had been the leadership of John Shuter, in charge for fourteen seasons and Surrey's longest-serving captain. Winchester-educated and an old-style amateur, his on the field performances were nothing out of the ordinary, but as a tactician, he was probably somewhat ahead of his time. The deliberate sacrificing of wickets against Nottinghamshire at Trent Bridge in 1887, though not original – Lord Harris had used the same ploy against Surrey in 1878 – led to legislation on the declaration. He assumed the captaincy in 1880 after a lean period in Surrey cricket and was instrumental in switching the dominance of county cricket from Nottinghamshire to Surrey.

> The Surrey Captain, as every one knows, is fully alive to every possible move of the game which can conduce towards a definite settlement of a match. His idea, and rightly so, is that the great object is to win a game even with the alternative of risking a defeat, rather than allow the play, like linked sweetness, to be long drawn out with the probable solution, the poor satisfaction of a drawn game.[20]

Successful captaincy, however, does not exist in a vacuum. He had the players, particularly the bowlers, to produce the results that made Surrey the leading county. None of Bowley, Beaumont, Sharpe or Lockwood were local products, but constant throughout the period 1885 to 1892, successively working alongside these four was George Lohmann. Born across the river, but having learned his cricket in Surrey, to The Oval faithful he would always be 'Our George'.

Cricket summed up the county season included the following:

> There are some who urge that a winter's cricket in Australia does no real harm. On the other hand, facts would seem to support the opposite view. At all events, of the four Surrey professionals who were with Lord Sheffield in the Colonies during the winter, none was in his very best form…
>
> Lohmann, well as he bowled, hardly gave one the impression of being quite as full of dash as usual, and Sharpe was so much out of form that he had to be replaced by Richardson…
>
> Though slightly less successful than last year, Lohmann bowled with excellent results, and when a great effort was wanted he was always equal to the occasion.[21]

The seamless passage from Sharpe to Richardson was to be significant for the future.

Despite Lohmann's 'less successful' season, he still finished sixth in the national averages, third in Surrey's after Abel's occasional slow round-arm partnership-breaking bowling and, of course, Lockwood, whose burn-out would begin later after an unsuccessful tour of Australia in 1894/95. For Lohmann, at the age of 27, his burn-out had already begun. In the autumn, tuberculosis – or consumption, as it was then known – was diagnosed. It would be two-and-a-half years before he played first-class cricket again.

In December 1892 he wrote to the Committee.

> A letter was received from Lohmann stating that he had been ordered to go abroad for the winter for the benefit of his health. The Secretary was instructed to write expressing the great regret of the Committee that he was obliged to leave England and hoping that he would soon return quite restored.[22]

The Club did more than that, however, paying for the trip and arranging for Maurice Read to accompany him to the Cape. It was a generous gesture, although not an entirely altruistic one. Surrey were the leading county and needed to protect their investment in the human resources that had made them so. The cost was £182.6.0 bracketed in the Accounts with Walter Read's usual £100, the professionals' £270 and other grants of £209.16.0.[23]

Before embarking on the voyage on Christmas Eve, Lohmann and Maurice Read spent a fortnight with Read's elder brother, Fred, in Torquay.

Lohmann's father wrote thanking the committee for the 'prompt, liberal and careful arrangements that have been made for my son's voyage to the Cape'.[24] In the New Year, the Committee approved the action taken by – for some unaccountable reason – the Football Sub-Committee. Maybe it was the next scheduled meeting and a quick decision was required.[25]

It marked, if not the end of an era, then at least, the beginning of a lengthy pause.

1 Bettesworth *op cit* 30 July 1896
2 *Clarion* 11 June 1892
3 *Cricket* 23 June 1892
4 Ib
5 9 June 1892
6 *Cricket* 26 May 1892
7 *Cricket* 14 July 1892
8 *Cricket* 7 July 1892. The reference is to George Bean, the Nottinghamshire professional, who had a similarly disappointing tour of Australia in 1891/92
9 *Lillywhite's* 1893 p 2
10 *Lillywhite's* 1893 p 107
11 *Cricket* 28 July 1892
12 *Cricket* 4 August 1892
13 *Cricket* 11 August 1892
14 *Cricket* 1 September 1892
15 *Cricket* 25 August 1892
16 *Cricket* 1 September 1892
17 *Cricket* 8 September 1892
18 *The Cricket Field* 17 September 1892
19 *Cricket* 15 September 1892
20 *Cricket* 18 August 1892
21 *Cricket* 8 September 1892
22 Surrey CCC minutes 15 December 1892
23 *Cricket* 27 April 1893
24 Surrey CCC minutes 22 December 1892
25 Surrey CCC minutes 19 January 1893

CHAPTER 11

SOUTH AFRICA – THE BACKGROUND

South Africa, renowned both far and wide
For politics and little else beside
Roy Campbell *The Wayzgoose*

Earlier South African Connections

LOHMANN'S RELATIONSHIP with South Africa was a mixed one. It was the scene of some of his most spectacular cricketing performances and also of his convalescence and premature death. He might have toured there on three possible occasions before he actually did so. Major Warton took a less than full strength team in 1888/89. Lohmann was a possibility for the tour but eventually withdrew on medical grounds.

Warton's team had played two matches against South Africa and were captained in the first by C Aubrey Smith, subsequently to achieve fame in another sphere in Hollywood, and by Monty Bowden in the second, who, although he played in only two Tests, became and remains, England's youngest Test captain. Thanks in the main to Johnny Briggs, they had been far too strong for their hosts, though *Cricket* was alive to the fact that without Lohmann, the side was considerably weaker than it would otherwise have been.

> Lohmann's withdrawal from the team on medical advice deprived Major Warton of one of his main supports… one of the most effective bowlers English cricket has produced of late years.[1]

Wintering in South Africa was not new for English cricketers. Brockwell and Mills of Surrey and Firkin of Worcestershire were there in 1889/90 and played for Kimberley against Natal in January 1890.[2]

There was a possibility of a further tour there in 1890/91. The initiative came from James Lillywhite and Lohmann was mentioned as team manager when Lillywhite, while seeking a guarantee of £3,000, suggested to the South African cricket authorities that his would be a much stronger team than Major Warton's had been. It would not have included Shrewsbury and Shaw who, in business terms, had now parted company with Lillywhite on account of his alleged failure to meet his share of the losses incurred on the 1887/88 tour of Australia. In an attempt to sound out local opinion, Lillywhite wrote to *The Times of Natal,*

> The idea is to get a guarantee for £2,500 to £3,000 and run the best places as is done in Australia where as much as £2,000 has been cleared for a single match both at Melbourne and Sydney, but as South Africa is strange to me any available information you can send will be gladly received… The team, I think, will be much more powerful than Major Warton's…[3]
>
> The Chairman W M Hopley (representing Western Province) stated he had received a letter from Mr Milton of Cape Town who informed him he had received a communication from Lillywhite, on behalf of Lohmann, and another from Briggs, each submitting offers to bring out an English cricket team next season. It seemed uncertain whether the Australians were really coming here or not, and it would be as well to ascertain this early, so that every scheme might not fall through.
>
> Mr Milton said the English teams offered better terms than the Australians.[4]

In the event, the tour was postponed because of the political situation in South Africa, Rhodes having occupied Mashonaland to pressurise the Transvaal.[5]

> Recent events in the Transvaal have led to the definite abandonment of the proposed trip to South Africa which James Lillywhite was negotiating in the interests of George Lohmann for the coming winter. I am given to understand, however, that the project is only deferred. There is every intention to arrange such a tour at the end of 1891.[6]

The intention was fulfilled, but without Lillywhite and Lohmann. Overseas touring sides had a novelty value for the cricket-following public and experiences of tours to and from Australia and Major Warton's earlier tour to South Africa had demonstrated the profits to be made from them. Cricketers from both hemispheres were keen to reap the benefits.

Lohmann would have been an obvious choice for that tour, had he not opted to go to Australia for a third time, on this occasion with Lord Sheffield's party. Earlier in 1891, it had looked unlikely that a tour of South Africa would take place, Lord Sheffield's tour now being a fairly firm arrangement and George Vernon, the Middlesex amateur who had headed the parallel tour of Australia in 1887/88 planning to repeat a tour of India he had undertaken two winters earlier. It was at this time suggested that Lord Sheffield's team should call at the Cape either on the way to Australia or on the way back.[7] In the event, the Vernon tour did not take place and the trip to South Africa went ahead under the management of Edwin Ash and the captaincy of Walter Read. In an era when qualification rules were less tightly drawn, it included the Australians, John Ferris, later to die in the Boer War, and Bill Murdoch.

At the South African end, there was heavy organisational and financial involvement by the Hon James Logan who was to play a significant rôle in Lohmann's later years. In fact, Logan advanced £750 towards the expenses of the tour, which he not unreasonably expected to be reimbursed at the end of it. It was not and he won the ensuing case in the Supreme Court against Read and Ash with costs.[8] *The Cricket Field* commented on the botched administrative arrangements for the tour[9] and supplied the scorecard from the *South African Sportsman*.

> The unfortunate lawsuit which was the sequel to the expedition of the last English team to the Cape, seems to have done a good deal of harm to the reputation of English cricketers in the eyes of the South Africans and it seems a hopeless task for an apologist to attempt to justify to them the system which permits amateurs to embark on the management of a tour as a commercial speculation. At the same time, it is difficult, by a mere perusal of the reports in the papers to understand the verdict given against Messrs Ash and Read, though their proceedings seem to have been, to say the least, far from transparently simple. If Mr Logan advanced the money for which he sued them as a mere loan, his way of doing it was effectively calculated to disguise his intentions. The action against Messrs W W Read and Ash by Mr Logan is thus reported by the *South African Sportsman:*
>
> SINGLE WICKET MATCH
> Played at the Supreme Court, Cape Town on Tuesday June 7, 1893
> Gentlemen of England

W W Read c Sir H de Villiers b J D Logan	0
W L Murdoch run out	0
'Daddy' Ash retired hurt	0
Mr Bridgette absent	0
Total	0

J D Logan not out	750
Extras	107
	857

Innings declared closed

Like most tours at this time, it was essentially a commercial venture, rather than a mission to improve the standard of South African cricket. Never slow to miss a money-making opportunity, the professional cricketers had endorsed the comforts of the Algoa Hotel in Port Elizabeth.

> We, the undersigned, members of the English cricket team have much pleasure in testifying our hearty appreciation of the Reception and Catering for our comfort of the proprietor of the Algoa House Hotel, Port Elizabeth and hereby assure our host (Mr John Constable) that it will be our pleasure to recommend the hotel as possessing all the comforts combined with an English House, and we at the same time express to him that we have been more comfortable and happy in his hotel than in any other during our stay in South Africa.[10]

The signatures of most of the party follow.

The tourists' visit was eagerly awaited. They were not short of invitations, as witnessed by the offer of £75 to 'favour Cradock with a visit', Cradock being a small farming community in the Karoo.[11] They declined the invitation, as they did one to Matjiesfontein.[12] At times, the rhetoric of anticipation was deflated by the reality of performance. There was, for example, some disappointment at Mr Read's batting. His reputation had preceded him, but when he was seen in the flesh he was found to be 'far from pretty or graceful, in fact it might almost be termed slovenly'.[13]

A huge discrepancy in standards was at times apparent: facing Ferris and Hearne, XXII of Pretoria were clearly way out of their depth and at lunch the score stood at 17 for 16.[14] That match at Berea Park was well attended, but the lack of a decent contest at times kept the locals away.

> Some scathing criticisms have been penned on the match between the English team and twenty-two of the Colony. The latter, in their two innings, only totalled 134, while four of the English team (two not out) made 201. The gate money on the last day amounted to thirty shillings – a striking proof of the public disgust.[15]

The one 'Test' match was played at Newlands on 19, 21 and 22 March. A different England team was to start a similarly designated fixture in

Adelaide within 48 hours of this one finishing. While simple logic dictates that there was no way both sides could be fully representative, 'England' – albeit strengthened in Cape Town by Ferris and Murdoch – won each by an innings, the Cape Town one by the rather narrower margin of an innings and 189 runs. Lohmann's Surrey colleague, wicket-keeper, Henry Wood had starred with 134 not out at no 8 in England's total of 369 and Ferris had bowled unchanged through both South Africa innings to take 13 wickets for 91, as the home side failed to reach a hundred in either.

There is little to suggest that South African cricket benefited, other than financially, from this tour. The gap in standards was just too wide. Over the next decade it was to narrow and George Lohmann would play a large part in that process.

However, his first visit to the Cape was not, as it would have been on any of the three previous occasions, to play cricket, but to allow his health to recover sufficiently for the purpose of playing again for Surrey in 1893. The optimists were confident that Lohmann would be back in England, fully fit at the start of that season. It was unrealistic. The reporter from the *Clarion* who had interviewed Lohmann that summer was perhaps more street-wise and better informed in matters medical.

> All cricketers and lovers of cricket will hear with profound regret of the illness of George Lohmann. To me it comes less as a surprise than a cause for sorrow, for when I last met Lohmann at Old Trafford I was concerned to observe the unnatural transparency of his complexion. I have seen that sign before and have learned to dread it.
> Well, George has gone to Africa, and we are told that he hopes to be back in May. I join in that hope. He will be badly missed by Surrey and by England, should he be unable to play. But May is not far off, and Africa is and I for one am anxious that so excellent a fellow and so sterling a cricketer should not return too soon.[16]

The costs of his stay in the Cape in an attempt to recover his health were met by Logan, a man with a colourful and interesting background in his own right.

For his remaining days, apart from two less than full seasons in England, Lohmann's life was to be inextricably linked with Logan, with Matjiesfontein and with South African cricket.

James Logan

JAMES DOUGLAS LOGAN was a classic entrepreneur. Born in Berwickshire in 1857, he had left Scotland to find a new life in Australia in 1877. It was a journey he never completed. Shipwrecked off the Cape, he abandoned his original idea and exploited the commercial opportunities that were available in the south of the 'dark continent'. He had worked as a clerk on North British Railways and Cape Town station was the obvious place to seek a job. Appointment as a porter was followed by rapid promotion to station master, then District Superintendent of the Touws River to Prince Albert Road section. He married Emma Haylett from a distinguished and influential Cape family. Their first home was the government-owned Frere Hotel in Touws River.[17]

The virtual absence of catering facilities on the long, slow and uncomfortable train journeys provided him with his first business opportunity. Georgina Lister, daughter of railway pioneer, Thomas Bain, the son of Andrew Geddes Bain, described a journey in the second of three trains to celebrate the extension of the railway to Beaufort West in 1879.

> It was difficult to get any food or drink owing to the crowds thronging the railway refreshment rooms where meals were provided... There were no washing facilities, and we had to sleep sitting bolt upright... The noisy and disorderly behaviour of some of the passengers was horrible and particularly distressed my father who hated drunkenness... Several men fell off the train and were injured and altogether it was an unpleasant journey for us and most exhausting.[18]

The paucity of refreshment rooms was to be remedied by Logan. Coincidentally it was broadly the same line of business as that followed by Lohmann's mother's first husband, Daniel Pattle, though on a much larger, nationwide scale.

It is possible that the Lohmann–Logan link was established through the agency of Walter Read who had captained the 1891/92 tour to South Africa. There is no firm evidence, however, of such a connection and arguments for it would be weakened by the loosening of diplomatic relations between Read and Logan as a result of the lawsuit and perhaps by the fact that the professional Lohmann and notional amateur Read were playing colleagues rather than friends. Consequently, it is more likely that the common factor was Edwin Ash, secretary to the Richmond Athletic Association. He was also involved in the lawsuit, but had stronger links with Lohmann who wrote regularly to him during his early days in South Africa.

Lohmann would, in any event, be a well-known name in South African cricket circles because of his popular association with earlier tours. Maurice Read had accompanied Major Warton on the earlier 1888/89 tour and while it is unlikely that he would have met Logan who at that stage was still getting his business empire established and had not begun to involve himself in cricket sponsorship, he would possibly have learned something of the healthy properties of the Karoo air. Whatever the origins of the link, it remains the case that Logan was able to offer what Lohmann required in the form of an ideal venue for medical treatment and convalescence and an association which led to a close personal friendship seems to have developed from there.

Logan had bought the area of the entire village of Matjiesfontein in 1883, when it was nothing more than a tin shed, and lots of land at a knock-down price of £400. The clear, dry Karoo air formed the ideal environment for a health resort which attracted wealthy invalids from all over the world, including Lord Randolph Churchill, the Duke of Hamilton, the Sultan of Zanzibar, Cecil Rhodes, Sir James Sivewright and Olive Schreiner all of whom Logan numbered among his friends. Today it would be called networking. Rather than collecting stamps or paintings, Logan collected people. He had members of the aristocracy, famous politicians and businessmen and a famous author. Lohmann would fit into the vacancy for a famous sportsman and in 1899 when General Wauchope's body was disinterred and brought from the near-homonymous Magersfontein, the set was complete.

Robert Toms' biography of Logan tends towards hagiography, scarcely surprising as it is based largely on Logan's own scrapbooks which are inevitably selective. The popular myth of the parsimonious Scot does not fit Logan. He was a man of great generosity, a philanthropist certainly, but not inclined to profligacy. He was aware of his own rights and prepared to fight for them, as evidenced by his recourse to the law courts on several occasions. Wealthy, but careful with his money, he bought influence and used it, neither the first nor the last in the history of mankind to do so.

In 1892, Logan was sufficient of an influence in the area where the borders between business and politics are indistinct to cause a parliamentary dissolution. By that time, he controlled ten refreshment rooms and came to an agreement with Sir James Sivewright, the Afrikaner Bond member, then Commissioner of Railways and Public Works, that all railway refreshment rooms would be leased to him for ten years, thus acquiring a complete monopoly of catering services. Existing contractors were given notice. They were not pleased. Neither was parliament which unsurprisingly took exception to the fact that the contract had been awarded without calling for tenders, consulting the cabinet or seeking the approval of the Attorney General.

The *Cape Times* admitted its earlier opinion of Sivewright had been overturned by events.

> We believed in Sir James Sivewright: we were mistaken. As he behaved to the shareholders of the Johannesburg Waterworks Company, so he has

> behaved to the greater trust reposed in him by the public of the colony. As a public man he is discredited.[19]

The railway authorities cancelled the contract. Logan sued for damages of £50,000. The Supreme Court awarded a notional £5,000. The split in the cabinet caused Cecil Rhodes to resign and form a new government. By 1892, Logan was a JP for the Achter Hex River area; by 1895, he was granted the monopoly of all refreshment rooms on the western section of the railway. In 1894, with the support of Sir James Sivewright, he had became MP for Worcester.[20] and continued to serve until 1907, under Rhodes who had also come to South Africa initially for the benefit of his health and who was a rather better known entrepreneur, becoming a multi-millionaire thanks to the diamonds of Kimberley and the gold of the Rand.

Known as the Laird of Matjiesfontein, Logan built his own private cricket ground and played an influential role in local, provincial and national cricket. He had guaranteed the expenses of the Western Province side which had won the Currie Cup in Kimberley in November 1892.[21] According to *Cricket*, Logan had 'blasted towns out of solid rock, raised luxurious and electric-lit hotels on waste-land, and reclaimed desert miles long doomed'[22]. Later, he was to establish a wines and spirits business at 6 Adderley Street in the centre of Cape Town.

Matjiesfontein

> ...the white-hot Karoo, a place of silence and desolation
> Edgar Wallace[23]

A local description of Matjiesfontein at the time of Lohmann's arrival is contained in a newspaper feature inspired by the presence there of Olive Schreiner.

> AFRICA'S ONE GREAT WRITER
>
> I write from Matjesfontein, the home of Olive Schreiner. Matjesfontein is a little railway station 195 miles from Cape Town and is reached by train in about twelve hours. It is situated in the middle of a sandy plain in the Karoo, surrounded by mountains. This little settlement in the desert consists of the railway station itself, to which there are attached very spacious refreshment-rooms.
>
> About fifty yards from the station and running parallel with it, there is a row of half-a-dozen houses belonging to Mr Logan, who is the proprietor of the refreshment-rooms. The occupants of these houses take their meals

> at the railway restaurant, to which they are summoned at stated hours by the ringing of a bell. Water to supply the little community is brought from a reservoir some miles distant, constructed by the enterprise of Mr Logan, a sturdy Scotsman who purchased land in the neighbourhood to the extent of twenty-seven square miles and is well called 'the Laird of Matjesfontein'.
> In the middle of the row of houses I have mentioned is the cottage in which Miss Schreiner lives, which Mr Logan has dignified by the name of Schreiner House.[24]

Olive Schreiner was resident in Matjiesfontein when Lohmann and Read arrived. An asthma sufferer, she, too, was there for health reasons. There is no evidence that she and Lohmann met, but as it was such a small community, the likelihood is that they did, though whether they shared conversations and whether he was impressed by her unfashionable but visionary feminism and anti-imperialism are matters for speculation.

C B Fry in his autobiography *Life Worth Living* described Logan and Matjiesfontein in the following terms:

> ...a stocky Scotsman with a long rectangular face and a pugnacious yellow moustache – a blend of genial hospitality, business-like energy and latent pugnacity...
> ...the whitewashed buildings and the large refreshment room, the prototype of Logan's far-flung catering business, and nearby a large square of gritty ground flanked on the side farthest from the station by Logan's house and a line of a few small houses. At each end of the square was a wire fence with two empty pillars of concrete like park gates, leading to the open grey Karoo. There was a stable half-way along the row of houses, with a rather frail green gate. The houses were all glistening white.[25]

It was here that Lohmann was to spend much of his time in South Africa, doubtless at times contrasting the azure blue skies, the eucalyptus, palms and agapanthus and the clarity of Logan's private reservoir with the grey panoply of London, the inner city environment of The Oval and the polluted Thames.

After Logan's death in 1920, the village fell into decline until it was bought and resurrected by David Rawdon half a century later.

South African Cricket

NOT MANY years before, South Africa had been one of the least appealing parts of Queen Victoria's expanding empire,

> ...a backwater filled with truculent Afrikaner frontiersmen and (in white eyes) unruly black chiefs, not nearly as attractive as North America or even Australia to prospective immigrants.[26]

Then came diamonds, then gold, then imperialism and with it, cricket, in South Africa and elsewhere in the world, the hand-maiden of British imperialist legacy and, although there was a small amount of Afrikaner and rather more native participation, the influence of the 'mother country' was by the far the strongest. England was the rôle model and it was to England that South Africa turned for the resources to improve the quality of her cricket. From the very beginning it was one of the functions of the South African Cricket Association.

> To encourage the professional talent of first-class order from England, or elsewhere, and should one centre or locality not be able to support alone such professional or professionals, to arrange for the removal or distribution of such professional or professionals from one locality to another, to coach local talent for certain periods in proportion to the contribution such respective localities can afford.[27]

Although racial segregation in South Africa was to be formalised and enshrined in Law from 1948 with the Nationalist Government of D F Malan and his successors, colour bars of varying degrees of formality were in place long before that. It was a society divided on racial lines and though there were no legal barriers to blacks and whites playing with and against each other, in practice it happened very rarely.

In 1891, there had been a separate tournament for Malays; in 1894, the coloured fast bowler Krom Hendricks had been included in the team to tour England, but then omitted on the grounds of race to conform to the wishes of Cecil Rhodes. So, there were two streams of South African cricket and any ultra-liberal who thought that a report on a Whites v Blacks cricket match was a pointer to racial integration, would be quickly disillusioned if the reading went beyond the headlines. The blacks were no more black than those of the Christy Minstrels mentioned in the report.

> There is but little doubt that the gentlemen who originated the above match succeeded in 'spoofing' most of the townspeople into the belief that the 'black team' was composed of genuine natives. The 'get-up' of the team was admirable, great attention having been paid to details, and as they drove through the town in the dray, a great deal of curiosity was evidenced to see this body of men which comprise such illustrious chieftains as Kreli and Sandilli etc. A great deal of amusement was afforded by the

> umpire, who was got up in regular Christy Minstrel style, not forgetting the banjo.[28]

The 'Black Team' were all white players who assumed names like Zwaartbooi, Piccanini and Gungubelle.

There is evidence of a genuine Whites v Blacks match, described in Professor André Odendaal's book *The Story of an African Game*, which took place at Queenstown in 1870 between an All Queenstown Eleven and a St Mark's College team. The polarisation of attitudes was summarised in the *Queenstown Free Press*,

> One of the most pleasing features of the game to our minds was the nice spirit in which it was carried on by both sides. There was no temper shown, no impatience, no complaints on the part of any one; everyone behaved himself as a gentleman.
>
> Among the talk of this unusual event we were surprised to hear some intelligent men, at least they called themselves such who thought the Europeans were bemeaning [sic] themselves in playing such a game. We cannot see it and must attribute such feelings to the abominable prejudice which would raise impassable barriers between one race and another. Occasional friendly games like that on Wednesday would, we are sure, promote kindly feelings between Kaffirs and English, and from all we saw and heard of those native players we certainly think there was nothing derogatory in Englishmen playing with them.
>
> They are far removed from the raw Kaffirs, in fact they are men who as far as book learning goes, are far better educated than many of their opponents. Several of them have been to England, and others have lived in Capetown; and at present we believe they are engaged in teaching at various mission stations.[29]

It was a rare example of trans-colour bar sport. Between then and the end of the century, only 'Krom' Hendricks and C B Llewellyn were serious contenders for international places – and far from successful in being included on merit. Not until 1991 and the dismantling of apartheid would the races of South Africa take the field on an equal footing. Until then, the two streams would run separately, sometimes in parallel, touching very occasionally, most notably in the D'Oliveira affair, before confluence in the late twentieth century. The black and coloured stream remained virtually unknown until the publication of Odendaal's encyclopædic and scholarly work while the white stream has inevitably been the better resourced, the better publicised and the better recognised internationally. The 1891/92 tour had included a fixture against a Malay Eighteen, but it was a rare oasis in a hundred years of white imperialist cricket.

A keen interest was taken in the game by those not allowed to mix with whites and compelled to make their own arrangements, but like the traditional Scots view that they will support Scotland and any team playing against England, *Imvo Zabantsundu* (Native Opinion), a Xhosa language newspaper and the first example of an independent black press commented, 'it is singular that the sympathies of the Native spectators were with the English'.[30]

For Logan – as for his contemporaries Abe Bailey and Solly Joel – cricket was just one of a huge panoply of commercial and imperial interests, but there can be no doubt about his influence. Like Derrick Robins and Kerry Packer in the following century, he was not part of the cricketing establishment, but was responsible for much of the financial underpinning which allowed it to function and develop.

1 *Cricket* 24 January 1889
2 *Cricket* 27 February 1890
3 *Cricket* 15 May 1890
4 South African Cricket Association – Inaugural Congress of Delegates 10 April 1890
5 Sissons *George Lohmann: The beau ideal* pp 32-33
6 *Cricket* 25 September 1890
7 *Bristol Evening News* 8 April 1891
8 *Midland News and Karroo Farmer* 9 June 1892
9 15 July 1893
10 *Cape Mercury* 8 March 1892
11 *Midland News and Karroo Farmer* 27 October 1891
12 The present day spelling of 'Matjiesfontein' has been used, except in direct quotations from contemporary sources when the 19th and early 20th century version of 'Matjesfontein' has been retained
13 *Midland News and Karroo Farmer* 8 January 1892
14 *Midland News and Karroo Farmer* 2 February 1892
15 *Midland News and Karroo Farmer* 22 March 1892
16 31 December 1892
17 *South African Directory* 1883/84
18 Burman *Early Railways at the Cape*
19 22 June 1893
20 Toms *Logan's Way* pp 77-79
21 *South African Sportsman* 4 August 1893
22 Sissons *George Lohmann: The beau ideal* p 43
23 *A Short Autobiography* p 109
24 *Midland News and Karroo Farmer* 15 November 1892
25 *Life Worth Living* p 128
26 Parry *Diamonds, Cricket and Major Warton*
27 Inaugural Congress of Delegates of South African Cricket Association 10 April 1890
28 *Midland News and Karroo Farmer* 25 November 1892
29 4 November 1870
30 Odendaal *The Story of an African Game* p 38

CHAPTER 12

CAPE PROVINCE (1893-95)

I fancied our monarch, Lohmann,
Was back with his mates again
...But Surrey will rise from her ashes,
And struggle against the fates,
When Lohmann, our pride and glory,
Is number'd amongst his mates
Albert Craig *A Vacant Place at the Oval* 1893

Lohmann and Read Arrive

REUTERS REPORTED the safe arrival on the *Tartar* of Lohmann and his friend Maurice Read in Cape Town stating that Lohmann appeared to have benefited greatly by the voyage and was 'almost well', a judgment subsequently proved to be excessively optimistic. Read would return in March; Lohmann in June. Meanwhile, they would proceed up-country neither being inclined to play any cricket.[1]

The passage from Southampton to and from the Cape was one which Lohmann was to make on several occasions over the next few years. The voyage took up to twenty days by liners of either the Union or the Castle line which were to merge at the end of the century and at this stage were working on a co-operative rather than competitive basis. The *Tartar* was one of the smaller vessels. Later the *Scot* was to reduce the passage time to 15 days and the slightly slower, but more economical *Norman*, launched in 1894 was to establish new standards in comfort and facilities.

The treatment of sports people as celebrities is a phenomenon associated more with the twentieth and twenty-first centuries than the nineteenth, but the beginnings of it were certainly there in the nineteenth century. W G Grace is the obvious example, according to popular legend, the best-known Victorian apart from Gladstone and the Queen, but Lohmann and other cricket professionals were not far behind. There is evidence of hero-worship in the press and in the poems of Albert Craig, but perhaps the main difference between the nineteenth century and later ones is that the celebrity-cult did not involve intrusion into private lives. *Cricket* had no interest in players' sex lives, gardens or living room decorations, but an exception seems to have been made in the case of Lohmann's medical condition and there are detailed reports of his and Read's activities, both before and during the journey, in Ceres, where they stayed initially, and subsequently from Matjiesfontein.

> It will be good news to learn that the *Tartar* with George Lohmann and Maurice Read on board, reached Lisbon safely yesterday on her voyage to the Cape via Madeira and Tenerife. During the last fortnight, as every one knows, Lohmann has been ill, and on the advice of an eminent physician, he has wisely decided to go abroad in the hope that he may be able to take his place in the Surrey Eleven next season. The mild climate at Torquay, where he stayed for the last fortnight, previous to his departure, appeared to do him a considerable amount of good and the salubrious air at Wynberg, in South Africa, where he is to make his first stay, at all events it is hoped, will work a great change in him. In Maurice Read, he will have a reliable and cheery companion, and the best wishes of every CRICKET reader will go with the pair for their early return to England. It deserves to be recorded that the Surrey County Cricket Club defray the expenses of the two cricketers.[2]

It was not Lohmann's first time out of England, of course. He had had three tours to Australia, all shared with Maurice Read who had also been on the earlier Shaw and Shrewsbury tour of 1884/85 and more significantly on Major Warton's tour of South Africa in 1888/89. Lohmann was obviously aware that the scenery would be different from that experienced in England, Australia and New Zealand, but he could not have helped being struck as they journeyed to the first port of call after Cape Town, the convalescent home in Ceres and later on to Matjiesfontein, by the parched, barren countryside, the yellow ochre earth, the hovering birds of prey, contrasting with the vineyards of Paarl and the fruit orchards of Ceres itself, rich in apples, pears and oranges.

Ceres, called after the Roman corn-goddess, was a small township of some 6,000 people of whom just under half were of European origin.[3] It had grown up in the previous century and had its origins in the expansion of stock-farming by European colonists. The sanatorium where Lohmann stayed was modern, having been completed in 1890. It became the Belmont Hotel in 1944, was destroyed, as was most of the town by the earthquake of 1969, but rebuilt the following year.[4]

> The latest information from South Africa... brings more hopeful news of George Lohmann. A letter received on Monday by the Secretary of the Surrey County Cricket Club shows that the two Surrey cricketers were, at the end of last month, located at Ceres, which is some eighty or ninety miles from Cape Town. By the advice of the doctor, Lohmann and Maurice Read moved up into the mountains from Cape Town, and with the most satisfactory result. Though they had only been there about a week when the letter was written, Lohmann had already made a material improvement. He had indeed put on flesh considerably and was in fact quite his old self again. What is most satisfactory is that Doctor Beck, on whose advice the pair left Cape Town, expressed himself most confidently that a few months in South Africa would effectually restore him to health. The great Surrey bowler seems even now to be contemplating a return to England at a much earlier date than at one time was thought likely... the two travellers seem to have got on to a very good pitch at Ceres... a few English people are temporarily settled there in search of health. Among them are F A MacKinnon and his wife...[5]

Maurice Read won the local quoits championship and the visit seems to have done the health of MacKinnon (otherwise the MacKinnon of MacKinnon, 35th Chief of the Clan MacKinnon) no harm at all. He was to live until his ninety-ninth year, dying in Scotland in 1947. He had previously played for Kent and in his one Test match appearance in Melbourne, distinguished himself by being in the middle of the first Test match hat-trick – by Spofforth. He now found himself in the company of one who had inherited Spofforth's mantle and who would take the fourth.

Ceres had been a staging post to permit gradual acclimatisation to altitude and after a few weeks at the sanatorium there, they travelled on to Matjiesfontein in March where all home comforts, including horses, carriages, guns and a billiard table, were provided. There was also company in the form of Logan himself and an Oxonian by the name of Browne Cave Browne. Read left for England in time for the new season, reporting en route to Dr Beck in Cape Town and Dr Sainsbury in London.[6] Lohmann, meanwhile, had written to the Committee 'giving a satisfactory account of his progress in Africa' and saying that he hoped to be back in the middle of June.[7] He was. The environment of the Karoo seemed to be having the desired effect on his health.

> A letter received from G A Lohmann during the last few days gives the comforting assurance that he is making the most satisfactory progress towards complete recovery. He adds that he is steadily regaining his strength and activity and altogether is a very different fellow to what he

> was just before he left England. He has not lost weight and, indeed, is much about his normal condition of twelve stones... he is going for a little cricket practice every day.[8]

The prognosis was optimistic, the reality less so.

His first match in South Africa in May 1893, for Matjiesfontein against the Railway Department, was, despite Frank Hearne's guest appearance, some way below the standard to which he was accustomed, but he was doubtless happy firstly to be playing at all and secondly to have turned in a match-winning performance, scoring 32 from 146, claiming nine wickets and having a hand in the other, a run out.

Back to England – Briefly

A MONTH later, while Logan was winning his case against Mr Read and his team in the Supreme Court in Cape Town, Lohmann was on his way home on the *Athenian*. He had pleasant memories of the journey, his fellow passengers and officers presenting him with a bat made from teak.[9] On reaching England on 15 June, fully intending to play some cricket, he made the short journey to the home of his friend, Mr Best, in Andover.[10]

The Committee took a keen interest. His return was reported to the Committee on the day of his arrival. The secretary accompanied Lohmann and Dr Sainsbury to a specialist, Dr Sainsbury wrote to the Committee on Lohmann's health. Lohmann himself also wrote, the Finance Committee agreed an emergency loan of £200, subsequently converted to a grant, and the player was informed that, were he to come to The Oval, he would be welcome in the Committee Room.[11]

Although he was still to play any first-class cricket in South Africa, his reputation was such that the media took a keen interest in his progress.

> Cricketers in England were rejoiced by the arrival this week from South Africa of Lohmann, the famous Surrey batsman. He left our shores last December for the benefits of his health, and returned on Monday in the Union liner, the *Athenian*. He has greatly benefited by his stay in South Africa, and has quite recovered his weight, and to look at him, no one would realise that there had been anything amiss with him. Lohmann stated in the course of an interview that he had had a splendid passage home, and speaks in high terms of the kindness he received at the Cape from Mr J D Logan, with whom he stayed for three months at Matjesfontein. The climate there, Lohmann says, is the best he has ever enjoyed, and he traces the improvement in his health to his stay in the district of the Karoo. Questioned as to his intention for the future, Lohmann stated that

> everything would depend on the report of his doctor in London. He said, however, that he scarcely thought he would play much this summer, and that he would certainly return to South Africa in the autumn.[12]

The last part turned out to be true, but hopes for a permanent improvement in his health were ill-founded. He suffered a relapse,[13] was compelled to remain indoors and within ten weeks of his arrival was on his way back to South Africa, on the *Mexican* leaving on 19 August.[14] *Lillywhite's* was to regret 'the loss of such a grand all-round cricketer as George Lohmann'.[15] The party which travelled to Southampton to wish him goodbye was optimistic that his health would be restored in time for him to play a full part in the next season.

> A small party of Surrey cricketers, among them General Marshall, many years President of the County CC, Secretary Alcock, F Read, brother of Maurice and Edwin Ash, of Richmond, who has twice himself visited South Africa, made the journey down to Southampton to bid Lohmann goodbye. They were rewarded too by seeing him depart in the best of spirits, and with the confident assurance that the second winter in South Africa would in all likelihood mean his return to England next summer fit and well enough to resume his place in the Surrey team.
> Dr Farr[16] of Andover, a great friend of Lohmann, who also saw him off on Saturday, and who has taken the keenest interest in his case, at all events reported in the most confident way of a searching examination he had made with another doctor on Friday so that there now seems real ground for hope.

In the event the optimism proved unjustified at least for the short term. Lohmann was to remain in South Africa for the whole of 1894. Although Richardson was to spearhead Surrey's regaining of the title that year, in 1893, they fell from the pinnacle they had occupied almost by divine right, losing half their matches and slipping to fifth place in the Championship. The anonymous sonnet in *Cricket* was not alone in drawing the conclusion that Lohmann's absence was causal not coincidental.

> LOHMANN'S LAMENT
> Have I not seen, the patriot hero cried,
> The Surrey bowling and that bowling wide,
> Their battle broken and their stumps upset,
> Beaten by Sussex and by Somerset.
> Oh! Mighty Notts, and mightier by the fall
> Of Surrey! Read and Lockwood, listen all,
> With or without me, lads, in all your matches,

> Look to you fielding well, back up and mind the catches,
> Keep your hearts up, bat well and never fear,
> You'll reign the champions for another year.
> He spoke and marked, how Briggs the twister slow,
> How Mold his fastest hurled upon the foe,
> No friend he greets, stretched out no hand to shake,
> But turned the brown cap sadly towards the Cape.[17]

Although, Lohmann played no first-class cricket in 1893, he continued to be alive to commercial opportunities by endorsing, along with Spofforth and Turner the products of John Wisden and Co, Cricket Goods Manufacturers.

> Dear Sir – I have given your Balls a thorough trial, and must say that I like them better than any others I have bowled with. They keep their shape and do not increase in size, which is a great fault with many, and a big ball is very difficult to manipulate.
> Yours truly, George A Lohmann[18]

1893 was also the year in which his elder brother, Stewart, played his only first-class match for the Players of the United States of America against the Gentlemen of Philadelphia at the Belmont Ground which, coincidentally, shared its name with that of the sanatorium at which George had stayed in Ceres. Stewart had taken a professional appointment with the Merion Club, having previously been with the Georgetown Club in Demarara (now part of Guyana).[19] Later he was to go to Jamaica where he umpired three first-class matches in 1895, then back to the United States where in 1905 he umpired the match between Philadelphians and MCC. His younger brother Joshua, who had also attracted the attention of the county, the previous season continued to play with the Surrey Colts.

Matjiesfontein Again

NINETEEN DAYS after leaving Southampton, Lohmann was once again in Cape Town and once again the press were taking an interest in his movements.

> George A Lohmann who was a passenger on the URMS *Mexican*, which arrived in Table Bay on Thursday midnight was interviewed by an *Argus* representative on Friday at the Royal Hotel, Plein-street, previous to his departure by the nine o'clock train to Matjesfontein, where he is once more to be the guest of Mr J D Logan. This is the second visit to South Africa of

the celebrated Surrey 'pro' his first trip being made with the same object as the present one – the recruiting of his health... Having acquainted the officials of the Surrey Cricket Club with this state of affairs, he resolved to re-visit the Karoo in the hope of getting his health completely restored. The sea voyage had apparently worked wonders with the great cricketer, for he certainly looked well and appeared to be in excellent spirits. Of course, he was almost inseparable from his host and it was pleasant to see how Mr Lohmann's old Cape Town friends recognised him. Every one who has the slightest acquaintance with him addresses him as 'George', which familiarity is quite pardonable owing to his general sociable disposition. Last night he was 'buttonholed' in the midst of an admiring and friendly circle and despite his assurances that he had nothing to say and furthermore disapproved of optimistic expressions of opinion, he was induced to chat a little for the benefit of local sportsmen.

How do you intend spending your sojourn in South Africa?

Mr Logan and I are going off tonight to Matjesfontein, where I shall stay long enough to get acclimatised, afterwards proceeding to Kimberley and Johannesburg. My headquarters will be on the Karoo, the air of which is the best I have ever breathed... Mr Logan's kindness has contributed in a great measure to my health being as near restoration as it is at present. He has a most genial heart and is one of the best sportsmen – in the proper sense of the term – in the world.

Being asked as to how long he had been unwell, he said: I retired in the 'close season' of 1892 owing to a slight chest infection. I first thought of visiting South Africa as the doctors said that a residence on the highlands of that part of your continent would prove beneficial to me. I intend to play a little cricket here now, he added, with a mischievous twinkle in his eye, for being fond of it, I cannot leave it alone altogether in that way.

Asked as to his opinion on the match recently played at the Oval for Maurice Read's benefit between England and the Australians, Mr Lohmann said: there was displayed some of the best cricket I have ever witnessed. W G Grace played in splendid form. The weather was very hot though, about 92 in the shade.

On the subject of sporting news, Mr Lohmann's verdict was a favourable one. He remarked: The way in which sporting news is reported in the English press is as near perfect as possible. Only dyspeptics object to it.[20]

Lohmann was clearly a man whose opinions were sought and respected, but more than that, was the object of something of a personality cult with a penchant for public relations and an appreciation of the cricketing public's thirst for stories about famous sportsmen. Two months later he was able to write to Edwin Ash that he 'was full of confidence, and in the best of spirits'.[21]

Lohmann's achievements on the cricket field were not unknown in the Cape Colony and by October, the *Argus* was alive to the possibility of Lohmann becoming a force in South African cricket, but also aware of the possible damage to the development of young cricketers if he were used predominantly as a player rather than as a coach.

> Now that Lohmann has joined the Western Province Cricket Club and the Cape Town Cricket Club, there is every possibility of his qualifying to play for the former Club against the Transvaal C C in the Currie Cup competition. If the great Surrey professional frequently plays during the current season at important fixtures of South African clubs, no doubt the gate money will increase by leaps and bounds, and the clubs concerned will of course benefit from a financial point of view. But while all will be pleased to know that Lohmann is identifying himself with local cricket, it may not be amiss to remind those teams who think of asking the demon bowler to assist them in their matches, that they may be doing cricket in this country a great injury. In England of late years, it has become the custom for many of the most obscure local clubs to induce a professional to play for them, for a consideration, to pull off an important match, and all sorts of ruses are adopted in order to qualify the great man in question… It may be retorted that supposing Lohmann plays, his services will be gratuitous, and therefore he would be an amateur, but all who wish success to South African cricket would do well to avoid inserting the thin end of the wedge. If the executives of our cricket teams think their men require coaching, they would be fully justified if their funds admit of the step being taken, to engage a 'pro' for training purposes, but there is a vast difference between coaching a team and playing for them…[22]

In both playing and coaching capacities, his contribution was to be significant. By the following month, his health had recovered sufficiently to allow him to play for the Western Province Club against Claremont. An innings of 29 and bowling figures of 25-13-20-7 demonstrated that the old skills were still there.[23]

The *Sporting Life* had a fuller report of the match and a full scorecard, attention which overseas club cricket would not normally expect to receive and the *African Review*, picking up on the report, brought the public up to date with a bulletin on Lohmann's health, cricket and preparations for a South African tour of England the following summer.

It was perhaps no coincidence that around the time Lohmann was beginning to involve himself in Western Province cricket, his patron was establishing a ground alongside the village at Matjiesfontein.

> At Matjesfontein Mr Logan is busy making a splendid field or ground, second to none in this country. It will cost, it is said, close on £800, and will have a beautiful bicycle-track.[24]

Cricket reported that Lohmann was playing in South Africa and would bring a team to England in 1894. That was undoubtedly the intention, but regrettably, although the tour went ahead and Lohmann played a part in the organisation of it, his health was not robust enough for him to accompany it and he was to stay in South Africa throughout the year.

1894

FOR LOHMANN'S patron, the year began on a pleasing note as he was elected MP for Worcester as a 'free and independent' Progressive candidate, replacing the sitting member, J M P de Villiers against whom he had stood unsuccessfully in an earlier election. His opponent had occupied the seat for fifteen years, but Logan, identifying himself with local farmers opposed to the Scab Act on the grounds of the cost of its implementation[25] and emphasising his working-class origins, gained sufficient local support to enter the Cape Colony Parliament where he became a friend and supporter of Prime Minister Cecil Rhodes. 'Plump for Logan', said his election posters when he stood for the Cape Parliament, 'The independent Friend of the Working Man. I was a Working Man myself once and am proud of it.'[26]

There were rumours that Lohmann was intending to settle in Australia and therefore might be co-optable by the 1894/95 English side touring there under the captaincy of A E Stoddart.[27] The story was at least credible, as there had been some interest at the end of the 1891/92 season in securing his services as a club professional and supported by the evidence of a letter from Lohmann himself to Rev Holmes, saying that he was planning to pay a visit there later in the year.

> Among the latest of many tales told about Lohmann's intentions is one that comes from Australia to the effect that he hopes to reach Melbourne during August. It is said that an engagement will be found for him in Queensland, the climate of which colony is supposed to be most likely to agree with him.[28]

Australia was doubtless a strong contender for Lohmann's future career aspirations. Despite the satisfactory arrangements at The Oval and the improving scene elsewhere, some aspects of the peripheral but, to a professional cricketer, important aspects of the game struck him as being distinctly superior.

> …cricket has improved all round, except in the matter of Players' dressing rooms. In many places they are so arranged that if a player wants to watch a match, he has to go out among the crowd… There can be no doubt that the grounds in Australia, at Sydney, Melbourne and Adelaide are better arranged for spectators and players than those in England and that we shall have in the end to follow their example. Even in the matter of luncheon arrangements they are better, which is a very important item to cricketers. At the Oval, however, we are well looked after.[29]

Interspersed with such speculation were reports that he intended to stay in South Africa for a couple of years.[30] For a semi-active Lohmann, uncertain of his future in the game or indeed as to whether he had a future at all, all options were open, although pragmatism and nostalgia combined to make The Oval clear favourite.

> George Lohmann is not going to spend the coming winter in Australia after all. He has decided, and wisely, as everyone will agree, I should think, not to risk a change when he has derived so great and, it is hoped, permanent benefit from his stay in South Africa. In a recent letter he writes most hopefully of the future. The successful result of Surrey's season has given him immense pleasure. 'How I should like a turn at the pavilion end' forms the last sentence of his letter.[31]

By February, plans were well in hand for a tour of England the following northern hemisphere summer. There was much enthusiasm, discussions at a high level and sound financial backing, Logan guaranteeing £500, increasing to £600 if necessary, although he was later to withdraw his support, and Cecil Rhodes, Prime Minister of Cape Colony, better known later for his financial sponsorship of education rather than sport, a similar amount.[32]

Although Lohmann had played no first-class cricket in South Africa at this time, his opinion was sought and valued on both cricket and related managerial matters. One of the final two candidates for the post of Tour Manager was H G Cadwallader, Secretary of the South African Cricket Association, who had expressed his willingness to do the job for expenses only. The other candidate, Simkins of the Western Province Union had asked for £25 per month and press rumours circulated that Cadwallader had asked for a similar amount. In a letter to the press, Cadwallader denied this and concluded that such rumours had started when he had met Logan in Matjiesfontein who had suggested that he would be foolish to accept the appointment on an 'expenses only' basis.[33] Lohmann had been 'standing by' and expressed the view that £25 per month would be reasonable. In the event, Simkins accompanied the team, but the relevance of the anecdote to the Lohmann story is that he was seen as

(Top) Campden Hill Road, Kensington, where George Lohmann first saw the light of day.
(Bottom) 16 Louvaine Road (Louvaine Academy), where Lohmann received his early education.

The Surrey team of 1892. (Back row:)T Richardson, E C Streatfeild, K J Key, J M Read, F Boyington (scorer); (Seated) H Wood, G A Lohmann, J Shuter (captain), W W Read, W H Lockwood; Front: R Abel, R Henderson.

Salcott House, from where Lohmann wrote to the Surrey committee, complaining about his 1889 'bonus'.

Newlands Cricket Ground, Cape Town, as it was in 1891.

July 11, 1891.] MOONSHINE. 13

CRICKETERS IN THE FIELD.

LOHMANN.

M.C.C.

George Lohmann on the cricket field as sketched by T. Downey in 1891

Lord Sheffield's team in Australia 1891-92.
Back row: H Philipson, W Attewell, G MacGregor, G Bean, J M Read, A Shaw (manager); Seated: A E Stoddart, G A Lohmann, W G Grace (captain), R Abel, R Peel; Front: O G Radcliffe, J Briggs, J W Sharpe.

Cricket Match played at The Oval between Surrey

First Innings Hants

Order of going in.	Name of the Batsman.	Figures as scored.	How Out.	Bowlers Name.	Runs.
1	L.G. Bonham Carter	1414	Bowled	Barratt	10
2	H.H. Armstrong	132	Bowled	Lohmann	6
3	E.O. Powell	1	Bowled	Lohmann	1
4	F.E. Lacey	4	c Abel	Barrall	4
5	F.W. Pember	141	c Wood	Lohmann	6
6	F. Walkinshaw	0	Bowled	Lohmann	0
7	E. Sheldrake	0	Bowled	Lohmann	0
8	Dible	0	Bowled	Lohmann	0
9	Young	0	c Roller	Barratt	0
10	C.E. Currie	0	Bowled	Lohmann	0
11	E. Barratt	3	Not	out	3
	Byes				
	Leg Byes	11			2
	Wide Balls				
	No Balls				
				Total of First Innings	32

Runs at the fall of each Wicket	1 for	2 for	3 for	4 for	5 for	6 for	7 for	8 for	9 for	10 for
	12	13	20	22	22	22	22	23	23	32

Scoresheets of a match dominated by Lohmann, Surrey v Hampshire at The Oval in 1885.
(reproduced by kind permission of Surrey County Cricket Club)

Order of going in	Second Innings Hants				
1	L. G. Bonham Carter	3423214111111411242	c Abel	Lohmann	40
2	H. H. Armstrong	4311433	Bowled	Bowley	20
3	E. O. Powell	22	Bowled	Lohmann	4
4	F. E. Lacey	14123 4121	c Roller	Barratt	19
5	F. W. Pember	1243141 7214124	Bowled	Bowley	30
6	E. Sheldrake	0	Bowled	Lohmann	0
7	Vible	0	c Roller	Lohmann	0
8	Young	23	c & Bowled	Lohmann	5
9	C. E. Currie	11111441	Not	out	14
10	E. Barratt	113	Bowled	Bowley	5
11	F. Walkinshaw	0	Absent	hurt	0
	~~Byes~~ Leg Byes	1124112			12
	Wide Balls				
	No Balls				
	Total of the two Innings			Total Second Innings	149

Runs at the fall of each Wicket	1 for 34	2 for 45	3 for 76	4 for 104	5 for 104	6 for 104	7 for 114	8 for 133	9 for 149	10 for

MILTON SMITH & CO. LITH. 13 & 15 DEVONSHIRE STREET, BISHOPSGATE

The bowling figures were 1st Innings: Barratt 14-5-17-3, Lohmann 13.3-9-13-7; 2nd Innings: Barratt 27-12-49-1, Lohmann 18-10-16-5, Bowley 24-8-47-3, Horner 13-5-16-0, Roller 7-4-9-0.

Lord Hawke's team in South Africa 1895-96.
Back row: E J Tyler, Sir Timothy O'Brien, A M Miller, T W Hayward, G A Lohmann; Seated: C B Fry, Hon J D Logan, Lord Hawke, C W Wright, C Heseltine, A J L Hill Front: S M J Woods, H R Bromley-Davenport, H R Butt.

Hon James Logan, entrepreneur extraordinaire.

The Wanderers cricket team coached by George Lohmann in 1897-98.
(Back row) W R Solomon, T B Parker, A Soames, E L Johnson, J E Greveson, Inset: G A Lohmann
(Middle row) A E Cooper, G Allsop, J H Sinclair, A Bailey (captain), E A Halliwell,
G H Shepstone, J H Piton (In front) L J Tancred, H M Colegrave.

Hotel Milner, Matjiesfontein, c1901, where Lohmann's short life ended.

MATJIESFONTEIN VILLAGE, C.P.

JOHN HALL

Almost a century later in 1987, Matjiesfontein Village is little changed.
Sketch by John Hall.

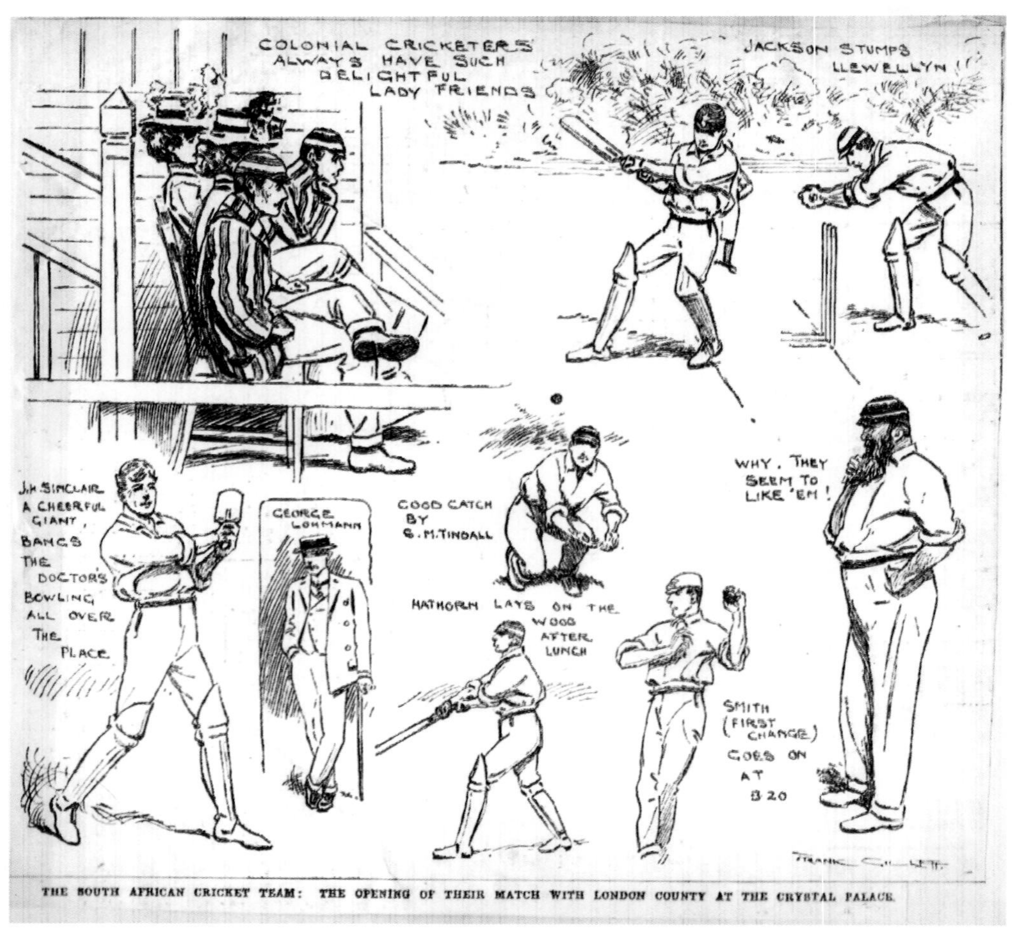

THE SOUTH AFRICAN CRICKET TEAM: THE OPENING OF THEIR MATCH WITH LONDON COUNTY AT THE CRYSTAL PALACE.

The South Africans against W G Grace's London County at Crystal Palace, May 1901. Newspaper cutting in Surrey Cricket Archive.

Joan Willamson, Joshua Lohmann's granddaughter, daughter of Winifred, Joshua's second daughter. Joan is therefore George Lohmann's great-niece. And appropriately her husband is called George! (reproduced by kind permission of Surrey County Cricket Club and Empics)

R.I.P. Lohmann's grave, Pieter Meintjies cemetery, near Matjiesfontein.

one with authoritative views on the financial side of the game.

An inter-state committee and a fortnight's practice before departure were suggested. Nominations were received from Western Province, Transvaal, Natal, Eastern Province, Kimberley, Orange Free State and Outside Districts. Fifteen were selected and the team departed for England on 11 April on the *Tartar*, a journey preceded by an on-board lunch attended by 'a number of gentlemen'. By this time they had doubtless cleared their minds of the subject of Krom Hendricks, who, on merit, should have been an automatic selection.

While the tour provided invaluable experience for the South Africans, it failed to capture the public imagination and was, in financial terms, said *Wisden* euphemistically, 'extremely disappointing'. Expenses were £3,600, receipts £500 and the venture was bailed out by South African friends in England. Sewell impressed with his batting, Rowe with his bowling and Halliwell with his wicket-keeping, but 'taking them as an eleven, there was nothing to lift them above the level of the commonplace'.[34]

The Hendricks Controversy

THE COLOUR question became a major issue with the potential selection of left-arm fast bowler, Krom Hendricks for the tour. He had made an impression when playing for the 'Malays' against Walter Read's team in 1891/92, Malays being a loosely used term to designate Muslims or Asians, not necessarily from Malaya itself.[35] There is still a Malay Quarter in Cape Town. Hendricks was not a 'Malay' – his father was Dutch, his mother from St Helena – but his skin was dark enough for him to be regarded as such. Walter Read had expressed the view that Hendricks would be a 'drawcard' in England and dubbed him 'the Spofforth of South Africa'.[36] His name had been among the nominations for the tour, but there were objections, especially in Cape Town, the *Cape Times* suggesting that the colour issue might be neatly circumvented if Hendricks were to accompany the party as baggage man. Hendricks was not impressed by the idea and wrote pointing out that he was not a Malay, that he had not been consulted about his availability and he would not dream of going as baggage man. The response of A B Tancred was, it can be assumed, typical of white, establishment opinion,

> ...after his impudent letter, I should certainly leave him out. If he wants to go on the same footing as the others, I would not have him at any price. As baggage man they might take him and play him in one or two of the matches when the conditions suited him. To take him as an equal from a South African point of view would be impolitic not to say intolerable.[37]

He did not go. Between them, Cecil Rhodes and the Western Province Cricket Union saw to that. As Rhodes, whose private secretary W H Milton was secretary of the Union and chairman of the selection committee, had contributed £500 to the costs of the tour it was the piper and the tune. There were rumblings of discontent in the British press and in the *Standard and Diggers News*, but ultimately there was no answer to money and power. Abe Bailey whose imperialistic stance was perhaps not as firmly formulated as it later became, summed up the position.

> I was strongly in favour of sending him, but I have yielded somewhat to the very good argument that, after all, our men are going to England to learn rather than with the hope of achieving any great glory. Under these circumstances, it was argued, it was not absolutely necessary to lift a coloured man upon account of the moral effect it might have in the whole coloured population.[38]

Later in 1897, the Union prevented Hendricks from playing for his own club side, the *Cape Times* supporting the decision by stating that coloureds were 'politically equal', but 'socially not so... both colours... should... pursue a policy of mutual exclusion'.[39]

Lohmann's views were based not on colour or racial politics and are scarcely surprising. They were based on the argument that the team should be selected on cricket merit and that Hendricks should have gone to England. Unlike Bailey, he had no hidden personal or political agenda. He could speak as a professional cricketer and from the liberal outlook that had been part of his upbringing.

> From a purely cricket point of view it would seem as if the exclusion of Hendricks, the coloured, was hardly wise policy. Lohmann, Frank Hearne and Mills were all, so my information goes, in favour of his accompanying the party. As a fast bowler Mills declares him to be considerably above the average, and as all the bowling at the disposal of the captain is of the slower kind, he would in all probability have been a great acquisition to the team.[40]

It was a rational, non-political view, but selection of South African national teams on grounds other than merit was something which was to remain largely unchallenged by the remainder of the cricket world for a century and more. Lohmann was a new boy in South Africa and though his opinions on cricket commanded respect, he was in no position to shape the country's politics.

Logan, however, who shared Lohmann's views, had more political clout and his withdrawal of financial support of the tour meant that the gap between receipts and expenditure was wider than it would otherwise have been.

> I found myself dealing with people with whom formerly I had had no negotiations on the subject of the guarantee and with the fact that the team which would visit England under quite different Management to that which I had been led to anticipate. When I, the original guarantor promised my five hundred pounds it was on the distinct undertaking made of course with Mr Cadwallader that the very best team... should visit England... Hendricks ought to have been included in the team; he was their finest bowler, but they would not have him because he was a coloured man... whether a man is white, black or yellow makes no difference to me nor does his particular trade or profession. What I want to see is the crack player and the crack sportsman.[41]

The tour was one in which ultimately Lohmann was in no way involved. It had earlier been suggested that he might be, along with Frank Hearne, either in a playing or managing capacity, but he judged it better for his health to remain in South Africa. In March he was living in Cape Town and intending to play in the Currie Cup.[42] In the event, he did not, and 'for certain reasons', declined an invitation to appear in what was loosely termed a 'test match' for All-Comers against the South African team.[43] He turned out for Matjiesfontein against Sutherland, about as near to a local derby as is possible in the largely unpopulated Karoo. He made a few runs and took a few wickets, but his next serious cricket was an appearance for the Cape Town Club against the Western Province Club on New Year's Day 1895.

Involvement in South African Cricket

BY NOVEMBER discussions on a tour of South Africa by an English team with Lohmann in a managerial capacity were under way.[44] In his association with Logan, Lohmann had certainly fallen on his feet. Logan was a wealthy man. His entrepreneurship in railway refreshment rooms and other ventures had ensured that. But he was also a generous man, underwriting the costs of cricket tours when the governing body was reluctant to do so and later making his villas available for the treatment of wounded soldiers serving in the Boer War.[45] There may have been a meaner side to his nature as demonstrated perhaps in his almost permanent flirtation with litigation, but the picture which comes across in his biography – albeit maybe somewhat slanted as it is based mainly on Logan's own scrapbooks, where what was retained and what rejected was obviously Logan's choice – is that of a self-made man, fighting hard for and generally getting what was due to him, then spending lavishly on whatever he chose, personal comforts certainly, but also 'good causes'.

'Laird of Matjiesfontein', an informal title, was one he would never have attained in his native Scotland. 'Semper paratum' reads the inscription on the coat of arms hanging outside the Laird's Arms – always ready. He was. His wealth might have exceeded that of some bona fide lairds, but his was 'new' money earned in 'trade' which in the eyes of a class-ridden British society, was a rank or two below 'old' money, inherited through several generations of landed gentry. Twice a year, on his birthday and on Hogmanay, he treated Matjiesfontein to a sumptuous feast. The menu for that held on his thirty-seventh birthday on 26 November 1894 at which Lohmann was very probably present was:

SOUP –	Mulligatawny
ENTREES –	Cutlets à la Jardinière
	Salmi of Duck & Green Peas
JOINTS –	Roast Beef & Yorkshire Pudding
	Roast Haunch of Mutton & Jelly
	Corned Beef & Carrots
POULTRY –	Roast Turkey & Ham
	Boiled Fowl & Parsley Sauce
	Roast Pheasant & Bread Sauce
VEGETABLES IN SEASON	
SWEETS –	Plum pudding & sweet sauce
	Orange & lemon jellies
	Cheese Dessert[46]

The wine list has not survived, but it would be nothing short of astonishing if it did not score high marks for both quality and quantity.

It was for Lohmann a happy environment in which his health continued to improve and by the end of the year, he was again ready for some serious cricket, preparing to play at Newlands in the New Year's Day local derby for the Cape Town Club against their major rivals the Western Province Club.

Meanwhile, Joshua continued to fly the Lohmann flag at The Oval, as he had since 1892, producing the goods for the Colts and, at nineteen, looked to be on the fringe of a first-class career.

> Is the mantle of George Lohmann, the famous Surrey cricketer, going to descend to his younger brother J S? Should the experience of the near future provide an answer in the affirmative, the result will give universal

> satisfaction to the public which follows cricket. Lohmann the younger, in any case is showing, just at the moment, all round form that is not likely to be overlooked by the Surrey authorities. Only last Saturday for the Stoics, against the Streatham Club at Streatham, he scored 201 out of a total of some three hundred odd, besides taking six wickets.[47]

A week later, he was to captain the Young Professionals against the Young Amateurs. He was turning out regularly for the Club and Ground side and played for Mr C W Alcock's XI against Richmond and District.[48] Three years later, attitudes had changed.

1895

LOHMANN'S NEW Year's Day appearance for the Cape Town Club was a satisfactory one. He scored 25 and took 8-70, continued to turn out for the Club and was well on the way to being fit enough for a return to first-class cricket. In March he was included in the Western Province squad for the Currie Cup. It was to be his first first-class cricket for two-and-a-half years.

The Currie Cup had originally been provided by Sir Donald Currie, owner of the Union steamship line, to be presented to the region which most excelled against Major Warton's 1888/89 tourists. It was won by Kimberley and from the following year was competed for by the provinces. In later times, the competition was to be played throughout the season, the provinces playing one another on a home-and-away basis. When it began in 1890, however, it was played at one centre, the holders having the right to stage it and play just the one match against one challenger to emerge from the other provinces. In an attempt to prevent any province monopolising the competition, the South African Cricket Association had decided after some debate at its General Meeting held on Friday 8 February 1895 and recorded in agonising detail in the *Cape Times* that the holders should not have home advantage for more than one season. The idea had come from the Transvaal contingent and might conceivably have been influenced by the fact that Western Province had won the trophy twice consecutively. It was moved by Mr Bailey and seconded by Mr Glover,

> That the winner of the cup shall not play a tournament for the same on its own ground more than one season after winning the cup and if thereafter any team or teams challenge the holders, the selection of the ground of play be left in the hands of the association, subject to its not being held on the ground on which the cup was last played for.[49]

Consequently, the 1895 challenge was held on Thursday to Saturday, 18 to 20 and Monday 22 April at Albert Park, Durban, the first of only three first-class matches played on the ground. Lohmann seemed to be back in his old form. Certainly there was no evidence of a lack of stamina. He sent down exactly a hundred five-ball overs in the match (47-20-72-7 and 53-29-59-1) and also made modest contributions of 13 and 18 with the bat. His first innings bowling performance had resulted in the challengers being dismissed for 134, to which Western Province had replied with 160. Transvaal's second innings 175 left the holders with a reachable target, but 7-40 by the promising eighteen-year-old all-rounder, James Sinclair, on whom Lohmann was to have an influence later, wrested the cup from the holders and saw it return to Transvaal for the first time since they had been the inaugural winners in 1890.

Lohmann's battle with the Transvaal opening batsman, Routledge, foreshadowed those he was to have in the following year's Test matches. Heavy overnight rain had preceded the match.

> In Lohmann's next over, Routledge was beaten by every ball... Routledge hit Lohmann for three 4s and a 2 in the next over... In Lohmann's next over Andrew caught Routledge in the deep...[50]

But for five missed chances, the Transvaal's first innings would have been lower and in summing up the match the following Tuesday, the *Cape Times* recognised that Lohmann and the Western Province team had been let down by their fielding.

> Lohmann and Rowe bowled very well, the former with exceeding bad luck.

Lohmann's dismissal in the second innings was nothing if not controversial. D C Davey, one of Natal's batsmen, was umpiring...

> ...Hings bowling, and Lohmann put his leg in front of the wicket. The game was at an exciting stage when the players were startled by a mighty 'How's that?' from Davey! Hings then appealed and the Surrey man was given out. It was felt that, after giving the cue, whether intentionally or not, he should not have given him out.[51]

Overall, however, the performance was highly satisfying. Reporting to the editor of *Cricket,* Norman Gale said,

> 'Our splendid George' is looking the picture of health, and the amount of work he did in this match shows how fit he is. He bowled unchanged

> throughout the first innings and altogether sent down 100 overs. Considering that it is two years since he took part in first-class cricket his form showed little or no falling off, and it is the feeling of good judges here that on his return to English cricket this season he ought to step back into his old position as one of the great bowlers of the age.[52]

The local support, however, had been with the Transvaal.

> A POPULAR WIN
>
> DURBAN. April 22 – [From our Correspondent]
>
> The victory of the Transvaal was exceedingly popular. The feeling here was very strongly in their favour for two reasons – firstly because of the inclusion in the Western Province team of a professional such as Lohmann; and secondly because of the way in which Western Province objected to play the tournament in Natal. The gates have been very satisfactory. Maritzburg totalled £193 but the expenses were heavy there, leaving only about £80 for the visitors. In Durban where the gate up to and including Saturday amounted to £260, expenses have been rigidly kept down and the local Union will therefore be able to hand over at least £200 to the visitors who have nevertheless been well entertained. An excellent feeling has prevailed all through among the cricketers…

Cricket was enthusiastic about the future of the game in South Africa, citing the influence of Lohmann and the 1894 tour of England as a catalyst to progress.

> The form in the Currie Tournament this year has too been of a higher order than has ever been seen in South Africa.
>
> George Lohmann's presence proved an immense attraction for the Tournament, and showed how widely he is known by all English-speaking people. I am glad to say, my informer adds, he is in magnificent health, and has apparently lost little of his old form.
>
> It was George Lohmann's first visit to Natal and he seems to be highly pleased with Durban and its capabilities as a sports centre. So satisfied, indeed, was he that he expressed his intention of making the town the venue for one of the test matches between the team he hopes to bring out next winter and a combined South African eleven.[53]

In the event, it did not happen. The Test matches were played in Port Elizabeth, Johannesburg and Cape Town. Durban had to wait until 1910, but at least there is a strong indication that Lohmann was giving serious thought to the future of South African cricket.

1 13 January 1893
2 *Cricket* 29 December 1892
3 1891 Census of Population
4 Ceres website
5 *Cricket* 23 February 1893
6 Interview with Maurice Read *Cricket* 20 April 1893
7 Surrey CCC minutes 20 April 1893
8 *Cricket* 27 April 1893
9 *Cricket* 8 June 1893
10 *Cricket* 15 June 1893
11 Surrey CCC minutes 15 June, 7 July and 31 August 1893
12 *Cape Times* 'Home Edition' 17 June 1893
13 *Cricket* 29 June 1893
14 *Cricket* 24 August 1893
15 1894 p 8
16 Dr Ernest Farr, a Medical Practitioner in Andover, about Lohmann's age, 37 on the 1901 Census of Population
17 10 August 1893
18 *Cricket* 23 March 1893
19 *Cricket* 20 July 1893
20 *Cape Argus* 9 September 1893
21 Sissons *George Lohmann: The beau ideal* p 44
22 21 October 1893
23 *Cape Argus* 20 November 1893
24 *Worcester Advertiser* 1 November 1893
25 *Midland News and Karroo Farmer* 23 January 1894 and Toms *Logan's Way* p 82
26 In Laird's Arms in Matjiesfontein
27 *Cricket* 25 January, 22 February 1894
28 *Cricket Field* 28 April 1894
29 Bettesworth *op cit*
30 *Cricket* 25 January, 22 February, 22 March & 7 June 1894
31 *Cricket* 13 September 1894
32 *Midland News and Karroo Farmer* 12 February 1894
33 *Diamond Fields Advertiser* 10 March 1894
34 *Wisden* 1895 p 335
35 Until the rigid classification of the Population Registration Act of 1950 into White, Coloured, Indian and African, terminology tended to be somewhat looser. 'European' may be regarded as being synonymous with white; coloured covers the rest, broadly 'Malay' or 'coolie' means Asian and 'native', 'Kaffir', 'Bantu' or 'Hottentot' black
36 Odendaal *op cit* p 74
37 *Standard and Digger News* 14 February 1894
38 Murray and Merrett *Caught Behind* p 16.
39 Murray and Merrett *op cit* p 18.
40 *Cricket* 3 May 1894
41 Toms *op cit* pp 48-49
42 *Cricket* 31 March 1894
43 *Diamond Fields Advertiser* 31 March 1894
44 *Cricket* 29 November 1894
45 Toms *op cit* p 119
46 *Cricket* 29 November 1894
47 *Cricket* 9 August 1894
48 *Cricket* 13 September 1894
49 *Cape Times* 9 February 1895
50 *Cape Times* 19 April 1895
51 *Cricket* 23 May 1895
52 Ib
53 Ib

CHAPTER 13

THE RETURN OF THE NATIVE (1895)

Best of Georges, come again
Norman Gale *The Hope of Surrey*

Will He... Won't He?

BY THE spring, Lohmann's return to England was anticipated with optimism and enthusiasm.

> A LETTER from George Lohmann, under date of Jan 7, from Matjesfontein, contains the qualifying assurance that the news of his recovery has not been overstated. He had, at the time of writing, just returned from Cape Town, where he had been testing his powers in the only practical way by playing in a match. He played for the Cape Town against the Western Province, and with no small success, making 25 runs besides taking eight wickets for seventy runs. The most cheery part of the letter is the statement that he went through the two days' hard cricket without feeling fatigued. He is looking forward, naturally to his home-coming next May and to his return to Surrey cricket.[1]
>
> GEORGE LOHMANN, who is according to all accounts returning to England next month with a view to take [sic] his place in the Surrey eleven, came down to Cape Town to assist the Cape Town Club against the Western Province in the Inter-Club Championship match on the 2nd of this month. Neither Lohmann, nor Mills, also of Surrey, did much with the ball on the first day of the match at all events. The latter, however, made amends by his batting, as with C Prince he put on 84 for the first wicket of Cape Town.[2]
>
> The news of the early return of Lohmann from South Africa has, it goes without saying, given great satisfaction, not only to the followers of Surrey but to the general public, which is never slow to appreciate zealous workers or... good sportsmen. Anyway Lohmann may be sure of the hearty

> welcome accorded to old favourites on his return to the scene of his former triumphs.[3]

By May, however, the optimism about Lohmann's return to England was being diluted.

> Last season began under evil auspices. Lohmann was unwell, and indeed, had had to be sent to South Africa during the winter, while it seems not unlikely even now that he will never be seen in county cricket again…[4]

Even if he were to return, he was unlikely to be the same bowler.

> Hardly is it likely that Lohmann will ever again be the magnificent bowler of old, a veritable Achilles of the cricket field…[5]

In the same edition of *Cricket*, there was a statistical analysis of twelve years of Surrey cricket. The bowling statistics whether analysed by all matches or by first-class matches only, showed that Lohmann had bowled almost as many overs and taken almost as many wickets as his bowling partners, Beaumont, Sharpe, Lockwood and Richardson between them, and at a lower average than any of them. It was an indication of the extent to which he had been missed, as was the fact that Surrey had slid to fifth place in the Championship in 1893, though under the leadership of new captain K J Key, had bounced back to win it in 1894 thanks in the main to the rising star Tom Richardson and Bill Lockwood. Meanwhile, Joshua Lohmann was turning in some reasonable performances for the colts, he and Higgins sharing a partnership of 172 for the first wicket against Brockwell Park at The Oval.

Rumours about whether and when Lohmann would return continued to circulate – until the end of May when *Cricket* was able to identify a date and a ship.

> So many different statements have been made and I am bound to confess in *Cricket* equally with other papers relative to the date of Lohmann's return to England that it is satisfactory to be able to make a definitive pronouncement on the subject on the authority of G A Lohmann himself from a communication received from him only this week.[6]

He would leave Cape Town on the Union line steamer *Moor* on 8 June and arrive in Southampton two weeks later, so would be in the Surrey team in a little over three weeks. In fact it was a little later than that. He was present at The Oval for the Middlesex match on 1 July, but his first appearance for Surrey was against Kent at Catford on 22 July.

> Considering that he had had little practice and could hardly have got over the effects of his voyage from the Cape, it was hardly reasonable to expect to see George Lohmann in the Surrey eleven which opposed Middlesex this week. He was present at the Oval on all three days looking, too, the picture of health. As Surrey has not a county match until the 15th of this month, Lohmann will make his reappearance in first-class cricket in the match between Gentlemen and Players commencing at the Oval on Thursday next. The *Sporting Life* points out as a curious coincidence that the last occasion in which the famous Surrey cricketer took part in an important match was at Hastings, in September 1892, when he helped the Players against the Gentlemen.[7]

The *Sporting Life* had overlooked the Western Province–Transvaal Currie Cup final in April – or perhaps that was not considered an important match. Meanwhile, Lohmann had some success in three Club and Ground matches, 43 and 5-50 against Addlestone – a match in which Joshua also played and opened the innings – 6-31 and 26 against Cane Hill Asylum and 22-8-16-10 as Nineteen of Horsell and Woking were despatched for 38.

> Since I wrote last week, George Lohmann who is to make his reappearance in first-class cricket at the Oval after a break of three years has played twice for the Club and Ground, and in each case with signal success. His all round cricket at Addlestone last Thursday, I am informed by one who took part in the match, showed all the infinite variety of old, and even ignoring his excellent batting and bowling, his fielding was quite up to his best standard. The great British Public is never unmindful of anyone who ministers to its enjoyment, and above all, respects and appreciates a thorough trier. And Lohmann's return to the scene of so many of his brilliant efforts, I feel sure, will be the occasion of a hearty welcome from cricketers of all kinds today.[8]

Additionally,

> George Lohmann's elder brother who has fulfilled engagements at Barbadoes [sic], Philadelphia and New York during the last few years, was well to the fore in the same team, with the bat as well as ball.

Joshua had also played a couple of matches with the 2nd XI.

Cricket ran a special feature on *The Return of Lohmann*, reminiscing on the past, commenting on a Lohmann-less Surrey and looking forward with confidence to the future.

> He was never forgotten. When Surrey lost the Championship, the wiseacres nodded sapiently and breathed the sigh: 'If only we had Lohmann!' When Surrey floated up again like a solid cork, the cry was : 'And without Lohmann too!' In this way the public appetite was whetted for the return of the wanderer.[9]

A turn at the Pavilion End

HIS FIRST first-class match after his return was the Gentlemen v Players fixture at The Oval on 11 July.

> The reappearance of George Lohmann in this match commenced at the Oval last Thursday could not fail to impart to it a special and widely felt interest.[10]

He opened the bowling with Richardson, had no wickets in his first spell, but returned to break a stubborn eighth wicket partnership, taking the wickets of the young amateurs D L A Jephson and H D G Leveson-Gower, both of whom had joined Surrey during his absence and both of whom would captain the county in later years.

He shared a lively partnership of 96 with Warwickshire wicket-keeper Arthur Lilley, took two further wickets in the second innings, including that of C B Fry and 'brilliantly caught' Murdoch before his second innings 'red inker' in a drawn match.

> Lilley and Lohmann enlivened the game, after a fluky start to their partnership, by some fine hitting, 30 runs coming in a quarter of an hour, and 50 in twenty-five minutes. In all they were together for an hour and the score had been increased by 96, when Lohmann was out for 47, a well played innings...
>
> George Lohmann's was a very satisfactory reappearance, as he made 58 for once out and took four wickets for 66 runs.

He did not play against Hampshire the following week, then, for the match against Kent, he and N F Druce replaced Smith and Lockwood, who had lost form, following his unsuccessful tour of Australia. His reintroduction was nothing if not dramatic. Six Kent batsmen failed to score as, on a pitch that was initially bowler-friendly, Lohmann and Richardson dismissed their hosts for 43 on their way to a ten wicket win inside two days. Lohmann had contributed to Surrey's reply of 191, before being stumped for 20.

> Lohmann hit very hard and his 20 on the tricky wicket was a capital display.[11]

Kent had seemed to be recovering at 118-0 in the second innings, then,

> Richardson and Lohmann, as on the previous day, could not be resisted, and no one of the last nine batsmen made double figures.
> Lohmann's reappearance was quite successful, he obtaining in all nine wickets for 90, but Richardson had ten for 76.

In the ten wicket win against Sussex at The Oval, Lohmann's single first innings wicket deprived Richardson of an 'all ten' (he had, however, already achieved this rare feat in a non-Championship match against Essex the previous season). In the fourth innings, Surrey required just one run to win, but a wide from Murdoch ensured that neither opening batsman was required to exert himself unnecessarily. Then at Derbyshire on a rain-affected pitch, Richardson and Lohmann led Surrey to an innings victory, bowling unchanged through both innings in a match in which the third day and most of the second were not required. On three previous occasions for Surrey, Lohmann and his opening partner had bowled unchanged through both innings of a completed match. He had done so once with Beaumont in 1889 and twice with Sharpe in 1890 and 1891. He remains the only bowler to have performed the feat in Surrey first-class matches on four separate occasions.

The 'Surrey poet' noted that the baton was changing hands.

> When George Lohmann sail'd away
> To a foreign shore
> Surrey griev'd, but yearn'd to see,
> See his face no more.
> Tom now takes our champion's place,
> Stands beside his gun;
> Yes, George Lohmann's mantle fell,
> Fell on Richardson.

Lohmann was not slow to appreciate the talent of his opening partner. The mental approaches of both were similar.

> In my opinion he is the best bowler in the world on a good wicket... If he could only get a footing on sticky wickets his average would be about half what it is now; as it is, about a third of the runs that are made off him are due more to accident than to intention. He is one of the best triers I have ever seen, and one of the best tempered.[12]

Even when in statistical terms his contribution was negligible, Lohmann could often be relied upon to provide some entertainment. Against Yorkshire, who bucked the trend of recent years winning by an innings and 30 runs, he brought a bit of life to the rapidly sinking ship of Surrey's second innings.

> Lohmann's innings of 2 in Surrey's second attempt yesterday does not appear on paper to contain any lively incidents, but as played it was an extremely lively chapter of accidents. After running a short run or two, the famous bowler drove a ball back to Wainwright, hardly a chance, next he drove a ball hard to Peel at mid-off, who should have caught it and he did in a sense for it cut his cheek open, next he again returned the ball to Wainwright who would not be induced to catch him out, having designs which are another story – soon told, for the next ball, Lohmann hit out wildly and was bowled over his wicket.[13]

Neither the heavy defeat, nor the loss of the whole of the second day to the weather were what Bobby Abel would have wished for his benefit match. Abel also remembers the match as a rare occasion on which a batsman was to dominate Lohmann's bowling.

> The Yorkshiremen, aided by J T Brown's batting and Hirst's bowling, beat us in hollow fashion by an innings. Brown's 83 was a grand display of batting on a difficult wicket, the manner in which he pulled good length balls off the middle stump to the boundary being truly astonishing. I have never seen our great bowler treated so lightly in the whole course of his career.[14]

A defeat by Lancashire in two days followed, Lohmann recording a 'pair' and helping create the statistical curiosity of no runs being added for the seventh wicket in any of the four innings. On this occasion the performances of Briggs and Mold outshone those of Lohmann and Richardson. Surrey's chances of reaching a victory target of 130 were sharply reduced as Abel, Maurice Read and Hayward were dismissed without a run on the board. When Lohmann was out it was 21-7. Despite Key's unbeaten half-century, there was no way back.

Kent were then beaten by 77 runs, but a defeat by Somerset by 53 runs was a blow to Surrey's Championship hopes, Edwin Tyler, who was later in the year to accompany Lohmann to South Africa, improving upon Richardson's earlier performance against Sussex by taking 10-49 in Surrey's first innings. Three run outs in the second ensured he had no opportunity of repeating the performance. A draw against Gloucestershire and an innings win against Sussex meant Surrey went into their last Championship match against Hampshire needing to win or draw to retain the title. Lohmann had scarcely scored a run or taken a wicket in recent matches and he was consequently 'stood down'.[15]

By his standards it had been a modest season – or part-season – and it was the first time since his début year of 1884 that he had been omitted from the team for a reason other than illness or injury. Also excluded were Key (Walter Read took over the captaincy), and Wood, replaced as wicket-keeper by Charles Marshall. Surrey won by an innings and 20 runs to take the title for the fifth time in six seasons since the formalisation of the County Championship in 1890, the eighth in nine if the preceding three years and the shared title of 1889 are included. The competition had been expanded from nine to fourteen counties with the result that the all-play-all formula was now abandoned in favour of counties playing different numbers of matches, so the calculations for placings became more complicated and were determined by wins less defeats as a proportion of finished matches. Surrey won under the new formula as they had under the old.

Lillywhite's was able to put Lohmann's rôle in Surrey's success into context,

> The return of George Lohmann from South Africa in the middle of the season helped Surrey at a rather critical time and on the wet wickets prevalent for a time he was very effective. But the great part of the credit for Surrey's success rested with Richardson.[16]

Summarising the season in his *Cricket Notches* column, Rev R S Holmes was less than laudatory about Surrey's success.

> The battle of the counties ended once more in favour of Surrey. Let it pass. Whilst ungrudgingly acknowledging their all-round superiority to all rivals, it is to be regretted that first place is not filled by some other county, by a county indeed to which such a position would be a novel experience. In the last nine years Surrey have been first no less than eight times. And why have they been?[17]

He goes on to answer his own question by referring to the popularity of the Australian matches which have attracted crowds – and, therefore, money – to The Oval. So the Surrey Club have been able to recruit bowlers from beyond their borders, thus buying success. The same observations have been made in more recent times of Arsenal, Manchester United and Chelsea and are part of the British penchant for knocking success. Interestingly, Lohmann, arch destroyer behind the majority of that success, does not merit a mention.

In statistical terms, Lohmann's performances were less impressive than they had been before his two-and-a-half year absence. He was older and less fit than in his hey-day and, however much he might have wished to deny it, his illness had affected him. There was another reason, however, and that was the improvement in the quality of the pitches. Replying, the following season, to a question from W A Bettesworth on the changes in the game since he began his career, Lohmann said, as an objective observation, rather than a justification of his own perceived decline.

> The wickets are, as a rule, much better. They last longer which is the reason why a side can go in for the fourth innings in a match and knock off 300. Such a thing would have been practically impossible ten years ago. Nowadays the best wickets are prepared so well that they are just as good at the end as at the beginning of a match.[18]

In Genesis, seven years of plenty were followed by seven years of famine. In Surrey's case the period of famine was rather longer. They were to surrender the title to Yorkshire and Lancashire for three years, regain it briefly in 1899 and again in 1914, then not see it again until their second golden period in the 1950s. In between were the days of Hayward, Hobbs and Sandham, a firm pointer in the direction of the theory that it is bowlers who win matches – and championships. Lohmann's contribution to that first golden age is scarcely measurable, though two-thirds of the 186 matches he played for his county were won. They were to do less well when he played for them no more.

1 *Cricket* 31 January 1895
2 *Cricket* 28 March 1895
3 *Cricket* 18 April 1995
4 *Cricket* 2 May 1895
5 *Cricket* 9 May 1895
6 30 May 1895
7 *Cricket* 4 July 1895
8 *Cricket* 11 July 1895
9 *Cricket* 4 July 1985
10 *Cricket* 18 July 1895
11 *Cricket* 25 July 1895
12 Bettesworth *op cit*
13 *Cricket* 15 August 1895
14 Abel *op cit* p 91
15 *Cricket* 5 September 1895
16 *Lillywhite's* 1893 p 107
17 *Cricket* 19 September 1995
18 Bettesworth *op cit*

CHAPTER 14

SOUTH AFRICA WITH LORD HAWKE (1895-96)

For fools rush in where angels fear to tread
Pope *An Essay on Criticism*

Arrival and Early Matches

AFTER THREE possible earlier visits to South Africa with English teams, Lohmann made it for the tour of 1895/96. He was a major organiser of the tour, having gained some experience of how it was done on his three tours of Australia with Shaw, Shrewsbury Lillywhite and Lord Sheffield. Clearly a man of some influence in South African cricket circles, he had been invited to attend the Annual General Meeting of the South African Cricket Association in Cape Town on 9 February 1895, the same meeting at which administrative arrangements for the Currie Cup had been set in motion. Taking rather less of the meeting's time, Lohmann, in better health than he had been for some time, crisply outlined his plans for the tour and sought the co-operation of the governing body in making contact with the minor associations.

> LOHMANN'S TEAM FOR SOUTH AFRICA
> Mr Lohmann, who was present, stated in answer to the chairman that he was at present in communication with well-known players in England, and he thought his proposal would come off. As far as South Africa was concerned, he was quite satisfied. The scheme had been favourably received by the Western Province and the Transvaal and he would be glad if the association itself would communicate with the smaller centres with which he was not in touch. He did not wish to mention the names of the cricketers in England who were likely to come over because there was

> another scheme on hand which people did not know of, and they wanted to get out of that so as to be able to come to South Africa. He thought it would be time to communicate with the smaller South African centres when he had definite news from England and could say that the team would positively come out.
> Mr Milton moved and Mr Smith seconded that 'Subject to satisfactory arrangements being concluded between the South African Association and Mr Lohmann, that Mr Lohmann's proposal to bring an English team to South Africa next season be approved.'
> This was carried unanimously.[1]

The South African Cricket Association had been established in 1890. Unlike Australia, sport was ahead of politics. Two decades later, an equivalent political initiative led to federation and the establishment of the Union of South Africa.

By June 1895, arrangements for the tour were well in hand.

> From a source which ought to be trustworthy I learn that the English team which George Lohmann, the Surrey cricketer, proposes to personally conduct in South Africa at the end of the year will in all probability play some sixteen matches there. The party are of course to land at Capetown and the tour will in all likelihood run to the middle or latter end of March, 1896. Matches, it is expected, will be played at Capetown, Kimberley, Bloemfontein, Johannesburg, Port Elizabeth, East London, Durban and Maritzburg. At Johannesburg, the intention is to have three matches – against Johannesburg, the Transvaal and South Africa respectively.[2]

Politics and military action in the Transvaal meant that it did not go ahead quite as planned.

Surrey and its cricketers made a significant contribution to South African cricket during that season.

> Surrey cricket will be well represented in South Africa during the coming winter, what with G A Lohmann in charge of an English touring team, and several of the minor lights under engagement in different parts. A week ago or so I mentioned the fact that Street and F E Smith had agreed to go to the Cape to assist the Western Province and Cape Town Clubs. And now comes the report that there is a good chance of George Ayres going to East London for the winter on a similar errand. Hayward, too, it is certain, is to form one of the team which Lohmann is personally to conduct, so that Surrey will be doing its fair share to the development of rising talent in South Africa during the long vacation.[3]

That may seem condescending, but it has to be understood in the context of a mentality that saw the world in terms of empire, of mother country and colonials. It does, however, suggest, what was subsequently proven, that at this stage in her development, South Africa was not ready for full-scale international cricket.

The tour did not get away to the best of starts. Lord Hawke, Sir Timothy O'Brien and Mr Hewett had made different travelling arrangements and had not arrived in time for the first fixture. The other tourists, fresh from the boat, still had to acquire their land legs, as well as accustom themselves to the different bounce of matting wickets and different light. There can be no doubt, however, about the enthusiasm with which the tourists were welcomed. Planning was meticulous and detailed. Large attendances were expected and materialised.

> The English Cricketers
> ARRIVAL OF THE TEAM
> The Union *S S Guelph* which arrived yesterday about two o'clock brought among her other passengers members of Lord Hawke's cricket team, which will tour this country during the next three months. Lord Hawke together with Sir T C O'Brien and Mr Hewett may be expected to arrive here on Tuesday next, but even if the *Moor* by which they are travelling, does not reach here in time to allow of these gentlemen taking part in the first match on Thursday, those who arrived yesterday, together with Lohmann who has been here for some time, constitute a formidable team in themselves, comprising as they do , such men as Messrs C W Wright, C B Fry, H R Bromley-Davenport, C Heseltine, A J L Hill, H Miller with Hayward, Butt and Tyler.

In an elaborate ceremony, Captain Tyson, captain of the *Guelph*, handed them over, saying they had been the life of the ship during the voyage. They were formally welcomed by Mr Attwell, the Mayor of Cape Town, and Colonel Schermbrucker representing the Mayor and Councillors of King William's Town. In the absence of Lord Hawke, Mr C W Wright replied on behalf of the tourists. He was quite confident they would have a pleasant time and that their memories of South Africa would long be treasured as particularly bright ones. Mr Nash, representative of the Western Province Union rose and welcomed the team 'most heartily'.

> No doubt the visitors would not find their opposition to be of first-class calibre, but Australia had once been in the same position and in twenty years or so, he would venture to predict that South African cricketers would be able to hold their own.

> The team were then conducted to the carriages that were in readiness and were driven to the hotels at which they are putting up, the amateurs to the Royal and the professionals to the St George.[4]

Colonel Schermbrucker was a friend of Logan who was to accompany the party which toured England and of which Lohmann was assistant manager in 1901. In the intervening five years he might have learned something about cricket, but at this time his ignorance was such as to be the subject of one of Lohmann's amusing anecdotes.

> I remember once bowling to Logan at practice and Colonel Schermbrucker, who had been in three ministries, was looking on. He was a great friend of Logan's but knew nothing about cricket. So when I happened to bowl Logan out, he thought that the batsman had done something clever, and shouted out in great glee, 'Bravo! Logan, that was good': Logan, who is a very keen cricketer, was of a different opinion.[5]

The Christmas Day edition of the *Cape Times*, amid information on church services and postal services over the holiday, reported on the tourists' practice at Newlands and the arrangements for the first fixture against a Western Province Fifteen.

> They seem to have overcome the difference in light and surroundings though they do not at all seem quite to have got in the way of playing on matting, though this will not take them long judging by the way they are shaping. The eleven formed of those who are at present here will probably be strong enough to cope with the Western Province XV, but it will be by no means a run-away game and it would not be a great surprise if the XV came out on top. The arrangements for seating the public are practically complete, and are most extensive. The catering has been left entirely in the capable hands of Mrs Stewart-Neave who has had two tents rigged up for tea and light refreshments, and several others for those who indulge in something stronger, while tables for public lunches are set up behind the pavilion, which are quite large enough to seat 100 persons comfortably. To avoid a crush at the time of the interval, lunch will be served at these tables from twelve to three. It is expected that should the weather only prove favourable, the attendance at the ground will be a record one.

It was and those who took advantage of special trains running at five minute intervals and enjoyed the band playing between 3 and 6.30 were able to enjoy the Western Province victory at which the *Cape Times* had hinted. Insufficiently acclimatised, Lord Hawke's team replied to Western Province's 115 and 130 with 79 and 92. Lohmann had 19.2-4-17-7 in the first innings and was 4-2-2-2 in the second overnight. He finished with 7-41, but the fourth innings target was beyond the tourists.

> The features of the day were the bowling of Lohmann for the Englishmen and Middleton for the Province. They each got seven wickets, Lohmann's costing only 17 runs and Middleton's 30.[6]

A one day scratch match the following Saturday was also lost.

Intermingled with the reports of cricket and Christmas celebrations, were multiple headlines of tension and rumours at the other end of South Africa.

> SENSATIONAL RUMOURS: TENSION AND ALARM: YESTERDAY'S MANIFESTO: FULL TELEGRAPHIC REPORT: MR LEONARD'S DEPARTURE: MAGNATES' WIVES LEAVING

Events in the Transvaal, however, were a long way off and did not affect cricket at the Cape, nor the detailed analysis of it in the Cape newspapers.

> Turning to the bowling which was considered the weak department on paper, we find that it has proved to be quite the reverse: in fact it is only in this branch that anything in the shape of a good performance has been accomplished. Lohmann easily heads the list here, and his performance in the first match will not soon be forgotten by those who had the good fortune to witness it. Seven wickets for 17 runs is a record of which anyone might be proud and his total for the match of fourteen for 60 is also far above the average, so far as to give somewhat of a facer to certain would-be critics who declared that he was too well known to local cricket to be effective.

A 'local contemporary' had suggested that South African batsmen were now 'reconciled' to Lohmann.

> Lohmann to whom our batsmen have now become 'reconciled' has even done better than this [i.e. C B Fry] ...by performing the same calculation it will be seen that his wickets have cost $4^2/_7$ runs apiece, and surely one can scarcely allege in the face of these figures that the batsmen against whom he was bowling had become 'reconciled' to his deliveries. Reconciliation in such a case must be understood to mean that they could play him with confidence, but it scarcely looks as though they have been able to do so, at least not yet.
>
> At the time of the first match it must be borne in mind that they have not

> had time for sufficient practice to enable them to become accustomed to the matting wickets, strong light and other differences which prevail in English and South African cricket. [7]

Matters improved for the match against a Cape Colony Thirteen when Lohmann distinguished himself with both bat and ball. To his 37, he added 27-13-35-3 and 22-7-40-8, as the Colony replied to the tourists 408, to which C B Fry contributed an impressive 148, with 118 and 162.

> After Hewett had been bowled first ball by Willoughby, to Lohmann and Hayward belongs most of the credit of laying the foundation of what eventually proved to be a record score for visiting teams to this country. For once in a way 'G.A.L.' showed the spectators that he really could bat, his innings being an exceedingly good display of cricket, though he never fairly got hold of Willoughby, when he frequently attempted to drive into the long field...
> The opposing bowling, bar Lohmann, was much below the standard of the last English team...
> With the exception of Hearne, Lohmann held the whip hand throughout, bowling wonderfully well in both innings...
> After the conclusion of the third match at Cape Town, the members of the team set off on January 4th for Matjesfontein where they enjoyed the hospitality of Mr J D Logan at his famous place in the Karoo Riding.[8]

Transvaal – Political, Military and Social Chaos

THE RECENT political history of South Africa is one of unrelieved complexity, the 'rainbow nation' of the Mandela era being preceded by centuries of inter-tribal enmity. In the Napoleonic Wars, the British had acquired the Cape as a highly convenient staging post on the voyage to India. Their presence and attempts at anglicisation of Southern Africa were acutely resented by the earlier white settlers, the Boers, and a century of Anglo-Dutch conflict overlay pre-existing enmities between local tribes.

Edgar Wallace, who was first a medical orderly, then a journalist in South Africa, summed up, albeit in simplified form, the political situation as he saw it.

> Home politics I understand... There were two parties in England – Conservative and Liberals. If the Liberals came in you had Home Rule,[9] and if the Conservatives came in you didn't... in South Africa politics were racial. On the one hand you had the psalm-singing, coffee-drinking Dutch,

> on the other hand the true-born Englishman with his inalienable right to do as he damn' pleased in any country at any time.[10]

R L Johnson, in his recent book, *South Africa: the First Man, the Last Nation*, sees a rather more complex picture.

> Unlike most African countries South Africa had no simple 'pre-colonial' period that ended in a clearly defined colonial conquest. Moreover, for a long time, there was no sharp division between the coloniser and the colonised, the victors and the vanquished – instead, the South African frontier was, like the American frontier, a continuously moving reality with a large penumbra of uncertainty in which shifting alliances and desperate compromises were the norm. There were far more actors of a variety of racial hues and political identities involved in this process than anywhere else on the continent. The influence – ultimately the dominance – of settler colonialism spread gradually, unevenly and in a far more complicated fashion than is allowed for in the mono-dimensional view of African nationalism today which asserts that the whole period since 1652 is a simple undifferentiated history of racial oppression.[11]

Throw into the cauldron the commercial interests, greed and get-rich-quick mentality catalysed by diamonds in Kimberley and gold on the Rand and the temperature begins to rise to boiling point.

Cricket with classic understatement reported that,

> ...the first of the two intended matches in Johannesburg was not played owing to disturbed times.[12]

Local reports were rather more detailed and alive to the interaction between politics and sport.

> There is considerable doubt about the future movement of Lord Hawke's team. It was intended that they should proceed to Matjesfontein and play a match against a local twenty-two, Mr Logan and the professionals, having already proceeded there; but it has been found impossible to raise a team, and Mr Logan with the professionals have [sic] gone to Kimberley.
> Lord Hawke, with the remainder of the team, remain [sic] in Cape Town, until arrangements for the continuance of the tour are completed. In the event of affairs in the Transvaal settling down, they will proceed to Pretoria; otherwise they will proceed to Maritzburg, a fixture for the 17th having been arranged provisionally.[13]

A thousand miles away, the Rand was in turmoil following the failure of the Jameson Raid on Johannesburg on 29 December 1895. Lionised in the popular British press, (The *Daily Mail* had a headline – 'God bless you, Dr Jameson! Here's your country's love to you') the activities of Leander Starr Jameson and his men were widely condemned subsequently and resulted in Jameson's being a guest of Her Majesty in Wormwood Scrubs having been found guilty on a charge of 'having unlawfully prepared a military expedition within Her Majesty's dominions to proceed against the dominion of a friendly state – to wit the South African Republic'. Supported at the time by Rhodes – 'die Bloedhond van Afrika', according to the Afrikaans press[14] and Prime Minister Chamberlain, it was an attempt to impose British Rule on the Boer State of the Transvaal, at a time when President Kruger was denying the franchise to 'uitlanders'. Strategically, Rhodes and colonial secretary Joseph Chamberlain withdrew their initial support, leaving Jameson isolated. The Raid was subsequently seen as a precursor of the Boer War and consequent 'Kruger Telegram' from Kaiser Wilhelm II, exposing British isolation in the international community and foreshadowing the first World War.

Headlines over the next few weeks proclaimed,

> TURMOIL ON THE RAND: TOWN IN A WILD FERMENT: NEARLY ALL MINES CLOSED: RUN ON THE BANKS: A LARGE ARMED FORCE

...and any press sympathy for the political rights of the 'uitlanders' was considerably diluted. Under the headline 'One Man's Madness', repeated in Afrikaans under, 'De Waanzinnigheid van Eenen Man', the *Cape Times* encapsulated what had become the common sense reaction to the raid.

> 'I am no longer pulling two ways,' Mr Hofmeyr remarked yesterday... 'JAMESON has decided me.'
> There is no cloaking the fact that this is the general verdict of Afrikanders. Dr JAMESON's 'colossal blunder' in taking the aggressive, instead of helping the political revolution in the Transvaal has checked the rising tide of sympathy with the 'uitlanders'. Had the act not been disowned promptly and fully by the Chartered Company and the Imperial Government (and the same will apply, no doubt, to the rumours from Bulawayo), the situation in South Africa today would be very serious. As it is, the question is reduced to the daredevil impulse of one man: and as that man is in so critical isolation, perhaps so tragic a situation we shall further comment...[15]

Oblivious to the international repercussions of the raid, Lord Hawke and his team travelled to Johannesburg. However, there could be no pretence that politics and sport could be divorced and the consequences were felt some time before they set foot on Johannesburg's Park railway station. Their train was stopped by armed commandos at Vereeniging, on the frontier of the Transvaal Republic. Luggage and personal effects were inspected, duty levied on virtually everything, including cricket bats. Sir Timothy O'Brien violently objected, a suspected revolver being carried by Hewett turned out to be a cylindrical toothbrush and all the captain's tact and diplomacy was required. Calm eventually prevailed and the party continued its journey, leaving bats as goodwill offerings with their interrogators.

Lord Hawke recalled that,

> ...we made such good friends with them that we presented them with a couple of bats and were loudly cheered.[16]

On arrival in Johannesburg, Lord Hawke, descending from the train and expecting to be met by Abe Bailey, his intended host, was approached by a gentleman who apologised for Mr Bailey's absence, adding that he was in Pretoria Prison. So were many of Johannesburg's erstwhile leading citizens, including the President of the Chamber of Mines and the President, Chairman and Secretary of the Wanderers Club, as well as a number of former and current committee members, including, in addition to Bailey, Solly Joel, who was later to play an important part in the Lohmann story.[17] The officials of the Transvaal Cricket Union had something of an availability problem and would struggle to raise a side.

Meanwhile, Lord Hawke had found alternative accommodation at the Rand Club and with an aristocratic arrogance that paid little regard to political sensitivities, took Sir Timothy O'Brien and Charles Wright with him to visit Bailey and other friends. Prison visiting arrangements seem to have been quite relaxed, as the visitors and prisoners dined and then played poker together.

There seemed little prospect of affairs in the Transvaal settling down. A week later the *Cape Argus* reported:

> Johannesburg January 15th
> About 2,000 armed Boers have just ridden through the principal streets headed with two Transvaal flags. At Eckstein's corner in Commissioner-street a large crowd collected and hooted at the summary way in which Boers ten or twelve abreast cleared the streets of all vehicles. Several burghers rode recklessly into the crowd, and a serious disturbance was at one time imminent.
> Late on Monday night, Commander Schutte searched Court Chambers for firearms and in two large water-tanks, thirty two Lee-Melford rifles were found all in good order...
> An attempt was made to burn down the offices of the Detective Department, occupied by ex-Detective Trimble. One of the inside doors was completely

> destroyed; also the oil-cloth on the floor and part of the flooring. Paraffine [sic] had apparently been poured all over the room, and the mystery is how the building escaped.[18]

Meanwhile, an adjacent column reported,

> Johannesburg January 15th
> The English team resumed their second innings this morning, and closed their innings at 268 for 8 wickets. The chief scorers were Hewitt, 36; Fry, 49; Hayward, 42; Lohmann, 14; O'Brien, 22; Hill (not out) 58; Wright (not out) 17.

The Wanderers' ground was not the modern stadium of today in the northern suburbs of Johannesburg at which Tests have been played since 1958, known as the 'bullring' from its circular shape and steeply banked wooden benches, now replaced by state of the art stands. It was the 'Old Wanderers', adjacent to Park Station and bounded by Loveday, Wolmarans, Keizer and Hancock Streets. Keizer Street has now been renamed Wanderers Street.

The site had been purchased by a group of 'randlords' so that the view to the north from their bungalows would not be obstructed. The Minister of Mines decided it should be used as an area for recreation and consequently the Wanderers Club was established in 1889. The unobstructed view did not last very long as the Johannesburg to Delagoa Bay railway line was built and Park Halt, subsequently Park railway station followed shortly afterwards.[19] The ground was in an open treeless veld with a small pavilion on the west side. As Johannesburg developed, however, the ground was surrounded by a corrugated iron fence, the pavilion was extended and trees planted beyond the boundary. The wicket was matting over hard earth and the outfield red dusty soil that suffered damage after heavy rains.[20]

From the neighbouring station trains leaving Johannesburg for the Cape and elsewhere were packed with both 'uitlanders' and what at the time were called 'Afrikanders' fleeing from the bombs and carnage. Conditions were horrendous. The issue of the *Argus* which reported on the cricket reproduced information from Johannesburg's *The Star*.

> THE RAILWAY RUSH
>
> A gentleman who has just arrived from Bloemfontein gives a brief account of the state of things... Railway carriages during the time of the great rush last week from the Rand, as seen by him from the station platform at the Free State capital. He states in the first place, that the misery witnessed by him was simply appalling – as was only natural considering the short

> time people gave themselves for preparation. The crush was so terrific that on each of two successive mornings two children were handed out for interment at Bloemfontein, having died on the journey from asphyxia. Several women also gave birth to children on the journey. The stench that arose as a consequence of the overcrowding in the carriage permeated the whole atmosphere of the station. It was agonising to witness the rush to obtain milk at the Bloemfontein buffet as there was a great number of children of such a tender age that they could partake of no other food but milk – and there was none to be had. The town of Bloemfontein was simply besieged by unwilling visitors... The hotels were crowded to suffocation and thirty women used one apartment as a dressing-room. It was amusing to note the signs of the hurry with which they had 'packed up their duds'. Several ladies had come away from Johannesburgh with only skirts, others with only blouses; and generally, many little articles apparently trifling but in reality of the highest importance had been neglected in the hurry-scurry. The misery and wretchedness, concluded the informant of the *Star*, was such as he would never wish to see again.

The tourists could not be immunised against the political situation. However, Lord Hawke and his team did not have an advance guard of ECB officials and Foreign Office Advisers to assess the security risk. Mercenaries of a kind themselves, they had ploughed on against the traffic to play cricket in Johannesburg. There was some rearrangement of the original schedule, but there does not seem to have been any suggestion that the tour should be abandoned amid the political and military chaos.

The team sought and were granted permission to picnic on the battlefield at Doornkop, the site of the Jameson Raid. It was, however, impossible to avoid the political situation and the occasion was not without incident.

> The English cricketers in South Africa had a peculiar experience during their stay in Johannesburg. Permission was given to them to visit the Doornkop battlefield, and the occasion was utilised on the scene of the disaster to Dr Jameson's followers. But their return was not so agreeable. Passing through Florida, the party was stopped by the Mining Commissioner. After being questioned they were allowed to depart, but had to walk to Maraisburg as the driver of the wagonette refused to take them on without the permission of the police. They reached town just in time to catch the Natal train, and left amid the cheers of a large crowd, assembled to see them off.[21]

Jeremy Lonsdale in a feature in *Wisden Cricket Monthly*[22] was not far wide of the mark when he said that, in a tour plagued from start to finish by doubts and uncertainties, no side since, even those visiting Pakistan in the late 1960s, has had to contend with anything on a similar scale. It is a position the ghosts of Lord Hawke's team can expect to retain unchallenged. No modern international side would begin, let alone continue, a tour in such circumstances. Natal, out of the war zone, would be less dramatic.

Natal

> The first match between Lord Hawke's team and Fifteen of Pietermaritzburg, was the occasion of quite a new batch of records for South African cricket. On the first day, Lieut Poore of the 7th Hussars, opened the ball with the highest individual innings made in South Africa against an English team. In addition, Lord Hawke's team created four records – firstly, by compiling more runs than they themselves, or the two English teams which preceded them, have ever made against a South African combination, secondly by scoring two 'centuries' in one innings; thirdly by producing the highest individual score made by any cricketer in South Africa; and fourthly, by making the highest aggregate for the City Oval. It was an eventful match for South African cricket.[23]

The match might have produced a number of records, but it ended as a meaningless draw. More significant perhaps was the following match against Fifteen of Natal, when Lieut Poore's undefeated 107 led the local side to a target of 228 after they had managed only 100 in the first innings, between Lord Hawke's team's 154 and 173. Lohmann, who was opening the batting regularly had made 36 and 31 and took 9-42 and 3-40. *Cricket* referred to 'the unexpected victory of the Colonials' and reported that,

> Great interest was taken in the match which was favoured throughout with splendid weather, and the attendance each day reached several thousands.[24]

Lieutenant Robert Poore was Irish by birth and in the early stages of a military career which was to see him reach the rank of Brigadier General, acquire a CIE and DSO and command the 7th Hussars at both the state opening of Parliament and coronation of King George V in 1911. He had previously served in India, having inter alia been ADC to the Governor of Bombay, Lord Harris, himself not unknown in cricketing circles. In 1895 his regiment had been posted to Natal and later in 1896 the Matabele Campaign would see him move further north. He was a distinguished sportsman, twice winning the West of India Tennis Championships at both singles and doubles and also excelling at polo, golf, squash, racquets, gymkhanas and rifle and revolver shooting.

He had arrived in South Africa with something of a cricketing pedigree, having already played first-class cricket in India, and would in 1899 have a single, but spectacular season with Hampshire in English first-class cricket. Lohmann took the view that he was by some distance the best batsman to face them on the tour. His 112 for the Maritzburg XV followed by the match-winning second innings 107 for XV of Natal so impressed Lord Hawke that there was an attempt to persuade him to join the touring party. H T Hewett had been obliged to return home on personal business and Hawke was a batsman short. Under pressure from the South African Cricket Association, the Natal Cricket Union and his superior officer, Colonel Paget, Poore declined the invitation and instead played for South Africa against England. Even at a time when international qualification arrangements were much more fluid, his credentials for doing so were a little thin, based solely on the fact that the 7th Hussars had been stationed in South Africa for nine months.

Lohmann questioned it, saying it was a great pity Poore had been chosen, as he was not South African, the length of his stay in South Africa was uncertain and it could only be discouraging to young local cricketers if they saw themselves shelved for a bird-of-passage like Poore. It was a valid point of view and finds an echo in reverse in England more than a hundred years later when there are concerns about first-class cricket being infiltrated by 'Kolpak' players many of whom are from South Africa.

He was perhaps failing to anticipate Abe Bailey's dictum, which the following year would allow Lohmann himself to represent Western Province against Transvaal in the Currie Cup, that good players should be allowed to play whatever their residential qualification. In the event, Poore's performances, batting at no 3 and usually finding himself at the crease fairly early in the innings were nothing spectacular. He averaged 12.66, Lohmann claiming his wicket four times in his six innings. He did, however, take one Test wicket, that of Lord Hawke in the first Test at Port Elizabeth.

Meanwhile, the tourists did not always endear themselves to their hosts who with limited resources had gone to a great deal of trouble to ensure that all went smoothly. Lieutenant Poore had for instance been involved in a sub-committee responsible for the arrangements for the ground which included negotiations with the local council, hire of marquees, refreshment facilities, purchase of new matting and negotiations with various authorities to arrange for the early closing of businesses and concessionary railway fares for both players and spectators.

At times the attitude of Lord Hawke's men verged on the arrogant and high-handed. In Pietermaritzburg,[25] they failed to attend a dinner and concert which had been arranged for them, complained about the quality of the pitches, put pressure on the umpires and Lord Hawke used his twelfth man to rest his fielders in rotation. C W Wright, the Nottinghamshire amateur, tried to sell balls at exorbitant prices when local supplies ran short as well as a supply of ghosted biographies of the players. There was no attempt to blur the social divisions of English society: Lord Hawke stayed at Government House, the other amateurs with the 7th Hussars and the professionals were left to find their own hotel accommodation.

Lohmann was to miss the match at King William's Town for reasons that were nothing to do with cricket or military hostilities. C B Fry describes the landing at East London.

> It was a formidable landing. We were lowered from the ship in a big basket into a tub, and the tub made for an opening in the coast which seemed to be obscured by a recurrent wave of prodigious size. This was the bar. We crossed the bar by an accurate piece of timing on the part of our skipper, who lay off until the right moment and then shot his cockleshell of a tub through a corner of the wave just as it subsided, and we found ourselves inland of a wall of water which quite obscured the ship from view.
>
> When I say 'we' I should say all of us except George Lohmann. George had been there before. Hours before we reached East London, George casually let it drop that he would be unable to land there, but would travel on the ship to Cape Town and join us later. Nothing would induce him to renew his previous acquaintance with the bar, where on some occasion, I suppose, the skipper had mistimed his spurt. When we were safely inside we were more sympathetic with George than when we left him on the ship.[26]

Cricket fields seemed a safer option than battlefields. The three matches against South Africa were at the time deemed Test matches – though only at the time of the third one did the local press start using the term – and that status has not since been revoked. There had been previous tours in 1888/89, 1891/92 and a subsequent one in 1898/99 at which point all eight Tests involving 'England' and South Africa had resulted in comprehensive defeats for the hosts. No Test matches were played on the tour to England in 1901 and it was not until South Africa had won the 1905/06 series by a 4-1 margin, that Test status was granted for matches in England. Journalists in the Cape had no doubt about the inferiority of South African cricket. For them playing cricket against the English tourists was a matter of gaining experience.

It seems fairly obvious then that these matches were against opposition that was not yet ready for international cricket and the spectacular nature of Lohmann's series statistics have to be seen in that context, as do the earlier ones of Johnny Briggs and, perhaps to a lesser extent, the later ones of Sydney Barnes.

The first Test at Port Elizabeth, beginning on 13 February, was preceded by Lohmann's spectacular and devastating demolition of Eighteen of Port Elizabeth.

> Lord Hawke won the toss and sent his opponents in at 12 o'clock in a gale of wind which handicapped the batsmen… Lohmann, with the wind at his back, proved unplayable, and took fifteen wickets for 38 runs.[27]

His final figures were 19.3-5-38-15 as the local side were almost literally blown away for 93. The reply of England's Twelve continued into the following morning when the last wicket fell at 162. Port Elizabeth managed to avoid an innings defeat, faring slightly better in the second innings with 108 and the tourists scored the required runs for the loss of three wickets.

> The Port Elizabeth men made a miserable show in the face of Lohmann and Fry, losing six wickets for 14 runs before lunch. Lohmann at the interval had four wickets for 5 runs to his credit.

Lohmann finished with 20.3-11-44-11; 26 wickets for 82 runs was a useful warm-up for the Test.

Cricket in South Africa at this time was on matting, but the matting was not uniform throughout the country. That used in Port Elizabeth was apparently thicker than its counterpart in Johannesburg or Cape Town and was laid over turf, As a consequence, it was bowler-friendly, which may partly explain Lohmann's phenomenal figures in the match against the local side, although he seems to have done well enough in Cape and Highveld matches too.

Regulations on the width of the matting, sweeping, stretching and rolling of the matting were introduced some time later for Currie Cup matches,[28] but there is no mention of thickness.

First Test Match

> It was looked upon as a foregone conclusion that the first match at Port Elizabeth being played on a turf ground to which the best men in South Africa are strange would be a gift to the Englishmen, especially as the pitch is the most favourable in the country for Lohmann's bowling. So it proved…

> Lohmann's marvellous performance with the ball was the great feature of the match. The light was certainly bad but by no means bad enough to explain away such a lamentable exhibition as they made against the famous Surrey bowler.[29]

An eclipse of the sun on the first day of the match, proved portentous as South Africa's batting was eclipsed by yet more spectacular bowling from Lohmann. Tom Hayward, his Surrey colleague, who had seen more of him than most, reckoned that Lohmann had never bowled better than he did on this tour. It was a compliment that could not extend to his batting. Lohmann opened the innings with Sir Timothy O'Brien, was caught for a duck and, dropping down the order to no 6 in the second innings, repeated that score. His bowling more than compensated.

The encounter was not referred to in the press as a Test match, equal prominence being given to the simultaneous Western Province Cricket Club v Simon's Town, but coverage was sufficient to allow a reasonable reconstruction to be attempted and was highly critical of the South Africans' unimpressive performance.

> The England v South Africa match started at 12 o'clock before a moderate attendance. The weather is exceptionally fine and a big crowd is expected this afternoon, business houses closing at 1 o'clock. Sir T O'Brien and Lohmann opened the innings to the bowling of Sinclair and Willoughby…[30]

By mid-afternoon, the England innings was completed. They had managed only 185 and Lohmann's bowling did not start auspiciously.

> Routledge and Hearne opened the African innings at a quarter-past four… Routledge, the Johannesburg batsman spanking the Surrey bowler to the boundary off his second ball and repeating the dose the last ball of the over… The pro. brought the first ten up by hitting Lohmann to the press tent for a quartette… Routledge put Lohmann over the fence for 6.

Lohmann's partner, Hugh Bromley-Davenport, fast left-arm, amateur, Eton and Cambridge, dismissed both openers, then Lohmann took over and disposed of the other eight, bowling seven and catching the other, as South Africa collapsed dramatically to finish 92 in arrears. England's second innings extended the lead to 318, way beyond the reach of the hosts whose,

> …efforts before Lohmann's superb bowling were feeble in the extreme, and in three-quarters of an hour the representatives of South Africa were

> dismissed for the paltry total of 30. Lohmann took fourteen wickets in the match for 48, a wonderful feat not even surpassed by himself.[31]

Lohmann's actual match figures were in fact 15-45. He bowled unchanged through both innings, 15.4-6-38-7 followed by an even more spectacular 9.4-5-7-8. He dismissed Cook, Middleton and Willoughby to finish the match with a hat-trick and complete the best innings figures by any bowler in 47 Test matches to date. His second innings figures and match figures remain records for Test matches at Port Elizabeth, and South Africa held the unenviable record of the lowest completed Test innings for a further 59 years. They were to repeat the 'achievement' in 1924 at Edgbaston, but not until New Zealand were all out for 26 at Auckland in 1954/55 were they rid of it.

> The air of South Africa, it would seem [sic], to suit George Lohmann's cricket 'down to the ground'. Consistently successful as his bowling has been for Lord Hawke's team, he fairly excelled himself in the second innings of the South African eleven at Port Elizabeth, when he took eight wickets at a cost of only seven runs. The South African team will have particular reason to remember him, as they were in and out within three-quarters-of-an-hour. With bated breath I would humbly submit to the heads of the statistical department, that this must be very near the shortest innings on record in a match of any importance...
>
> Nor is it only as a bowler that Lohmann has been furnishing material for the cricket critics in South Africa. On the occasion of the visit of Lord Hawke's team to Kimberley, a scratch match was arranged to fill up a spare afternoon between eleven locals and a scratch eleven composed mainly of the English team. Six wickets were down for 65... Lohmann outstaged the remaining batsmen and finally carried out his bat for 115. How he must have hit will be understood when I add that his figures included five sixes and seventeen fours.[32]

Second Test Match

THE SECOND Test, the first played at the Wanderers began on Monday 2 March, a week later than originally planned, 'it having been found impossible to make the necessary arrangements for the removal of the wounded now lying at Wanderers before that day'.[33] An attempt to bring forward the match in Pretoria originally scheduled to follow it was only partially successful, the Pretoria Mechanics Cycling Club declining to give up a meeting with the result that the tourists' match was restricted to Wednesday and Friday, sandwiching the Cycling Club meeting on the

Thursday. President Kruger declined Lord Hawke's invitation to attend the match.

It was all against the macabre background of the aftermath of a huge dynamite explosion which had taken place less than two weeks before. Many had been killed and the Wanderers premises had been converted to emergency hospital facilities. As Lonsdale said, cricket, though not impossible, was hardly tactful.

Lord Hawke was to recall later that 'the whole of the Wanderers Hall which was our pavilion, stank of iodoform and was full of wounded'. However, sharing the premises with doctors, nurses and undertakers was no deterrent to the cricketers and amid surrounding newspaper headlines of 'Explosions – Relief Fund – Arson – Disturbances' and 'Dynamite Inquiry', Lohmann's and England's feats were recorded for posterity.

The Test bowling record of 8-7 lasted eighteen days. On the second day of the Johannesburg Test, bowling at first change for some reason best known to Lord Hawke, Lohmann surpassed it with 14.2-6-28-9. This time it was to survive until 'Laker's match' at Old Trafford in 1956. Hayward's 122 had helped England to what was, in the context of the series, a massive 482.

> After lunch the wickets dropped one after the other before Lohmann who took nine wickets for 28 on a perfect batsman's wicket. 331 runs behind, the South Africans followed on.[34]

> The English fielding throughout the match has been very fine, and Lohmann's superb bowling of yesterday was followed doing a good piece of bowling this morning.[35]

Although the statistic was one which would not have been recorded at the time, Lohmann had taken just sixteen matches to take one hundred Test wickets.

Alongside the uitlander–Afrikander conflict were the non-military, parish-pump-style, but long-standing and acrimonious battles between the cricket authorities in Western Province and the Transvaal and, of course, the ongoing 'native question'. The system of selection, as in England, was that the host venue selected the team but, for players from other centres, only from those nominated by those centres.

Transvaal caused a controversy by selecting Krom Hendricks, the coloured fast bowler, who two years earlier had declined the tour to England as 'baggage man'; Western Province were having none of it, as he had not been among their nominated players. He did not play. The enforced omission of Middleton further weakened the side.

> Some such result was not unexpected as the South African Eleven was by no means representative... Middleton was ordered to Cape Town to take part in a club match and his recall by the executive of this club gave rise to a great deal of unpleasantness...
>
> The South African innings opened well, and 70 was put on the board by Sinclair and Lieutenant Poore for the loss of one wicket when Lohmann going on beat the latter first ball for a useful 20. Sinclair was as it proved top scorer leaving with the total four for 77. Few of the others played Lohmann with any degree of confidence... Lohmann came out with the splendid analysis of nine wickets for 28 runs – on a batsman's pitch too.[36]

Between the second and third Tests, en route from Johannesburg to Cape Town, there were matches against Griqualand West at Kimberley and Mr James Logan's Twenty-two at Matjiesfontein. On the latter occasion, there is no doubt that the cricket was secondary to serious socialising. Lohmann played for Logan's team and in festival mood, hit C B Fry out of the ground, twice hit Tyler over the fence, 'well on the way to Kimberley' according to one report, before he stepped out once too often and was stumped after making 64 of an eventual total of 277. Logan, 'greeted with loud applause', made two before being bowled by one of Lord Hawke's lobs. In the two-and-a quarter hours remaining Lord Hawke's team reached 183-9.

> After the game, the teams were royally entertained by Mr Logan and a most enjoyable evening was spent.
>
> Lord Hawke's team, to judge by the elaborate accounts of the entertainment in the South African papers, must have had a high old time of it on the occasion of their match against Mr J D Logan's team on March 6th. The Lord of Maffesfontein [sic] as Mr Logan is called in South Africa, played a very prominent part in getting Lord Hawke and his merry men out there, though this is only one of many forms in which he has shown his interest in the development of the game. 'The Laird', as I had occasion to remark at the time, was in England last summer, and it goes without saying, took the opportunity to witness some of the best matches in London. He has a son who, according to rumour, is not unlikely to turn out a good player.[37.]

The match against Western Province was presumably rather more serious. Eleven-a-side this time, rather than Eleven against Fifteen in December and the only first-class match of the tour outside the Test matches, Lohmann added to his tour haul with 6-48. The match was drawn, the final day being washed out completely.

Third Test Match

THE TOURISTS fielded a weakened side at Newlands, C B Fry being unavailable. According to the *Cape Argus* he was considering settling in Bulawayo. The same newspaper reported that he had completely recovered from the effects of his experiences on a pony,[38] having fractured his right fibula in a riding accident. Hewett had already returned home. The discrepancy between the teams was so huge that it was to make little difference.

> ...there was no great excitement about what would be the result of the match. Nevertheless, it was still possible for the South Africans to win some glory and they collected together about their strongest team.[39]

England won by an innings and 33 runs, Lohmann taking 7-42 in the first innings. Play was extended on the second day, playing regulations being less rigid than they have subsequently become.

> The umpires then called time, but a finish was called by the spectators.[40]

Lohmann finished the three-match series with 35 wickets at 5.8 each.

Postmortem

AS THE team left for home in the Union steamship *Pretoria*, *Cricket* had its reservations about the wisdom of the tour, but despite the Shakespearean mis-quotation, recognised that some good had come of the trip in cricketing, if not political, terms.

> It was very unfortunate they should have visited South Africa at a time when things were so unsettled everywhere. Their double visit to Johannesburg, in particular, forcibly illustrated the axiom that 'misfortunes come not as single spies but in battalions'. All the same, considering the differences in conditions they have done fairly well. The best wish anyone can offer is that their trip has done something to help on the development of Cricket in the various cricket centres of South Africa.[41]

Summing up the tour twelve months later, *Wisden*, too, was alive to the political background and had no hesitation in pointing to the principal reason for the team's success.

> Excellent as the batting was, the success of the eleven was mainly brought about by the effective bowling of George Lohmann who had the splendid record of 157 wickets for less than seven runs each. The Surrey professional accomplished his best work in the eleven-a-side games with South Africa, taking in the three matches no fewer than 35 wickets.
> At one time it was feared that the disturbances in the Transvaal would seriously affect the tour, but such happily was not the case. The finances no doubt suffered in consequence, but we understand there was no loss. George Lohmann undertook the business management of the tour.[42]

Lillywhite's was more specific both about Lohmann's performance in the context of that of the team and the disturbances and their effect on the tour.

> Lohmann's bowling was quite out of the common... When it is noticed that the nearest approach to him was Mr H R Bromley-Davenport with 46, the full force of his remarkable performance will be felt
> ...at the conclusion of their two engagements in the Western Province came the startling news of Jameson's raid. This caused the postponement of the third fixture which was to have taken place at Johannesburg, and even when this match did come off the 'gate' suffered tremendously...
> Once more, when they were just about to visit Johannesburg, came the news of the fearful explosion in that city; this necessitated a second postponement.[43]

Well into the next century, Lohmann's bowling on that tour remained in the memory of S M J Woods who had played for Australia against him in 1888, then having spent four years at Cambridge University, alongside him on this tour.

> George Lohmann was a marvellous bowler on matting wickets. He got three times as many wickets as anyone else...
> Mr Logan looked after us splendidly during our trip, and as all the profits went to our dear friend George Lohmann who was suffering from weak lungs and was resident there in Magersfontein [sic], we all returned thoroughly happy and delighted with our tour.[44]

C B Fry, who had joined the tour on the recommendation of Ranjitsinhji and was to say later that the experience turned him into a candidate for the Gentlemen's Eleven and for England,[45] was in no doubt as to Lohmann's quality.

> George Lohmann was in a class by himself... perhaps the greatest medium pace bowler England has ever had. He had a lovely rhythmic action, and to

> my mind ranks with F R Spofforth, the Australian, as a consummate artist in disguised variation of pace… He was a handsome fellow with an Anglo-Saxon complexion, browned to the colour of a cup of tea with cream in it. He had a pale gold Anglo-Saxon moustache, but his eyes were of a lambent brown such as one sees amongst the Meridionals.[46]

Lohmann did not return immediately to England at the end of the tour, deferring his departure until early May, reaching England in the *Norman* on Friday 22. *Cricket* commented,

> George Lohmann has decided to stay on in South Africa for the time being. It was hardly expected that he would return to England with the main body, and it will probably be a few weeks before he makes his first appearance in English cricket.[47]

There were also concerns about the effects of excessive touring, not only for Lohmann, but for his distinguished contemporaries too.

> Briggs, Lohmann and Peel are not yet Australianized although projects for buying the services of all three of them were seriously discussed in colonial cricket circles a few years back, when the supply of mature colts seemed about to become exhausted. Had any of these projects come to anything, it would only have been fair retaliation for the capture of Ferris…
>
> It would be easy to mention others whose play has not been improved by these winter trips. Why did Sharpe's bowling fail after his visit to Australia with Lord Sheffield's team? Did Lohmann's trip with the last team do him any good?

For Lohmann, at any rate, it was his last tour as a player.

1 *Cape Times* 9 February 1895
2 *Cricket* 6 June 1895
3 *Cricket* 12 September 1895
4 *Cape Times* 23 December 1895
5 Bettesworth *op cit*
6 *Cape Times* 27 December 1895
7 *Cape Times* 31 December 1895
8 *Cricket* 30 January 1986
9 in Ireland
10 *A Short Autobiography* pp 90-91
11 p 62
12 *Cricket* 30 January 1896
13 *Cape Argus* 8 January 1896
14 *Land en Volk* 9 January 1896
15 *Cape Times* 2 February 1896
16 *Gutsche* Old Gold p 78
17 Ib

18 *Cape Argus* 16 January 1896
19 Taylor *Lucky Jim* pp 104-6
20 Walltext in exhibition of Club history at 'New' Wanderers
21 *Cricket* 27 February 1896
22 'England's Tour Problems' January 1985
23 *Cricket* 25 February 1896. Major Poore had 112; CB Fry 153; Sir T C O'Brien 118; Lord Hawke's team's second innings total was 433-9
24 *Cricket* 30 January 1896
25 The capital of Natal, usually referred to in contemporary accounts by the more popular abbreviated form of 'Maritzburg'
26 Fry *Life Worth Living* p 117-118
27 *Cape Argus* 10 February 1896
28 Sub-Committee on Currie Cup Rules, appointed 17 December 1902
29 *Cricket* 26 March 1896
30 *Cape Argus* 14 February 1896
31 *Cape Argus* 15 February 1896
32 *Cricket* 27 February 1896
33 *The Star* 27 February 1896
34 *Cape Argus* 4 April 1896
35 *Cape Argus* 5 April 1896
36 *Cricket* 9 April 1896
37 *Cricket* 16 April 1896
38 21 March 1896
39 *Cricket* 16 April 1896
40 *Cape Argus* 24 March 1896
41 *Cricket* 26 March 1896
42 *Wisden* 1897 p 387
43 *Lillywhite's* 1897 pp 219-220
44 My Reminiscences – *The Cricketer* – 14 July 1923
45 Fry *op cit* p 105
46 Ib p 129
47 *Cricket* 16 April 1896

CHAPTER 15

TEN YEARS LATER (1896)

People say they used 'to go and see Lohmann and Richardson bowl'. Today, does anyone go to see anyone bowl?
D R Jardine Letter to *The Times* 5 July 1947

Prelude

THE 1896 season was anticipated with some enthusiasm. Surrey celebrated All Fools' Day with a comic cricket match on Thames Ditton Village Green when a team of Surrey professionals, captained by Richardson, took on a team of comic entertainers. The skipper for the day limited himself to one over and Bobby Abel and Maurice Read reversed their traditional roles, Read stonewalling and Abel slogging wildly. It was all for charity and the team were aware of their social responsibilities.

> During the afternoon the players took round collecting boxes for the Thames Ditton and Surbiton Cottage Hospital on whose behalf the match had been organised, Richardson himself reminding the spectators that they never knew when they might be there themselves.[1]

Read, Lohmann's great friend, although he turned out here, had retired from the first-class game at the end of the previous season. Albert Craig, the 'Surrey poet' was looking for some appropriate eulogy and was seemingly less than impressed with the *Daily Mail* journalist's parody on Longfellow's 'A Psalm of Life'.

> Lives of all great 'Pros' remind us
> That there always comes a time
> When they, fattening in the waistcoat
> Settle in the 'Public' line

Publics where the cockney sportsman
Mad with cricket on the brain
While he drains a glass of bitter,
Hears their yarns about the game.[2]

It was all light-hearted stuff. Lohmann was still in South Africa, resting from the winter tour and awaiting better weather in England. For him, what lay ahead was anything but light-hearted. He had a three match Test series and a benefit to which to look forward, but 6,000 miles away in late April, how could he anticipate the drama of the year that lay ahead?

Under the heading 'CRICKET GOSSIP Latest About the Surrey Men and the Oval Programme', the *Daily Mail* eagerly looked forward to the season.

> ...The Oval too will be the arena for one of those test matches England v Australia on August 10. Another attractive fixture is Gentlemen v Players on July 6. Nor must I omit to refer to George Lohmann's benefit, the match with Surrey's great rivals, Yorkshire, on July 30.
>
> ...The eleven will comprise all the old favourites except of course Maurice Read. Lohmann will not be back for the opening matches, as he is staying in South Africa till the east wind and cold damp weather have quite departed. George is in rare form as his South African averages show, but it is to be hoped that he is not overworking himself. We know how these winter tours have on several occasions sadly interfered with some of our best men, notably Sharpe and Lockwood. 'Staleness' from overwork is the bowler's deadliest bane.[3]

The same newspaper also looked forward to yet another Australian tour to England

> IT PAYS THEM TO COME
>
> Nominally, the Australian teams that come to England consist entirely of amateur players. As a matter of fact and necessity, the team is run on strict business principles, and very proper principles too.
>
> The manager, who must be a man of influence in the cricket world and 'know the ropes' thoroughly, selects his men, and having completed his team he then arranges the fixtures in England. As a rule, the Australians take half the gate money at each match, but when the ground is a small one, they will stipulate for a larger share. Considering that as much as £3,500 has been taken as gate-money at the Kennington Oval, the receipts of the team in a good season must be considerable, as they will play between thirty and forty matches.
>
> After deducting all expenses – the cost of the voyage to and from Australia, and the travel and living expenses in England which amount to

> a considerable sum – there still remains a surplus for division at the end of the season.
> What each man receives depends of course on his arrangement with the manager but £500 is not by any means an extraordinary bonus for a member of the team to take.
> It is asserted that the first Australian team to visit England cleared £800 at the end of the season.
> The amateur, of course, receives no salary and may not share the gate-money, but there is nothing to prevent him accepting a liberal amount for expenses.[4]

The figures quoted and the relatively favourable treatment of the tourists compared with that of the home players were to feature prominently in the thinking of those plotting the later August revolution.

Lohmann returned to first-class cricket on 1 June in a fixture against Somerset at The Oval which Surrey won by ten wickets inside two days. Opening the bowling with Richardson, he found wickets less easy to come by than they had been in the South African Tests the previous winter, and he was overshadowed by his younger and faster colleague who captured thirteen wickets in the match compared to Lohmann's two. However, he contributed 36 with the bat and his reappearance on the Surrey scene was the cause of a great influx of spectators.

> There was a big crowd present some time before the match commenced and they extended a warm welcome when Lohmann appeared. But after luncheon the people streamed in from buses and trams and the electric railway, and soon after three there was scarce standing room left at any point from which the game could be seen…
> George Lohmann, after Brockwell's retirement, was the first to make any prolonged stay at the wicket and he steadied the game for the Surrey side. He was at sea with Woods's bowling for some little time, but gradually increased the score with singles and played himself into form. But the Somerset captain broke through his defence at the finish. Having given him a full toss, then a remarkably short-pitched one, he then sent down a splendid length ball which spread-eagled the wicket…
> Surrey are a great side and they deserve hearty congratulations on yet another splendid win in the championship.[5]

Derbyshire followed and were dispatched by an innings and 57 runs, again within two days. This time, however, Lohmann was among the wickets, 29-12-51-6 and 25-9-54-4, and once again, he and Richardson formed a match-winning combination. A rain-affected wicket helped, though not as much as might be assumed, and some of the Derbyshire batsmen contributed to their own downfall.

> The excellence of Lohmann and Richardson's bowling was responsible for the dismissal of a good many batsmen, but there were certainly one or two who lost their wickets more through bad play on their own part than any particular good cricket of their opponents...
> I should not like to say which bowled the better yesterday morning, Lohmann or Richardson. Both got a tremendous amount of work on the ball and both appeared very difficult to play, and although Lohmann got the most wickets, Richardson certainly bowled the most good balls...
> A great deal of rain had fallen overnight, and consequently the wicket might have been expected to play very treacherously when play resumed yesterday. Oval wickets do not go in for that sort of thing, however. They have been too well looked after to take any unnatural advantage of the batsman and beyond a little natural kicking in the morning, after a wet night, they usually play as truly and easily as it is possible for respectable wickets to do under the circumstances.[6]

At this stage of the season, Surrey had played nine matches and won nine, five by the margin of an innings. They failed to make it ten out of ten. The Bradford rain saw to that. After a first day wash-out, a rain affected pitch resulted in a low scoring match. Lohmann was again among the wickets for Surrey, Wainwright, Jackson and Hirst for Yorkshire. Lord Hawke's final day declaration almost led to a result, but time was against it and the match ended in a draw with honours even.

> Lohmann came out with the superb analysis of seven wickets for 61 runs, his bowling after the interval being particularly fine, as he took four or five wickets while scarcely any runs were hit from him...
> The great match between Yorkshire and Surrey was drawn with neither side able to claim any decided advantage. Now we shall have to wait until July 30 to see the great rivals in competition; on that day they meet at Kennington Oval, and given fine weather there should be a monster attendance to see the final tug of war and to fill the pockets of George Lohmann.[7]

Before that, however, there was some Test cricket to be played for which Lohmann and Richardson warmed up with wickets in comfortable wins against Hampshire and Leicestershire, before coming unstuck and losing by three wickets against Lancashire at Old Trafford.

First Test Match

LOHMANN HAD made his Test début in the equivalent match ten years earlier, but had not played against Australia for more than four years, the last occasion having been in the Adelaide Test of March 1892. So it was perhaps with more than usual anticipation that his reappearance was awaited by the thousands trekking to Lord's on Monday 22 June, as near as makes no difference the summer solstice and the longest day. For George Trott, captaining Australia for the first time it must have seemed it.

England's lead at the end of the day was 233, which remained the highest for all Test matches until 2005 when South Africa led Zimbabwe by 284 at Newlands. Any Surrey faithful who had crossed the river would not have been disappointed, as their two idols, Tom Richardson in the morning of his long career and George Lohmann in the evening of his on a good pitch on which the tourists had chosen to bat, demolished their guests in 22.3 overs for a paltry 53, Richardson 6-39, Lohmann 3-13. This turned out to be the only occasion on which Lohmann and Richardson played together for England. Richardson had begun his Test career in Lohmann's absence in The Oval Test of 1893. His impact had been immediate and in six Test matches, he had taken 42 wickets.

Lohmann was not expecting to open the bowling.

> Not even the players knew who the other bowler was going to be and Lohmann was walking to his place in the field when W G gave the ball to him. Lohmann was difficult from the first, and often beat the batsmen in his pace… Richardson and Lohmann carried everything before them.[8]
> As Richardson and Lohmann walked back to the pavilion at the end of the innings they received just the ovation they deserved for their respective performances… both men bowled with rare skill and judgment, hardly a loose ball coming from either end.
> On an almost perfect batting wicket, with all the encouragement derived from gaining first innings – an incalculable advantage under the conditions which prevailed – a first-class batting side was disposed of for the meagre, the miserly meagre, total of 53.[9]

Lohmann contributed just a single to England's reply of 292, Abel enhancing Surrey's contribution with 94. Australia did rather better in the second innings and, thanks to what was at the time a Test record partnership of 221 by Trott and Syd Gregory, redeemed themselves to an extent and managed to set England a target of 109. Abel again top scored as England cleared the arrears for the loss of four wickets. Lohmann had taken no wickets in the second innings, Hearne and Richardson dividing the spoils between them.

On only one occasion since – in Verity's match in 1934 – have England beaten Australia in a Test match at the subsequently self-styled 'Home of Cricket'.

Although it could not have been known at the time, it was Lohmann's last Test match.

> Only a short time previously he had made 251 not out for Reigate Priory against Horley and it seemed as though his health had been restored. His recovery, however, was only partial, and this, coupled with an unfortunate disagreement with the Surrey County Cricket Club caused him to drop out of the game.[10]

Surrey Lose Momentum

Oh! Full Surrey Twilight!
John Betjeman *A Subaltern's Love Song*

AFTER SURREY'S outstanding start to the season, the defeat by Lancashire marked the beginning of a less successful period which saw them eventually slip to fourth place in the table. It was the converse of 1892 when they came from nowhere to win the title. Now, having seemingly no obstacles to yet another Championship, they fell away dramatically.

Comfortable wins against Hampshire and Middlesex were counterbalanced by defeats by the latter, as well as by Kent and Sussex. Lohmann continued to take wickets, though not at the same rate as Richardson, including a second innings 6-36 against Hampshire and, in a losing cause against Middlesex at The Oval, 5-59 and 4-70. He was less consistent with the bat, but retained the ability to contribute when it mattered, his highest score of the season coming at The Oval against Sussex when an undefeated 86 took Surrey to within 43 runs of a fourth innings target of 424. He also made 63 not out in the innings victory over Middlesex at Lord's, his last appearance there, a week after his final appearance on the same ground in a Gentlemen v Players fixture.

> After Mr Read had succumbed to a splendid catch in the slips by Mr Stoddart, Lohmann and his captain completely collared the bowling and caused the score to rise rapidly.
>
> To Lohmann who was eventually the top scorer and retired unbeaten, Surrey owe the largest share of their thanks for the fairly favourable position in which Surrey finished their innings. Coming in with the score at 190 for 7 wickets, he quickly got to work scoring freely in every direction from all the bowlers tried – Hearne, Rawlin, Phillips, Mr Stoddart and Mr Bromley-Davenport. Whilst

> he drove cleanly, hard and often, and occasionally cut finely out of point's reach, his most effective stroke was a leg-hit, almost square, into which he put tremendous power. It was a splendid display of fearless batting and was invaluable to the side.
>
> How hard Lohmann hit may be judged from the fact that in his 63 were twelve 4s, two 3s and four 2s.
>
> Mr Warner found it extremely difficult to get a run off either Lohmann or Richardson.[11]

Cricket reported on 1 August that Richardson had taken his 200th first-class wicket of the season. It was the second of three seasons in which he was to do so and part of 1005 he took over four consecutive seasons. There is no mention of Lohmann or the fact that Lohmann had topped 200 in three consecutive seasons. Understandably, the magazine was looking forward not back...

Second Test Match

AT OLD TRAFFORD on 16-18 July, Australia had levelled the series with a three wicket win. Grace selected from fifteen on the morning of the match. Lohmann was not included, neither was Gunn, Lohmann, according to the press because of a slightly strained leg, though J N Pentelow says 'he did not feel quite well enough', and Gunn 'on account of some little personal matter'. The *Daily Mail* was more concerned about the inclusion of Ranjitsinhji and of MacLaren and Briggs, attributing the latter to the fact that they were Lancashire men and calling for an end to the arrangement where the team for each Test match was selected by the authority of the ground hosting the fixture.

> What had MacLaren done to earn his place in the team and why was Briggs included? We may be told for an answer that they are Lancashire men, but the cold fact remains for the Lancashire executive to ruminate on... MacLaren and Briggs were the most conspicuous failures.
>
> Gunn, it is said, lost his place on account of some little personal matter – he did not play for the North of England and was invited only at the eleventh hour to be at the ground.
>
> There should be some form of permanent national committee for electing the all-England team.
>
> Again, what was Ranjitsinhji doing among that sacred band? It is true that he learned all his cricket in England, that he is perhaps the best batsman alive, that he insisted on the Australians being consulted, and that Trott returned a sportsmanlike 'Yes'.

But all the same, the Australians were playing England, not England and India...[12]

Lohmann did not participate in the Surrey–Notts match in early August a week before the Third and Final Test match, nor in the match against Essex at Leyton later the same week.

Lohmann's Benefit

THE YEAR will be remembered as that of the 'regrettable incident',[13] but on a happier note, despite the match being sandwiched between the Surrey v Australians and Surrey v Notts Bank Holiday fixtures, neither of which would the committee allow him to choose, Lohmann enjoyed a successful benefit, the proceeds being almost £1,100, more than twice or three times what professionals could expect to receive about that time. The 1897 Annual Report recorded,

> The proceeds of the Yorkshire match were given to G A Lohmann in recognition of the brilliant services he has rendered to Surrey cricket. In addition to the nett proceeds of the gate, a sum of £615.4.6 was subscribed by members and others.

The match attracted 33,000 paying spectators and produced net proceeds of £625.1.3 from which was deducted an advance payment of £200 made in 1895. The Committee added a further £50.[14]

It might have been better. Two years earlier in August 1894, Arthur Shrewsbury, whose financial shrewdness was not in question, had advised Lohmann to begin negotiating for a benefit as soon as possible.

> Hear Mr W Read is going to have a Benefit and I should not be surprised if he got a £1,000 (Barnes will if he is lucky get between £300 and £400). The sooner you arrange about yours the better for you and the longer you delay the worse for you. You would have a big Benefit if you could take it within the next year or so – Take my advice and don't delay it.[15]

Twelve months later, *Cricket* reported,

> The report that George Lohmann is to have a benefit at the Oval next summer is, *Cricket* readers will be glad to learn, correct. As it seems pretty certain that we shall have another Australian team over here in 1896, there is every likelihood that the precedent set by Maurice Read will be followed and that Lohmann will choose the match between England and Australia.

> There could hardly be a more appropriate fixture in view of the high reputation he has alike on Australian and English grounds.[16]

It was a decision taken some time previously. In the event, it did not happen. Lohmann's connection with the England–Australia match at The Oval is remembered for different reasons and despite the report in *Cricket*, the Committee had effectively renegued on what they had decided in November 1894. Lohmann had acted on Shrewsbury's advice and despite his not having played for the county for two seasons the Committee responded with a generosity that reflected Lohmann's contribution to the county's success between 1884 and 1892.

> A letter was read from G A Lohmann stating that he hoped to return by next summer and asking for a benefit match. Secretary was instructed to reply that the Committee were glad to hear he was returning to Surrey cricket, that they would be glad to give him a benefit match in 1896 and that in the event of a visit from an Australian team they would be glad to give him the match between England and Australia.[17]

However, by July 1895, the goal-posts had moved and,

> It was resolved that G A Lohmann be allowed any match but the Bank Holiday match in 1896 for his benefit.[18]

In the event, Lohmann chose the match the previous week-end against Yorkshire on 30, 31 July and 1 August. It was, said the *Athletic Cricket News Annual*, 'a bad date' for a benefit match.[19] In the circumstances, he did well enough, collecting somewhat less than his friend Maurice Read who had been awarded the England–Australia match in 1893, but more than Walter Read whose 1895 testimonial proceeds had been boosted by £200 from the Committee (contrasting with the £50 or 50 guineas traditionally contributed to the benefits of professional players). Bobby Abel had received £621, disadvantaged perhaps by having his benefit the same year as Walter Read's testimonial.[20]

The match itself resulted in a win for Surrey by an innings and 61 runs, Yorkshire having the disadvantage of having to bat on a wet wicket. Lohmann's own performance was not spectacular, a duck and two wickets for 45 and unable to field in the second innings because of a hand injury sustained while attempting a caught and bowled. Tom Hayward distinguished himself with 164. *The Times* had previewed the match by saying that 'upon this game the championship really depends'. They could not have been more wrong. Having lost heavily, Yorkshire went on to be County Champions. The newspaper was, however, suitably adulatory towards the beneficiary.

> It is George Lohmann's benefit match. Lohmann, who entered the eleven in 1884, has become one of the greatest cricketers Surrey ever possessed, alike in bowling, fielding and batting: and although his illness affected him, he is still a first-rate player.

On the first day, 12,420 paid for admission and a collection on the ground raised £89.[21]

While the streamlined marketing and events programmes of Benefit Committees were for the future, Lohmann did have some support from his patron James Logan who collected £25 from the passengers of the *Norman*, and his step-brother, Joseph Pattle who, under his stage name of Charles Pond, was playing in *Othello* at Covent Garden and raised £100.

Pond himself had had a colourful career and would continue to do so. A decade older than George, he had followed his step-father into the City, beginning as a messenger boy and, benefiting by tips he picked up from investors, made an alleged £250,000 by the time he was 19. However, he lost it as quickly as he earned it. Ambitious to become a millionaire, he entrusted half his fortune to a broker, the other half to a solicitor. The broker absconded, the solicitor shot himself. A change of career followed and Joseph Pattle, entrepreneur and amateur entertainer, was metamorphosed into Charles Pond, professional entertainer.

He began in music hall and was shortly topping the bill at the London Alhambra and continued his act with a depiction of cockney characters and recitations and monologues of his own composition.[22] He is credited with being the inspiration behind the Moss Bros dress hire business. The firm had been in business since the 1850s as retailers of high quality clothes and formal wear, but in the early days of his stage career, Pond needed attire for his performances and, his misfortunes leaving him short of the necessary finances, persuaded the brothers to hire their suits to him. News spread quickly, others in the entertainment business followed suit and a long-lasting niche market was born.

Lohmann did not play in the matches between his benefit match and the Third Test in which Surrey met with mixed fortunes, winning by an innings against Nottinghamshire in the Bank Holiday fixture and losing by a similar margin to Essex later the same week. In the light of events of that week and the following one, it may be significant that William Gunn was not included in the Notts XI.

1 *Daily Mail* 2 April 1896
2 *Daily Mail* 6 April 1896
3 22 April 1896
4 4 May 1896
5 *Daily Mail* 2 & 3 June 1896
6 *Daily Mail* 5 & 6 June 1896
7 *Daily Mail* 10 and 11 June 1896
8 *Cricket* 25 June 1896
9 *Daily Mail* 23 June 1896
10 Note by F S Ashley-Cooper to Bettesworth 'Chat' 1910
11 *Daily Mail* 20 July 1896
12 20 July 1897
13 *Wisden* 1897 p 247
14 Surrey CCC minutes 21 March 1895, 4, 18 June, 3 September 1896
15 Letter from Arthur Shrewsbury to George Lohmann, dated 21 August 1894
16 *Cricket* 15 August 1895.
17 Surrey CCC minutes 18 November 1894.
18 Surrey CCC minutes 18 July 1895
19 Sissons *George Lohmann: The beau ideal* p 53
20 Sissons *The Players* p 158
21 *The Times* 31 July 1896
22 Obituary in *The Performer* 21 October 1931

CHAPTER 16

TROUBLE AT MILL (1896)

Third Test Match and the Professionals' 'Strike'

Thy tones shall wake the slumbering throngs
Who patiently endure
And teach them that the labourers' wrongs
The labourers' strength can cure
The First Blow *The Clarion*

OF THE historical significance of the so-called 'strike' of 1896 the *Daily Telegraph* had no doubt.

> In more than one respect the cricket season of 1896 has proved noteworthy, but future historians of our national game will have difficulty in pointing out an incident equally sensational in character to that which was recorded in our columns on Saturday. To cricket chroniclers of the days to come ...the present year will be known as that of 'the strike'. Absolutely unique in itself, entirely unexpected, except to a few persons behind the scenes...[1]

This was not the first 'strike' of professional cricketers. Nottinghamshire professionals had taken such action in 1884, Lohmann's first year on the county circuit, and shortly afterwards, a withdrawal of labour in Australia had precipated eleven changes to a team between the first and second Test matches.

> In Australia, however, nothing is complete without a strike.[2]

Compared with skilled artisans such as fitters, coalface workers and bus drivers,[3] who could expect about £2 per week, professional cricketers were reasonably well paid, although, of course, they had a shorter working life and heavier travel and accommodation expenses; compared with other sportsmen and entertainers they were not. The encyclopædic survey of poverty in London undertaken by Charles Booth[4] contains an interview with the acting secretary of the Cricketers' Fund Benevolent Society, an organisation established[5] to alleviate the poverty suffered by retired cricketers in old age and/or ill health and of widows and children 'left destitute'. He makes the point that while Adelina Patti, the contemporary soprano, might get £500 for a single night, professional cricketers would do well to get £10 for a three day match, about half of which would go on travel and accommodation, the cost of which, except for international matches, was met from their own pockets. Rather than pay professional cricketers their entertainment value, clubs preferred to accumulate large reserve funds, in Surrey's case, around £40,000.

Lohmann was on the Management Committee of the Society, was financially literate, aware of the position of the average 'pro' in the national pay picture and, as already demonstrated in his previous dealings with Surrey, alive to his professional worth and that of his fellow 'strikers'.

In a bitter interview with the *Daily Mail*[6] which infuriated the Surrey committee, Lohmann's colleague Henry Wood gave some information on the financial position of the professional cricketer, stating inter alia that he had never been able to save anything from his earnings and that most of his fee for away matches was absorbed by travel and accommodation expenses. He was aware, moreover, that amateurs could receive £20, £30 or £50 per match in expenses, compared with typical annual pay for an English professional of perhaps £150. Dr Grace got thousands for going to Australia, the professionals who accompanied him around £3,000 between them. Maurice Read had left the county because the Committee had declined his request for winter pay. Lohmann received £300 a year but that was exceptional. Other professionals were paid by the match with no retainer. Wood's own benefit had realised £350; he had been 'shoved aside' for Mr Shuter's testimonial. The report added that leading jockeys could make £20,000 a year, baseball players up to £1,000 and that the Australians, amateurs all, were grossing around £500 for the tour. Under pressure from the committee, Wood claimed he had been misreported. The *Daily Mail* claimed he had not, giving him an opportunity to retract any of the statements. Wood did not do so and although he was reprimanded by the Committee, neither the facts nor the figures were denied by himself or any party involved.

The basic facts of the strike are that a dispute over pay which had been bubbling all season came to the boil when the team for The Oval Test match was selected and four Surrey professionals – Abel, Hayward, Richardson and Lohmann – along with William Gunn of Nottinghamshire – wrote to the Surrey committee in the following terms.

> We the following players having been asked to represent England v Australia on August 10 and two following days do hereby take the liberty to ask for increased terms viz. twenty pounds. The importance of such a fixture entitles us to make this demand. Trusting this will meet with your approval...

Surrey declined to be held to ransom, calling up reserves and refusing to pay more than the £10 which had been in force since the first Test match played in England in 1880. The importance of that fixture and the haste with which it had been arranged led the Committee to pay £20 on that occasion without any prompting from the players or any one else. The following peremptory telegram was sent to Leyton where Surrey were playing Essex.

> Fee for playing England v Australia £10 or you are out of the match

The following statement was issued by Surrey to the press.

> August 7, 1896
> Sir, – I think it best to place the facts before you.
> Gunn, Lohmann, Abel, Richardson and Hayward refused to play for less than £20.
> The Committee offered them the same terms as they had at Manchester, i.e. £10 and expenses – they only got £10 at Lord's.
> This they declined.
> Your representative took the names of the team away with him.
> Yours faithfully
> C W Alcock

One of the Surrey committee, unnamed and at first reluctant to be interviewed, dismissed the matter laconically.

> We have no dispute whatever with the men; we have simply replaced them.[7]

A classic demonstration perhaps of the theory that cricket is a game played by professionals and run by buffoons. The terse statements hid a more complex story. Although popular cricket history refers to the saga of August 1896 as a strike, the reality is that it was nearer a lock-out, the threat of exclusion from the team, coming from the Surrey committee rather than the professionals. The team, copied from the official list at The Oval, excluded the rebels and included the names of MacLaren, Pougher and Hirst or Mold. Neither the replacements, nor the replaced were given the full facts.

One professional who had been wired to when it had been decided not to accede to the terms asked by Abel and the others replied that he would be only too pleased to play, but was now excluded after all, said that while he was naturally disappointed that he was not playing he was glad that some approach to a reconciliation had taken place between the Surrey man and their committee. 'Had we known how the matter stood,' said he, 'probably we should have been in with them. But we were merely asked if we would play and we said we would. Of course we did not know but that somebody was not able to play.'[8]

Bobby Abel, when, interviewed by the press was apparently astonished to learn he had been replaced.

The news that a remodelled eleven had been chosen, omitting the four Surrey men and Gunn came as a bolt from the blue upon one of the players at least, Robert Abel, the popular 'little Guv'nor' of the Oval enthusiasts. He was seen at his residence near the Oval, and he was at first most reluctant to utter a word. But when our representative told him the news that a new eleven had been chosen, and their names had been officially communicated to the *Daily Mail*, he relinquished his policy of silence in sheer astonishment. Asked whether the dissatisfaction was of long duration, he replied that it was.

'So you seized the opportunity,' suggested our reporter, 'and calculated to get the club at your mercy, and to get higher wages for the future?' – 'No, that would not be a fair way of putting it. We had no desire to get the club at our mercy. It was only in respect of this match that we asked for better remuneration.'

'But why for this match?' – 'Well, I need hardly say it is a match of unusual importance. It is a matter of great anxiety to us when we know we are playing for England in a critical encounter. And our best and hardest play is required of us. That's why the application was made in this particular match.'

It was an angle taken up by the *Daily Mail*.

WHO ARE TO BLAME?

Later enquiries would suggest that to call the situation a strike by the professionals is perhaps not to do the players justice. They made their application, without threat of refusal to play so far as can be ascertained, and the Surrey club's reply was to set about engaging alternative players. Could not a meeting have settled the dispute and is it the players, or may it be the club who have endangered England's laurels?[9]

Whether there was a refusal to play or not is perhaps debatable. There is no suggestion of it in the letter signed by the five professionals, but at the meeting at which it was considered on Thursday 6 August was a letter from Lohmann earlier the same day from Leyton (he had obviously accompanied the team there, notwithstanding the fact that he was not playing in the match) purporting to represent the position of the five.

> Dear Sirs
> In answer to your note I beg to inform you that we i.e. W Gunn, R Abel, T Richardson, T Hayward and myself are willing to play for England against Australians on Monday and two following days provided we are paid the sum of £20 each.
> Yours faithfully
> (sgd) G A Lohmann

Although the note to which Lohmann is replying has not survived, it was clearly an invitation to clarify their position. Would they still play if they were not offered £20? The implication of Lohmann's reply is that they would not and the committee responded accordingly.

Gunn was simply told his terms were not acceptable. Abel, Hayward and Richardson relented on the first morning of the match and were reinstated in the team. Whether Lohmann's letter represented the undiluted views of his colleagues is questionable. Gunn was to say later that he would have played for £10 and the other three voted with their wallets and opted for half a loaf rather than no bread. Lohmann, obviously the ring-leader, still smarting perhaps from his treatment over his benefit match, was left isolated.

On the first morning of the match, the *Daily Mail* informed its readers that this was not the first time in the summer the issue had been raised.

> A HIGHER SCALE FORMERLY GRANTED
> The subject of increased payment we are informed was raised in connection with the Surrey and Australians match, and the executive of the county club on that occasion consented to pay on a higher rate than the usual scale.

What the report does not say – probably because the journalist concerned was not aware of it – is that the headlined word 'formerly' represents a time scale as short as that between two items on the Agenda of the same committee meeting. It was earlier in that meeting that the committee had approved the request in a more obsequious letter from nine Surrey professionals written on July 13, before the Surrey v Australians fixture. It read,

> We the undersigned members of the County eleven beg to ask the favour that in future the fee for playing against the Australians be ten pounds. In asking this we are not unmindful of your kindness to us in the past. Trusting you will be able to grant our request.
> We beg to remain Gentlemen
> Your obedient servants

It was clearly the kind of language which appealed to the committee. Abel, Lohmann and Richardson were signatories to the letter. Abel and Richardson had played in the match which the Australians had won by seven wickets two weeks previously. It was immediately before Lohmann's benefit match and he had sat it out.

The start of the Test on Monday 10 August was delayed by rain, which allowed the press additional time to collect comment and opinion. Among those whose views were sought was Lohmann who filled in some background to what, behind the scenes, had been an acrimonious season.

> What is of importance to know is that the subject of extra pay for the England v Australia matches was not raised last week for the first time.
> LOHMANN MAKES A STATEMENT
> to the effect that several of the professionals who were engaged for the first test match at Lord's talked over the question of remuneration and it was decided that after the match had been played, and not until then, the MCC should be asked to pay them a larger sum than £10. When the Manchester match came on all the same professionals were not chosen and as it was away from London they had not an opportunity of consulting so that no joint action was taken in the matter. Abel and Richardson, however, on their own initiative approached the Lancashire committee and asked for £5 expenses in addition to £10 for the match; but so far they have heard no more about it. Then, says Lohmann, they naturally decided that if chosen for the next match, they would ask definitely for £20. Accordingly, when Abel, Hayward, Richardson and himself received an invitation to play last Saturday week, they immediately wrote to the Surrey committee to say that they could not accept that amount and made a demand for £20. It was, therefore, not the professionals who deferred action until the eleventh hour but the Surrey Committee, who did not consider the matter until Thursday.[10]

Whether the rebels had wished it or not, they had caused major national publicity and a torrent of correspondence to the press which had eventually to be halted by editorial decree. There was general public sympathy for the players' cause – which seems to have elicited some support from trade union professionals – though perhaps slightly less for

Lohmann who, it was felt, had received generous treatment during his illness and had, only a few days previously, enjoyed a lucrative benefit.

> There was less sympathy perhaps with Lohmann, the general impression being that he had been handsomely treated by the club especially during his three years' illness...
> I noticed that most of the striker's champions seemed to be Radicals; indeed one friend informed me that outside the Electric Railway that morning, a number of men who have a suspicious resemblance to union pickets had earnestly besought people not to go to the Oval. I should add, however, that most fair-minded people considered that the cricketers had chosen an unfortunate moment to push their claim. Meanwhile the rain had begun and the long period of weary tribulation set in...

Lohmann, his livelihood threatened by those whose kudos he had been instrumental in enhancing, was summoned before a special meeting of the committee and compelled to apologise and agree to the following letter appearing in the press,

> August 12 1896
> To the Committee of the Surrey Club
> Gentlemen
> I beg to express my sincere apologies for my refusal to sign the document placing myself unreservedly in the hands of the committee (in company with Abel, Hayward and Richardson) on Monday morning. At the same time my colleagues signed the withdrawal of the position taken up I expected William Gunn to be here, and having associated myself with him, merely desired to wait until his arrival before taking any action. I would add that when the original letter was being drawn up my idea was that a request was being preferred instead of a demand being made, and that the expression 'demand' which I now see to have been so unfortunate was inserted against my wish and better judgement. Whilst tendering my apologies I wish to express my heartfelt gratitude to the Surrey Club for the great many kindnesses I have receive at their hands, both in times of health and sickness.
> My career as a cricketer has been so entirely bound up with the Surrey Club that I should regret it if any action of mine caused a rupture with the Club with which my happiest days have been spent, and to which I am so indebted.
> I am, gentlemen, your obedient servant. Geo A Lohmann.

In a contest between master and servant, the servant could not be expected to win. 'Obedient' was in this case not simply a polite way of signing off. He did as he was told – or he took the consequences. The repercussions were significant. Notionally the apology was accepted, the other four all played Test cricket again, though perhaps less than might otherwise have been the case. Lohmann did not, though it is probable that because of his health he would not have done so anyway. It was, however, his last season for Surrey. There were other reasons for that, but it is likely the ill-feeling remained in the background.

Even without Gunn and Lohmann, England won on a rain-affected pitch by 66 runs, the damage being inflicted by Hearne and Peel who had declined to join the strikers. On a pitch ideally suited to Lohmann, 40 wickets fell for fewer than ten runs each.

It seemed to be a satisfactory conclusion, but the repercussions were to rumble on for some time. Inevitably attitudes differed, ranging from sharp criticism of the strikers, through ambivalence, to support.

The 'Establishment' Position

CRICKET COMMENTED simply that the England team was not definitely decided upon until Monday morning.[11] *Baily's*, the monthly sports magazine concerned with horse racing, hunting, shooting and fishing rather than cricket, was unsympathetic,

> They should remember that county clubs have been built up by liberal contributions of private individuals and by hard, wholly unpaid work of amateurs, and that in the bad times there did not exist as far as I know – a single case when players have not received their full pay…
> …we may dismiss the matter with the expression of the deepest regret that, at a time when the eyes of the world were focused upon English cricket, and at the time when the heartiest co-operation was requisite to successfully engage the colonial team English cricketers should have been caught discussing and haggling over the pounds, shillings and pence of a cricket match with its most sordid surroundings.[12]

Some Surrey members expressed similar views when regretting that cricket seemed to be following running, cycling and boxing, and lots of other so-called 'pastimes', and becoming nothing but a money-grabbing concern.[13]

The dispute was translated into terms of Capital v Labour, Amateur v Professional, Owners v Hired Hands. Charles Alcock, the Surrey secretary, both in an interview with the *Daily Telegraph* on the first day of the Test Match and his subsequent book, was as ever the ultimate in diplomacy and, as that newspaper commented,

> One satisfactory feature of the whole lamentable business was to be found in the attitude of Mr C W Alcock and the committee which he represents. Not a word escaped those in authority which was derogatory to the players or which could be construed to be an expression of ill-feeling towards any of the professionals.[14]

There was, however, an iron fist in the velvet glove.

> It is a question of principle, not of money, that is involved. In refusing to accede to the demands of the professionals, the committee were not animated in the slightest degree by any personal feelings. The point really is whether the Surrey Club is to manage its own affairs or whether the professional players are to do so and dictate their own terms. The Committee had no desire to treat the men shabbily and I don't think that any one could accuse it of such conduct.

Later, in his *Surrey Cricket, its History and Associations*, Alcock was to write,

> The Surrey Club committee very naturally felt that such an ultimatum ought not to have been hurled at them on the very eve of the match, and by their own men… Looking at the action of the players from the most favourable point of view, the best that one could say is that they were badly advised… From a Surrey standpoint it seemed regrettable that the third and last of the three Test matches, and particularly that on their own county ground, should have been chosen as the occasion for presenting such an ultimatum.[15]

Wisden had taken a similar line,

> …the Surrey committee declined point blank to be dictated to. It is betraying no secrets to say that they felt greatly aggrieved, on the eve of the most important match of the season, at being placed in a difficulty by four of their own professionals. However, they did not hesitate for a moment as to the course to be pursued… in our judgment the match committee took a just as well as a popular course of action.[16]

So, unsurprisingly, had *The Times,*

> …the refusal of Lohmann, Richardson, Hayward, Gunn and Abel to play will produce a feeling of both anger and regret in all who take an interest in the game… The Surrey Committee naturally refused to be dictated to by professional cricketers… and the consequence is that they have

reconstructed the English eleven. Had the professionals shown more tact by approaching the Surrey Club in a less dictatorial manner… the professionals should have sought some other means than an attempt to force the hands of Surrey in a week preceding such a great test at cricket as England v Australia. The representative character of this last match is much injured. Mere loyalty to the Surrey Club should have prevented the Surrey professionals from adopting the course they have chosen to follow.[17]

Seeing Both Sides

HISTORY TENDS to be written from an establishment point of view, since generally the landlord tends to be more literate than the serf, and the establishment commentators, like Alcock, *Wisden* and *The Times*, on the 'strike' have been virtually unanimous in conceding that the England Five had a case, but spoilt it because of the timing and nature of the 'demand'.

The professionals, if they have erred in their method of ventilating what is certainly a grievance, have brought the subject of their cricket remuneration very prominently before the public. There has long been a strong feeling that the rates of payment be revised since the 'gates' and general profits of the matches have in these last ten years so enormously increased; and the discontent is no longer hidden since the professionals see the amount of money the Australians are making…[18]

The press, while generally seeking a balanced presentation, took the side of the players, the *Daily Telegraph*, then less right-wing than it has subsequently become, saying that working men could not afford to play for honour any more than a doctor could serve his patients or a Government minister serve the nation free of charge.[19]

The strength of the case was almost incontrovertible, supported by the subsequently influential A C MacLaren, even if that support was articulated later rather than at the time. The Australian 'amateurs' were making huge sums from the tour, as they had on previous trips, so were their English equivalents and the host clubs themselves were coining in revenue from large gates of which a very small proportion found its way into the pockets of those paid to provide the entertainment. What was criticised by Alcock was not the justification for the claim, but that Surrey were presented with an ultimatum in the form of a peremptory 'demand' 'on the very eve of the match'.

In fact, neither is true. The issue had been brewing all summer. Even before the arrival of the tourists there had been press comment. Dissatisfaction with pay was not new on the circuit and the matter had been raised a week earlier as soon as the team was known on Saturday 1 August. This was scarcely the 'very eve of the match' – which started on 10 August – and it would have weakened the case and doubtless influenced selection if the players had raised it before the announcement of the team.

In a letter to the *Sportsman* reproduced in the *Daily Telegraph*, which preceded but has received less publicity than Lohmann's apology, the four Surrey players set out the course of events in some detail.

> SIR – As we, the undersigned, have been blamed for waiting until the eve of the test match before approaching the committee on the question of remuneration, we would like with your permission to state the facts. Abel, Hayward and Richardson were told on Friday night, July 31 that they had been selected to play, but it was the following day, August 1 that we received official intimation. On the Monday following (August 3) all four of us, with Gunn drew up a letter and sent it to the committee. This letter was duly received by Mr Alcock on the same day, and during the day the Secretary wrote to us acknowledging receipt of our letter and stating that its contents would be considered by the committee the following Thursday (August 6). The public were made aware of our position on the Friday, and they apparently came to the conclusion that we had waited until the eleventh hour before making an application, whereas the fact is we asked for increased remuneration as soon as we received the invitation to play and our letter was received by the Surrey committee one week before the date of the match.
>
> We would like to take this opportunity to say that we have no grievance whatever against the Surrey committee but we express the hope that in the future professionals will receive a higher wage in these important representative matches. We applied at Lord's after the first test match and were refused. At Manchester, we asked for our expenses, which up to the present, we have not received.
>
> We are, sir, yours etc
>
> (signed) T RICHARDSON, G A LOHMANN, R ABEL
>
> August 11 T HAYWARD[20]

Writing 25 years later, A C MacLaren was able to offer a different, but complementary angle.

> There had been a rumpus over the amount of money to be paid for the services of the professionals, the professors very rightly being of the opinion that £10 was not enough, and a fortnight before the game they had notified the Surrey County Cricket Secretary that they would not play for less than £20. George Lohmann, Tom Richardson and Bobby Abel were the three

> Surrey representatives... There was a lot of uncertainty on the morning of the match... and it is necessary for me to mention that I received a telegram from the Surrey Committee asking me to play if wanted. This telegram was despatched before the actual demand was made by the professionals, and not after the rumpus, as reported in the press. I replied to the Committee that I must have yes or no. Then a reply was received inviting me to play for England, some ten days or so before the game took place.
>
> The Surrey Committee now decided to leave out the professionals named above, and proceeded to fill their places but on the morning of the match it was agreed to accept the services of Richardson and Abel. Feeling that I had rather forced the Committee's hand, I wrote to the Secretary, Mr Alcock, offering to stand down owing to the difficulty of the situation, and the Committee appreciated my desire to assist matters, but A E Stoddart paid me the greatest possible compliment by refusing to play if a place could not be found for me, and I could not persuade him to do so. That was the only reason the Middlesex amateur did not turn out in this game...[21]

MacLaren's memory is not quite infallible after a quarter of a century in that he omits any mention of Hayward and Gunn, a fortnight before the game is a slight exaggeration and there may well have been other reasons for Stoddart's withdrawal. On the other hand, it is quite clear that his sentiments were with the professionals and, most significantly, the demand was not last minute and the Surrey committee was preparing contingency plans well in advance.

While the *Daily Mail* was prompted to criticise the players for a 'lamentable want of patriotism', it was only too willing to give free rein to the views of the players, spectators and its correspondents most of whom were in full sympathy with the rebels. One of the four Surrey players, who declined to be named, but there is a one in three chance that it was Lohmann (Abel's views being given elsewhere) put the case.

> In the cricket world it has been no secret that the Colonials are doing very well out of the gates, and that the English players have watched the growing profits of the visitors with envious eyes seems to be an explanation of which some confirmation may be found in the following interview.
>
> A SURREY PLAYER'S VIEWS
>
> One of the recalcitrant Surrey players who did not care to consent to give his name as the speaker, was seen by a *Daily Mail* reporter in the vicinity of the Oval. He said... 'We have put in for more money than we are getting. We have been offered the same as was paid at Lord's and Manchester, namely £10 each and expenses. That offer, so far as we Surrey men are concerned isn't really so good as formerly, because what expenses can we charge, living, as you might say, next door to the Oval?'

'...The Australians will probably take away £1,700 or £1,800, and the Surrey Club will benefit probably to the same extent or more. We professional cricketers in England do not get anything like adequate payment for our services. The rate of remuneration that prevails now is much the same that was in existence long before cricket was the game it is now. The enormous crowds which now follow the game
BENEFIT THE CLUB
and, in fact, everybody but those who have done at least their fair share towards bringing the game to its present state – the professional players'.
'But isn't the present moment a curious time to select to raise the question of payment?'
'Not at all. The most natural time. The time when most is likely to be made out of us without anything like an adequate return; and the time when our services will be most missed and therefore more truly valued. If our services were better valued they would be better recompensed... What I want to know is, will the Surrey Club jeopardise this match – the greatest match in the history of cricket, you might say – for the sake of a few pounds out of their takings? Why, the amateurs who are playing will be paid more than us professionals.'
'Amateurs paid?'...

The Players' View – and Some Public Support

THERE WAS nothing new in the discrepancy between amateurs' 'expenses' and professionals' wages. Surrey issued a statement on W G's remuneration at The Oval and A E Stoddart withdrew from the match and it is a matter of speculation whether he did so in sympathy with the professionals, to allow MacLaren to play, because of a heavy cold or because his own expenses were under investigation. If the latter, then again this was nothing new. On the 1891/92 tour of Australia, the *Bulletin* had picked up an item from the English press.

> London DAILY NEWS says that A E Stoddart of Sheffield's team refused £1000 to join the present team when it was organised, Query: What did Stoddart get, how much more of an amateur is Stoddart then Grace?[22]

A popular couplet at the time had it,

> Ye gentlemen of England, your honour do not stain,
> But call your pay expenses; and gentlemen remain.

One correspondent asked rhetorically,

> …what think you would be the opinion of many a well-paid amateur if he were offered £10 expenses and the rest of his stipend in the 'glory of victory'?

Others were no less trenchant.

> Honour does not find the families of professional cricketers in food and drink.
> The professionals must be aware that huge sums are taken from the British public as gate money; but they do not know what becomes of it, nor what constitutes an amateur's expenses.
> It is absurd to suppose that for a two or three days' match the expenses of one man would reach £50…[23]

Joe Public, brought up at a time when the Victorian family environment resembled the structure of society in that the expectation was that children should be seen and not heard, now welcomed the opportunity to give an opinion. The weather prevented any play before 4.55, affording journalists plenty of time to seek the views of those who were beginning to enjoy the benefits of a developing democracy.

> Another *Daily Mail* representative, eschewing the society of his fellow-pressmen, and even of the cricketers, amateur and professional, made his way amongst the crowd on the ground, and this is the story he has to tell of the opinions heard expressed by members of the public, who, after all, are the people who keep cricket in its latest and highest development going, and who supply the money which goes to pay players' wages and amateurs' expenses:
> Surely never was the patience of an enormous crowd more severely tried than yesterday at Kennington Oval. Not only was the match one of first-rate interest and importance, but the interest curiosity [sic] prevailed to see the personnel in the England team and to know the decision of the executive committee…
> 'Look here,' said one man, 'what's brought these thousands of folk together? Isn't it to see Richardson, Abel, Hayward and the others play. It's only right therefore that they should have their fair share of the profits.'[24]

The *Daily Telegraph* found public sympathy was on the side of the players, including large numbers of Surrey members who, said one of their number, had great sympathy with the underpaid professionals, but were so widely dispersed that they were unable to exert any influence in the area where power was focused.

> ...in this kind of organisation, the committee and officials are practically supreme and uncontrolled.
> But I should be now glad to see our pros treated not only with justice but with generosity. We are a very flourishing concern with plenty of money and could well afford, I am certain, to pay our players better than we do.[25]

An anonymously written poem in *Cricket Rhymes* by 'Century' put the players' viewpoint in a firm but light-hearted manner

> Now this is what the 'pros' all say:
> 'Why should we receive less pay?'
> Than those who just for pleasure play?
>
> 'Tis we who draw the people here
> 'Tis we who cause the crowd to cheer
> When we professionals appear.
>
> The Oval ground belongs to us,
> And that is why we've made a fuss
> That we may all these things discuss.
>
> ...As we have reason to believe
> The so-called 'amateurs' receive
> A deal more than for us they leave...

Likewise, the *Clarion*, true to its political colours, was impressed by the new rules published by the *Morning Leader* ridiculing the whole situation.

> 1. The use of a separate door for professionals must be continued out of consideration for the professionals themselves, for there is no doubt they would be struck dead if they used the same door as the amateurs.
> 2. The system of distinguishing between the two classes by placing the prefix 'Mr' and his initials before the name of an amateur, and giving the unadorned surname of the professional in this way –
> Mr X Y Z Simpkins lbw 0
> Snooks not out 1000
> is to be held right as far as it goes but is insufficient. In future, therefore, professionals will be numbered like convicts and known only by their numbers.

11. Professionals must lunch alone in some convenient shed. The food will be brought in a bucket and the public will be admitted at sixpence each to see the animals fed. The money so provided will go towards providing champagne for the amateurs.
20. Should any professional ask for more, he is hereby denounced as a mean unpatriotic hound, of whom the country should be ashamed.[26]

The Timing and Nature of the 'Demand'

CERTAINLY THE communication from the players appears peremptory, but the significance of the word 'demand' has perhaps been exaggerated. Lohmann did not cave in with the other three Surrey players, but held out and later withdrew the word, saying he would have preferred 'request'. Nevertheless, the word was part of the union-management negotiating vocabulary at the time, as evidenced by a number of random news items in that year.

> At a meeting convened by the London Building Trades Federation and the United Builders' Labourers' Union held in East-street, Walworth yesterday, a resolution was adopted promising support to the strikers till they were successful in their demands.[27]
> The medical men of Hersham and Walton (near Kingston) recently gave notice to the friendly society of the district that after next month they would not attend patients for four shillings as before, and also that they would not accept men earning thirty shillings a week as club patients. These demands are not assented by members...[28]
> ...it was unanimously decided to remain out on strike until the Victorian Steamboat Association concedes the men's demands.[29]

The language of parts of the sporting press certainly saw parallels between the actions of the professionals and the labour disputes which characterised the period.

> ...it seems a pity that the professionals had not combined and assumed an unbroken front at that period, for there is no denying the justice of their demands...
> ...their share of the spoils is only infinitesimal compared with the princely sums the Australians pocket and the amount which falls to the club on whose ground the match is decided...
> ...certain amateurs being able to feather their nests to much more purpose than the pros...[30]

The word 'demand' would not have seemed out of place to anyone involved in the process of pay determination, any more than it does in the Laws of Cricket which provide that the captain of the fielding side may 'demand' a new ball.[31] However, to those whose horizons were restricted to the walls of the Surrey committee room, it might have been considered insolent and discourteous. The situation is not dissimilar from the use in European summit meetings of the French verb *demander* which has sometimes been misunderstood – perhaps deliberately on some occasions – as it has the force of 'to ask for' rather than the English 'demand' which has a somewhat stronger force in its dictionary definition of 'an insistent and peremptory request, made as of right' than it has in the language of labour relations.

Furthermore, strikes and industrial action were part of the climate at the time and while the possibility of withdrawing their labour may not have loomed overlarge in the minds of the five, their action was taken in a year which had seen industrial action by the builders, doctors and steamboat employees referred to here as well as by cabmen and carpet-workers. In recent years, strikes by dockers, gas workers and matchgirls had resulted in improved pay and conditions. The power of organised labour was on the march and in the social context of the last decade of the nineteenth-century, the 'demand' by professional cricketers should not have seemed out of the ordinary. Before concluding their letter with the word, they had courteously 'taken the liberty of asking for increased terms' and 'trusted that it would meet with the committee's approval'. It was not their 'demand', but Surrey's telegram in response that was peremptory.

Judged solely from a financial perspective, the Committee's stance lacked logic and was indefensible. What they were implying was, firstly, that while £20 had been appropriate in 1880, half that amount was now the correct rate of pay and, secondly, the pay for a Test match should be the same as that for a county match. But, as Charles Alcock had said, it was not about money. He was right. It was about power, the power which lay with those who pulled the purse-strings, the power to decline to accede to a reasonable 'demand' because it was contained in a letter which was perceived to be clumsily worded and contained an insufficient amount of brown-nosed, social deference.

Had there been more solidarity among the players, the outcome might have been different. Matches can be played without committees and without establishment press comment. To play them without the players is a different proposition. Hearne, Lilley and Peel did not associate themselves with the rebels (Lilley was to say afterwards in his *Twenty Four Years of Cricket* that the request was justifiable but he could not accept the means[32]) and Abel, Hayward and Richardson soon caved in. Their financial position was different from that of Gunn and Lohmann who certainly did not need the money and to whom an additional £10 would have made very little difference. The former was well established in the family bat-making business and the latter about to receive the proceeds of a substantial benefit.

Neither were greedy men, a point emphasised in Gunn's case by Basil Haynes and John Lucas in *The Trent Bridge Battery* which mentions he lived in 'The Park', a select residential area of Nottingham.[33] In a letter to the *Daily Telegraph*, Gunn pointed out that it had never been his intention to withdraw from the team if the request for increased remuneration were not granted.

> SIR–Whilst expressing regret that any misunderstanding has arisen between myself and the Surrey committee, I may say that as far as I am concerned in the matter, I only acted along with the others in asking for an extra payment in consideration of the importance of the match, and the increased strain involved in playing such a fixture. What was asked was a sum of £20 per man, the same as paid in such matches a few years back.
> In the request we forwarded to the Surrey committee it was not stated that I would not play for the £10 offered; neither did I refuse to play on those terms, but merely solicited the committee to consider the payment of the higher sum. In reply I received the following telegram. 'Committee regret they cannot accept your terms – Signed, Alcock, Oval.' Up to this moment I have received no further communication whatever. I also wish to state that the remarks in the papers said to be made by myself and others respecting the payment of amateurs' expenses and the Australians' share of gate money are entirely erroneous, no such remarks ever having been made. I feel that these are matters which neither I nor any other player has anything to do.
> I am, Sir, your obedient servant,
> Wm Gunn
> Nottingham August 10

That it was a matter of principle rather than finance for Lohmann is perhaps demonstrated by the fact, that, having forgone his fee, he maybe recognised that he would have no further opportunity to play international cricket and made an offer to purchase the match ball. Bobby Abel tells the story in his autobiography. Australia had been 19-8 and 25-9, but Trumble and McKibbin had hung around for a while, the latter with 16 at no 11 recording the only double figure score of the innings. However, with the total on 44, Abel took the final catch of the match to dismiss McKibbin and still had the ball on arrival at the pavilion. Arthur Duke, from the cricket ball manufacturers, offered £5, Lohmann £6. Abel declined both and retained the ball as a souvenir of the match.

Alcock had maintained his stance on a matter of principle, that of not yielding to the dictatorship of the proletariat. Principles are fine, if they can be afforded and the proletariat, as represented on this occasion by a handful of professional cricketers, could perhaps not afford too much to be bound by principle. Yet two of them could and held out for the principle of recognition of their professional worth. They lost the battle, but won the war. It was a watershed in the history of Committee-player relations. Two years later, Test match pay was brought into line with the sum the 'strikers' had sought. The way was paved for the era of the respectable professional. After the match at the same meeting at which the apology was extracted from Lohmann, the Committee resolved to award Hearne and Peel £5 each for their bowling performance. Magnanimity and generosity, certainly, but also a demonstration of where the power still lay.[34]

The Fag-End of the Season

PEACE RESTORED with Surrey, at least officially, Lohmann was included in the team for the following match against Kent at The Oval. It was won by a comfortable ten wickets as was the last match of the season against Sussex. It was not enough, however, to arrest a slide to a final fourth place in the Championship table behind Yorkshire, Lancashire and Middlesex. There were defeats by Lancashire at The Oval and Somerset at Taunton and draws with the Australians and with Gloucestershire at Clifton when Lohmann had 5-48 after the first day was washed out. His contribution to the win against Sussex was 6-58 and 5-67. Although it was not known at the time, this was his last match for Surrey. His first victim for Surrey had been W G Grace; among his last was C B Fry.

The first-class season concluded with two appearances for the South of England at the Hastings Festival, final ones against the Australians and then the North of England. Although his performances were eclipsed by Hearne's 6-8, Lohmann was doubtless satisfied to sign off with 4-63 and 4-45, his last wicket Tom McKibbin, the most successful Australian bowler of the tour. Hearne again dominated the attack, taking 14 wickets for 64, Lohmann returning a more modest 3-47 and 1-9.

> Lohmann also bowled exceedingly well and did not have the best of luck.[35]

His final first-class victim was George Hirst at the beginning of a long and distinguished first-class career. He was to become perhaps the leading all-rounder of the first part of the twentieth century and as a master of the craft of swing and seam bowling, a respectable professional cricketer and a direct heir of George Lohmann.

The Reigate Festival and Surrey's match against the Gentlemen of England with Two Professionals were ruined by rain, although once again, Lohmann could count C B Fry among his victims, bowling him for four, and against Richmond and District,

> On a difficult wicket the home side made a very poor show for in less than an hour and a half they were all disposed of by Richardson and Lohmann for the wretched aggregate of 45.[36]

The past and future met as Lohmann took 8-19, Richardson 10-22. On Saturday 24 October the former sailed for South Africa on the *Norman*. As he left, rumours were circulating that he would not return – rumours vigorously denied in *Cricket*.

> Lohmann leaves England again for the winter to get the full benefit of the seasonable climate of South Africa. As irresponsible chatter has very unfairly attributed to him all kinds of plans. I can authoritatively say that he intends, all being well, to return to England early next summer. His intention, indeed, is to be over here in time to take part in Surrey's first match of 1897.[37]

Whatever the intention at this stage, 'irresponsible chatter' was proved subsequently correct. Though they were to twitch briefly in 1897, the curtains had finally closed on Lohmann's Surrey career.

1 10 August 1896
2 *Bulletin* 20 February 1892
3 Robson *Twentieth Century Britain* p 165
4 Now in the Archives of the London School of Economics
5 There are conflicting accounts of the origins of the organisation. Sometimes called the Cricketers' Fund Friendly Society, *Wisden* (1880 p 15) dates its foundation from 1857 with reorganisation in 1864, whereas Scores and Biographies (vol 15) says it was 1862.
6 10 August 1896
7 *Daily Mail* 8 August 1896
8 *Daily Mail* 11 August 1896
9 *Daily Mail* 8 August 1896
10 *Daily Mail* 11 August 1896
11 *Cricket* 13 August 1896
12 Booth *The Father of Modern Sport* p 201
13 *Daily Telegraph* 10 August 1896
14 10 August 1896
15 p 206
16 *Wisden* 1897 p 247
17 *The Times* 8 August 1896
18 *The Times* 10 August 1896
19 10 August 1896

20 12 August 1896
21 *The Cricketer* 30 July 1921
22 5 March 1892
23 *Daily Mail* 11 August 1896
24 Ib
25 *Daily Telegraph* 10 and 11 August 1896
26 *Clarion* 15 August 1896
27 *Daily Mail* 11 May 1896
28 *Daily Mail* 18 May 1896
29 *Daily Mail* 28 May 1896
30 *Cricket and Football Field* 15 August 1896
31 Law 5.4
32 Sissons *The Players* p 179
33 Sissons *The Players* p 180
34 Surrey CCC minutes 12 August 1896
35 *Football & Cricket World* 7 September 1896
36 *Daily Mail* 15 September 1896
37 *Cricket* 29 October 1896

CHAPTER 17

WESTERN PROVINCE AND THE CURRIE CUP (1896-97)

A challenge Cup which would mark and
commemorate the visit of the first English team
Sir Donald Currie

ON HIS return to South Africa after the eventful English season of 1896, Lohmann resumed the association with the Cape Town Cricket Club he had begun two years earlier. The Club had been established in 1888/89, had expanded rapidly and within five years had a membership of more than 180. Two professionals were employed and a fixture list of more than seventy matches organised, which had expanded to about 300 by 1897/98.[1] Among the most important were three Mother Country v Native Born and three against their main rivals the earlier established Western Province Club.[2] The encounter with the latter played over two Saturdays, 27 February and 6 March 1897, was a prelude to the Currie Cup tournament at the Wanderers in Johannesburg.

The previous week's match against Diocesan College had provided but limited practice. Cape Town declared at 231 for 3, Lohmann opening the batting and contributing 63. The College were then dismissed for 26. He took a catch but his bowling was not required. The Western Province match was more of a challenge. In a low scoring encounter, on the first day, Western Province were all out for 74 and Cape Town replied with 52. Lohmann opened both batting and bowling and followed his 5-45 in 22 overs by being stumped for six. The following week, Province declared at 171 for 7 and Lohmann's second innings at no 5, ensured the draw.

> Lohmann made the capital score of 63 for which he batted an hour and a half and his score included seven 4s.[3]

Lohmann was coach to the provincial side and there was objection on two counts to his inclusion in the team to contest the Currie Cup, firstly that he was a professional, and, secondly, that he did not have the required residential qualification. However, Abe Bailey, captain of the Wanderers Club, overruled them on the grounds that quality of cricket was more important and a good cricketer should not be barred, qualification or no qualification. No inter-provincial tournament at the time could be complete without inter-provincial bickering and, sure enough, there were objections to Western Province playing all their matches on what was perceived to be the better ground. However, as George Allsop, who was at the time secretary to the Transvaal Cricket Union, pointed out, where there were four teams competing and only two grounds available, one of the teams had to play all its matches on the same ground.

The competition got under way on Saturday 15 March, Western Province playing off with Eastern Province, Natal and Griqualand West for the right to challenge the holders, Transvaal. There had been no contest for the Cup the previous year. The tour by Lord Hawke's team had dominated the season and left little space for the resumption of domestic rivalries. The political situation in the Transvaal might also have been a factor.

> The Currie Cup competition is not receiving much attention this year. The holders (Transvaal) are likely to retain it undisputed for another year. It is well that it is so. The fag end of the season is on us, and the visit of the English team has given us a surfeit of cricket for one season. The competition will be all the keener next season.[4]

In the first match against Eastern Province, Lohmann started as he was to continue.

> The attack this morning was shared by Lohmann (railway end) and Rowe… The Surreyite immediately dismissed Cook… Lohmann was well on the spot this morning and captured four wickets at a cost of 48 runs.[5]

Western Province went on to win by an innings and 7 runs.

In the second match, he and Rowe bowled through both innings, Lohmann finishing with 16.4-5-44-4 and 23.1-7-44-5 and Rowe 17-6-33-5 and 24-17-15-5, as Griqualand West collapsed for 80 and 65, Province winning comfortably by an innings and 338 runs.

Eastern Province and Griqualand West were effectively making up the numbers. Natal had also beaten them both convincingly on the romantically named Pirates Lower Back Ground and now met Western Province for the right to challenge Transvaal in the Final. Eastern Province and Griqualand West did not play each other in what would have been a dead rubber, effectively agreeing to share the wooden spoon.

Western Province were favourites to beat Natal, though Lohmann warned against making assumptions about the result of any match.

> Before the above match was played, Lohmann, when asked what he thought would be the extent of the Western Province victory, replied – 'I cannot understand you up here; you all regard it as a certainty that the Western Province are going to meet the Transvaal in the final. Cricket is most uncertain, and you can never calculate on anything till the match is over. Natal will certainly give us a good game; it is certainly no walkover.' The result showed clearly that Lohmann had not over-estimated the merits of the Natal team, despite its defeat.[6]

A washed out first day resulted in a damp pitch and Natal, having won the toss, invited their opponents to make first use of it. Their bowlers made an ideal start. Despite Abe Bailey's magnanimity in allowing Lohmann to play in the tournament there had been some local opposition to his inclusion and,

> To the great delight of the crowd, who were not satisfied with the inclusion of Lohmann in the Western Province team, the famous Surrey player was caught and bowled off the second ball of the match...[7]

However, Western Province's first innings total of 185 proved to be more than enough, as Lohmann and Rowe once again combined to twice bowl out their opponents cheaply and, while the margin of victory was narrower than it had been in the first two matches, a difference of 136 runs was convincing enough and set up the anticipated Transvaal–Western Province Final.

Transvaal were favourites to retain the trophy, but Lohmann was instrumental in upsetting the form book, supported by some outstanding fielding. He bowled throughout the second innings, finishing with 32-6-61-5 to follow his 49-13-96-5 in the first. Over the four matches of the tournament, he had bowled more overs and taken more wickets than anyone else – 34 at 12.26, marginally behind Llewellyn and Rowe and clearly was a major influence in the successful challenge. Press reports suggested a huge public interest which continued up to the time of the departure for home of the new trophy holders, a large crowd assembling to see them off at Park Station.[8]

It is likely that during his two weeks in the Transvaal, Lohmann made the initial contacts that led to his appointment to the staff of the Johannesburg Waterworks Company and a new rôle as coach to the Wanderers Club.

1 *Cape Argus* 25 February 1898
2 *South African Sportsman* 4 August 1893
3 *Cape Argus* 8 March 1897
4 *Cape Argus* 22 March 1896
5 *Cape Argus* 16 March 1897: Lohmann's official figures were 4-49
6 *Cricket* 22 April 1897
7 Ib
8 *Cape Argus* 30 March 1897

CHAPTER 18

NEGOTIATIONS FAIL (1897)

I didn't wish to travel steerage
George Lohmann

Déjà vu – But a Different Result

AS QUEEN VICTORIA'S Diamond Jubilee Year dawned, the Will he? Won't he? ping-pong of 1895 resumed, but this time the outcome was different. After the acrimony that had characterised the end of the 1896 season, there was always likely to be a doubt as to whether Lohmann would return at all. For the last four seasons, he had been in South Africa in May. He had not played in 1893 and 1894 and had started the following two seasons late. On those occasions, health had been the only factor. Now there were others. Then the media had been optimistic – over-optimistic even; now pessimism – or realism – prevailed.

Early in the year the Secretary of Surrey County Cricket Club,

> ...reported that he had received a letter from G A Lohmann in which he stated that he had booked his passage for England in the *Scot* leaving Cape Town on 24th March 1897.[1]

Cricket reported,

> The English cricketers who have been wintering in South Africa will be most of them either on the way or be on the eve of starting for home. Some months ago it was reported that George Lohmann had booked his passage in the *Scot* which was to leave Cape Town yesterday...

That departure was on 24 March. At the time Lohmann was involved in the Currie Cup Final in Johannesburg. Two weeks later the report was corrected,

> The announcement that George Lohmann was leaving the Cape in the *Scot* on March 24 was a 'little too previous'. At any rate he was still in Cape Town at the end last month…

Three weeks later there was no firm information.

> Rumour has it that, after all, George Lohmann will not be seen in English cricket this year. It was stated freely outside the pavilion on Tuesday that a well-known Surrey player had received an intimation from Lohmann that he would not return to England for the coming season. In any case there is no news that he has left South Africa up to date.[2]

The following week *The Times* referred to,

> George Lohmann… who has not yet returned from South Africa and may not return this season at all.[3]

and *Cricket* confirmed,

> It would seem, after all, as if G A Lohmann had terminated his connection with Surrey cricket. So far as one can hear, the executive of the County club at all events have given up the idea of seeing him return this summer to take his place in the Surrey Eleven. That he will be a loss to Surrey cricket goes without saying and, under certain conditions, his bowling is bound to be greatly missed. But there are hundreds who would like to hear that he was returning for the season and for his own sake alone.[4]

A week later all hope had been abandoned,

> Any idea of George Lohmann's return to resume his place in the Surrey eleven seems now to have been given up by those who ought to know. Presumably he has made up his mind to settle permanently in South Africa and there seems to be little chance that he will be seen again on English ground at least in first-class cricket.[5]

It was reported to the Surrey AGM,

> With regard to George Lohmann the executive had done all they could, and had offered to pay his fare from and to the Cape.

In fact, they had not. It would have been quite possible to meet Lohmann's proposal, but they chose not to do so. As in the case of the 'strike', principle, rather than money, was at stake, but this time Lohmann, not Alcock, was to decide what those principles were.

> The absence of George Lohmann from Surrey cricket this season... is regretted by those on whom rests the responsibility of the county's affairs... But, after all, the matter would seem to be one of principle, and quite unconnected with any incident of last year, as some of the papers seem to think. The Surrey committee, it may be stated, offered Lohmann, in the event of his deciding to come to England this summer, fifty pounds, which represents a sum in excess of his second-class return passage from the Cape, and this in addition to the usual fees for the matches in which he played.[6]

Behind the scenes in the committee room,

> The following telegram from G A Lohmann was received:
> 'Will come hundred addition usual fees reply Lohmann.' The recommendation of the Match Committee. 'That the offer of £50 be adhered to assuming that that amount will cover second class fare out and home, if not he be offered an amount sufficient to cover second class fare out and home' was adopted.[7]

Then,

> The following telegram from G A Lohmann dated Matjesfontein April 30 was read: 'Cannot accept offer sorry Lohmann.'[8]

In May the press was confidently reporting,

> NOT THIS YEAR We have it on good authority that George Lohmann the famous Surrey cricketer, will not return to England from the Cape to take part in cricket this season.[9]

Yet, Lohmann did return, but at his own expense. In a balanced article which harks back to the previous year, the popular *Daily Mail* put the case for both Surrey and for Lohmann, seeing that for the latter as somewhat stronger,

> George Lohmann is in England again, but not to play first-class cricket. When it was announced at the opening of the present season, that Lohmann's services would not be available for Surrey County Cricket Club as heretofore, the facts were not published. Although this cannot be described as an interview with 'Our George', Lohmann spoke freely to the writer and appeared to feel keenly what he deemed the ungenerosity of the Surrey executive. The facts are these. When it was mooted to the famous bowler that his services on the 'tented field' were again in request

for 1897, he wrote from his South African home stating that he would come for ordinary playing fees and expenses and £100 for travelling expenses. The Surrey Secretary was instructed to write back and offer £50 instead of £100. This offer Lohmann could not see his way to accept, and in that sense he replied because, as he whimsically said in recounting it, he 'didn't wish to travel steerage'.

The question inevitably arises among sportsmen: Has Lohmann been treated quite fairly in this matter? It is true that there are two sides to every question; but were the terms he asked the Surrey executive exorbitant from a sporting standpoint? It is well known that the Surrey CCC is one of the wealthiest cricket combinations in existence; but equally true it is that the Lohmanns, Abels and Richardsons are the men who have been mainly instrumental in making it so.

Again George Lohmann was more than loyal to the county of his adoption until his health broke down and he was driven to South Africa in favour of a fresh constitution. Yet his powers as a cricketer are but slightly impaired, and although the rise of Richardson as a bowler was a positive godsend to Surrey, occurring as it did nearly coincidentally with the loss of Lohmann, it would be idle to say that the county has not suffered severely from the lack of their best bowler, and not only their best bowler but one who was for a term of years by way of being the first trundler, as he was the first fieldsman and one of the most dashing bats in all England.

So much is indeed evident by the recent falling-off in Surrey cricket. It is by no means the certain quantity that it was during what may be termed 'the Lohmann period'; and defeat this year at the hands of Yorkshire, Gloucestershire and Somerset have caused the County's partisans to give themselves pause and reflect sadly upon the halcyon days of Lohmann's prowess. Conceivably the great bowler's powers are a shade less conspicuous than they were. Conceivably, too, many would argue that the County have done much for Lohmann in the past and that it would not have been 'worth-while'. Perhaps not. But on which side lies most of the obligation – on Surrey for 'discovering' Lohmann or on Lohmann for allowing himself to be 'discovered'? It is true that cricket is and ought to be a pastime and not a mere money-making enterprise. Professional players, however, like professional workers, must live. It must be borne in mind, too, that Lohmann is a Middlesex man by birth, not a Surreyite, and that he must have been sorely tempted many times to throw up the service of his adopted county for that of the shire of his birth. It is to his honour that he never left Surrey until ill health drove him to the Cape – whither, by the way, he will return at the end of this summer.

Lohmann is in capital spirits and is very sunburnt. Looking closely into his face, though, it is noticeable that he is not the splendidly strong fellow he once was. But he is good for plenty of first-class cricket yet.[10]

The dispute about the amount the club was prepared to pay towards travelling expenses was clearly one of principal rather than money. £50 would have covered second-class return fare by the western route. £100 would have left sufficient change for incidentals en route.[11]

On the very same day, a copy of the newspaper had found its way into the Committee room.

> The attention of the Committee was directed to certain statements of G A Lohmann in an interview published in the *Daily Mail*. A letter suggested to be sent in reply by the President was read. It was resolved that no action be taken in the matter.[12]

Stalemate in the power struggle. The Committee had had enough of verbal ping-pong and moved on to the next business of sending a message of congratulation to the Queen on the completion of the sixtieth year of her reign. The next mention of Lohmann in the minutes is the report of his death.

'Plenty of first-class cricket' was not on the Agenda, but he did play a little with Andover where he had friends in Dr Farr, who had seen him off on his first visit to South Africa in 1892, and Mr Best with whom he had stayed on his return the following year. Dr Farr was Medical Officer to the Andover Board of Guardians, a member of the Andover Town Council and in the Diamond Jubilee honours when four new magistrates were appointed, became a JP. He was a subscriber to the Andover Cottage Hospital (coincidentally, so was Major Poore), so he was clearly a distinguished local citizen.[13]

Andover – and Repercussions for Joshua

LOHMANN PLAYED for Andover in a drawn match against Deanery on the Andover Recreation Ground. He opened the innings and made 69. No bowling figures are included in the press report. If he did bowl, he did not take any wickets.[14] He also turned out in a charity match when the Landowners and Tenant Farmers took on the Corn Merchants and Millers in aid of the Agricultural Benevolent Institution. His friend Mr Best was one of the umpires.[15]

Joshua Lohmann had played for Surrey Young Amateurs in 1892 and distinguished himself by scoring an undefeated double century and taking six wickets for the Stoics against Streatham. As a consequence, he had first been engaged as a ground bowler for the 1893 season, the first year of George's absence in South Africa, making a number of appearances for the Club and Ground Eleven. Aged 17, he had previously played for

Norwood Middle Class School and remained on the Surrey staff until 1897, playing early season for the 'Next Fourteen' against the 1st XI and then regularly for the Colts and Club and Ground side. Like his brother, he was a medium-pace bowler, middle order batsman and slip fielder.

He was not re-engaged for 1898. There were doubtless other reasons, like his not having made the senior Eleven in five years, but it is difficult to avoid the conclusion that the Club's increasingly acrimonious relationship with his elder, more distinguished, brother was not unconnected with their decision to dispense with his services.

1 Surrey CCC minutes 21 January 1897
2 *Cricket* 29 April 1897
3 *The Times* 4 May 1897
4 *Cricket* 6 May 1897
5 *Cricket* 13 May 1897
6 *Cricket* 15 July 1897
7 Surrey CCC minutes 27 April 1897
8 Surrey CCC minutes 6 May 1897
9 *Andover Advertiser* 21 May 1897
10 *Daily Mail* 1 July 1897
11 In 1913 fares were 1st class: £28 7s; 2nd class: £23 2s; 3rd class £10 10s (advertisement in *South African Who's Who* 1913)
12 Surrey CCC minutes 1 July 1897
13 *Andover Advertiser* 8 January, 19 February and 25 June 1897
14 *Andover Advertiser* 30 July 1897
15 *Andover Advertiser* 6 August 1897

CHAPTER 19

THE WANDERERS AND THE WATERWORKS (1897-98)

Bring my terug na die ou Transvaal
(Take me back to the old Transvaal)
Sally Marais

IN AUGUST 1897, Lohmann sailed once again for South Africa by the *Norman*. On the same passenger list were the Premier of Natal and his wife and Mr and Mrs S B Joel.[1] It is probable that both the coaching appointment at the Wanderers and the job at the Waterworks which were to occupy Lohmann's time for the next year came from the contact with Solly Joel who had his fingers in several pies of which these were two. The Waterworks position was not a sinecure, as evidenced by a business trip to Natal, but it was one which enabled him to become professional coach and take time off to play cricket on Wednesday afternoons.

Johannesburg was to South Africa what Sacramento had been to California some fifty years before. R L Johnson describes it as follows:

> By 1898 the Rand was already producing more than a quarter of the world's gold and Johannesburg was booming. Its society had a rough frontier character: there were a lot of guns, fighting, drinking, drunken brawls and prostitution, unsurprisingly in a population with nearly a hundred men for every woman. This burgeoning population needed not just brothels, but houses, food, clothes, health, hygiene and entertainment; needed it right away and had the money to pay for it. Johannesburg, even today, has never quite lost that mining-town feel, a place of almost professional shallowness, where people come to make money, where they flaunt material wealth with glitz and glamour and judge others very largely on whether they have nice houses or cars, a place bereft of interesting scenery or much high culture so that the only thing in town was to have fun with

> other people and with money. A hundred years on, prostitution, glitz and guns remain central features.[2]

In his list of the needs of this artificial and unbalanced society, Johnson could have included water. Almost overnight Johannesburg had grown from being a few villages to a major gold rush city and the water supply was insufficient to meet the need, a situation which had been exacerbated by the drought of 1895. Consequently a Water Works Commission was established to examine ways in which Johannesburg could be supplied with good quality drinking water. A geologist named Dr Draper had discovered a plentiful and stable supply at a farm called Zuurbekom which was sufficient for the city's requirements for almost thirty years when it was replaced by the Vaal River system.[3]

Rand Water, the current administrative body, was established in 1903 but was preceded by the Johannesburg Waterworks, part of the Johannesburg Consolidated Investment Company, of which Solly Joel was Chairman. There was an earlier body in which Sir James Sivewright was involved and according to the *Cape Argus* [4] there was evidently some malpractice, a story at least consistent with the same man awarding the railway catering franchise to James Logan. There is no suggestion that Lohmann had been involved in either of those questionable ventures, however, and he doubtless saw Joel's offer of running the two jobs in tandem as an opportunity to combine his business acumen with his talent for playing and coaching cricket.

About the same time as Lohmann was appointed it was reported from Johannesburg,

> RAND WATER SUPPLY
> The Town Council has appointed a Committee to meet Mr Woolf Joel to discuss the expropriations of the waterworks, Mr Joel having expressed a desire to meet such a deputation. The motion in favour of the town undertaking an independent water supply was postponed for a week.[5]

It was a large and significant business operation.

> The Johannesburg Consolidated Investment Company are inviting applications for a quarter of a million 5 per cent debentures in the Johannesburg Waterworks for the purpose of improving the machinery, extending the water supply to the mines and liquidating existing liabilities.[6]

The combination of the two appointments was clearly an attractive one. The influence of Joel and Bailey is self-evident, but this was not simply a question of 'who you know'. Without his cricketing ability, Lohmann would probably not have come into contact with either and, though he was well remunerated, in cricketing terms the Wanderers Club was very much in his debt when he left for the Cape twelve months later.

Lohmann, of course, had had previous contact with the club and doubtless fond memories of it, having taken his 9-28 there in the 1895/96 Test match and played in Western Province's Currie Cup winning side the following year. Like the MCC, it was the establishment at play, though an establishment based not on inherited wealth, but on the *nouveau riche* establishment of the Randlords of the gold mines, epitomising the theory that cricket follows money. As Richard Parry has said,

> ...in late nineteenth century South Africa nearly everything followed the money as the discovery of diamonds and later gold sucked hundreds of thousands of people into the sparsely populated interior. The frontier quickly became the metropolis.[7]

Abe Bailey was captain of the Club, George Allsop Vice-Captain. Jimmy Sinclair was on the committee. In Pretoria, William Quaife had agreed terms as professional, but later withdrew to be replaced by Albert Trott.

Although Lohmann's health and general physical fitness were no longer sufficiently robust to stand up to regular and continuous first-class cricket, he was still able to make a significant contribution to Wanderers' performances both in the league and friendly matches. His impact was immediate.

> George Lohmann has been giving the West Rand people a taste of his calibre – 96 (not out) and five for 16 against Roodeport being a fair Sunday's work.[8]

Later in the month,

> A fairly strong team under the captaincy of Mr G Allsop journeyed to the Marie Louise, Roodeport, and engaged a local team in a friendly contest. The home team defended their wickets to the bowling of Messrs Lohmann and Nordon who easily disposed of the eleven for the small score of 52. Lohmann took 6 wickets for 25 and Nordon 4 for 20.[9]

An internal match, Bailey's Team v Allsop's Team followed where,

> ...though he was knocked about a good deal by Halliwell and Sinclair, Lohmann came out with the capital analysis of eight wickets for 71.[10]

In the vanguard of pioneering competitive club cricket on the Rand, one difficulty faced by the Wanderers was that if they fielded a full-strength side it was unlikely any opposing side would be of the right calibre to give them a decent game.

> The match at the Wanderers on Wednesday afternoon drew a fairly large number of spectators, and if a good game could be put on for the mid-week half holiday, it would tend to popularise the game here a good deal. The Wanderers can put such a strong team in the field every Wednesday afternoon – including Lohmann, Sinclair, Halliwell, Allsop, Bailey, Shepstone and Fleischer – that it will be impossible to get teams with any pretentions to cope with them, and interest will die out in matches between scratch elevens. It would not be a bad idea to get up a match between Home-born and Colonial elevens and play it out. This should last three weeks at least and a couple of well-balanced teams could be got together under this head.[11]

The club responded and arranged a number of such fixtures. On the whole they were well balanced though Sinclair's 249 in one match rather upset the equilibrium. It received very little press coverage, most sports reporters being at Pretoria Races.[12] Conversely, in a later match, Lohmann's freak dismissal prevented him from making a contribution with the bat.

> Lohmann had the misfortune to be bowled by French in an unfortunate manner. He played the ball on to one of the nails in the matting and the ball rebounded and hit the wicket.[13]

Apart from these Home Born–Colonial encounters, opposition tended to be fairly weak. In the first league fixture spread over two Saturdays (as they were and still are in club cricket in South Africa and Australia), Wanderers beat a team called the Australians – presumably expatriate Antipodeans looking to cash in on the gold rush – by an innings and 102 runs. Lohmann had 21-4-65-3, Sinclair 12.3-2-29-6.

> The feature of the concluding stage of the match on Saturday was the grand form J H Sinclair displayed with the ball and in the course of a dozen overs he captured six wickets for only 29 runs. There is no doubt that the few 'wrinkles' Lohmann has taught him have largely increased his ability to get wickets as well as keep down the runs.[14]

So, a few weeks into the job, Lohmann was already demonstrating his ability as a coach. Presumably, 'wrinkles' are variations and the press comment seems to be evidence that it was from Lohmann that Sinclair learned the art and craft of the 'hanging-ball'.

Parallels between the styles of Sinclair and Lohmann were drawn later in Beldam and Fry's analysis of 'great bowlers and fielders' when it is recalled that because of the extra bounce on matting wickets, particularly when stretched on the fine gravel at Kimberley or the red dust of Johannesburg, many balls from both bowlers, having beaten good batsmen, passed harmlessly over the bails.

In between the serious club cricket there were some relaxing Sundays at Barnato Park where Solly Joel hosted the kind of country house cricket to which he could never have dreamed of aspiring in the London east-end of his younger days. The cricket was seemingly not of a high standard, but in the context of the hospitality and the socialising that did not matter a great deal. It was symbolic of empire and social superiority and pertinent that the opposition were not bank staff, but bank officials. This was not the kind of cricket that broke down social barriers, but the sort which built them up and reinforced them.

> The Banks team were a poor lot and had no chance against their powerful opponents. Prior to starting cricket the visitors were afforded an opportunity of a stroll through the tastefully laid-out park grounds although the mansion is not quite complete.
>
> Unfortunately for the fielders the grass had only just been burnt off the cricket field and someone jocularly remarked that he thought Mr Joel must have an interest in one or other of the local laundries, but the pitch itself was all right. Needless to say the teams were entertained in the most hospitable manner by Mr Joel who was nobly seconded by Mrs Joel, Mrs H F Strange, Miss Maxwell, Miss Smith and Miss Douglas – not a little of the success of the lunch under the trees depended on the kindly ministrations of the unselfish ladies.[15]

In a more competitive fixture at the Wanderers on Christmas Day, Lohmann played for Beves's XI against Sinclair's XI and celebrated the festive season in style.

> ...on the Wanderers front ground and the combinations being made up of our strongest men, considerable interest was taken in the contest. Beves won the toss and sent Lohmann and Slatem in to the bowling of Sinclair and Dante Parkin. At 38 Slatem retired[16] for 26. Lohmann was joined by Morton and took the score to 216, Morton making 37. The Surreyite had been scoring freely, and received loud applause when he passed the century, and continued in a fast scoring mood until he reached 145, when Sinclair held him off Norden. This is Lohmann's best score since his arrival here, although he has been very near in sundry matches in the country.[17]

A fortnight later when League cricket resumed, the Lohmann–Sinclair duo was immediately on song.

> Sinclair opened the bowling from the Garden End and with his second delivery got Walshe caught at long slip. Lohmann bowled from the Station End and with the last ball of his over Dickenson was cleverly caught at short slip by Sinclair.[18]

Lohmann finished with 2-36, Sinclair 6-56 in the first innings of this fixture against Stray Klips, from Kimberley, which continued two weeks later, the Wanderers winning easily by an innings and 68 runs, Lohmann 7-24 in the second innings, including five clean bowled.[19]

On the intervening week-end, he had turned out for S B Joel's XI against the Press at Barnato Park and seems to be the only player on his team to have made a significant contribution. His 8-20 and 30 not out in a total of 58 could not prevent this side losing by two runs.[20] Picking up the report some time later *Cricket* reported that Lohmann had permanently settled in the Transvaal. That may have been his intention, the combination of the Waterworks and the Wanderers, if not exactly a 'dream ticket', certainly offering him a not unattractive lifestyle among some new found friends of influence. His declining health, however, meant that soon he would once again seek the clearer air of the Karoo.

In February, he turned in another excellent performance against Pretoria, albeit in a match in which Wanderers were obliged to follow on.

> George Lohmann was bowling well, his first thirteen overs realising as many runs, six of which were maidens…
> George Lohmann bowled remarkably well and had Solomon accepted the chance that A B Tancred gave him, before he reached double figures, he would have come out with a much better average than he did.[21]

He had 4-43, then having failed in the first innings, demonstrated his batting skills in the follow on,

> George Lohmann who scored 72 might have been caught when he had 24 to his credit and he again escaped with a life at 38. With these two exceptions his innings was an excellent one, and he aroused the enthusiasm of the spectators by his dashing cricket, hitting all round the wicket in fearless style.

There followed a week of misfortune. Lohmann was injured in a trap accident on Friday 11 February and the following Tuesday, the Wanderers pavilion burned down. Damage was estimated at £8,000. In 2004, albeit on the site of the 'New Wanderers', it happened again.

> Lovers of cricket will be glad to learn that George Lohmann who was driving with Mr Wyatt yesterday when the serious trap accident occurred, escaped with a severe shaking and several bruises. The injuries to Mr Wyatt were more serious than was at first supposed and on being conveyed to the Hospital, it was found that his ankle was badly fractured.[22]

But the show must go on – and it did, without a pavilion and without Lohmann who was compelled to miss a week-end's cricket. It mattered little as on the first day of the match against Pirates, the club formed by A B Tancred and P H de Villiers, and Wanderers' major rivals in Transvaal cricket, play was restricted by rain and Wanderers won the toss. Lohmann had recovered sufficiently to play the following week.

> The return match between Wanderers and Pirates was commenced Saturday afternoon but only an hour and a quarter's play was possible owing to the heavy storm. The home team won the toss, which was a huge stroke of luck for them, as neither Sinclair nor Lohmann could appear for them on Saturday, whereas they will both be able to take their places when the game is resumed on Saturday next.[23]

On the Sunday, he was fit enough to turn out for S B Joel's XI against the Exotics at Barnato Park when he was again of a different standard to the opposition.

> The Exotics had first innings, but were all dismissed for 37 runs, thanks to the excellent bowling of George Lohmann who took seven wickets for seventeen runs.

Joel's team scored 156 and second time around, the Exotics managed 52 to succumb by an innings and 67 runs.[24] Then Lohmann played for Abe Bailey's XI against Pretoria in a benefit match for A E Trott who was coaching at the Union Club. It was in days long before the fast M1 link between the two cities a journey of six hours by coach at the time, maybe longer if the intervening Six Mile Spruit and Jukskei River were in flood.[25] Lohmann took 3-25 in a total of 64.[26]

Furthermore, in addition to his on the field performances, he played an invaluable rôle as coach.

> With a view to encouraging and developing the talents of the younger players your Committee with the kind assistance of several patrons of the

> game, engaged the services of George Lohmann for the current season with satisfactory results, a number of young players having been brought out whose form shows good prospects for the future.[27]

He was exceptionally well paid but seems to have repaid the investment. *The Star*'s report on the Wanderers Annual General Meeting expressed some astonishment.

> We knew that George Lohmann, who was acting as professional and coach to the Wanderers Club last season was receiving something a bit out of the common in the way of remuneration but it was a bit of a surprise to find that his salary totalled up to no less than £450. Say that his engagement lasted seven months, it panned out at close on £65 per month, which we should say is about the highest wage ever received by any professional. The whole of the sum of £450 that was paid to Lohmann did not come out of the Club funds, as there was a special subscription got up amounting to £250.[28]

Among the young, talented players mentioned were Ernest Halliwell, Louis Tancred, lob bowler J H Piton and sprinter T B Parker, now at the end of his athletics career. But standing out above all of them, both literally and metaphorically, was 6ft 4in Jimmy Sinclair, the youngest of Abe Bailey's mature team. Although Lohmann's coaching may have improved Sinclair's bowling, the youngster's batting talent would very probably have developed the same way with or without Lohmann as his mentor.

He is generally credited with being by some distance the biggest hitter of his day and there are several stories of his feats. The one concerned with hitting a ball to Cape Town by landing a ball in a passing coal-truck is perhaps apocryphal, but there is less doubt about his ability to clear the trees as he regularly hit the ball clean out of the ground.[29]

The Natal Tour

TOWARDS THE end of the season, Bailey took a team to Natal to play against opposition of varying quality. The match against Natal itself was deemed first-class, but there was little serious competition in the preceding fixtures. In a one sided encounter with the Garrison side in what the *Cape Argus* headlined as 'A Hollow Victory', Bailey's team came out easy winners, scoring 283 in response to the Garrison's 95, then bowling them out again for 38. Lohmann had 47, 2-33 and 5-23, Sinclair 8-53 and 5-15.

> ...nothing could have been more pronounced than the absolute inefficiency to cope with the grand bowling of Sinclair and Lohmann who disposed of the whole team for the paltry total of 38.[30]

Maritzburg were then beaten fairly easily, Lohmann taking 4-60 in a nine wicket win, his protégé, Sinclair providing some entertainment in the scratch match which followed by scoring 139 in 45 minutes before being caught on the boundary.

> Sinclair sent the ball clean out of the ground on no fewer than thirteen occasions, making nine 6s off Maurice Hime, off whom in 4 overs no fewer than 82 runs were scored. The spectators enjoyed the performance immensely and every stroke by the young bat was loudly applauded.[31]

Lohmann's last first-class match was played for A Bailey's Transvaal XI against Natal in Durban on the ground known as 'Lord's'. The start was delayed by half an hour, as Lohmann had complained that the pitch was too long. It was measured and he turned out to be right. It was – by half-an-inch.[32] *Cricket* says three-and-a-half.[33] Either way, it can surely have made little difference, even for one of Lohmann's accuracy. Additionally, the stumps had been placed too far apart with the result that one of the batsmen had a fortunate escape when the ball passed through the wicket without removing the bails.

In a drawn match he made 9 in his only innings, had 23-10-33-3 and 27-5-72-3, opening the bowling with Sinclair who had 26-9-65-5 and 34-6-82-2. The torch had been passed on.

There was, however, one more match – against a Durban XI. It was drawn, Lohmann scoring 61 and taking 2-23. Apart from his occasional appearances the following season in Matjiesfontein, it seems to have been his last cricket.

Had he not been a professional, he would probably have played for Transvaal, strengthening their chances of wresting the Currie Cup from Western Province which he had helped the latter win twelve months earlier. It remained an amateur competition, though the arguments for the inclusion of professionals were made as they had been elsewhere and would be in many sports in many countries over the next century.

> When George Lohmann came back here it was understood that he was to take up a position in a big office in town, which, while allowing him to devote a great deal of his time to cricket, would also enable him to enjoy the amateur status he had hitherto enjoyed in this country, and assist the Transvaal in trying to regain the Currie Cup from Western Province, who have to thank Lohmann more than anybody else for winning it for them

> at the end of last season. Lohmann, however, has accepted the position of professional to the Wanderers Club and so the Transvaal will not be able to play him on their team which is much regretted.
> In Pretoria a few days ago we had a chat with Mr A B Tancred on the subject of allowing professionals engaged in the different centres during the season to play in the Currie Cup matches, and were pleased to find that he shared the view we have always held, that any centre enterprising enough to get out a professional should have the full benefit of his skill and be allowed to play him in inter-state matches.[34]

Lohmann accompanied Transvaal's Currie Cup team to Cape Town.[35] In the competition for the right to challenge Western Province for the trophy, they lost to Border but won the other two. Griqualand West also won two, but Transvaal qualified by virtue of the head-to-head between them. It must have been with mixed emotions that Lohmann watched Western Province win a low scoring encounter by eight wickets as his former teammates, Middleton and Rowe shared the spoils between them.

Although *The Star* had commented on the amount of Lohmann's pay, it was quick to praise his contribution to the Wanderers' season.

> In the Averages presented for the First League matches Louis Tancred comes out first with the capital average of 37.1.
> Lohmann with a batting average of 20 and a bowling average of 12 did capital work and on these run-getting wickets to go through a season and finish up with your wickets costing you but twelve runs apiece is a performance of which any bowler might be proud.[36]

The report went on to say that Lohmann had now joined the ranks of the amateurs. He was elected unopposed as vice-captain for the 1898/99 season, having been defeated by twelve votes to nine in an election for the captaincy by George Allsop, the previous season's vice-captain.[37] It was an appointment he was never to take up. He had a heavy cold in July and visited Natal on Waterworks business in August, but the dust storms of the highveld caused his health to deteriorate and precipitated a return to the Cape. He was replaced by Sinclair as vice-captain.

Some Influential People

INITIALLY THROUGH his connection with Logan, but also because of the respect in which he was held as a world-class international cricketer, Lohmann mixed with people who, in terms of wealth and influence, were at the very top of South African society. He had every advantage, of course, being a white man in a society structured on the basis of colour, in a way which was not open to, for example, Gandhi who arrived in South Africa in the same year, or any of the successful Indian businessmen and lawyers seen as a threat to white supremacy and unceremoniously segregated. Nevertheless, even in the narrow band of white South Africans, he could justifiably consider himself in the upper stratum.

Abe Bailey

THE WANDERERS captain at the time of Lohmann's involvement was Abe Bailey, an entrepreneur who amassed a fortune from the goldmines of the Witwatersrand. Born in South Africa of Yorkshire and Scottish parentage, he had married Caroline Paddon (Kate according to the *South African Who's Who* and the local press) in 1894, settling £50,000 on his bride, the daughter of a wealthy Kimberley merchant, who had a similar sum in her own right.[38]

He once proudly announced to a distinguished gathering at the Mansion House in London: 'I did not come out of the top drawer. I am the son of emigrants: I love South Africa with all my heart, for it was there that I was able to rise from the bottom of the ladder.' He was acquainted with, though not a close friend of, Cecil Rhodes, and shared his imperial vision.

Lohmann would have met Bailey on the 1895/96 tour, but for a large part of that season he was out of circulation, his involvement in the Reform Committee, the organisation behind the Jameson Raid, causing him to be a guest of President Kruger in Pretoria Prison. He was not, however, in the country at the time of the Raid, which Jameson launched without the knowledge of the Committee. Bailey and Lohmann again came into contact at the Currie Cup tournament in March 1897, when Bailey agreed to Lohmann's playing for Western Province despite the question marks over his amateur status and residential qualification. He was a major influence in Transvaal cricket at the time and in March 1898, led the tour to Natal, of which Lohmann was part.

He organised and managed the 1904 tour to England and was President of the Wanderers Club in 1911. The triangular tournament of 1912 was his brainchild and he was a founder member of the Imperial Cricket Conference which in later years was metamorphosed into the current International Cricket Council. He firmly believed in cricket as the 'Empire Game',

> ...a symbol of imperial endeavour, made all the more powerful by its subtlety and mannered conventions, and the difficulty these represented for those not educated in its complexities.[39]

Outside cricket, he had a distinguished war record, reaching the rank of Major, earning King's and Queen's medals and six clasps. He was one of the co-owners of the *Rand Daily Mail* from 1902 and one of the first people in the Cape to have an automobile.

In politics, he was returned to the Cape House of Assembly as MP for Barkly West on the death of Cecil Rhodes.

He was an organiser of the 'British Party' in the Transvaal, subscribing to the ethos of white supremacy throughout the whole of South Africa. On the Bantu question, he described himself as 'Boer to the backbone' and consistently opposed Indian claims for equal rights in land ownership in Natal and the Transvaal. He donated the Fairbridge Library, of which he was a benefactor, to the South African Library in Cape Town to which he added a wing to house it. He was knighted (KCMG) in 1911.

Possibly as an expansion of Bailey's liberal streak, or more likely as a reaction, his son Jim (by his second wife, Catherine) was the founder of *Drum*, a platform for black journalists and banned and banished South Africans, and major opponent of the apartheid régime. Another son, John, married Diana, daughter of Sir Winston Churchill.

Caroline died in 1902. His second wife, Lady Mary Bailey (Catherine – according to the Abe Bailey website) was a renowned aviator who in 1927 flew solo from Croydon to Cape Town.[40]

On his death in 1940, he left estate valued at £10 million.

Solly Joel

SOLOMON BARNATO JOEL, who in 1898 suffered the double tragedy of his uncle Barney Barnato's suicide and his brother Woolf's murder, was a senior member of Barnato Bros, Director of de Beers Consolidated Mines and Chairman of JCIC. The two deaths placed 'Solly' at the head of the Barnato family interests.

He was not an active cricketer as Bailey was, but, a millionaire by his early twenties, his wealth and position in the higher échelons of Johannesburg society ensured that he was influential in the Wanderers Club, the focus for sporting and leisure activities of the Randlords.

He was the youngest of three brothers and, unlike Bailey, came from a working class background, his uncle Barney Barnato having emigrated to the Transvaal from London's east end. He had worked behind the scenes of the Music Hall stage and occasionally on it. The legality of some of Barnato's activities was highly suspect and, according to the *Oxford Dictionary of National Biography*, likely to be more objective than accounts by family members, there is evidence of attempts to influence the course of justice by bribery and corruption and substance to the charge of dealing in stolen diamonds. He had, according to Colin Newbury, his biographer in that publication, fought and cheated his way to the top with all the pugnacity of an East End Londoner on the make, and backed by some luck and legal and illegal handling of goods, had made of the JCIC a dubious and speculative trust. Those who live by the sword are likely to perish by the sword and such activities are probably not unconnected with his own suicide and Woolf Joel's murder.

His nephews had inherited at least some of the genes. One of them, Isaac, escaped prosecution by fleeing Kimberley for England and early in his life, Solly Joel had begun to demonstrate the initiative and enterprise which was later to take him into the millionaire bracket. With his brother, he trained racing pigeons to return to their home loft, then sold the birds, thus conditioned, to unsuspecting market customers. The birds returned very soon after the sale and frequently were sold again in the same day… with similar results.

Barney Barnato, had in June 1897, committed suicide by jumping into the Atlantic from the *Scot* off Madeira when on his way to England. There was a suspicion that he was being blackmailed. Solly, who was with him at the time tried to save him, but only succeeded in catching hold of his trousers as he fell into the sea.[41] The Southampton coroner's verdict as recorded in Joel's biography was death 'by drowning while temporarily insane'. The *Dictionary of National Biography* is rather stronger, suggesting mental instability, alcoholism and paranoia. The name of Barney Barnato lived on in the Barnato Memorial Trophy and the inter-provincial Barnato Tournaments, competed for by non-white cricketers.

Within a year the Joel family had suffered a second tragedy. In March 1898 a Kurt von Veltheim, according to Thelma Gutsche's book, a 'questionable character',[42] who had earlier interviewed Barney Barnato in Cape Town, had gained access to the office of Woolf Joel, elder brother of Solly, in Johannesburg. He had apparently tried to interest Woolf in a scheme for kidnapping President Kruger. In the presence of his manager, Harold Strange, in his younger days a noted swimmer, Woolf received him. Von Veltheim began his customary blackmailing tactics, the discussion became heated and in a melodramatic scene, all three drew revolvers. Woolf Joel was shot and died instantly, but Strange ducked and escaped. Von Veltheim was arrested and tried, but acquitted.

Lohmann went to meet Solly Joel at Bloemfontein on his return from Cape Town, an action less associated with an employee or business associate than with a friend.

> The special train which brought Mr and Mrs Joel from Cape Town reached Park Station a few minutes after 2 o'clock on Wednesday, having made the run through in forty-three hours. On the train drawing up Mr Joel was assisted to alight on the side opposite the platform. He looked very ill and dejected and at the sight of the crowd of sympathisers he completely broke down and had to be supported from the train to his carriage, his face being hidden from the public by a handkerchief. Mr George Lohmann travelled with Mr Joel from Bloemfontein, whither he had specially gone to meet the train.[43]

Joel was later to travel to England with the intention of settling there permanently. Also in London temporarily, having travelled to see their son who had broken his arm playing football, were Mr and Mrs Logan.[44] Lohmann remained in South Africa continuing his business career with a trip to Natal, having been out of action for nine or ten days with a heavy cold.[45]

Joel was involved in horse-racing, both in England and South Africa, and his membership of the principal racing clubs, the Automobile Club and Royal London Yacht Club, and English residences at Maiden Erlegh, London and Newmarket suggests that neither his business nor his turf activities were entirely unsuccessful. He married the Lancashire-born actress, Nellie Ridley. He donated substantial sums to the National Playing Fields Association and endowed the Chair of Physics at the Middlesex Hospital Medical School.

Shortly after his return from England in August 1897, Joel had been involved in an unsavoury incident at the Johannesburg Empire during an interval in a music hall performance. A jockey with a grievance over a steward's enquiry at Krugersdorp Races sought out Joel and 'lowered his head which he shoved with some ferocity and force against Mr Joel's chin' – a head-butt in the more concise language of today. The details of the incident are marginal to the Lohmann story, but what is significant is that in Joel's party were Harold Strange, later to be present when Woolf Joel was murdered, the Governor of Lorenzo Marques, and Mr George Lohmann[46] – a sure sign that Lohmann was welcomed into the upper strata of Johannesburg society.

Lohmann's influence was felt long after his departure. The official history of the club records that the Wanderers never had a more distinguished or popular professional. It may perhaps also be said that no professional had a year which off the field was affected by events outside his control, such as a traffic accident, a fire, a suicide and a murder.

1 *The Star* (Weekly Edition) 7 August 1897
2 Johnson *South Africa: The First Man, The Last Nation* pp 94-95
3 Rand Water website
4 22 June 1893
5 *Cape Argus* 17 February 1898
6 *The Star* 15 January 1898
7 Parry *Diamonds, Cricket and Major Warton*
8 *The Star* 18 September 1897
9 *The Star* 2 October 1897
10 *The Star* 9 October 1897
11 *The Star* 16 October 1897
12 *The Star* 30 October 1897
13 *The Star* 18 December 1897
14 *The Star* 23 October 1897
15 *The Star* 16 October 1897
16 i.e. 'was out'
17 *The Star* 1 January 1898
18 *The Star* 15 January 1898
19 *The Star* 29 January 1898
20 *The Star* 22 January 1898
21 *The Star* 12 February 1898
22 Ib
23 *The Star* 19 February 1898
24 *The Star* 26 February 1898
25 Hall & Schultze *The Cricketing Brothers Tancred*
26 *The Star* 5 March 1898
27 Wanderers Club Annual Report. *The Star* 29 January 1898
28 20 August 1898
29 Gutsche *op cit* p 88
30 *Cape Argus* 3 March 1898
31 *Cape Argus* 7 March 1898
32 *The Star* 19 March 1898
33 7 April 1898
34 *The Star* 30 October 1897
35 *Standard and Diggers News* 24 March 1898
36 20 August 1898
37 *The Star* 20 August 1898
38 *Midland News and Karroo Farmer* 12 April 1894
39 Murray and Merrett *op cit* p 12
40 Sir Abe Bailey website
41 *Andover Advertiser* 25 June 1897
42 *Old Gold: The History of the Wanderers Club* p 95
43 *The Star* 19 March 1898
44 *The Star* 2 and 9 July
45 *The Star* 16 July and 20 August 1898
46 *Standard and Diggers News* 23 September 1897

CHAPTER 20

THE TWILIGHT YEARS (1898-1900)

Rage, rage against the dying of the light
Dylan Thomas

Lord Hawke's Second Tour 1898/99

WHILE LOHMANN was in Johannesburg, back at the Cape, the fourth tour by an English team was anticipated with enthusiasm in the South African press.

> AN ENGLISH CRICKET TEAM FOR SOUTH AFRICA
> The decision of the Western Province Cricket Union to accept the splendid offer by an unknown gentleman to bring out a first-class cricket team for the season 1898-9 will meet with the approval of every lover of the national game. Of course the matter is not definitely settled and it has yet to receive the approval of the South African Cricket Union, but there is no reason to apprehend that there will be any difficulty and the proposal is such a generous and sportsmanlike nature that it defies refusal. The name of the gentleman who made the offer is not yet public property, but it was made known in committee last night, and evidently gave every satisfaction, for all opposition to the proposal was immediately dropped, and a vote of thanks was conveyed to the gentleman concerned.[1]

It came as no surprise when it was announced three months later that the Hon James Logan was the gentleman concerned.[2] He continued to expand his business empire, a large advertisement for 'James D Logan & Co Ltd, Wholesale Wine and Spirit Merchants, Cape Town' appearing regularly in local newspapers.

Arrangements for the Currie Cup were also put in place.

By August, the Honorary Secretary of the South African Cricket Association was able to report with some relief,

> An offer has been received from that very good sportsman Mr J D Logan of Matjesfontein to bring out an English team during the coming season, he guaranteeing all expenses, provided only that such terms are granted him by the different centres as were given to Lord Hawke's team in 1895-96 and any profits made on the tour accrue to the Association. At a meeting held at Capetown during the tournament it was decided to accept this generous offer and to leave the arrangements of the tour with the Western Province Cricket Union, that body being more in touch with Mr Logan, and the Association.[3]

It was an offer impossible to refuse – relief from any financial and organisational responsibility and entitlement to the profits, the cricketing equivalent of owning a gold mine and exploiting it with cheap labour. Lohmann, already in South Africa, was to manage the tour. Lord Hawke's first tour had coincided with the Jameson Raid. His second took place as the storm clouds of the Boer War were gathering.

As late as October, the tour was still in doubt, Logan writing from England,

> I am very much afraid that it will be utterly impossible for me to bring out a team this season. Of course I could bring one out, but I fear it would be one not acceptable to the cricketers of South Africa, and I think it will be better not to have one at all than one which would not come up to our expectations. I am going to have another interview with Lord Hawke and there might still be some small hope of my raising a team, but I am afraid the chances of my doing so are very remote. Dr Grace will not entertain the idea of going out, as he says he is getting too old for touring about.[4]

In the event, the pessimism was unfounded. The tour went ahead and it was a measure of Logan's continued influence on the game that the press referred to 'J D Logan's English team'[5] and that plans for the Currie Cup were put on hold until it was known whether the team would be visiting South Africa. In the event they did and there was no tournament that season.

The *Scot* docked in Cape Town on 20 December and Lohmann was among the party who welcomed them. Christmas Day was celebrated with plum pudding and strawberries and cream, Lord Hawke presenting the professionals, Lohmann and A A White, the umpire who accompanied the tour, with a silver-mounted card-case and the amateurs with 'charming silver pencils in red or blue enamel cases with the name, date and giver neatly inscribed thereon'. On New Year's Day, there was a picnic (for the amateurs only) at the Government farm at High Constantia and, in a rare and temporary dismantling of class barriers, professionals and amateurs dined together in the evening at the Royal Hotel.

There was then some cricket, two Test matches eventually, plus three other first-class matches and a number of non-first-class fixtures 'against odds'.

By 1898/99 Lohmann was too sick to play any cricket, other than the occasional match at Matjiesfontien. The Surrey professional Ernest Hayes, who was in South Africa for that season, though not as part of Lord Hawke's team, kept a diary record of his visit – *My trip to South Africa Nov 1898–April 1899* – tucked inside his album of press-cuttings. It contains the following comment.[6]

> I was delighted to see old friends again altho it was painful to see how poor Geo Lohmann had wasted away and how terribly ill he looked.

The tour took its toll in other ways. Pelham Warner was to mention later that he enjoyed his conversations about cricket with Lohmann on the long railway journeys and 'long' could mean anything up to 55 hours, leaving Kimberley at 9 am on Friday and arriving in Bulawayo at 4 pm on Sunday.

South African cricket at the time was in organisational chaos. The Western Province 'Malay' team were under the impression they had won the Barnato Cup, only to be told that it had not been played for this year and would not be played for until the following year.[7] Administrators' counterparts on the other side of the colour bar were not setting the ideal example. Eastern Province asked for nominations for the first Test scheduled for Port Elizabeth on 14, 15 and 16 January. Transvaal had declined to make any on the grounds that the team should be selected by a committee of the various unions. Eastern Province did not disagree, but pleaded that pressure of time left them no alternative. Western Province claimed they were only informed of the arrangements in early December and that Lord Hawke's team were in South Africa only because of a cyclone in the West Indies.

In fact, the tour had been mooted twelve months previously. In the event time ran out and the Test match did not take place, a match against Cape Colony being played instead. Cricket is not alone in being subject to internal parish-pump style politics and unseemly wrangling, but on few occasions have they caused Test matches to be cancelled. This was one of them.

> The collapse of the first test match at Port Elizabeth is another evidence of the chaos among the different centres of South Africa. These continual bickerings and 'developments' can do no good to the sport, or to those

> responsible for their origin. The slinging about of all sorts of insinuations, the application of boycotting, and the jealousness of some centres as against the others, are all things that leave a bad taste in the mouth.

Selection practice was the same as in England in that the cricket centre hosting the match picked the team, but in England,

> ...every one did his best loyally to support the national team as picked... Lord Hawke may well wonder what sort of sportsmen our cricketing world is composed of... In the meantime the tour will go on, and a succession of victories will give the impression in England that we are in a worse condition than ever, whereas with a little sacrifice of personal feeling a united front might have been shown to our visitors and something achieved worth recording in our cricket history. A more sorry and deplorable washing of dirty linen in public has certainly not been seen hitherto, and for our credit's sake let an appeal be made urgently to sink all differences and remember the cricketing honour of South Africa is at stake.[8]

On the field, the South Africans gave a better account of themselves than they had three years previously. Both Test matches were lost, but by narrower margins. They followed similar patterns in that in each case, South Africa gained a first innings lead only for England to rally in the third innings and bowl them out cheaply in the fourth. P F Warner made a century on début at the Wanderers, carrying his bat through a completed innings in the process.

Bowling honours were taken by Albert Trott who was making two Test appearances for England (he had been omitted from the 1896 Australian side which toured England and transferred his allegiance by taking a position on the ground-staff at Lord's) and an emerging Schofield Haigh who had 6-11 at Newlands as South Africa were bowled out for 35.

For the hosts, the biggest impression was made by the improving Jimmy Sinclair, now on a bigger stage than that on which he had played with Lohmann at the Wanderers the previous season. He followed South Africa's first Test fifty at the Wanderers with her first Test century at Newlands, having earlier taken 6-26 to bowl England out for 92.

War Clouds Gather

IN A repeat of the social match that had taken place three years earlier, against XXII of Matjiesfontein, Lohmann opened the innings for the hosts, made 43, took 5-48 and a catch at extra slip. The usual Logan-hosted banquet followed.

Lohmann was well enough to turn out for Matjiesfontein in the match which was part of the celebrations for the Queen's birthday on 24 May.

> At 9.30 am a move was made to the pretty cricket field where an interesting match was played between elevens representing Matjesfontein (captained by G A Lohmann) and the Civil Service (captained by Mr A W Odendal). Owing largely to a masterly 85 (not out) by the famous ex-Surrey cricketer and the deadly bowling of the young Mr Logan in the first and by the Laird... in the second innings, the Matjesfontein eleven won handsomely by an innings and 46 runs.[9]

In early October 1899, Lohmann made what was probably his final appearance on a cricket ground as a player, making three and taking none for seventeen in seven overs for Matjiesfontein against Murray Bisset's 'Bashi-Bazouks'.[10]

Cricket in South Africa, despite the chaos and internal dissensions and although still below the standard of that in England and Australia, continued to improve. The two Test matches which survived the internal politics were won by Lord Hawke's team, though with not quite the ease they were three years before. Some, however, regretted the advance of professionalism, and warned about taking the game too seriously.

> WORK OR PLAY? A WORD ON PROFESSIONALISM
> A man who has made a study of the game is willing to exhibit himself for a given sum and thus the transition is effected and the playing of cricket becomes a mere matter of business. The professional cricket player, if we do not regard him as a trainer, is a public entertainer, pure and simple. He plays cricket as Irving would play Shylock or Miss Marie Lloyd sing any of her myriad songs, that is in a very small measure because he likes to do so, but chiefly because he is hired and paid for the purpose. A great deal lately has been said about the conduct of the professionals of the Western Province team. Their striking for a higher rate of pay has been variously commented on, but most agree that such a proceeding was detrimental to our national game. We would put it to our readers. Is now professionalism in itself degrading? Does it not point to a decrease of sporting instinct which is claimed to be a part of the national character. To a state of anaemia in the descendants of a generation of sportsmen. Cricket, like all other games, first invented for the exercise of the limbs has, like many other games, declined to the level of a show. No doubt many ardent cricketers will disagree with our view, and we shall be told that professionalism tends to improve cricket. Yes, but in what way? Without a doubt they make it more difficult to play and longer to learn. But what advantage do they add to the

> game by so doing? What great pleasure can a man derive from standing up against a highly paid expert who bowls like a field-gun. Methinks there was more fun in the single-wicket game we used to play on the tennis-lawn when we practised over-arm bowling against our sisters. That was indeed cricket.[11]

Highly paid expert George Lohmann would have agreed with very little of this. All the evidence is that he enjoyed his cricket and worked at it to achieve the highest standards.

Soon the news from South Africa would be not of Lohmann, nor of Lord Hawke and his cricketers but of Ladysmith, Mafeking and Spion Kop. The fighting did not extend as far west as Matjiesfontein, though a few shots were exchanged with roving Boer commandos. The area served as a remount station and hosted a number of famous regiments, including the Coldstream Guards, the 17th Lancers, the Middlesex Regiment and the Duke of Edinburgh's Own Rifles. The turret at Logan's hotel housed a machine gun and was used as a look-out post. Lord Ironside and Douglas Haig were billeted at Logan's private residence and the Milner Hotel was for a time the headquarters of the Cape Command and later a convalescent Home for officers.[12]

Lohmann played his part acting as press censor, a job which required a measure of education and judgment, involving the examination of telegrams and other dispatches and purging them of any information on troop movements, transport and supplies or any propaganda likely to give information to the enemy.[13] An educated man with capacity for judgement, he doubtless performed his duties with skill and efficiency.

1 *Cape Argus* 25 January 1898
2 *Cape Argus* 7 April 1898
3 Honorary Secretary's Report 29 August 1898
4 *The Star* 8 October 1898
5 Press cutting in South African Cricket Association minute book
6 Unpublished MS in Surrey Cricket archives
7 *Cape Argus* 9 January 1899
8 *Cape Argus* 11 January 1899
9 *Cape Times* 31 May 1899
10 *Cape Times* 6 October 1899
11 *Cape Argus* 7 January 1899
12 Toms *op cit* p 114-119
13 *Daily Mail* 17 August 1901

CHAPTER 21

THE FINAL TOUR OF ENGLAND (1901)

My native land, good night
Byron *Childe Harold's Pilgrimage*

Disjointed Preparations

A SOUTH AFRICAN touring team had visited England in 1894, but had played no Test matches and only a limited amount of first-class cricket on a trip which had been a financial disaster. In 1901 the Boer War was still in progress, the newspapers full of reports of atrocities, such as the murdering of prisoners. There had been an intention to send a touring party to England for the 1900 season, but there was some reluctance on the part of the constituent members of the South African Cricket Association to finance it. However, Logan's offer to underwrite the venture, as he had done previously, brought about a change of mind, albeit in a dignified and diplomatic manner.

> The Honorary Secretary was instructed to communicate with the centres dissenting from the idea of sending a South African team to England during 1900, informing them that there was every probability of the expenses of the visit being guaranteed without the various unions being called upon to subscribe and asking if this in any way affected their decision as to the sending of a team.[1]

Correspondence followed and by the end of August the required change of heart had been brought about in all but one of the constituent unions and it was resolved,

> That a South African team be sent to England during the English season

> 1900 in terms of Mr Logan's offer. The team to be purely an amateur team and selected by the Association.

and,

> That it be an instruction to the Honorary Secretary to write to Lord Hawke sending him a copy of the resolution and requesting him to arrange a first class tour, advising Mr Logan of so doing.[2]

In the event, the Boer War intervened, the tour did not take place and the minutes of that meeting remained unconfirmed until 21 January 1903. There were, however, unminuted negotiations and the tour materialised a year later in 1901, much to the dismay of Arthur Conan Doyle who had strong reservations about the propriety of men playing cricket when there was a war to fight.

Meanwhile, at the end of 1900, Lohmann was to demonstrate that, whatever the feeling in the other direction, Surrey was still on his Christmas card list,

> 'A Merry Christmas and prosperous New Year' above the signature of George Lohmann came as a pleasant reminder that the brilliant Surrey cricketer of a decade ago is not unmindful of his friends in the old country. The familiar handwriting gives his address as Matjesfontein, Cape Colony.[3]

It was to be his last Christmas.

Although the original intention was that the touring party should be selected by the South African Cricket Association, the deferment of the tour for a year and the war, resulted in that plan being modified and the tour became more of a privately-sponsored venture rather than one financed and organised by the national governing body. As such, it was no different from overseas tours by English teams to both South Africa and Australia, but the *Natal Witness*, whose colony could be perceived as under-represented, perhaps had a point when it commented critically on the composition of the side, particularly the inclusion of Logan's son who had played no first-class cricket before and played none afterwards.

There was no need to respond to that criticism, but had the Laird chosen to do so, the text may well have made reference to pipers and tunes. The theme, however, was taken up in the English media.

> The South African cricketers at present in this country are not, as many people imagine, a recognised representative team of that colony. The tour is a private one, the players having been selected by Mr Logan, and not by the South African Cricket Union. In fact a Natal paper recently stated that

> only half-a-dozen of the players sent out would stand a chance of being selected for South Africa in a representative match in that country against one, say, from England or Australia.[4]

The team had arrived at Southampton on the *Briton* on Friday 4 May. Rudyard Kipling, born in the same year as Lohmann, was on the same boat. His company was accidental, but in view of his poetic comments on 'flannelled fools at the wicket', not inappropriate or indeed incompatible with some of the attendant unfavourable publicity.

The Times, however, in welcoming the team, was happy to publish their response to Conan Doyle's comments, as they pointed out that most of them – including the management – had made their contribution to the war.

> THE SOUTH AFRICAN TEAM
>
> The South African cricketers reached Southampton yesterday in the Union Castle liner *Briton*. They were accompanied by the Hon J D Logan who is in charge of the team, and George Lohmann, the old Surrey player who will act as Assistant Manager. They will remain at Southampton and practise there until after the Hampshire match with which they will start their tour on the 16th inst. Amongst those who met them was Mr A J L Hill, the well-known Hampshire cricketer. Mr Murray Bisset will be captain of the side and he will have with him Messrs A Bisset, A Reid, A Graham, J J Kotze, G Rowe, D Logan Jun. (of the Western Province), J H Sinclair, E A Halliwell, L J Tancred, G Hathorn (of the Transvaal), W Shalders (Griqualand West), B C Cooley (Natal) and C F Prince (Border). In the course of conversation several players expressed regret that a controversy should have been raised by Dr Conan Doyle respecting their visit to this country while war was being carried out in South Africa. It was pointed out that eight of the 14 players have seen active service, whilst others have been members of various town defence forces. The Hon J D Logan has also borne arms and, as captain of the Matjesfontein Rifles, was present at the battle of Belmont. Mr Sinclair, who is regarded as the batsman of the side, served with General French's scouts. Of the team which visited this country seven years ago, Halliwell and Rowe are the only ones to renew acquaintance with English cricket. The colonials had counted on the assistance of Llewellyn – who has now qualified for Hampshire – when that player was not engaged for the county, but it is understood that the Hampshire executive will not release him from Hampshire engagements. They contend that it would be a bad precedent, and, moreover, would spoil his bowling for Hampshire. The South African team is purely an amateur one and firmly representative of Cape cricket. Their colours – red, blue and orange – are identical with the colours of the South African war medal ribbon, and the permission of Sir Forestier

Walker had to be obtained before they could be adopted. The members are looking forward keenly to their opening match and, on hard wickets at any rate, hope to hold their own against the majority of the counties. The Hon J D Logan left for Scotland last night to arrange fixtures there.[5]

However, although the early part of the tour was covered in some detail, the South Africans' poor results and the one-sided nature of some of the early encounters caused that newspaper's interest to diminish and the later part received few column inches. The question of adapting to turf was a significant one and the improving quality of the pitches and the consequent changing balance between bat and ball was one to which some sections of the press drew attention.

THE EVER-GROWING EVIL OF COLOSSAL SCORES
Although only six days of the season have yet gone by, there have already been eight individual scores of over a hundred, a result probably as much due to the excellent work of the ground man as to the skill of the batsman. It is doubtful whether this superlative excellence of our cricket grounds is altogether an unmixed blessing. Certainly it is better for a first-class match to be played on a good ground than on a bad one, but on such wickets as were obtainable last year at the Oval, Birmingham and Brighton, the perfect condition of the pitch gave the batsmen such an enormous advantage over the bowler that quite an undue proportion of matches were drawn, and centuries were scored with such frequency as to savour monotony.[6]

Lohmann would not have found the pitches as responsive to his wiles as those on which he had started his brief career. Doubtless, had he been fitter, he would have risen to the challenge, but he was by this time a very sick man and must have known that this was a final opportunity to say a last farewell to friends and family in England. Mentally, however, he was alert enough to express lucidly, but diplomatically, opinions on the tour and the political background to an interviewer from the *Daily Mail*,[7] a publication with which he had been associated during the 'strike' of 1896 and again during his brief visit to his native land in 1897.

FROM BATTLEFIELD TO CRICKET PITCH
EXPERIENCES OF THE SOUTH AFRICAN ELEVEN
The South African team of cricketers who have been in England some few days enter upon their fixture list at Southampton today. The tour has been promoted by the Hon J D Logan who selected the team – an amateur one – after consultation with prominent Colonial cricketers, and who has accompanied them to England. George Lohmann who was so popular a member of the Surrey XI before he went out to the Cape some nine years

ago, is acting as Manager for the team in conjunction with the captain, Mr Murray Bisset.

In an interview with a correspondent of the *Daily Mail* Mr Lohmann explained that the idea of bringing over the team originated before the commencement of the war; but in consequence of the serious aspect which the position at the Cape assumed, the trip was postponed.

'We were sorry not to fulfil our engagements,' said Mr Lohmann, 'but we felt that the English supporters of the game would understand why we didn't come. This year we thought we could be spared.'

'But, of course, whether you came or stayed away, you scarcely expected to please everybody,' suggested the interviewer, in reference to the strictures passed on the members of the team by Dr Conan Doyle for having left South Africa before the war has been finished. 'Are you all very angry about it?'

Apparently, Mr Lohmann for one was not angry. He merely said that Dr Conan Doyle seemed to be labouring under the mistake of imagining that the members of the team had seen no service on the battlefield, whereas most of them had served many months in some capacity or other.

'And what did you do yourself there?' he was asked.

'I? Oh, I was Press-censor at Matjesfontein,' replied Mr Lohmann, and it seemed as though the mention of the fact aroused a slumbering censorial instinct, for he added, 'Get the name of that place right for once; it is nearly always mis-spelt here at home.'

A reminder was next given of the fact that this is the second South African XI which has visited England. The first team came in 1894. They improved in play after the start, and developed into a very fair side, but it was a wet season, and cricket in that year was more or less unreliable.

'They are a young team in a sense,' continued Mr Lohmann, 'but there are brilliant cricketers among them. Mr Murray Bissett [sic][8] captained the South African XI when they came to the Cape, and as skipper displayed perfect tact and judgment. He is a very good bat, and in every respect we are glad to have him with us. In Helliwell [sic] we have one of the best wicket-keepers in the world, and a very fair understudy in C F Prince.'

'I assume the team are all Britishers?'

'No. As to nationality we have a Dutchman whose name is J J Kotze but his sympathies are decidedly British, for he has been to the front with our forces, as have also his father and other members of the family. We have had some capital practice on the Hants County Ground. A little practice was generally necessary, for most of the team. As you know, in South Africa, cocoa-nut matting pitches are used, and these have troubled some of the best English batsmen who have visited the Cape.'

' I dare say you can sum up in a word or two the main differences between the two kinds of pitches.'

He could: 'The light, pace and footing are very different.'
'And are your men getting used to the change of conditions?'
'I think so, and I believe they will develop into a very good side.'

The Social Scene

THE TOUR was punctuated with several dinners where the hosts and tour management were in their element and the cricketers, especially the professional ones, if invited, doubtless felt slightly less comfortable. The one at the Crystal Palace on the first evening of the London County fixture may be regarded as not untypical.

DINNER TO THE SOUTH AFRICANS

Last night at the Crystal Palace the South Africans were entertained to dinner by the London County Club. Lord Suffield, the President was in the chair, and among the other guests in addition to the cricketers, were Sir Walter Peace, the Hon J D Logan, the Hon Colonel F Schermbrucker and Mr C E de Trafford. Dr W G Grace, Mr W L Murdoch, Mr W Gardiner and Mr A Schenk were also present. The chairman read letters from Mr Chamberlain and the Lord Chief Justice expressing regret at their inability to be present. Lord Suffield, in giving the toast of 'The King', mentioned his keen interest in colonial cricket tours. Other speakers were Mr J D Logan, Dr W G Grace, Colonel Schermbrucker, Mr A Schenk, Mr W L Murdoch, Mr Murray Bisset, Sir Walter Peace and Mr H V L Stanton.[9]

London County were the team established in 1899 by the Crystal Palace Company. W G Grace had been persuaded to take on the post of secretary/manager, persuasion accompanied by a salary of £600 per annum, 1/- of every guinea collected in gate money and membership fees and free education for his son at the Crystal Palace School of Engineering.[10] His final falling-out with Gloucestershire enabled him to devote his full attention to his new job, having originally intended to combine it with the continued captaincy of his native county. In 1900, first-class status was granted by MCC and the reputation of Grace was such that he was able to attract some of the best cricketers. When Halliwell and Sinclair, newly arrived with Logan's Team, were recruited to play against Warwickshire on 9, 10 and 11 May, the players they were replacing were C B Fry and K S Ranjitsinhji.

It is perhaps no coincidence that *The Times* report on the play the day after the dinner contains the opinion that 'the fielding of both sides left room for improvement'.[11] There is no mention of Lohmann. The likelihood is that he chose to absent himself from this and similar functions. If so, it seems a sensible decision. The prospect of sitting through nine or more after-dinner speeches is one which would not fill most cricketers with enthusiasm and his relationship with Grace probably remained prickly from the 1891/92 tour of Australia and the 'strike' of 1896.

E A Halliwell was to write later in the year on learning of Lohmann's death.

> To me it did not come as a great surprise for, being in daily contact with him for many months, I naturally saw the rapid ravages that fell disease was making. This was one of the reasons he did not go about more during his visit to England last summer. You knew him as a powerful man and he purposefully refrained from allowing you to see his shadow.[12]

Lohmann himself was all too aware of his decline. From Darlington where he was staying while the team played in Dublin, he wrote to Mr A J Webbe,

> I am fairly well but cannot walk very far as it makes me blow so hard – it is rather dreadful, but I must make the most of a bad job, and as I am with such nice fellows, I must not complain.[13]

However, notwithstanding Lohmann's absence, firm links seem to have been already established between the tourists and the London County set-up and as well as Halliwell and Sinclair, a number of the other tourists, namely, Hathorn, Prince, and Tancred turned out for Grace's team over the course of the summer, Sinclair in particular distinguishing himself with 8 for 32 against Derbyshire and 108 not out against Warwickshire.

In view of his now semi-permanent indisposition it is unlikely that Lohmann had any part in the travelling and logistical arrangements for the dinner in Harrogate hosted by the Yorkshire Club when acquaintance was renewed with captain and president, Lord Hawke. It was also an occasion which saw Logan in York, believing the event was the following evening, Colonel Schermbrucker in Darlington, having caught the wrong train at King's Cross and a chaotic evening characterised by Yorkshire's first entertaining of an overseas touring side and three-way telegraphic communication between the three towns.[14]

The Cricket

> Their own cricket is by no means to be despised. Naturally they cannot hope to compete with our counties yet, but they have plenty of fine batsmen and their bowlers are improving.[15]

SUCH WAS Lohmann's verdict six years earlier. Since then, the South Africans had continued to improve and Lohmann himself, as coach to two senior cricket clubs and participant in domestic and international competitions, had played no small part in that improvement.

The early results of the tour were not entirely successful. A heavy defeat by Hampshire was followed by a win against London County. The South Africans were then swept aside in two days by Kent at Beckenham (where Lohmann doubtless recalled the different circumstances of his first first-class century fifteen years before) and at Leicester and then lost heavily to Warwickshire at Edgbaston, where he perhaps took the opportunity of seeing and saying a last farewell to his sister Augusta who was living in Birmingham at the time.

From a cricket viewpoint it was not the best of starts, but there were mitigating circumstances in the unseasonal weather which, in turn, could not have been other than detrimental to Lohmann's health.

> With only one victory in five matches, the South Africans can hardly be said to have come up to expectations. Their batting has, except in a few instances, been disappointing, and the bowling is by no means up to first-class form. The cold east winds which prevailed until the last few days have, however, proved inimical to the health of the men, who have certainly not so far shown their best form, and when the genial summer breezes come along a very different tale of their abilities will in all probability have to be told.[16]

Matters improved a little against a strong MCC side at Lord's and although the match was lost by 53 runs, the weather had improved sufficiently for the bowling to attract favourable comment from the press and for the best of the fielding to revive memories of Lohmann in earlier years.

> Although the MCC put a decidedly strong team into the field against the South Africans they did not give a particularly good account of themselves, and left off with very little the better of the game. For a side which includes Grace, Ranjitsinhji, Hayward, Storer, Chinnery, Murdoch and Albert Trott to be dismissed for 168 runs would lead one to suppose that the wicket was not playing satisfactorily, but as a matter of fact there was very little fault to be found on that score. The success met with by the South Africans was in the main due to the excellence of their fielding. Special mention must be made of the catches which dismissed Grace and Chinnery, but the work generally was most neatly and expeditiously performed. Shalders must have been receiving lessons from George Lohmann in the art of making lightning catches in the slips, for one of his efforts yesterday was quite the equal of those brilliant performances, which used to cause the crowd to cheer so heartily in the palmy days of Surrey cricket.[17]

However, the batting again let them down and they sacrificed a strong position.

> The South Africans are certainly a most disappointing team. After proving the quality of their bowling and fielding by dismissing the powerful MCC side opposed to them for scores of under 200, their batting broke down badly and they were beaten by fifty-three runs.[18]

They then moved on to beat Derbyshire, thanks to Murray Bisset's career-best 184, and, as the tourists continued their winning streak, Cambridge University were disposed of by the convincing margin of an innings and 215 runs. A better pitch and weak bowling conspired to produce a team total of 692, the highest by a South African team in England. However, the dustcart was not far behind the Lord Mayor's show and they came unstuck against Somerset, losing by 341 runs.

In the north, winter had continued until mid-June.

> There has been snow in the Grampians, and snow and hail have fallen at Leak [sic] in Staffordshire. In the North during the last four days, the temperature has barely risen above 40 deg and even in London at four o'clock yesterday morning it was down to 45 deg. At breakfast time it had risen to 50 deg.[19]

In the non-first-class fixture against Liverpool and District, Llewellyn was able to make one of his rare appearances for the side and made a difference with a half-century and 6-51 and 6-79. Without him the tourists' erratic form continued with a five-wicket defeat by Lancashire at Old Trafford.

By now, however, the weather had begun to change. July was characterised by a heatwave and conditions more familiar to the South Africans. Fixtures with Surrey, the leading county side of the 1890s by some distance, and Yorkshire, under Lord Hawke, the heirs apparent to that position in the decade just beginning, had been scheduled for July and August respectively, but those matches apart, the schedule was frontloaded with the strongest oppositions. It was thus largely to be expected that this combination of the fixture list, adjusting to turf pitches and unseasonal weather led to disappointing results. So it was a season of two halves: the South Africans, having by the midpoint completed two-thirds of their first-class matches, could look forward to weaker opposition in more favourable weather on pitches to which they had now adjusted.

Against Surrey at The Oval, Sinclair shone as did Tom Richardson, Lohmann's erstwhile opening partner and successor as darling of the

Surrey crowd. No longer the force they had been in Lohmann's heyday, the brown hatters were still strong enough to finish in the top half-dozen in the Championship and to win the match by 59 runs.

It is not clear whether Lohmann was present at the match. None of the contemporary press accounts mention it. In particular *Cricket* says nothing and neither the Surrey minutes nor Annual Report have any reference to Lohmann's being either at the match or at the associated dinner. Two conclusions can be drawn: firstly, that because of his failing health, Lohmann was deliberately keeping a low profile and secondly, the 1897 split had not been forgotten and he was *persona non grata* with Surrey.

Following a thrilling tie at Worcester, the tourists beat Northamptonshire by five wickets in a non-first-class fixture. They lost to a strong Yorkshire side, then proceeded to win three matches in Scotland before producing their best performance of the tour in their last first-class fixture against Gloucestershire at Clifton. On a less than perfect pitch they scored 234, then proceeded to dismiss their hosts for 40 and 89, Sinclair, bowling through both innings with Rowe and finishing with match figures of 13-73.

Overall, the tourists had won five of their fifteen first-class fixtures, tying one and losing the remainder. Of their ten non-first-class matches, they had won eight and drawn two, not including the 'holiday' matches in Scotland which were considered as being outside the official programme.

The relative merits of Sinclair and Llewellyn as all-round cricketers are open to discussion, but in the context of the tour the debate would be a sterile one, as the latter was a fringe member whereas Sinclair played a full part.

J H Sinclair

IN ITS preview of the tour, the *Daily Telegraph* pointed to the attributes of Lohmann's protégé.

> Whatever the collective merits of the team may be, there seems to be no doubt that J H Sinclair is a very fine bat. Standing nearly 6 ft 4 in, he has great physical advantages, and his record at home is so good that his success here seems merely a question of whether, having learned all his cricket on matting wickets, he will readily be able to adapt to turf.[20]

Sinclair's reputation had preceded him and provided him with the opportunity for pre-tour match practice when he was invited to play for

London County against Derbyshire. On his first appearance in a match in England, he made an immediate impression.

> J H Sinclair, of the South Africans, was the bowling hero of the day. Indeed, he made the Derbyshire batting look very poor stuff indeed. He is a fine strapping player with the elasticity of youth in his vigorous frame. Slightly over medium pace, he keeps a good length and gets plenty of work on the ball.[21]

The *Cape Times*, commenting in rather more detail, gives a generally laudatory, but not entirely uncritical profile of Sinclair's tour. He is not yet the finished article, but the influence of his mentor is apparent.

> Sinclair, by his improved batting, clearly justified his claim to be considered the best all-rounder. He has done a lot of useful run getting of late, but even now is not in his old-time form. He has developed a tendency to use a crooked bat at times, especially when tackling a fast bowler, and moreover he is occasionally very rash. Sinclair is, of course, a magnificent hitter, but he is, or can be, a sound reliable batsman of the most approved type. If only he could be persuaded to play as he played in the Easter tourney, at Johannesburg – when opposed to George Lohmann, George Rowe and Middleton – he would take a deal more shifting than he does at present, and the cables would shortly be flashing the details of some great century or other of his across the waters. With regard to his bowling there can be no question that on his day, he is quite the most difficult of our four attackers. Yesterday for instance he kept a splendid length, varied his pace very cleverly, and made 'em turn both ways.[22]

Similar comments had been made about Lohmann in his heyday.

C B Llewellyn

'BUCK' LLEWELLYN was the only coloured cricketer to play Test cricket for South Africa until the dismantling of apartheid in 1991. Krom Hendricks was obviously good enough to do so but was excluded by the system. Though of similar parentage, a white father and mother from St Helena, it was perhaps significant, at least for cricket and political purposes, that Llewellyn was of somewhat lighter pigmentation, Wilfred Rhodes describing him as 'like a rather sunburned English player', though Llewellyn's daughter's later protestations that her father was white can safely be disregarded.[23]

Lohmann was of the opinion that, had Llewellyn been available for the full tour, rather than just joining the team for just the one match, the team would have had more success.

> Poor Lohmann who, as assistant manager of the team had his last experience of public cricket before his untimely death at Matjiesfontein, thought highly of the side and expressed the opinion that if they could always have commanded Llewellyn's service they would have been a match for any of the counties.[24]

It was a view questioned by *Wisden* but the weight of evidence is on Lohmann's side. Had the tour taken place the previous season as originally intended, the likelihood is that Llewellyn would have played a full part. However, his omission from the 1901 party was not a political or racial issue, but occasioned by the fact that, by the end of the 1900 season, Llewellyn had qualified by residence to play for Hampshire (Major Poore's county; perhaps Llewellyn's gravitation there is more than coincidence) and the county committee was naturally reluctant to release him from his professional obligations, except on the rare occasions when the South Africans' fixtures did not clash with Hampshire ones. Consequently, he was able to play for his county as 'Llewellyn' and for Mr Logan's team as 'Mr Llewellyn'.

In the first two matches of the tour, he was successful under both titles. The team had almost a week to acclimatise and to begin to make the adjustment to turf pitches. It was a coincidence – fortunate for Llewellyn, perhaps less so for the tourists – that the first fixture was against Hampshire. The first day was nothing if not traumatic.

> The South Africans had a severe experience in the opening match of their tour at Southampton yesterday, Hampshire staying in all day, and in five hours and a quarter putting together the huge total of 538. The batting honours of the day were carried off by Llewellyn whose driving and placing on the leg side were very good.[25]
>
> Yesterday's cricket at Southampton... would seem to foreshadow many a long day's leather hunting for the colonials during the next three months.[26]

Llewellyn compiled a first-class career best of 216, including thirty fours, nine threes and three twos and with amateur, John Greig (then 'Captain', but later secretary of Hampshire and later still, 'Canon') took part in a fifth wicket partnership of 219 in an hour and fifty minutes. The South Africans lost by an innings and 51 runs as Llewellyn finished the match with a spell of four for six.

He then switched sides and played for the South Africans in the next fixture against W G Grace's London County at the Crystal Palace and, to bring the wheel full circle was to play for London County later in the season. His impact on this occasion, however, was with his bowling, 6-140 and 7-101, including the wicket of Grace in each innings. It is a measure of Grace's continued influence on the game that his permission seems to have been required for Llewellyn to be released by Hampshire to play for the tourists. It is reported that 'Dr Grace sportingly allowed C B Llewellyn, a South African Test player, now with Hampshire, who was not a member of the touring team, to play against them'.[27] In a match which did not form part of any competition and where the question of eligibility would not normally arise, it does seem unusual that team selection should be subject to the permission of one's opponents. Or were other issues involved?

> Mr Llewellyn is the best all-round cricketer of the South Africans and his success in batting, bowling and fielding was the chief cause of the South Africans' success yesterday.[28]

He had 88 in the second innings and the fact that he was twice stumped in the match is perhaps a clue to his batting style.

The question of Llewellyn's eligibility to play in the Currie Cup was one which was to exercise the South African Cricket Association in later years. Transvaal had wished him to play in the 1903 Currie Cup on the grounds that he played as an amateur and any payment to him was for his duties as a clerk in the Wanderers Club office. Western Province however, objected on the grounds that Llewellyn was employed by Hampshire as a professional cricketer and, as such, ineligible. So, Western Province, supported by Eastern Province and Griqualand West, opposed by Transvaal and Border with Natal abstaining, carried the day by three votes to two and he was excluded on the grounds of professionalism.[29] The minutes do not say so, but the likelihood appears to be that there was a racist element there as well.

The team left Southampton on the *Scot* on 31 August.[30] Logan was not with them, his wife was ill, thus detaining him in England.

Reviewing the 1901 tour, *Wisden* pointed out the gap in class between South African and Australian cricket. At this stage in its development, South Africa was very much the poor relation of the three nations now playing Test matches, which would soon become founder members of the Imperial Cricket Conference. It was not, nor did it claim to be, a representative South African side and, hampered by the unfamiliarity of turf wickets, cold weather early on the tour and a programme front-loaded with the stronger fixtures, could perhaps be excused for a hesitant start. The tourists' fixtures received less media attention than the simultaneous first-class and county programme, though their improvement during the tour was mentioned. In the London County match, *The Times* took the view that,

> The South Africans are a good side, both in batting and bowling; but if they want to win matches, they must learn to hold the catches.[31]

but, a couple of days later, was constrained to point out,

> The feature of the game was the brilliant fielding of the South African side.[32]

and, a fortnight later, was able to comment,

> ...the South Africans' bowling and fielding were splendidly keen.[33]

Against the background of the Boer War, the tourists could retrospectively see themselves as rungs on the ladder of progress which would take their country to their first Test victory in 1906 and their participation in the triangular tournament of 1912. Although he would not live to see the end result, George Lohmann would doubtless take a professional pride in being part of that process. He would have been equally satisfied with the way in which he had influenced Sinclair's development.

Although Lohmann's playing days – and indeed the majority of his active life – were now behind him, he remained the yardstick against which aspirant bowlers were measured. An emergent Wilfred Rhodes, who, under the iron rule of captain and President Lord Hawke, along with George Hirst and Schofield Haigh formed the great Yorkshire triumvirate of the day, was already attracting comment from the press and his peers.

> The tendency of the day in the cricket press is to extol the man of the hour at the expense of his fellows, both contemporary and past greatnesses... In my humble opinion, Rhodes is not so good a bowler as poor old Johnny Briggs. He seems to lack very much the infinite cunning, the variation, and resources of the wily John. He is more of a length bowler than Briggs was, in fact he keeps a better length than any bowler we have seen, and he varies his flight with great skill. The ball seems to be coming right up to you. And then suddenly to drop a foot shorter than you expect. Our own side formed diverse opinions of his skill. One said: 'He's no better than

> Cranfield or Blythe.' Another: 'He's a great bowler. You have to play against him to appreciate his worth.' Another of the team said: 'You can play him all day provided you don't take liberties.' Personally, I think it nothing short of heresy to compare him with George Lohmann.[34]

The comparison may be unfair and premature as Rhodes was a left arm spin bowler as opposed to a right arm medium-pace one and would still be gracing the first-class scene almost thirty years later, but it is significant that the gold standard for bowling had been established by Lohmann.

1 Minutes of South African Cricket Association 12 June 1899
2 Ib 31 August 1899
3 *Cricket* 31 January 1901
4 *Titbits* 8 June 1901
5 4 May 1901
6 *Daily Mail* 6 May 1901
7 16 May 1901
8 Bisset, 25 at the time was later to be knighted and pursue a distinguished political career. At the time of his death in 1931, he was acting-Governor of Rhodesia
9 *The Times* 21 May 1901
10 Pearce *Cricket at the Crystal Palace* p18
11 22 May 1901
12 *Cricket* 30 January 1902
13 Sissons *George Lohmann: The beau ideal* p 62
14 *Cape Times* 29 August 1901
15 *Cricket* 4 July 1895
16 *Daily Mail* 1 June 1901
17 *Daily Mail* 4 June 1901
18 *Daily Mail* 5 June 1901
19 *Daily Mail* 19 June 1901
20 6 May 1901
21 *Daily Mail* 14 May 1901
22 Ib 29 August 1901
23 Merrett *Sport and Race in Colonial Natal*
24 *Wisden* 1902 p 467
25 *The Times* 17 May 1901
26 *Daily Telegraph* 17 May 1901
27 Pearce *op cit* p 30
28 *The Times* 23 May 1901
29 4 April 1903
30 *Cape Times* 17 August 1901
31 23 May 1901
32 25 May 1901
33 5 June 1901
34 Ib

CHAPTER 22

DEATH ON THE KAROO (1901)

Cry, the beloved country
Alan Paton

IN ENGLAND the winter was bitterly cold and preparations were under way for the coronation of Edward VII. In Matjiesfontein, the summer solstice was approaching and arrangements were being made for George Lohmann's funeral. He had died in Matjiesfontein on the morning of Sunday 1 December, the cause of death phthisis pulmonatis and cardiac failure, the informant a medical orderly, the doctor, John A Robertson, the duration of his last illness, four days. His occupation – none. The place of his intended burial, Peter [sic] Meintjies, nr Matjiesfontein.[1] Alas, poor George. Partly on account of his wife's illness, Logan had delayed his return from the tour of England. He was in Cape Town when he received the news of Lohmann's death. The *Cape Times* carried a full report.

> The death of Mr George Lohmann, the great Surrey cricketer whose name is indissolubly connected with the heyday of Surrey's glory in the cricket field, took place at Matjesfontein yesterday. Upon receipt of the news in Cape Town, the Hon J D Logan made suitable arrangements for the funeral, which takes place at Matjesfontein. By last night's mail train, wreaths from the following were forwarded to Matjesfontein: Hon J D Logan, Mrs Logan and family, Lieutenant Colonel Hon F Schermbrucker, Mr S M Wright, Mrs Miss and Mr Jas Wright, Dr J A Robertson, South African Cricket Team, Messrs Harry Attridge, George Page, Harry Newsome, William R Morgan, A W Waddington and others. The deceased cricketer was in the prime of life, being in his thirty-seventh year, and but for the fell illness which first made itself felt at the close of 1892, he should still have represented his old county. Poor old George Lohmann, cheerful comrade, best of fellows, all will miss him (writes our Sporting Editor). Since he has been in South Africa, and it has been on and off over seven years,[2] he has made innumerable friends and, it is quite safe to say, no enemies. We all knew, and he knew

> too, that his years were numbered, but still the wonderful progress he made at first led to the belief that he had baffled the doctors, and that his complaint was capable of cure. A season in England, however, dissipated these ideas. Since then, with the exception of a year he passed on the Rand, he had been the guest of the Hon J D Logan MLC at Matjesfontein, when he was the recipient of every care and attention. I saw him about a fortnight ago in Adderley Street and he told me the trip to the Old Country had done him good, although his wan looks and appearance rather belied his statement. He then spoke very hopefully about the future. We discussed cricket of course and he said he was very satisfied with the result of the tour, which he said had served to raise South African cricket in the public mind, and he expressed himself most hopefully of the future of cricket in this country. Of what he has done for cricket in South Africa during his sojourn here it is impossible to say too much. He was always willing to give advice, and to illustrate the meaning of his remarks, and his performances here on eventful occasions, when he bore the brunt of the bowling, also did more than his share of the work in the field, and then batted well, served as a splendid example of pluck and determination to those who were playing with and against him. The news of his death came down yesterday morning, and the Hon J D Logan, who is staying at Sea Point, was at once communicated with. He was very much cut up at the news, but immediately made suitable arrangements for his friend's burial.[3]

Among those who sent wreaths were Logan's friends, the Wright family of Sea Point, with whom he was staying at the time. Lohmann too had stayed there at their home on his visits to Cape Town.

It is suggested by Langham-Carter that 'the army doctors treated Lohmann in his illness, and he was ministered to by a medical orderly named Edgar Wallace who would later become a famous novelist'. That Wallace later became a famous novelist is not in doubt, that army doctors treated Lohmann is certain as Dr Robertson[4], who appears on Lohmann's death certificate had been recruited for the purpose of ministering to troops at Matjiesfontein in the Boer war, but that one of the medical orderlies should be Edgar Wallace is dubious. Certainly he was in South Africa, certainly he was a medical orderly, but before the time of Lohmann's final illness, he had become war correspondent of the *Daily Mail* and was being sent to where the action was. There is evidence from Logan's scrapbook that Wallace reported the death of Queen Victoria in January 1901 from the telegraph room at Matjiesfontein station. He witnessed the Battle of Belmont in which Logan was involved, but an itinerary, following the action at Magersfontein, of the Orange River, Mafeking, Beira, Salisbury, Bulawayo, London, Johannesburg, Pretoria and Cape Town in the months preceding and following Lohmann's death took him to the end of the Boer war in 1902 and suggests that he was not in Matjiesfontein in December 1901 and his visit earlier in the year does not warrant a mention in his autobiography.

The funeral took place the following day, Monday 2 December. There were obituaries in both the British and South African press. E A Halliwell unconsciously spoke for many when he wrote,

> He had his faults (and who has not?) but at heart he was one of the best and I feel his death muchly.[5]

The N1, popularly known as the 'national road', which runs from Cape Town to Johannesburg, was not complete in 1901, but it can perhaps be perceived as a powerful symbol of George Lohmann's contribution to South African cricket, linking its two most influential centres, Western Province and the Transvaal.

It is entirely appropriate that Lohmann's final resting place should be a short walk from this road in Pieter Meintjies, the cemetery for Matjiesfontein, situated some ten kilometres south-west of the village. Apart from the cemetery, the road and the parallel railway line and fences to contain (not always successfully) the native ostriches, little has changed since pre-historical days when Africa was joined to South America and Australasia. An article in the *Australian Cricket Journal*[6] is entitled *A Lonely Grave on the Karoo*. Lonely, it is not. The cemetery itself could scarcely be more isolated, but as Lohmann rests in a peace unparalleled by most graveyards, he is surrounded by his contemporaries, people he would have known in Matjiesfontein, many of them young, having come to the area for health reasons, but, like Lohmann, having enjoyed little more than and sometimes less than half the Psalmist's threescore years and ten.

Among the purple statice flowers which at the coast would be called sea lavender and which now cover the largely neglected graves at the end of the sandy dirt track under the clear blue skies of the Karoo which become purple in the late afternoon lie victims of railway accidents, tuberculosis and the Boer War. In death as in life, Lohmann is surrounded by friends and colleagues, some just ordinary people, others like General Wauchope, whose memorial dominates the small cemetery, of some distinction. Wauchope had a distinguished military record in campaigns in the Ashanti Wars, the Sudan and the Nile, died in the battle of Magersfontein on 11 December 1899 and was exhumed and brought to the near homonym, Matjiesfontein, to add distinction to what was essentially Logan's private graveyard, an extension of his private village. Also buried here is John Maitland Grant, a friend of Logan, District Engineer of Cape Colony Railways, killed in a railway accident in 1891. Finally Logan himself, who died in 1920 and his family are also here, their graves two rows in front of

Lohmann's, relatively obscure and unadorned compared with his.

Few, if any professional cricketers – or anyone else for that matter, barring royalty, archbishops and the aristocracy – have been finally pavilioned in such splendour as George Lohmann. The memorial is in white marble with an elaborate inscription, verging on the hagiographic. It is flanked by two ionic columns, surmounted by a laurel wreath to denote victory and a broken wicket symbolising the end of an innings.

Separately, at the foot a horizontal marble cross has been placed with an apt biblical quotation (Isaiah 57:19). Some sources say it was placed there by Lohmann's fiancée.[7] If that is so, her identity remains a mystery. There is no mention of any one who might have been a fiancée in any of the reports of his death, his obituaries and the lists of those who sent wreaths. Nor did Lohmann leave a will, either in England or South Africa. He must have been aware for some time that death was imminent and had marriage been on his mind, it seems likely he would have made provision for a lady who in other circumstances would have become his wife.[8] He must have been reasonably wealthy, having received a generous benefit and been well paid as a professional cricketer, coach and employee of the JCIC. As a guest of Logan in Matjiesfontein, his living expenses would have been negligible. It is possible that on his last tour of England in 1901, he distributed some of his wealth to his family, but there is no evidence of this.

As with the mysterious girl in Melbourne, there seems to have been an attempt to make any relationship more serious than it actually was. It is more likely that the cross at the foot of the memorial inscription was the personal tribute from Logan, his Scottish Presbyterian background filtering through in the Old Testament verse.

In the bottom right hand corner of the memorial, erected in 1904,[9] is the name of R Cane and Son, the leading monumental masons in South Africa. It has been suggested that the elaborate nature of the memorial stone was such that it might have been beyond the capacity of Cane's team and that the work was undertaken by Harold Adams Acton, a London sculptor, who was working for Cane at the time.[10]

The inscription on the stone and the financing of it were the subject of an undignified and unseemly wrangle between the Surrey Club and Logan. Once the appropriate message of condolence had been sent to Lohmann's father, the club decided that a memorial should be erected 'by the Surrey County Cricket Club': Logan suggested that 'and his friends in South Africa' be added. Such an inscription was entirely appropriate. Lohmann had spent a quarter of his life in South Africa and towards the end, his friends in South Africa had been a more important part of it than his former employers. Surrey were not impressed and wished 'the tombstone at least to be erected by the Surrey club alone'. The funding had initially been agreed as £25 by the club and £25 by Logan. When the latter increased his contribution to £125, the weightings in the negotiating equation had changed. Money had talked. Logan had his way.[11] There were other donations. The history of the Wanderers Club proudly reports a contribution of £1.

After Logan's death in 1920, the graveyard, like Matjiesfontein itself lay forgotten and neglected. In 1973, the Surrey Yearbook included a letter from John Penney of Cape Town,

> On a holiday in the Karoo about 150 miles from Capetown some months ago I came across a gravestone in a lonely graveyard... Many years ago during the last century it was possible to book a ticket from London to Matjesfontein return. The purpose of such an expedition was to help people suffering from bronchial problems to recover in the dry Karoo of the central plain of South Africa. The area is once again becoming popular since the town of Matjesfontein and the Lord Milner Hotel have been completely restored by a very talented and sympathetic person by the name of David Rawdon.

At the end of the tour of England in 1901, George Lohmann would have known there was no purpose in his booking a return ticket, but would surely be happy today with the way he is commemorated and with the restoration of Matjiesfontein to something approaching its former glory. In 1993 the cemetery was one of nine sites declared national monuments by the Minister for Arts, Culture, Science and Technology.

1 Death certificate
2 actually nine
3 2 December 1901
4 Toms *op cit* p 119
5 *Cricket* 30 January 1902
6 Vol 1, no 2 December 1985
7 Ib
8 There was a photograph in Logan's private collection, recently sold at auction, of a black lady with the inscription 'Lohmann's wife'. She is elderly and unattractive and the possibility is that she was cook and laundress to the cricketer and the reference is a jocular one
9 *South Africa* 7 May 1904
10 *Australian Cricket Journal* Vol 1, no 2 December 1985
11 Surrey CCC minutes 18 December 1901; 20 February, 17 April 1902; 21 May, 15 August 1903

CHAPTER 23

THE FAMILY AFTER GEORGE'S DEATH

For life goes not backwards nor tarries with yesterday
Kahlil Gibran *The Prophet*

Stewart and Joshua

STEWART LOHMANN died in Croydon in 1931. Joshua, having left Surrey at the end of the 1897 season, about the same time as George, took himself off to the United States for a professional appointment with the Staten Island Club and then joined the 1897/98 goldrush to the Klondike in Northwest Canada.[1] By September 1898 he was back in New York, playing against Pelham Warner's tourists, but his stay on the other side of the Atlantic was short-lived. In early 1901 he was back in England, married to Florence with an eight month old daughter and living in Tittenley, Staffordshire. On the Census of Population for that year, he is described as a professional cricketer.

In 1910, he was professional for South Shields in the Durham Senior League, a competition of which the constituent clubs remained remarkably constant until reorganisation in response to the ECB's Premier League initiative. Although the club had a modest season, winning eight matches, losing ten and drawing four and finishing eighth out of twelve, in a season when Durham City were champions and Chester-le-Street runners up, Joshua enjoyed modest success with both bat and ball with a few 'five for's and fifties. Against Wearmouth,

> The hero of the match was Lohmann who secured five wickets for 55 runs and was top scorer with 57 not out.[2]

According to Sissons, however, relying on *Grass Roots: A History of South Shields Cricket Club* by Clive Crickmer, his fondness for the bottle was a limiting factor.

> It was no secret that Lohmann liked his beer and the companionship of the public bar... he frequently arrived at the ground straight from the County Hotel and would sometimes make a bee-line back there still wearing his flannels after losing his wicket... it could no longer be ignored or tolerated when Lohmann supped too deeply on the eve of a game and spent the night sleeping it off in a police cell.[3]

A club official paid the fine, Joshua repaid it from his talent money, but his contract for 1911 was withdrawn and, according to Sissons, he left the club at the end of August. While family recollections confirm a drink problem, there is no evidence that it affected his play. He missed no matches and was still there after the end of August, playing in the away fixture at Durham City on 3 September. South Shields lost the match, confirming Durham City as Senior League Champions. Joshua made 10, took three wickets and two catches, but played no more in the north-east after that.

Instead, the following year he took himself off to South Wales, signing as professional for Llanelli (or Llanelly, as it was then styled in the local press), playing at Stradey Park, more famous for another sport in a community which boasted some 30,000 souls and about thirty chapels, Anglican, Baptist, Wesleyan and Methodist, each holding at least two services every Sunday. The temperance lobby would have been strong and it can be assumed that Joshua's drinking habits would not be the subject of general approval in the town.

He did not have the greatest of summers, despite close season optimism,

> NEW CRICKET PRO
> The Llanelly Cricket Club during the coming season will have two professionals. Simpson, who did so well last season has been re-engaged, and instead of Holsinger, they have engaged Lohman [sic] who was in excellent all round form last year. He ...should be a great acquisition to the team.[4]

Evidence seems to be that he was a good team man. He took the collection for fellow professional, Simpson, and the Neath professional, Davies, in a joint benefit match against Neath at Stradey Park and also performed with some distinction in the match.

> A collection made on the ground by Lohmann realised £4 7s 9d...
> The professional with his first ball of the match had the Neath captain caught at slip by Lohmann... Up to this period the best bit of play in the field was seen at silly point by Lohmann who... smartly held a drive off Ward.[5]

He made eight, batting at no 5, so seems to have continued his middle order batting in addition to his close to the wicket fielding, but his bowling played less of a part than it had done in County Durham. The club's supporters were disgruntled. A letter to the *Llanelly Star* complained,

> As a follower of cricket for over 28 years I should be glad if the committee of the Llanelly Cricket Club would inform me why they employ two professionals and then do not use their talents.
> Llandovery scored 259 last Saturday. Simpson was called on for a very few overs, and, although taking one wicket, was dismissed to deep extra cover.
> Lohmann was called upon, although a fairly fast bowler, but was placed in the envious position in the field of square leg.
> Spectators pay to see cricket, and if the Llanelly Cricket Club are in the happy position of having a strong amateur side, why go to the expense of professionals?
> I am etc
> SPECTATOR
> Llanelly, Aug 30

They did not, however, appear to be a strong amateur side. The *Star* bewailed the fact that they had played Swansea four times during the season and lost all four, regretting the weakness of the attack and commenting that 'the bowling has been feeble all through'[6].Now aged 36, the same age as George when he died, Joshua seems to have done little to compensate for that weakness. He appears not to have played again.

He is remembered with no great affection by the family. He married Florence Pritchard but, though never formally divorced, they lived apart for many years, and correspondence between the two was routed through solicitors. His drink problem continued until his death in Liverpool in 1946, just two weeks before that of his widow in the same city where she had gone to sort out his affairs.

The Pattle Brothers

THE FORMER Joseph Pattle continued treading the boards with some success, his *Fully Licensed Man* being recited more than 11,000 times. Among other recitations were *Eving's Dorg 'Orspital, Who'll buy a Blood Orange?*, and *On Strike,* written in 1906, which could perhaps have served as a fitting accompaniment to his half-brother's activity ten years earlier.

> Now I'm a paper-'anger by trade I am and wild 'orses can't drag me from paper-'anging
> The very last time I picked hup my tools was seven year ago
> They tried it on wiv me but it didn't come orf
> They didn't know 'oo they was a-deal in wiv
> I got the money what I arsked afore I started on me job which was the stripping of a wall
> I called up the foreman
> What's the matter wiv you? 'e says
> I says, 'Look at this old bell wire in the wall'.
> 'Pull it aht' 'e says
> 'What?' I says
> 'Pull it aht' 'e says
> I says, 'You'll pardon me, that's plumber's work'. And I lays dahn me tools.
> And when I lays dahn me tools, I lays 'em dahn.

Stanley Holloway recorded the monologue in 1957. Though less well known than *Wallace the Lion* and *Pick oop tha Musket*, it was in distinguished company.

> Pond ended his days in poverty, living in a bed-sitting room the furnishings of which were restricted to little more than a bed and a grand piano. In his later days he lapsed into eccentricity and was often to be seen in Charing Cross Road, but never without a top hat. He died in 1931.[7]

Henry Pattle, aged 47, had a less adventurous, but perhaps more stable life than his younger brother, remaining in the City. In 1901, calling himself Harry, he was married to Louisa and living in Dorking.

Augusta

FOR FAIRLY obvious reasons, the family name was Anglicised to 'Loman' during the First World War, some two centuries after their ancestors' arrival in England with the Elector of Hanover.

George's father, however remained 'Lohmann' until the end of his life in 1919. He died at 2 Upper Beulah Hill, Norwood, on 25 October of what his death certificate describes as 'senile dementia 4 months'. He was 86. The informant was Walter Quaife, son-in-law, a name which will be not unknown to those familiar with the history of Sussex or Warwickshire cricket. Quaife's second marriage was to Augusta Elizabeth, the younger of George's two sisters, in King's Norton in 1904. In evidence given at his earlier divorce case in 1902,[8] Quaife stated that they had met fourteen years before, placing the beginnings of the relationship very firmly at a time when he and George Lohmann were playing with and against each other.

Quaife and Lohmann first opposed each other almost two decades previously in 1885 when they were both young professionals with their respective counties and continued to do so on several occasions after that. In July 1887, the pair had played together for the Players of the South against the Players of the North at Beckenham and in August 1887 at Hove they each scored a century (coincidentally Quaife was c Lohmann and Lohmann c Quaife) and three weeks later were the subject of what Lillywhite's *Cricketers' Annual* records in its catalogue of 'Curious Incidents',

> Quaife, the young Sussex professional, in playing forward to Lohmann at the Oval, in the Surrey match on August, the ball beat him altogether and he lost his balance. Thinking he had been bowled from the noise of the ball hitting the wicket, which it did without dislodging either of the bails, he left his ground apparently under the impression that he was out and was promptly stumped by the Surrey wicket-keeper.

It could not have happened today: the umpires would have been obliged to intervene under Law 27.7 *Batsman leaving wicket under a misapprehension*. The Surrey wicket-keeper on this occasion was Henry Wood who nine years later was to spill the beans to the *Daily Mail* on the treatment of professionals. Coming events cast their shadows before and as well as the Lohmann–Wood newspaper interviews, perhaps we have here the beginnings of the Lohmann–Quaife relationship. Then, as now, professional county cricketers were a tight-knit community, but then, unlike now, they were not accommodated in four and five star hotels during away matches and had usually to finance their board and lodgings from their match fee. It is likely that informal reciprocal accommodation arrangements existed and though it is impossible to say with any certainty, it is at least within the bounds of possibility that the future bride and groom, then aged 18 and 23 respectively, met in this way.

During the intervening seventeen years, Walter and his younger brother, William (W G) had left their native Sussex for Warwickshire, a move which resulted in years of acrimony between the two county committees. Walter had also met, married, had three children by and divorced Alice Birch, a schoolmaster's daughter from Islington.

Before the Matrimonial Causes Act of 1857, divorce was almost unknown and, at around £700 for an uncontested case and into four figures for a contested one, the preserve of the very rich. In the wake of that Act, the number of divorces rose from about two per annum to about 200, the social stigma and the influence of the church keeping the number within bounds. Changing attitudes resulted in an increase to about 20,000 by 1961 and since then there has been a tenfold rise to some 200,000. So, a century after the Quaife v Quaife case, divorce has become almost the norm, but at the beginning of the twentieth century it was relatively rare and court cases were not dismissed in a couple of lines, but were newsworthy items for the local and national press.

Court papers on divorce proceedings are closed for a hundred years, presumably to protect any surviving relatives, though with rare exceptions, there was and is no bar to media coverage. Those on the Quaife divorce cover a period from August 1901 to March 1903[9] and, only recently available, reveal a tale which a century later would have billboards for the tabloids screaming 'Cricket Pro in Love Nest with England Star's Sister'.

Augusta was mentioned in the petitioner's submission as living in an adulterous relationship with Quaife at 4 Wyndham Road, Edgbaston. Walter and Alice had two children, Beatrice, born in March 1893 and Arthur Walter in May 1897. A third was on the way and this was a turn of events clearly not to Walter's liking. He suggested an abortion, Alice's absence to be disguised under the veneer of a holiday. He would make all the arrangements. Abortion was illegal at the time, so it can be surmised that Quaife had been through the process before or had access to sources who knew what was to be done.

Among the grounds for divorce were adultery, desertion and cruelty and there were elements of all three here, though the court papers quote 'adultery coupled with cruelty'. Walter's conduct towards Alice was less than exemplary as he taunts her with having no spirit, with not having relationships with other men, saying that it was her own fault that she was pregnant, calling her a fool and an idiot, threatening to have her confined to an asylum, employing such physical violence as caused bruising to her arms and breasts and finally saying that he could not have two wives and as he loved Augusta Lohmann, he would opt for her. Quaife, through his solicitors, had made a formal denial of the charges, but at the hearing counsel for Alice Quaife demonstrated otherwise, saying,

> …the parties were married on March 9 1892, at St Andrew's Church, Islington, and that there had been three children issue of the marriage. The respondent was the well-known cricketer and a member of the Warwickshire eleven. The parties had lived happily until after the birth of her first child in 1893, when the petitioner became aware that her husband was corresponding with a Miss Lohmann. He had wished this lady to accompany him to the seaside but she had declined to do so. The petitioner, on discovering what

was going on, wrote to the lady and to her father and the correspondence ceased. In 1898, the petitioner discovered that her husband was carrying on an intrigue with another lady; but after they had both admitted it, she forgave them and that intimacy entirely ceased. After that the petitioner lived on fairly happy terms with her husband although she never felt that she had his affection. In November 1900, however, on one occasion when she had to correct one of the children, the respondent threatened to assault her and offered her £2 a week to leave him. In April 1901, the petitioner discovered that she was *enceinte*, and the respondent then urged her to take drugs, and when she refused urged her to undergo an illegal operation. During the month of June he was continually taunting her, and told her that he intended to live with Miss Lohmann and that no power in heaven or earth would prevent him. He also suggested to her that if she had been a woman of any spirit, she would have left him years before. Finally, on June 18, matters reached a climax. Some discussion arose about Miss Lohmann, and the petitioner suggested that she (the petitioner) seemed to be in the respondent's way. He replied that he or she must leave the house; and on her suggesting that she would go he flew at her, pressed his knee against her abdomen and forced her into a chair, telling her that she was mad and must be kept under control. As a result of his violence she was much bruised and had to call in a doctor. Two days later he left home and had since been living *maritalement* with Miss Lohmann.

The petitioner was called, and in cross-examination admitted that she had had in her possession for years drugs for a specific purpose and had purchased them herself.

Mr Le Bas (counsel for Quaife) intimated that he was not in a position to dispute that his client had been living in adultery since June 20 1901.

Evidence was given on the bruises and the adultery.

The respondent was called, and denied that he had ever suggested to his wife that she should either take drugs or submit to an illegal operation. In November 1900, his wife when in a passion struck one of the children, and he did threaten to strike her if she did it again. On June 18 his wife spoke to him about Miss Lohmann, and threatened to commit suicide by cutting her throat. As she was rushing from the room he caught her by the arms and held her down until she was calmed.

Cross-examined – His wife had told him that she had obtained the drugs under medical advice, and he was aware that she had used them. He had never committed adultery with Miss Lohmann until after the date on which he had finally left his wife. His wife had wished him to give up Miss Lohmann, but he had declined to do so.

Mrs Mary Quaife, the wife of William Quaife, now in Australia with Mr

> MacLaren's eleven, said that her brother-in-law always seemed to treat his family with kindness and consideration. The petitioner had never complained about his conduct until after he had left her.
>
> Other rebutting evidence having been given, counsel addressed the Court on behalf of their respective clients.
>
> The PRESIDENT said that he might at once dismiss the charge of an illegal operation, as such a charge as that would require very different evidence to prove it than that which had been given, the more so as the petitioner had herself admitted having taken drugs for a long time past. There was no corroboration of such a serious charge, and he was glad to be able to relieve the correspondent of it. With regard to the threats in November 1900, there did not appear to be much in that; but with regard to the scene of June 18, 1901, the respondent appeared to be totally responsible for what had occurred. He had admitted to his wife an affection for Miss Lohmann, and had thereby assaulted her in a most deadly way, following it up by the use of physical violence. The charge of adultery was admitted and there must therefore be a decree nisi, with costs and the custody of the children.[10]

The divorce was made absolute on 30 March 1903. The cost of the court proceedings, met by the defendant, were almost £120 and maintenance payments set at £1 per week, so although he played in only four first-class matches in 1901 and none at all after that, Walter needed a continuing income to support two families. He and Augusta were married in King's Norton Registry Office on 12 March 1904. She was now 34, although she claimed on her marriage certificate to be 31. Their first child, Dorothy, was born on 13 August, so the marriage was clearly accelerated by, perhaps even occasioned by Augusta's pregnancy, the social stigma of illegitimacy and bearing an illegitimate child being as significant then as it is insignificant now. Some time later they moved to Ipswich where Walter continued his cricket career with Suffolk and was in business as an 'Athletic Outfitter'. The business was an offshoot of the family business which Walter had established with his rather better known brother, William. The firm later became Quaife and Lilley when another famous Warwickshire professional became involved and survived in that form until it was sold in the 1960s by William's son, Bernard, who had taken over the business.

A second daughter, Phyllis was born in 1909. According to the birth certificate it looks as though by this time Augusta is using her second name of Elizabeth. At some stage over the next ten years they moved to London to look after Walter's ageing father-in-law.

The Family after George's Death

1 *Cricket* 30 March 1898
2 *Newcastle Daily Chronicle* 29 August 1910
3 Sissons *George Lohmann: The beau ideal* p 58
4 *Llanelly Star* 4 March 1911
5 *Llanelly Star* 22 July 1911
6 9 September 1911
7 Obituary in *The Performer* 21 October 1931
8 *Birmingham Daily Post* 12 March 1902
9 High Court of Justice – Probate, Divorce and Admiralty Division
10 *The Times* 12 March 1902

CHAPTER 24

BOWLING ANALYSIS – AND EXTRAS

A bowler of infinite variety
A splendid field and a resolute batsman
From Lohmann's epitaph at Pieter Meintjies

UNTIL THE early part of the nineteenth century, all bowling was underarm, the Laws specifying that the hand had to be below the elbow. The history of bowling through that century is one of gradual transition from that style through roundarm to the acceptance and eventual domination of overarm bowling. Underarm bowling was a rarity in the twentieth century and the wheel came full circle when in the 2000 Code of the Laws of Cricket, underarm bowling became illegal 'except by special arrangement before the match'.[1] The first known reference to roundarm bowling is in the *Sporting Magazine* of 1807. It became known as 'Sussex bowling' or 'throwing style' and was first introduced to the game by John Willes of that county. According to cricket folklore it was his sister who first gave him the idea, her voluminous crinoline preventing her from bowling in the conventional way and obliging her to adopt a roundarm style. When Willes tried it for Kent against the MCC in 1822, he was no balled for throwing and left the match determined never to play the game again. Whether he did or not, he had made his contribution to the evolution of the Laws. MCC subsequently authorised the raising of the arm to the level of the shoulder.

By 1862 there had been some experimentation with 'overhand' bowling and the controversy of forty years earlier was resurrected at a higher level, this time above the elbow. Edgar Willsher of Kent was no balled for doing just that; as a result play was abandoned for the day, umpire John Lillywhite was replaced and the Laws changed again in 1864 to allow the hand to be raised above the elbow. Hence, what is now the universally accepted method of delivering the ball had only legally been in use for twenty years when Lohmann began his career and was still at an elementary level of sophistication. He learned from his predecessors and contemporaries, moved the art of medium pace bowling forward and whether they realised it or not, bowlers of the twentieth century owed him much.

In 1882, Australia had won a famous Test match at The Oval. It was a watershed in the history of the game, though in establishment circles the view persisted that the game was essentially about batting, that bowlers were there simply to put the ball into play and fielding was a chore to be endured between innings. The 'colonials' had demonstrated that bowling and fielding skills have their part to play in winning matches and the legalisation of overarm bowling within the preceding twenty years had paved the way for a new approach in which Australian bowlers, especially the 'Demon' Spofforth, were pioneers.

The launch of Charles Alcock's weekly magazine *Cricket* the same year and the competition between *Wisden* and the Lillywhite publications meant that analysis of cricket style and tactics became more sophisticated.

In Lohmann's day, bowling was based very much on off theory, few fielders being placed on the leg side. The 'pull' as pioneered by Walter Read was relatively novel and leg theory was not to be perfected until some time into the next century.

Lord Harris who had captained England in the first Test against Australia on English soil was not slow to acknowledge the Antipodean influence.

> ...a bowler tries, he is not always successful of course, to get the batsman to play forward at short balls, and back at pitched up ones, in the hope that the ball may take whichever break may have been put on and so beat the bat. Spofforth has wonderful power in putting on break, chiefly from the off... their [Spofforth and Palmer] chief excellence is in bowling a good length; neither break or direction of themselves are much use. A good length is everything; it makes a batsman 'feel' for the ball. When to a good length direction and break are added you have found a first-class bowler... I might add that they [the Australians] always bowled to hit the sticks. Now when the Australians first came here we had got into a slovenly kind of artifice. We did not always bowl dead on the wicket but bowled a great deal to the off for catches. Good batsmen playing with judgment made fine scores off this kind of bowling and became a little puzzled when Spofforth and the other Australians went at their stumps with every ball.[2]

It was a sound basis for the science of bowling which George Lohmann was to take further forward and increase in sophistication. He was in his early teens, playing for the Alma Club, when in 1878 Fred Spofforth began teaching England a few lessons – lessons he was to repeat in 1880 and 1882. In his 'chat' with W E Bettesworth, Lohmann denies using any particular bowler as what would today be termed a 'rôle model', but he does admit to an enthusiasm for taking his sandwiches to The Oval and watching cricket and while it cannot be said for certain that he saw Spofforth at that time, the likelihood is that as a young cricket enthusiast, he would have been at the Kennington Oval on occasions when the master-bowler was playing there and his cricketing intelligence was such that he could not fail to learn something. From an early age, he acknowledged the need to learn from other, more experienced bowlers.

> As a small boy at school I used to get many wickets, and I always had a slight idea of varying my pace. Of course, when I began to play in better cricket, I saw that other bowlers did certain things which were effective, and I tried to do as they did. But I always bowled in about the same style as I do now...[3]

Writing towards the end of the century, the Hon R H Lyttelton says of Spofforth,

> I regard him as the greatest bowler the world has ever seen. He has tried and succeeded in all paces, except, perhaps, the very slow; and has bowled in two hemispheres on every variety of wicket, and against the leading batsmen of the world... In 1878 he was a first-rate fast bowler; in the subsequent years he was a bowler who had mastered every trick of the trade; he learnt variety of pace and variety of length; he studied the whole art and there was nothing to be mastered. So perfect was his command of the ball that Blackham earned undying fame by proving to the world that however fast the bowling, provided it be accurate, a long-stop could be dispensed with. So very rarely did he send down a half volley on the leg side, that Boyle had no hesitation in standing only a few yards from the bat, in front of the wicket on the on side. Both these methods were absolutely new to English cricketers... Spofforth did not bowl for maidens but for wickets...[4]

Similarly, Lohmann was soon to develop the art of mixing the skills of fast and slow bowling and mastering the art of flight, cut and variation of pace. The terminology may be a little different, but consciously or otherwise, Lyttelton draws a parallel between the two bowlers.

> From the year 1884 to 1892 there was hardly a victory gained by Surrey for which Lohmann was not largely responsible. He was generally bowling with variety, break and good length. Lohmann was one of the players who made cricket an attractive game to watch. He did not bowl

for maidens, so the other side did not often play a slow game. Bowling... was his speciality: and I have frequently, during the last few years, felt that to win back our old position as bowlers it is absolutely necessary that Englishmen should copy Lohmann's method of variety of pace, pitch and indifference to being hit. If a bowler can make the ball break, take odd curves and come off the ground at different paces, you find the batsman mistime, because he expects some eccentricity, and is deceived by a plain long-hop or ordinary ball... The real merit of Lohmann's bowling... was its deceptive length. Every ball to the spectator appeared to be right up, even a half-volley, because the flight of the ball was high in the air at first, but it dropped rapidly, and the batsman attempting to hit found himself far from the pitch of the ball and struck under it rather than over it.[5]

However, who better to comment on Lohmann's bowling than Lohmann himself who contributed the following page to the 1890 *Wisden*[6].

The chief characteristics of an effective bowler are good length, break, a tendency to rear up quickly from the pitch, and a deceptive delivery. This last is perhaps more important than any of the others, as, for instance, a ball which a batsman imagines is coming faster or slower than it really is very often proves fatal through his failing to time his stroke. I think this is the reason why so many men are bowled by 'yorkers', while some return the ball tamely to the bowler or poke it up by playing too soon. A good length ball loses half its terrors if bowled over after over on a good wicket, as a batsman becomes accustomed to it, and soon begins to punish this orthodox ball. But if the bowler is able to put one in now and then which is, from the style of his delivery, apparently a very fast ball, but really a slow or medium one, the batsman will not dare to take any liberties and will probably feel a little abroad. Some batsmen are puzzled by a ball which pitches on the off and breaks away from the wicket and which consequently is only half hit, and there may be a catch on the off side. The same rule applies to this ball as to any other – its frequency will lessen its destructiveness; therefore it should be varied by a break from the off to the wicket, one with nothing at all, or a fast 'yorker' and the batsman, not knowing what is coming next, does not feel so confident or determined as he would do if he had sent the same ball down continually. Care should be taken to make the delivery of these different balls as much alike as possible.

I think it is necessary for a bowler to understand at least the theory of batting, as he is then able to find out the batsman's weak points and bowl accordingly. You cannot lay down any hard and fast rule to break through all defences, for what one man has great difficulty in playing another will score from. The wickets are in such good order nowadays that in dry weather it is no easy matter to get really first-class batsmen out, and you must rely on some little artifice such as I have tried to explain. The ball that takes by surprise is usually the fatal one, and it is the unexpected that batsmen have most reason to dread.

W G Grace writing in *Cricket*[7] emphasises the value of a sideways-on action and of variation in pace.

The great Australian bowlers first taught us the power of a ball bowled slower or faster without a perceptible change of action.

Commenting on Spofforth's mastery of the art, he goes on to say,

Lohmann today is equally effective; and it is simply ludicrous to watch batsman after batsman walk into the trap. After the trick was done one could not help saying: 'What an absolutely simple ball to have been bowled by!' – but all the same, it was a triumph of the bowler's art.

Consequent advice is to bowl straight, bowl a good length, try to get some break on the ball, learn something about the nature and condition of the wicket on which you are bowling, seek for the weak spots in the batsman's defence. As examples of those conforming to these suggestions, he mentions Lohmann, Attewell and Turner as 'three of the most finished bowlers we have at the present time'. More than a century down the road, bowling coaches would still regard those time-honoured basics as the starting point.

Charles Turner, the Australian bowler whose career ran parallel to Lohmann's for a while, was a New South Welshman and in style a direct descendant of Spofforth, bowled in a similar way. When *Wisden* included both Lohmann and Turner in their Six Great Bowlers of the Year, there were comments on the similarity of their styles and approach. Neither was fast, Turner being timed at 55 mph by the Woolwich Arsenal,[8] but both owed their effectiveness to variations in pace.

Lohmann's contemporary, Johnny Briggs, was also aware that a successful bowler needed to put some thought into his bowling, vary his pace and do something in the air, as well as off the pitch. There was a need to,

...feel every finger on the ball – it is only by that means you can work properly... It is all moonshine to suppose that cricket bowlers rely upon the ball touching the ground to work a break... Unless he is capable of putting a little headwork to his bowling he will not long be connected with first-class cricket.[9]

Richard Daft called Lohmann 'a wonderful head bowler', Anglo-Australian colleague Sammy Woods too, analysing 'the greatest English bowlers I played against from 1888 to 1910' commented on his break and variations of angle and pace, though he does not specifically mention the slower ball.

> George Lohmann was a great bowler, especially on a bad wicket, medium pace with one a bit faster. He, on a bad wicket, bowled round the wickets getting lots of break, just enough the width of the bat [sic] He would deliver the faster one which one thought was going to be played to leg. But it pitched on the off stump and if it didn't bowl you it was out if it hit your leg. A great bowler and I dare say the finest ever seen, not excepting R E Foster, Tunnicliffe and Braund.[10]

Sir Pelham Warner was at the beginning of his playing career as Lohmann's was coming to an end, but he too, as founder and editor of *The Cricketer*, had an appreciation of Lohmann's place in the bowling hierarchy and of his technical skill.

> Among the great bowlers of all time Lohmann ranks among the very greatest…
> At the end of the eighties and early nineties Lohmann was the dominating figure in the Surrey eleven. He was a perfect model of a slow to medium bowler with a fine control of length and a master of flight. His action had the slightest suspicion of strain about it, for just before delivering the ball he seemed, as it were, to halt, but his arm was very high and his control of length and break perfect. He made the most of every inch of his six feet, and he was the most flighty bowler we have ever seen. The ball was constantly dropping feet shorter than one anticipated. Lohmann combined with this deceptive flight a quick off-break, and occasionally, a faster ball which went a little with his arm and which he was very fond of bowling on sticky wickets.[11]

Less technical perhaps, but no less complimentary is Rev R S Holmes' later appreciation of Lohmann's art.

> Was there ever a greater bowler of his type? I doubt it. Right-hand medium with an occasional faster ball and a very high delivery, he was a master of length and of flight. He made the ball break very quickly from the off and he could also turn it from leg, though he seldom, I think, did so. He was full of artifices – always trying some fresh device, always varying his pace – never content just to keep the runs down. His object, all the time, was to get the batsman out; and he worked untiringly for this purpose. On the

> field, with the ball in his hand, he was the deadliest of enemies. Off it, he was the most genial of friends.[12]

C B Fry, who toured South Africa with Lohmann in 1895/96, played against him on a number of occasions. His sporting and literary achievements render him a reliable source and he has perhaps the most valuable technical analysis of Lohmann's bowling. Like Johnny Briggs, he acknowledges that the art has a cerebral input.

> He made his own style of bowling and a beautiful style it was – so beautiful that none but a decent cricketer could fully appreciate it. He had a high right-over action which was naturally easy and free-swinging... owing to his naturally high delivery, the ball described a pronounced curve, and dropped rather sooner than the batsman expected. This peculiarity he developed assiduously into a very deceptive ball which he appeared to bowl the same pace, but which really, as it were, held back, causing the unwary and the wary to play too soon. He was a perfect master at varying his pace without betraying the variation to the batsman... he was full of artifices and subtleties, and he kept on trying them all day, each as persistently as the others, one after another. With all his skill he would never have achieved his great feats but for his insistence on purpose. He was what I call a very hostile bowler; he made one feel he was one's deadly enemy. He was by far the most difficult medium-pace bowler I ever played on a good wicket.[13]

W G Grace has a not dissimilar appreciation, though his description of Lohmann as a 'roundarm' bowler is puzzling. All contemporary evidence suggests his arm was high. It can only be assumed that 'roundarm' is used either to mean 'round the wicket' or as the opposite of 'underarm' of which there was still a little around at the time.

> ...today he has no superior as a bowler. Since he first represented his county in 1884, his bowling has been the theme of admiration in England; and very good judges in Australia have said he is the best bowler that ever visited them. He has the enviable and exceptional power of rising to the occasion; and the better the company the better he performs.
>
> He bowls right-hand, round arm, above medium pace – indeed he might almost be classed as fast – has a beautiful action and keeps a splendid length; and he alters his pace without altering his action, which is one of the strongest characteristics of a first-class bowler. His command of the ball is half the secret of his success. To a right-hand batsman he bowls on or just outside the off-stump, and breaks back very quickly, but now and then he puts in a very fast one with a break from leg. Should a left hand batsman

> follow, especially if he can hit well on the leg side, he pitches everything on the wicket or off-stump, varying it with a faster one, breaking slightly from the off to the leg. But the ball he has been as successful with as any is a simple straight good-length one without any break. The batsman expects something exceptional from him every ball and never thinks that he will treat him with such an easy one, and so while he is looking for the break his wicket is bowled down.[14]

H S Altham points out that it is significant that W G Grace and C B Fry both classify Lohmann as the greatest medium pace bowler they played against and their combined experience covers over half a century.

There was no provision for the taking of a new ball during an innings before 1907 and the seam on the ball was less prominent and the lacquer less glossy than they were to become in the twentieth century. Swing and seam bowling were not therefore part of the bowler's weaponry. Swing was later to be developed by George Hirst, reverse swing later still and while the 'break' and 'work' on the ball described in contemporary accounts, included an element of 'cut' allied with finger spin, later developed and perfected by Sydney Barnes, Lohmann used everything available to him at the time – change of pace, change of angle, flight and, of course, pitches uncovered and less well manicured than those on which his successors were obliged to bowl.

The distinction between finger- and wrist-spin and between spin and cut was not as clear as it is today and Lohmann was to say, in his 'chat' with W A Bettesworth,

> It is a curious thing that on a perfect wicket a leg break bowler can get some work on the ball, but I have never seen an off-break bowler who could do it except Richardson.[15]

It is generally accepted in the game that one of the most valuable opinions on how the ball and wicket are behaving is that of the wicket-keeper. Henry Wood who kept to Lohmann probably more than anyone else when asked which bowler was the most difficult to take, replied,

> Well, I think Lohmann was the worst, because he made the ball come back so quickly and one was very likely to lose sight of it. He used to bowl a ball which pitched just off the off stump and missed the leg stump by a hair's breadth, and it was very difficult to take that, especially if the batsman turned it ever so little.[16]

While Lohmann and most of those who commentated on his bowling have invariably pointed to variations of pace and flight, there is not much indication of how he did it without varying the pace of the delivery arm. If he followed the example of Spofforth, whom he had seen, and against whom he played in 1886, then it was by holding the ball more loosely in the fingers or gripping only half of the ball so that the speed of the ball was disguised by the speed of the arm or alternatively by bowling a finger spun off-break rather than a seam-induced off-cutter. Flight and the famous 'hanging ball' the technique of which was passed on to Jimmy Sinclair would have been achieved by varying the point at which the ball left the hand.

But in addition to all his technical skill, Lohmann had another string to his bow – psychology, the ability to 'talk a batsman out' – not the art of full-blown sledging that it was to become in Australian mouths in the next century, but an attempt at gentle, mental disintegration which worked more often than not. In his 'chat' with Lohmann, W A Bettesworth reproduces the words of Stanley Scott who played for Middlesex from 1878 to 1893, a period covering the whole of Lohmann's pre-South Africa first-class career.

> He seems to me to be more fertile of resource than any man I ever played against. After being hit he will smile and give you another to hit. Often he used to say to me 'When are you going to have another hit?' although he knew as well as I did that it entirely depended on him. He knew one's favourite ball, and one had it lots of times – generally once too often.[17]

It was part of Lohmann's psychological strategy, part of his cricket brain. Maurice Read, his closest friend in the Surrey team who played alongside him through ten seasons and three tours of Australia and accompanied him on his first trip to South Africa, had plenty of opportunity to witness the Lohmann approach at close quarters.

> …often when on good wickets we could not part the batsmen he has said to me, 'Look out, I'm not going to bowl at the sticks now' and then he would send in anything in order to get the batsmen to hit.[18]
> This 'neither fast nor slow man'[19] embodies very aptly and beautifully the kind of bowler George Lohmann was. No previous bowler of any period has enjoyed quite such command of pace and spin as he. Agile as a panther, he never bowled two consecutive balls alike. A 'fast' bowler in that sense of the word he never was, yet the batsman did not know what kind of ball was coming next and as the ball 'always came with his arm' his off- and leg breaks were almost equally dangerous. 'We shall not look upon his like again'.[20]

In a similar vein, F S Ashley-Cooper was to write,

> He combined the art of the slow bowler with that of the fast, and was, with perhaps a couple of exceptions, the best match winner England has possessed during modern times.[21]

In the decade in which Lohmann played Test cricket from 1886 to 1896, England's main bowlers were Briggs, Peel and himself, although Richardson had begun to make an impact towards the end of that time and neither Briggs nor Peel was on the 1895/96 tour of South Africa. Overall, Lohmann has the lowest Test bowling average (10.75) of the three, although of course, it is artificially deflated by his performances in South Africa. Briggs' final Test career average (17.74) also owes something to his 15-28 at Newlands in 1888/89, while Peel's (16.81) does not benefit from performances against the weakest of the Test-playing countries.

Against Australia alone, however, Lohmann still has the lowest average (13, against Peel's 16.8 and Briggs' 20.5). However, Briggs and Peel were both on the 1894/95 tour which Lohmann missed through illness and Briggs on the 1897/98 tour. On both occasions, scores were much higher than they were on Lohmann's three tours of 1886/87, 1887/88 and 1891/92. It is perhaps a circular argument. Maybe if Lohmann had still been fit for the later tours, the scores would not have been quite as high. It is all hypothetical.

The picture is again different in the matches in which all three or two of the three played together. Lohmann and Briggs played together in ten Tests, Lohmann and Peel in eight, and there were five Tests in which all three featured. In terms of both average runs per wicket and strike-rate, the northerners emerge marginally superior.[22] That is not to say that Briggs and Peel were necessarily 'better' bowlers; one would need to take account of whether the wicket favoured spin-bowling, whom they dismissed, in what circumstances etc. Statistics – particularly cricket statistics – rarely prove everything. On the other hand, they rarely prove nothing either and it can be said without serious fear of contradiction that, irrespective of bowling figures, the trio operated as a unit which contributed to making the decade between 1886 and 1896 one of the most bowler-dominated in the history of the game.

Batting and Fielding

AT A time when fielding was regarded, especially by the amateurs, as an activity to fill the time between batting and bowling sessions, Lohmann was one of the first Englishmen to follow the Australian example and acknowledge and pioneer the importance of this aspect of the game. His slip fielding especially was world-class, as a number of knowledgeable commentators have indicated.

> Many great slip fieldsmen have appeared since his day but never a greater, his activity being cat-like, and his hands supremely safe.[23]

W G Grace describes him as,

> ...a marvel: he seems to be able to get to everything within six feet of him; and anything he can reach he can hold. Time after time I have seen him go head over heels in trying for an almost impossible catch; but rarely if ever did he lose hold of the ball.[24]

Henry Wood, again perhaps better equipped to comment than most, says on the subject of short slips,

> Men like Abel and Lohmann are like cats, and in addition to taking what comes straight to them manage somehow or other to bring off the most astounding catches. Lohmann had a way of throwing himself at the ball, and seemed to be able to stretch almost any distance. He would sometimes throw himself right off his feet and land on his knees, and make a catch which no other man would have thought of. I have sometimes wondered whether his illness is not partly caused by the great strain which he must often have put upon himself at slip.[25]

He was not quite infallible, however. Even Homer nods occasionally and F E Lacey, later knighted for his services to the game as secretary of MCC, recalls an incident in a Gentlemen v Players match at Scarborough.

> I was fielding at short-slip... and the man who was standing extra-slip had to leave the field. Lohmann came out as substitute. Now Lohmann was, of course, about the best short-slip in the world and I was very glad of a chance to give up my position. I asked him to take my place while I went extra-slip where I felt more comfortable. The very next ball was a 'gaper' to Lohmann at short- slip and he missed it![26]

The incident must have been in 1892, the only occasion Lohmann played in the Scarborough version of Gentlemen v Players. A cynical view might be that Lohmann, fielding as substitute for the opposition, might well be clever enough to disguise a deliberate drop as accidental.

There is some inconsistency in the literature as to whether Lohmann was a specialist short-slip or extra-slip. P F Warner in *The Book of Cricket* describes Lohmann as the greatest 'extra slip'. The sensible conclusion is that he excelled at both. Techniques are not worlds apart. The coaching mantra is that first (short) slip watches the ball from the bowler's hand, while second (extra or cover) slip watches the edge of the bat.

However, notwithstanding the occasional lapse, Lohmann's reputation as a fielder was such that he was invited to contribute a feature to the 1893 edition of *Wisden*. He advocates more fielding practice and the development of fielders for specialist positions, as well as encapsulating his own approach to the game.

> A FEW WORDS ON FIELDING
> BY GEORGE LOHMANN
>
> ONE fact that has struck me during the seven or eight years I have played the game is that the keenest cricketers are the best fieldsmen, and for the simple reason that they are always watching the game very attentively and are always on the alert, consequently they start more quickly to get to the ball when more negligent fieldsmen would think to themselves, 'Oh, I couldn't have caught that – if I had tried.' To try is the thing. How often have we seen Woods, Briggs, Stoddart, Maurice Read, Gunn, Abel, Attewell, Peel, and others bring off catches on the off side and stop balls that have appeared at first almost impossible.
>
> Now, we have all heard cricketers remark, 'Oh, I like fielding there – I rather fancy myself in that position,' and it should be the object of a captain to discover the place best suited to different fieldsmen. Sharpe is a most notable instance of being a brilliant field at mid-off, but moderate in other places. On the other hand we have Abel (whose ability at short-slip all the cricket world knows) equally as good in the country as in the position in which he usually stands. I have seen him make some very fine catches near the boundary, and I can only say that unfortunately there are not many Abels about.
>
> Most men can ground-field well, because the leading enclosures are in such good condition nowadays (especially that at Old Trafford, Manchester) that there is little difficulty in picking a ball up quickly…
>
> One little piece of advice before I close – that is, that captains of local clubs (we all know that far too many catches are dropped) should allow two bowlers at one net and the others out in the field. After the batsmen have had their turn, put a good hitter in to send catches, and in four or five weeks, those fieldsmen will want catches instead of wishing to avoid them.[27]

In today's terms, despite such accolades as 'the world's greatest all-rounder', Lohmann was a 'bowling all-rounder', as his first-class career record of 1,841 wickets and 7,241 runs indicates. He was in the top flight as a bowler and slip-fielder, but, if perhaps not international standard as a batsman, probably good enough to hold a place on his batting alone at county level. He saw himself primarily as a bowler and, on his own admission, batting as very much his second suit.

Nevertheless, that second suit was stronger than many players' first.

> ...it must not be forgotten that even if he had never taken a wicket in the course of his long career he would always have deserved his place in the team for his batting and fielding alone. In fielding he was unsurpassed.[28]

However, he had an uncanny ability to produce the goods when it mattered and did so on a number of occasions.

> If not exactly a sound batsman, Lohmann was a daring and dashing cricketer who was always at his best when runs were needed.[29]

Fry believed Lohmann did not fulfil his potential as a batsman, reporting Lohmann's attitude that, except when he had to, he did not care for making runs as he maintained it affected his sense of touch, the ball feeling like a lump of dough after a while instead of the notes of a piano.[30]

It is batsmen who take the glamour in cricket – and the knighthoods. It was once said that the last bowler to be knighted was Sir Francis Drake. Now Sir Richard Hadlee and Sir Alec Bedser are in the frame. In different circumstances in a different era, so might Lohmann have been. He blazed the trail for others to follow.

1 Laws of Cricket 24 1(b)
2 *Cricket* 24 September 1885 – reproduced from interview with Lord Harris from *Daily News* of 22 September under 'Workers and their Work'
3 Bettesworth *op cit*
4 *Giants of the Game* pp 27-28
5 Ib pp 59-60
6 p xlvii
7 'Forty Years of Cricket'. *Cricket* 30 October 1890
8 Sissons *George Lohmann: The beau ideal* p 29
9 Richard Hobson *Johnny Briggs Remembered*
10 'My Reminiscences' – *The Cricketer* 1 September 1923
11 *The Cricketer* 25 August 1925
12 *Cricket Memories* p 63
13 *The Cricketer* 23 August 1941
14 Grace *Cricket* p 336
15 Bettesworth *op cit*
16 Bettesworth *Chats on the Cricket Field – The Cricket Field* 31 March 1894
17 Bettesworth *op cit*
18 Bettesworth *op cit*
19 Norman Gale *The Hope of Surrey* see Appendix D pp 329–330
20 Standing *Cricket of Today* p 3
21 Note by F S Ashley-Cooper – to Bettesworth 'Chat' 1910

22 Peter Caswell 'Fresh Light on Some 19th Century Bowlers'. *Cricket Lore* Aug 2001 p18
23 P F Warner *The Cricketer* 25 August 1925
24 *Cricket* pp 258
25 Bettesworth *Chats on the Cricket Field – The Cricket Field* 31 March 1894
26 Bettesworth *Chats on the Cricket Field – Cricket* 5 May 1898
27 *Wisden* 1893 p xlix
28 Bettesworth *op cit*
29 P F Warner *The Cricketer* 25 August 1925
30 Fry *Life Worth Living* p 130

CHAPTER 25

PERSONALITY AND POLITICS

...a gentleman to his finger-tips
W G Grace

A Popular Man with a Sense of Humour

> 'Our George' as the Surrey crowd loved to call him was a tall, fair-haired, good-looking man with very broad shoulders, who loved cricket with a rare enthusiasm, and he had every claim to be considered the finest all-round cricketer who ever played for Surrey. He was a charming man with nice manners and everyone who knew him felt keenly his early death from consumption in December 1901.[1]

THUS WAS Lohmann summed up a quarter of a century after his death by Sir Pelham Warner, establishment man par excellence and critical of Lohmann's rôle in the 1896 strike. He came to know Lohmann very well on Lord Hawke's 1898/99 tour of South Africa and found his enthusiastic talk about cricket on the long train journeys undertaken 'positively delightful'.

Of Lohmann's charm and attendant sense of humour, there is ample contemporary evidence.

> An amusing story is now going the rounds about George Lohmann and Abel, two congenial spirits, who were once playing in an all-England match against a local twenty-two. The ground was connected with a sort of fair, where Aunt Sallies, cocoa-nut shies and similar attractions were provided. The last man of the twenty-two went in with only a few runs wanted to win and the ball was hit down to the cocoa-nuts where Lohmann was fielding. Quite equal to the occasion and without looking at the ball, he threw up a cocoa-nut to Abel, who whipped off the bails, running a batsman out, and pocketing the cocoa-nut, and the eleven retired to the tent with the blushing honours of victory still upon them, their opponents being quite unconscious that the game had not been won in a legitimate way.[2]

Similarly,

> Cricketers are not above a little game of spoof. In the *Diggers News* yesterday appeared an account of a single wicket match at the Wanderers between G Allsop and J H Sinclair, stating 'that it drew a fairly large crowd to Kruger's Park, and that it was played under the usual conditions of singlewicket matches'. The names of the fielders and umpires were given, and the huge hits of J H Sinclair described. All spoof! The 'match' was played on a table in the Social Club, with a contrivance called parlour cricket brought out by George Lohmann. It is intended to send to the *Diggers News* the date of the return match.[3]

He was also a respected story-teller. Alfred Gibson recounts, albeit second-hand,

> It was in an up-country match in Australia – all the funny things happen there! – and Pilling finely stumped a batsman off a ball from George. To general amazement the umpire stentoriously gave 'Not out!' When asked whether he knew the game, he smiled sardonically. He said, 'Bowling I holds with, catching I holds with but when it comes to bowling a man from behind – no, you don't catch Joe Robinson napping, even if you do come from England.'[4]

Likewise, in his interview with the *Cape Argus* on his arrival from England for the second time in 1893, he keeps an admiring circle of followers entertained with the following tale.

> I remember that on one occasion we were playing at Hobart, Tasmania. We had got about four or five wickets down against the Tasmanian eighteen when a fellow walked in to bat and came straight up to me – I was bowling at the time – saying 'I've got a bet on for 'a tenner' that I make four runs.' I replied 'All right. Look out! I'll give you one on the leg side.' His rejoinder was 'Which side is that?' 'Outside your legs' I retorted. 'All right' says he 'I don't know much about it but I'll try.' The first ball I bowled he missed but the next he hit to the boundary, which of course counted for four runs. What was my astonishment to see him, immediately after his achievement, walk to the pavilion! I called for him to come back, telling him he wasn't out but had made four runs. 'It's all right,' he assured me, 'I'm going to look after that bloke I made the bet with.'

His meeting Solly Joel in Bloemfontein following Woolf's murder is the mark of a humane man, a humanity and an ability to relate to people reflected in his several magazine and newspaper interviews. All contemporary evidence points to his geniality and popularity. There is little support for the view of David Lemmon, the author of Surrey CCC's official history, that Lohmann was not the easiest of men – except when it came to financial negotiations.

A Ladies Man?

IT HAS been suggested by Sir Home Gordon, joint author (with Lord Harris and Lord Hawke) of the W G Grace Memorial Biography, that Lohmann had 'a weakness for women'.[5] There is little evidence of this beyond the quite unconvincing references to a lady in Melbourne in 1892 and the equally tenuous possibility of a fiancée and/or housekeeper just before his death in 1901. However, unlike their counterparts of the following century, prominent entertainers and politicians were exempt from the intrusions of the tabloid press into their private lives, so there can be no certainty. It is all too easy to suppose that because a man is attractive to women, he is also attracted by them, a reasonable assumption in the case of a Beckham or a Best, but not invariably so.

Doubtless his wealth and fame as an international sportsman would have been an attraction and there seems little doubt that he had charm, good manners and breeding. Tall and well built (5ft 10ins and 12st 10lbs), photographic evidence and contemporary interviews suggest that his Aryan good looks and brown eyes would have made him physically attractive to women. On the 1891/92 tour of Australia, when he was 26, before tuberculosis had ravaged his complexion, the *Bulletin* opined,

> Stoddart and Lohmann are the best-looking men in the English eleven.[6]

It was on the same tour that W G Grace remarked that all the ladies were in love with George following a demonstration of his picnic organising skills.

Did he respond or was he differently inclined? Certainly he had a number of close male acquaintances especially Maurice Read and his Andover friends, Dr Farr and Mr Best, but whether there were any sexual overtones to any of these relationships is a matter of speculation. There are further clues in the fact that he complemented his good looks by smart dressing, being 'rather point device in his accoutrements',[7] and that he never married. None of this, however, is remotely conclusive. Despite Victorian prurience, press reports of sexual activities tended to be restricted to those that found their way into the courts. The only sensible conclusions are that we shall never know and, in the context of his personality, politics and contribution to cricket, it matters not in the least.

A Socialist?

HIS FATHER was active in local politics, being a committee member and librarian of the local Liberal Club and Institute.[8] In an interview with the *Clarion*, a left-leaning satirical newspaper of the time, Lohmann admits to admiring the publication very much.[9] That may just be courtesy, but it is probably more than that as the interviewer concludes that he has clearly read it and while that would not necessarily make him a socialist, it does point to his being something of an anti-establishment figure, prepared to challenge the existing order and improve the lot of the professional cricketer. He remained, however, a sportsman not a politician.

He was certainly not a full-blown Marxist, nor a cloth cap socialist à la Keir Hardie, uniting the workers of the world and intent on breaking down social structures based on class in England and colour in South Africa. Not much headway was made in that direction by any one before the First World War. Had he lived, however, he would doubtless have welcomed the eventual changes of the twentieth century, the gradual erosion of a society based on class and its replacement with one in which upward mobility is based on ability and later changes in the treatment of women and ethnic minorities, in short the 'rise of the meritocracy'.

That was all for the future. The socialism with which Lohmann was marginally involved was more concerned with the rights of professional cricketers in a society sharply divided by class. Lohmann was aware of his professional worth. So were many of the professionals he played with and against. The difference was that Lohmann was an educated, articulate man and equipped to do something about it. The 1870 Education Act and organisations such as the WEA would have a role to play, but it would take time and two world wars for a rigid class system with its roots in the feudalism of the Middle Ages to yield to the pressures of the liberal political thought of Lohmann's time.

Unionism and a Sense of Public Duty

THE PROFESSIONALS' strike did not lead to unionism in cricket, the Professional Cricketers' Association not coming into being until 1967. At a time when large-scale trade unionism was becoming the norm in most industries, professional sport lagged behind. Wray Vamplew, the Director of Research in Sports Studies at the University of Stirling and President of the European Committee for Sports History, has suggested that further research is required to determine whether such disputes were the tip of an iceberg of underlying labour unrest. Cricket was perhaps different from association football where the Players' Union was established in 1914, in that there was no maximum wage and that the professionals played with and against those who were perceived by society to be their superiors.

Several factors, says Vamplew, militated against unionism among cricket professionals, among them, the competitive nature of the sport, so that professionals v professionals is perhaps more significant than professionals v the Establishment, and the brevity of their careers which meant time was more profitably spent maximising earnings rather than contemplating collective bargaining.

The capital-labour, management-shop floor division is thus less distinct than in the conventional industrial model and there is perhaps not the same homogeneity of interest as for example, miners or shipyard workers. There is competition on the equivalent of the shopfloor and the interests of professionals of the calibre of the 'Oval Five' had much in common with one another, but perhaps not so much with the rank and file cricket professional. The Surrey committee were not taking a huge risk when they gambled that Lohmann, Gunn, Abel, Hayward and Richardson were easily replaceable with players of sufficient, if not parallel, calibre.

Vamplew suggests that the situation in cricket was not dissimilar to that in racing where there is little common ground between the well-paid top échelon and the vast underlying army of underemployed jockeys. Although Lohmann was always keen to encourage up-and-coming young cricketers and there was recurring antagonism between him and the amateurs, certainly Grace and probably Read, it is clear that in the matter of his own financial interests, he had more in common with Gunn, Shrewsbury and company than the journeyman of the cricket world dependent on payment on a match-by-match basis. While he was in sympathy with the position of common or garden cricket professionals, he was obviously conscious of the fact that they were a mixed group with several levels of ability and that he himself was part of a talented upper layer. Democracy was tempered by meritocracy.

According to Anthony Meredith in *The Demon and the Lobster*, his experience and level-headedness in fiscal matters made him something of a father-figure in dressing rooms.

His business acumen and knowledge and willingness to give advice to those who sought it meant that, although his parting from Surrey caused some acrimonious feeling in the committee room, his loss was keenly felt by his former professional colleagues.

He was involved in the Cricketers' Fund Benevolent Society, his Stock Exchange background providing the financial acumen to play a key rôle in an organisation whose objects were:

(1) The relief of the Cricketers being members of the Society who, from old age, illness, accident or other infirmity, are incapable of following their profession.

(2) The temporary assistance of widows and children of such members left destitute.

Any one deriving a livelihood from the game was eligible. There was an annual subscription of a guinea, following an age-dependent admission fee of £2.10.0 to £10 and benefits were up to £1.10.0 per week for injury and 6/- per week pension, subject to five years' membership.

It is inappropriate to superimpose the social structure of the early twenty-first century on the late nineteenth. It was a time when class mattered and unlike that of the majority of his professional colleagues, Lohmann's background was professional and middle class, rather than artisan and working class and his parental background and stock exchange experience had produced a financial literacy which was superior to that of most of his colleagues. Not only was he a better player than most of his contemporaries; he was better educated, more articulate and aware of his social responsibilities. The stand he took in 1896, was instrumental in paving the way to a doubling of the Test match fee to £20 per match and towards respectable professionalism.

1 *Cricketer* 25 August 1925
2 *The Star* 9 July 1898
3 *The Star* 9 October 1897
4 *Some Cricket Yarns in Cricket's Silver Lining* p 287
5 Barker *Ten Great Bowlers* p 59
6 30 January 1892
7 *Clarion* 23 July 1892
8 *South London Press* 3 May 1884
9 23 July 1892

CHAPTER 26

IN SICKNESS AND IN HEALTH

Everyone who is born holds dual citizenship,
in the kingdom of the well and the kingdom of the sick
Susan Sontag

CURRENT ATTITUDES to fitness are ambivalent. Gymnasia and health clubs have been one of the boom industries of the last decade or more, there is far more awareness of the risks inherent in tobacco and alcohol and greater attention to diet and sexual health, but drug abuse is prevalent and obesity is at record levels. Physiotherapists, fitness advisers and specialist medical and surgical practitioners are now part of the professional sports scene and in scientific terms a great advance on the former 'masseur' or well-intentioned amateur with a bucket of cold water and 'magic sponge', yet television and private transport have reduced many to couch potatoes. It is partly the result of affluence. In some ways we are more fit than our ancestors of three or four generations ago, in others far less so. It is beyond question that the decline of manufacturing and related industries has reduced levels of what might be termed 'natural fitness'. No longer is it possible to whistle down a coal mine and summon a fast bowler; no longer do the successors of Tom Richardson maintain their fitness by walking seven miles to The Oval and the same distance back again each match day. It is rather push-ups in the gym on non-match days, having parked the sponsored car as near as possible to the entrance. The major difference from George Lohmann's day, however, is not that this generation is fitter or less fit than its predecessors, but that reductions in atmospheric pollution and almost immeasurable improvements in hygiene have reduced exposure to the killer diseases of the nineteenth century.

George Lohmann was not the only, nor by any means the youngest, cricketer to die of the disease known in the nineteenth century as 'consumption' and thought to be relievable by clear, dry climates such as that of the Karoo. As Lohmann was launching himself into his first-class career, cricket was mourning the death of William Blackman of Victoria of that 'insidious disease'. He was just twenty-two years old.

Percy McDonnell was not to see 40, Archie Jackson died at 23, the life of Duleepsinhji was similarly curtailed. Bob Appleyard missed two seasons, but happily survived. Outside cricket, tuberculosis claimed the lives of John Keats in his mid-twenties and D H Lawrence in his mid-forties. It was the stuff of opera and romantic fiction, embracing characters such as Verdi's Violetta, Puccini's Mimi and Helen Burns in *Jane Eyre*. In the nineteenth century it was incurable and responsible at various times for between eight and fifteen per cent of all deaths. By the late twentieth century, that figure had fallen to 0.1%.[1] It was the cancer or AIDS of its day. Although almost eradicated in the west, it accounts for three million lives per annum in developing countries.

Tuberculosis is caused by the tubercle bacillus mycobacterium tuberculosis, is spread through the air and affects principally the lungs, though other parts of the body can also succumb. Early diagnosis by X-ray, drugs and lung operations have resulted in the disease now being curable and higher standards of hygiene mean that the incidence has been greatly reduced. In the nineteenth century when antibiotics and anti-microbial medicines were unknown, the only cure was fresh air. In most cases, including Lohmann's the 'cure' was temporary, deferring the inevitable.

Lohmann was a smoker at a time when medical knowledge was unaware of the dangers. That could not have helped. Nor could the polluted London atmosphere. It is estimated that in the 1890s, 200 tons of soot per day were pumped into the air.[2] The industrial revolution had brought with it slum dwellings, overcrowded and poorly ventilated. Standards of hygiene in what was locally called 'marvellous Smellbourne' were also low. His 'overwork' as a bowler has no direct connection with the onset of the disease, except insofar as it would have ultimately caused exhaustion, reducing his resistance to any infection going around.

Lord Harris, in his interview with the *Daily News* in 1885, said,

> ...we should not forget that the spring and autumn work of cricket is hard on the professional. The grass is often wet and he has not his patron's army of boots and shoes to fall back on. Also he becomes very hot with the exertion of bowling and has not a servant as we have to bring us an overcoat after an easy morning's shoot. Consequently pulmonary disease attacks the professional cricketer who rarely makes old bones. Popular as the game is it offers no substantial reward for excellence.[3]

His Lordship's opinion may tell us more about the class system than medical science, but it does give an indication of the vulnerability of professional cricketers to long-term health problems.

Towards the end of the century, there was a better understanding of the disease.

DECREASE OF CONSUMPTION

At a meeting of the Sanitary Inspectors' Association held on Saturday night at Carpenters' Hall, London Wall, Dr Newsholme, Medical Officer of Health of Brighton lectured on the 'Prevention of Tuberculosis'. A quarter of a century since, said the lecturer, tuberculosis was regarded as constitutional or inherited, aggravated by finding unfavourable conditions of life. We know now it is due to a specific microbe introduced into the system from without, and that its entrance could be prevented by appropriate means. Before 1860 the annual death rate was 2565 per million and for the five years ending 1890 only 1635.4. The poorer classes, from overcrowding and numerous other causes were more susceptible to the attack from the 'tubercle bacillus' than the rich.[4]

It remained uncurable until well into the following century, though numerous quack remedies appeared in the pages of the nineteenth century press, such as that for some kind of inhalation mechanism called the 'ammoniaphone' which, it was promised, would last a lifetime, cultivate the voice and immediately relieve asthma, bronchitis and consumption. Despite alleged endorsement by their Royal Highnesses, the Prince and Princess of Wales and Princess Louise and the Rt Hon W E Gladstone, the device does not appear to have revolutionised medical science.

Nor does 'Ayers' Cherry Pectoral'. The manufacturers and copy writers between them may well have gone part way to identifying the causes and found something to relieve the symptoms of coughs and colds, but it was still a long way from being a cure.

DO YOU WANT CONSUMPTION?

We are sure you do not. Nobody wants it. But it comes to many thousands every year. It comes to those who have had coughs and colds until the throat is raw, and the lining membrane of the lungs is infected. Stop your cough when it first appears and you remove the great danger of future trouble.

AYERS' Cherry pectoral

stops coughs of all kinds. It does so because it is a soothing and healing remedy of great power. This makes it the greatest preventative to consumption. It is not a question of many bottles and large doses. A few drops will often make a complete cure. Don't neglect your cough. You cannot afford to run the risk. Ayers' Cherry Pectoral will soothe your throat and quiet your inflamed lungs.[5]

A leader on 'The Consumptive' in the *Cape Argus* on 19 April 1899 commented on the number of passengers bound for South Africa. The disease was 'communicable' rather than 'infectious' and there was a need for the rigorous cleaning of ships and disinfecting of cabins but not for the 'perfect and complete isolation' of hospital ships.

The climate of South Africa, at least that unaffected by the industrial pollution of gold and diamond mining, was seen as a powerful antidote to tuberculosis. The *Cape Argus* of 16 June 1898 contains a long report on a plan to build a home for consumptives. An anonymous donor had given £5,000 on condition that another £5,000 was raised to build a home in or near Kimberley,

> Several prominent residents of Kimberley, having observed a great increase in the number of phthisal cases resorting to Kimberley with the hope of prolonging life, and seeing that the majority of these on arrival cannot avail themselves of the full advantages which the climate offers and which is essential if health is to be at all restored, formed themselves into a committee.

The detrimental effect of tobacco smoke on the lungs was known about, but the 'medical authorities' or, at least, the 'medical authorities' as misrepresented by an industry, not yet subject to the control of the Advertising Standards Authority, suggested that damage could be minimised by the use of cigarette papers.

> Save Your Lungs... Smoke only Ramses Cigarette Papers... The only Paper recommended by the Medical Authorities...[6]

More seriously, medical science was beginning to get to grips with the disease and by the new century, there were reports on Dr Koch's new theory that it was spread by sputum and infected droplets passed by air, rather than caught from animals or milk.[7] All too late, however, to prolong the life of George Lohmann and many of his contemporaries.

1 Nissel *People Count* p 121
2 Walltext at Turner, Whistler, Monet exhibition, Tate Britain 2005
3 *Cricket* 24 September 1885
4 *The Times* 4 January 1897
5 *Cape Times* 31 March 1899 *et passim*
6 *Cricket* 18 July 1895 *et passim*
7 *Daily Mail* 26 July 1901

CHAPTER 27

THE LOHMANN LEGACY

When thou, O Man! hast passed away
And crumbling into dust, hast joined
Thine atom to the ceaseless round
Of time – then shall this silent force
Work on…
Suffice it for us now
To carve a name – or details yield
In the vast plan, worked out by Time
To fill eternity
A Mountain Reverie *Cape Argus* 18 March 1898

Bowling and Fielding

LOHMANN'S PROWESS as a bowler was still in the public mind a decade after he had been at his peak in English cricket. The Whit Monday MCC v Middlesex fixture in 1901 was played for the benefit of Lohmann's erstwhile adversary and colleague, William Gunn. It was the adversarial side that was recalled when the *Daily Telegraph* recalled Gunn's batting at The Oval in 1892.

> It was a tremendous game and the way he and Barnes played for an hour and a quarter against Lockwood and George Lohmann – both of them at their best on a wicket which helped them – was one of the most unforgettable things in modern cricket.[1]

Lohmann was a major factor – it would not be an overstatement to say the major factor – in Surrey's success and a significant part of England's, in the decade spanning the mid 1880s to the mid 1890s, demonstrating that it is principally bowlers who win matches. In so doing, he was the catalyst for a change of emphasis from the gentleman-amateur-batsman to the professional bowler and the public, particularly at The Oval, idolised him. The bowler was no longer there just to put the ball into play. Bowling had become a craft, a science and Lohmann played a major part in moving it forward.

It is at least arguable that Lohmann was England's greatest bowler and Peter Hartland has recently undertaken a detailed statistical analysis,[2] looking at a number of factors such as career averages, performances against Australia, wickets in a season and wickets in a match. From the maelstrom of statistical machinations, Lohmann emerges top of the pile. Variations in conditions, the balance between bat and ball at different eras make it impossible to 'prove' anything by such statistics, but it is incontrovertible that if Lohmann was not England's greatest ever bowler, then he is certainly to be numbered among the best.

Raw pace allied with accuracy is generally a match-winning combination especially in low grade cricket on pitches of indifferent quality. However, the higher the standard of batting and the flatter the pitch the less effective it is likely to be. Self-evidently spin-bowling is less effective on a pitch unresponsive to spin. Consequently, the medium pace bowler who can make the ball 'do' something in the air or in earlier days of the game on a rain-affected pitch comes into his own. It is an art which Lohmann took over from Spofforth, ran in parallel with Turner and passed on to men like Barnes, Tate, Bedser, Appleyard and Underwood.

Indeed, there is an almost uncanny parallel between Lohmann and Bob Appleyard. In Stephen Chalke's and Derek Hodgson's biography of him, Appleyard tells how a blistered right index finger, caused him to experiment with bowling off the second finger which he found he could do with resultant increase in pace, but no change of action. Sir Colin Cowdrey could have been writing about Lohmann when he wrote,

> He possessed astonishing accuracy, bowling from a great height. A slow-medium off-cutter was his stock ball, and by way of contrast, a genuinely spun slow off-spinner – and he could throw in a lethal yorker. He pursued each batsman's weakness with a tenacity and zeal all his own… Appleyard was rarely mastered.[3]

Appleyard was born a quarter of a century after Lohmann died. He also missed two seasons as a result of tuberculosis. It can only be coincidence, though there does seem to be something of a genetic succession.

Lohmann also perfected the art of slip fielding. He missed catches occasionally, as all slip fielders do from time to time, but probably fewer than most, and paved the way for future generations where competence in slip-fielding is an accepted part of the modern game.

Professionalism

THE AMATEUR-PROFESSIONAL divide was part of the cricket scene long before Lohmann arrived on it. It reflected the divisions of society and would continue to do so until its abolition a century after his birth when divisions between the social classes had become more blurred, gentlemen and players were no more and all became 'cricketers'. It was long overdue. Lohmann, however, was an untypical professional, in that he was middle-class, educated and financially literate. He was aware of his value to his employers and in a stronger negotiating position than the journeymen working-class players of earlier decades, dependent on payment by the day or by the match in their playing days and on benefits and hand-outs from their seemingly benevolent employers to fill the gap between retirement and death, not infrequently by their own hand or in the workhouse or asylum.

By contrast, Lohmann, who was nearer the intellectual equal of his employers – indeed, probably the intellectual superior of many of them – was not going to be demeaned and humiliated. When 'demands' or requests were rejected, he was in a financial and professional possession to put up two fingers and go and do his own thing. He was perhaps the yeast in the rise of cricket's meritocracy.

The stand of Lohmann and his colleagues in 1896 had highlighted the position of the cricket professional. Lord Harris's analogy of the agricultural labourer and skilled artisan was only partially relevant. Skilled artisans have an important rôle to play in society, but do not generally attract five-figure audiences. Five years later, the *Daily Telegraph*, in its review of a new book by Captain Philip Trevor[4] deplores the idea of player unionism, but acknowledges the need for a fairer distribution of proceeds between 'owners' and 'workers'.

> In his concluding chapter Captain Trevor deals with cricket as a profession and forcibly points out how precarious is the lot of the professional cricketer. The pay of the great professional is disproportionate to his skills and the money he attracts into the coffers of those who pay him; while the pay of the ordinary professional varies undesirably in accordance with the locality in which he is employed. These two propositions are beyond dispute and the remedy suggested is as follows:
> 'Let a percentage of the gross takings (including all money paid for stand tickets) of every day's play in every first-class match be set aside to form "A Professional Cricketers' Good Service Fund" and let that fund be administered by the MCC on the military principle of "batta".' The MCC would divide the men into classes at the end of the season and apportion the fund in shares according to merit, those in Class I counting as generals,

> and those in the lowest class as privates. The scheme is decidedly ingenious, and would certainly tend to improve cricket in the weaker counties, where the professional, whatever his merit, has no chance of reaping the big benefits common in Yorkshire and Lancashire. A trades union of professional cricketers – a development not unknown in football – would be disastrous. But, if it is to be prevented, some steps towards the removal of flagrant inequalities will have to be taken sooner or later.

Neither the MCC, nor the succeeding governing bodies of the game ever did respond to the initiative and the sky did not fall down when the Professional Cricketers' Association was established as late as 1967, but the efforts of that body and the economic laws of supply and demand have ensured a more equitable distribution of the cake between 'ordinary professionals' and led to the rewards of the 'great professionals', while not comparing with those available in football, tennis and golf, being above those of the 'skilled artisan'.

A spectator, at The Oval, expressing his opinions to the *Daily Mail*'s reporter at the time of the 'strike' was reported as saying,

> I don't like to see it... I don't like to see the players come out at one door and the gentlemen at another. If they're good enough to associate with gentlemen on the field, they're good enough to do so in the pavilion.[5]

Amateurs and professionals were to share dressing rooms after the First World War, but the social distinctions remained and almost seventy years were to elapse before the abolition of the Gentlemen–Players divide. In 1937, a Commission appointed to investigate the 'problems at present confronting the first class counties' was still able to recommend,

> ...That every effort be made to include more amateurs in county teams whose presence is desirable for obvious reasons.[6]

The reasons may have been obvious in 1937 when class structures were more rigid than they have subsequently become and even on the eve of formal abolition, the Editor of *Wisden* was still able to write:

> By doing away with the amateur, cricket is in danger of losing the spirit of freedom and gaiety which the best amateur players brought to the game.[7]

The inheritors of George Lohmann's influence were perhaps less concerned with freedom and gaiety than the maximisation of their talent and earning respect and a decent living from the exploitation of their skills. It is at least arguable that part of what was achieved in the game in the wake of the Packer Revolution in 1977 had its roots in Lohmann's approach to cricket as a profession eighty years earlier. He had challenged the establishment; he had challenged W G Grace, almost the same thing. Like Agamemnon, he had trod the purple carpet, previously reserved for the gods. Like Agamemnon too, he paid the price, but he had played his part in ensuring better treatment for his successors.

A new hierarchy was to arise where the distinction was not between amateurs and professionals, but between capped and uncapped players. A century was to elapse before the demolition of the wall in the Surrey dressing room dividing them. The dismantling of its counterpart in Berlin had preceded it, but on a shorter time-scale than the process begun by George Lohmann a hundred years before.

Lohmann and his colleagues had paved the way towards the recognition of paid employment in cricket as a respectable profession. They did not aspire, however, nor would it have been realistic to expect it, to the dismantling of a whole social edifice.

> Amateurs continued to dominate the county cricket club committees and to provide the powerful MCC with its leadership. The view was commonly held and for much too long that the game could not survive without amateur ideals, and that professionals could not be trusted with positions of authority. This was one of the unfortunate features of the Victorian legacy. During the nineteenth century the majority of professionals had sprung from proletarian roots, and had therefore fallen easy prey to the snobbery of bourgeois and aristocratic amateurs. The relationship between amateurs and professionals was essentially a master-servant one. Cricket was a menial profession and therefore no gentleman would play it for money.[8]

Keith Sandiford goes on to mention that professionalism is more a state of mind than an emphasis on financial returns, a sentiment with which Lohmann and his colleagues would have concurred.

The power-struggle was not won, however. The Surrey Committee demonstrated that they were still in control by rewarding Hearne and Peel for their bowling in the 1896 Oval Test. In some ways, the situation has changed little. Although the PCA and international captains are now consulted, the real power still lies with those who hold the purse strings, the national governing bodies, the ICC and, of course, the sponsors. Players are still required to endure nonsensical fixture lists, both domestic and international and, the antiquated nineteenth-century benefit system has survived into the twenty-first. As one recently retired county captain has said: 'We are all slaves to the system.'[9]

Having played his part in the emancipation of the professional cricketer in England, Lohmann was able, albeit perhaps indirectly, to influence a smoother transition to the recognition of his emerging counterpart in South Africa. He had, of course, already started to do so before the final rift with Surrey and, such was his reputation, possibly before he set foot in the country. The founding fathers of South African cricket had recognised the value of English professional cricketers as coaches and while the Currie Cup in its early years remained strictly amateur, the introduction of Lohmann as a professional saw the beginnings of the road to professional dominance. In 1895/96 and again in 1898/99, South Africa's amateurs had been annihilated by Lord Hawke's mercenaries; Logan's tour of England of 1901 was comprised of amateur cricketers; the Currie Cup Rules were amended in 1903 to allow professionals, provided they had a birth qualification for the province they wished to represent[10] and Abe Bailey's tour of 1904 had de facto professional players and a first-class programme. Within eighteen months South Africa had won her first Test match.

1 27 May 1901
2 *Cricket Lore* Volume 5 Issue 5 December 2003
3 *No Coward Soul* pp 24 and 32
4 15 May 1901
5 *Daily Mail* 11 August 1896
6 *Wisden* 1938 p 184
7 1963 p 138
8 Sandiford *The Professionalisation of Modern Cricket* p 270
9 Adam Hollioake in conversation with the author – July 1997
10 Minutes of South African Cricket Association 12 October 1903

APPENDIX A: GEORGE LOHMANN'S CAREER STATISTICS

TEST MATCHES

BATTING AND FIELDING

Matches	*Innings*	*Not Outs*	*Highest*	*Runs*	*Average*	*50s*	*Ct*
18	26	2	62*	213	8.87	1	28

BOWLING

Balls	*Maidens*	*Runs*	*Wickets*	*Average*	*Best*	*5wI*	*10wM*
3830	364	1205	112	10.75	9-28	9	5

ALL FIRST-CLASS

BATTING AND FIELDING

Matches	*Innings*	*Not Outs*	*Highest*	*Runs*	*Average*	*100s*	*50s*	*Ct*
293	427	39	115	7247	18.67	3	29	337

BOWLING

Balls	*Maidens*	*Runs*	*Wickets*	*Average*	*Best*	*5wI*	*10wM*
71724	6812	25925	1841	13.73	9-28	176	57

ALL FIRST-CLASS BY SEASON

BATTING AND FIELDING

	Matches	*Innings*	*Not Outs*	*Highest*	*Runs*	*Average*	*100s*	*50s*	*Ct*
1884	10	17	3	69	271	19.35	0	1	4
1885	24	34	2	92*	571	17.84	0	2	15
1886	26	36	5	107	728	23.48	1	2	32
1886/87(Aus)	11	17	2	40*	212	14.13	0	0	12
1887	25	36	3	115	843	25.54	1	5	23
1887/88 (Aus)	8	13	0	39	173	13.30	0	0	10
1888	29	40	1	80	628	16.10	0	3	45
1889	27	39	3	79	557	15.47	0	3	33
1890	32	47	4	57	832	19.34	0	3	49
1891	25	36	1	61	809	23.11	0	3	23
1891/92 (Aus)	8	11	1	102	222	22.20	1	0	9
1892	23	34	3	73	557	17.96	0	4	33
1894/95 (SA)	1	2	0	18	31	15.50	0	0	1
1895	12	19	5	47	159	11.35	0	0	16
1895/96 (SA)	4	6	0	8	14	2.33	0	0	6
1896	23	33	6	86*	540	20.00	0	3	19
1896/97 (SA)	4	6	0	44	91	15.16	0	0	7
1897/98 (SA)	1	1	0	9	9	9.00	0	0	0

BOWLING

	Overs	*Maidens*	*Runs*	*Wickets*	*Average*	*Best*	*5wI*	*10wM*
1884	218	116	313	18	17.38	5-35	1	0
1885	1267.1	590	2037	142	14.34	8-18	9	3
1886	1715	809	2425	160	15.15	8-43	15	3
1886/87 (Aus)	813.3	391	1028	59	17.42	8-35	7	3
1887	1631.2	737	2404	154	15.61	8-36	16	6
1887/88(Aus)	646.3	364	755	63	11.98	7-43	7	2
1888	1649	785	2280	209	10.90	8-13	25	9
1889	1614.1	646	2714	202	13.43	9-67	21	8

1890	1760.1	736	2998	220	13.62	8-65	21	5
1891	1188.3	445	2065	177	11.66	7-20	20	8
1891/92 (Aus)	*137.4							
	†283.3	178	640	40	16.00	8-58	2	1
1892	1213.4	431	2316	151	15.33	8-42	13	4
1894/95 (SA)	100	49	131	8	16.37	7-72	1	0
1895	500.2	166	904	64	14.12	6-34	3	0
1895/96 (SA)	133	46	251	41	6.12	9-28	5	2
1896	766.4	258	1512	93	16.25	7-61	7	2
1896/97(SA)	211.2	65	417	34	12.26	5-44	3	1
1897/98 (SA)	50	15	105	6	17.50	3-33	0	0

Note: 1884-88: 4-ball overs
1889 onwards: 5-ball overs
except 1891/92† when 6-ball overs were the norm, except for the two matches against
**New South Wales when 5-ball overs were bowled*

TEST MATCH BOWLING AVERAGE, STRIKE RATE AND WICKETS PER MATCH

Lohmann tops the all-time, all-comers tables in both bowling average and strike rate and, although trans-generational comparisons are meaningless because of differences in the quality of pitches and of the opposition, he is so far ahead of the second-placed that it seemed worthwhile to give the top four in each case.

Bowling Average

	Tests	Wickets	Average
G A Lohmann	**18**	**112**	**10.75**
S F Barnes	27	189	16.43
C T B Turner	17	101	16.53
R Peel	20	101	16.98

Strike Rate

	Tests	Wickets	Strike Rate
G A Lohmann	**18**	**112**	**34.19**
S F Barnes	27	189	41.65
Waqar Younis	87	373	43.49
Shoaib Akhtar	43	169	44.71

More significant perhaps as an indication of domination is the average number of wickets per match, given that the maximum is a finite 20. In this table, Lohmann stands comparison with any of his contemporaries or near-contemporaries.

Average Wickets per Match

	Tests	Wickets	Average per Match
S F Barnes	27	189	7.00
J J Ferris	9	61	6.77
T Richardson	14	88	6.28
G A Lohmann	**18**	**112**	**6.22**
C T B Turner	17	101	5.94
C Blythe	19	100	5.26
F R Spofforth	18	94	5.22
R Peel	20	101	5.10

and, finally, a few modern bowlers judged by the same criteria

M Muralitharan	110	674	6.12
D K Lillee	70	355	5.07
R J Hadlee	86	431	5.01
S K Warne	145	708	4.88
G D McGrath	124	563	4.54

Figures at March 2007

SURREY'S PERFORMANCE IN MATCHES CONTRIBUTING TO COUNTY CHAMPIONSHIP DURING LOHMANN'S CAREER

	Played	Won	Drawn	Lost	Position
1884	18	9	5	4	
1885	20	12	4	4	
1886	16	12	1	3	
1887	16	12	2	2	1st
1888	14	12	1	1	1st
1889	14	10	1	3	1st=
1890	14	9	2	3	1st
1891	16	12	2	2	1st
1892	16	13	1	2	1st
1893	*16*	*7*	*1*	*8*	*5th*
1894	*16*	*13*	*0*	*2*	*1st*
1895	26	17	5	4	1st
1896	26	17	2	7	4th

The figures in italics are for those seasons when Lohmann did not play.

LOHMANN AS A MEMBER OF WINNING TEAMS

Every cricket match won by one team is lost by the other. A draw or a tie is a draw or a tie for both sides. The average cricketer therefore would expect over the course of a career to be on the winning side on about as many occasions as on the losing side. It is a measure of the superiority both of Lohmann and the teams he played for in first-class matches that he was on the winning side on more than three times as many occasions as the losing one.

	Played	Won	Drawn	Lost
for Surrey	186	120	28	38
for other teams	89	49	23	17
Test Matches	18	15	–	3
Totals	**293**	**184**	**51**	**58**

APPENDIX B: CHRONOLOGY

1714	Ancestors come to England with George I
1863	Father marries Frances Pattle (née Watling)
1863	Elder brother Stewart born
1865	**Born at 3 Campden Hill Road, Kensington**
1866	Family move to Battersea
1867	Sister Julia born
1869	Sister Augusta born
1875	Younger brother Joshua born
1876	First plays cricket for Church Institute Club
1881	First plays for Alma Cricket Club
1884	**First-class début**
1886	**International début**
1886/87	**First tour of Australia**
	First bowler to take eight wickets in Test innings
1887/88	**Second tour of Australia**
1890	Takes 220 first-class wickets
1891/92	**Third tour of Australia**
1892	Breakdown in health
1892/94	Convalesces in South Africa
1894/95	Plays for Western Province
1895/96	**Tour of South Africa**
	First bowler to take nine wickets in Test innings
1896	Players' 'strike'
	Last season in England
1896/97	Again plays for Western Province
1897/98	Coach at Wanderers, Johannesburg
	Johannesburg Waterworks Company
1898/99	Manages Lord Hawke's tour of South Africa
1898/1901	Boer War
1901	Assistant Manager of South African team in England
	Dies at Matjiesfontein
1904	Augusta marries Walter Quaife in Birmingham
1919	Father dies in Upper Norwood
1931	Stewart and Charles Pond, half-brother, die
1946	Joshua dies in Liverpool
1956	Jim Laker breaks Lohmann's sixty-year-old record
2007	Lohmann remains top of all time world-wide Test bowling averages and strike-rate statistics

APPENDIX C: THE LOHMANN FAMILY TREE

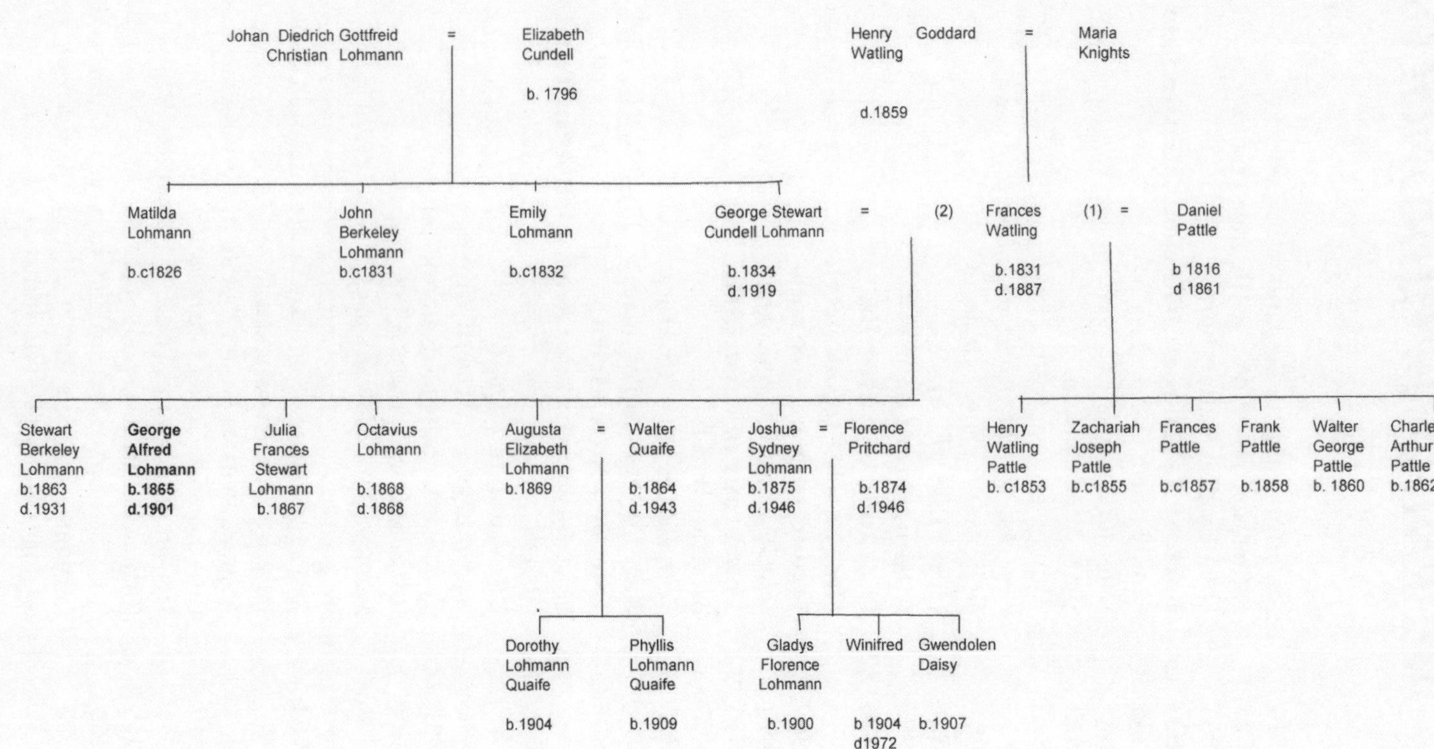

APPENDIX D: OBITUARIES AND OTHER TRIBUTES

PROFILE from *Cricket* 27 August 1885

GEORGE ALFRED LOHMANN

A South Londoner, himself, by every association, to South London belongs the credit solely and wholly of the cricket training of the young professional who has done such good service for Surrey, with bat as well as ball, during the last two seasons. Born in 1865, on June 2, Lohmann first saw the light at a period of Surrey cricket when Jupp and Tom Humphrey had just made their reputations as two of the best batsmen of the day. All his early practice was had on Wandsworth Common, and, in fact, the whole of his cricket until he was fifteen or sixteen years of age was learned on the Common. A member of the Church Institute Club which played there, it was with it that he first showed any signs of ability as a cricketer, and for three successive seasons (1876-77-78) he won both the average bat and ball given for the most successful batsman and bowler of that society. Though he played little in the two following summers he became connected with the Alma Club in 1881, and he was not only actively connected with it at the time when he first appeared at the Oval, but is still a member. His introduction to Surrey cricket was a little out of the ordinary course. Indeed he came up to the test practices of last year without any credentials and without a testimonial of any kind. In fact he was not at all fancied as a cricketer by many in his own neighbourhood, and it was really the favourable impression created by his promising all-round form at this preliminary trial of Colts which gave him his first step in promotion as a professional cricketer. His unmistakable keenness and evident ability procured him the immediate offer of an engagement as a bowler at the Oval, and the commencement of last season found him regularly attached to the ground staff of the Surrey Club. Losing no opportunity of practice his cricket steadily improved, and in the numerous Colts' matches played at the Oval during the early part of May he rarely failed to show to advantage, with either bat or ball. Against Surbiton and District, in particular, his all-round cricket was very promising, and it was in a great measure due to his form on this occasion that he was elected to represent Surrey, against Leicestershire, at the Oval, in the third fixture of the season. Though only moderately successful in the earlier matches he made his mark with a capital 24 not out against Gloucestershire, and also had the satisfaction of getting Mr. W. G. Grace caught from his bowling in the second innings. At the end of the same week he figured even more prominently against Cambridge University, and his second score of 69, though not faultless, was a very promising display of batting. His stand with Wood, indeed, entirely altered the aspect of the game, and, while they were together the two professionals added as many as 95 runs to the Surrey total. So far Lohmann had been more successful as a batsman, and it was not till nearly the close of the season that he reappeared in the Surrey XI. His first achievement, too, on his return was with the bat, and he signalised his re-instatement with an exceedingly well-got thirty-two against Lancashire at the Oval, the highest score in Surrey's first innings. The three last matches on the Surrey programme of 1884, too, proved his capabilities unmistakably as a bowler, although he was also fairly successful with the bat, in particular against Yorkshire, in which match he got nineteen runs in very good style. The wickets just at the close of last summer helped the ball materially, and Lohmann advanced his reputation considerably as an all-round cricketer by the judgment he showed as a bowler in most of the later fixtures. The victory of the Surrey eleven in the closing match of the season against Sussex at the Oval was indeed, in a great measure, due to his effective bowling. Varying his pace with considerable skill and getting a lot of work on to the ball, he puzzled the Sussex batsmen completely, and altogether in the two innings was credited with nine of their wickets at a cost of only 58 runs. Though unsuccessful with the bat in the opening match against Essex at the Oval. Lohmann began this season very auspiciously as a bowler. He was not put on at all in the first innings of Essex, but in the second the Essex batsmen could do nothing with him, and in all seven wickets, five of them bowled, fell to him at the very small expense of thirty-three runs. His best score during the early part of the summer was one of 86 against Oxford University, at Oxford, and runs were got at such a rapid rate while he was in that 100 were added in an hour. Though for a time, after this he was comparatively unsuccessful with the bat, he has recently, several times shown capital cricket and more than once at very important periods of the game. His plucky play with Mr. Horner won Surrey a most exciting match at Gravesend against Kent with one wicket to fall, and too much praise could hardly be accorded to him for his excellent score of 34 not out. The following week, against Notts, at the Oval, he played sound cricket for his thirty; and again, a little later, showed to the greatest advantage against the Kent bowling, carrying out his bat for 92 in the second innings without a mistake. In the early part of the season his bowling proved very effective, and in the first few matches he got a large number of wickets. His best record was at Southampton, where he secured twelve for 31 runs. The heavy work, though, of the Surrey programme seems of late to have told on his bowling, and his only notable performance of late has been this week at Taunton, where he was credited with eight Somersetshire wickets at a cost of 57 runs. With care, Lohmann ought to make a first-class all-round cricketer. He bowls fast round, with a high delivery. And when the wicket helps him at all gets a lot of work from the off. He is not afraid of pitching the ball up as so many bowlers are, and varies his pitch and pace with judgment, his slow ball being particularly dangerous. He is likely, too, to train on into a good batsman. He plays the ball hard and can hit freely, although a little more discretion in his hitting, which will come with experience, will improve his play materially. Lohmann is also a capital field anywhere.

SIX GREAT BOWLERS OF THE YEAR *Wisden* 1889

GEORGE ALFRED LOHMANN was born on June 5 [sic] 1865 and first played for Surrey in 1884. He is by general consent admitted to be one of the best bowlers and most accomplished all-round cricketers ever seen and he fairly challenged comparison with Turner by what he did during the season of 1888. Lohmann and Turner are indeed very much alike. They bowl with remarkable skill and judgment; their batting and fielding are invaluable to their side, and they both have that peculiar electrical quality of rising to a great occasion. It has often been said of cricketers of proved skill, that the match has been too big for them, but certainly no match was ever too big for George Lohmann or Charles Turner.

THE HOPE OF SURREY by Norman Gale *Cricket Songs* 1894

When Surrey ladled out defeat,
Who did it?
When Notts and Yorks and Kent were beat,
Who did it?
Lohmann did – George Lohmann –
Something like a yeoman
Neither fast nor slow man,
George.

Surrey wants you – come again!
England wants you – cross the main!
Say Goodbye to
Capetown sky, you
Best of Georges, come again.

Though bowlers good as you should come
(Not likely!)
From you to them shall fancy roam?
Not likely!
Soldier, sailor, tinker

Ev'ry proper thinker
Knows you are a clinker,
George!

Surrey wants you – come you back!
England wants you – homeward tack!
Say Goodbye to
Capetown sky, you
Best of Georges, come you back.

May warmer heavens make you whole
For Surrey!
How men would roar to see you bowl
For Surrey!
Nursed and helped and mended,
Truly kept and tended,
Come and be our splendid
George.

Surrey wants you home again!
England wants you – cross the main!
Say Goodbye to
Capetown sky, you
George of Georges, come again!

OBITUARY FROM *The Times* 2 December 1901

A Reuter telegram from Cape Town dated yesterday says:
'Mr George Lohmann, the famous cricketer, has died of consumption at Matjesfontein'. George Lohmann, who was in England as recently as last summer, when he accompanied the South African cricketers as Assistant manager, returning to the Cape in the middle of October, was at the time of his death in his 37th year. He was born in Kensington, and so qualified by birth to play for Middlesex. It was in Surrey, however, that he received his early cricket training with the Church Institute Club at Wandsworth-common, and it was for Surrey that he made his first appearance in county cricket in 1884. In June of that year, he made his first half-century in first-class cricket against Cambridge University at the Oval. So rapid was Lohmann's advance that in the next season he was credited with nearly 100 wickets at a cost of less than 14½ apiece; but his best season was in 1888 when he secured 209 wickets at a cost of a fraction under 11 runs each, though he surpassed the number of wickets a couple of seasons later, when 220 batsmen fell to his deliveries. The cultivation of off-theory was largely due to him and with a high delivery following on a long swinging run he would vary his pace and character of the ball considerably his aim

being to deceive the batsman without regard to maiden overs. He was one of the greatest bowlers ever seen, whilst with the bat he was almost as successful. A powerful hitter, he was severe on loose balls, and in the field his reach made him a fine fielder in the slips where he frequently brought off remarkable catches. He visited Australia three times, and no English team until the breakdown of his health after the season 1892 was complete without him. A long sojourn in South Africa caused his absence from the Surrey side in 1893 and 1894, but he returned during the summer of 1895, not with his old form, yet a sufficiently able cricketer to render a useful service to his county in 1895 and 1896. In the later year he appeared for England against the Australians at Lord's, was left out at his own wish at Old Trafford, and was not included at the Oval in connexion with which game the unfortunate 'strike' occurred. A few days earlier he had received his benefit from his county in the shape of the Yorkshire match at the Oval. This season was his last in first-class cricket and he subsequently returned to South Africa, where he secured a post with Mr Logan, the patron of sport by whom the latest interchange of visits between the Cape and the mother country was organised.

OBITUARY FROM THE *Daily Mail* 2 December 1901

DEATH OF GEORGE LOHMANN

SURREY'S GREATEST CRICKETER SUCCUMBS TO CONSUMPTION

George Lohmann, perhaps the greatest allround cricketer that ever lived has, says a Reuter's Telegram, from Capetown, died of consumption at Matjesfontein at the early age of thirty-six.

Those who knew Lohmann will not be surprised at the sad news, for when he was over here last summer with the Hon J D Logan's team of South African cricketers, it was evident from his appearance that he was in the clutches of the most insidious of all diseases, and he himself was fully aware of the fact that he was paying his last visit to his native land. Uniformly bright and cheerful, however, he discharged his duties as manager of the South African team in such a thorough manner as to make the tour a complete success, and never a word of complaint passed his lips, although the cold, easterly winds that prevailed during May must have been a sore trial.

George Lohmann who was born in Kensington in 1865, and made his first appearance for Surrey in 1884, was for ten years the most popular cricketer that ever played at Kennington Oval. As 'George' he was known, not only to his intimates, but also to the crowd that lined the ropes and his appearance at the wicket was always the signal for the loudest cheer of the day. Whether engaged in batting, bowling or fielding, Lohmann was always working his hardest and the Oval spectators who dearly love a genuine 'trier' made him their idol.

His greatest fame was, of course, earned as a bowler, but his fearless hitting as a batsman has often turned the fortunes of a game and as a fieldsman, he was probably the finest short slip that England has ever produced.

In bowling Lohmann was never content merely to keep the runs down, he was never satisfied unless he got wickets as well, and probably no man better knew the weaknesses of particular batsmen....

It was in 1892 that failing health first obliged Lohmann to leave England to settle in South Africa. In 1895 he returned again to this country, but the year after was compelled to go back. In South Africa he won golden opinions from all with whom he came into contact, and was as popular as he was in England. When the war broke out he was made Press censor at Matjesfontein, a fact which he seemed to take great pride in relating during his recent visit to this country.

OBITUARY FROM *Cape Daily Telegraph* 3 December 1901

Cricket enthusiasts throughout the world will learn of the death of poor Lohmann with feelings of the utmost regret. 'George' as he was familiarly called, passed as a brilliant comet across the cricket hemisphere. He was, during the zenith of his short career, regarded as the only rival to the great champion, W G Grace. As a bowler he was truly magnificent. It is doubtful whether England ever possessed a better. He ranked as a 'medium' as regards pace, but he held in reserve a deadly 'slow' as well as a deadly 'fast'. In fact he bowled with his head and could make his hands do almost what he liked with the ball. As a batsman he became brilliant. His punishing powers were great and during seasons when centuries were not as common as they have since become, George Lohmann added his contributions to the list. In the field he was magnificent. In fact he excelled in all departments of the game, and when his health broke down, Surrey's great loss became Great Britain's loss. Lohmann settled in this country some six years ago for the benefit of his health and was engaged by Mr Logan at Matjesfontein. The dry Karoo climate prolonged his life but, we believe, a cold caught during his recent trip to England with the South African team, brought back the old lung trouble, and poor Lohmann died on Sunday. The news of his demise will be received with regret by all British cricketers.

EPITAPH ON GRAVE

GEORGE ALFRED LOHMANN
BORN JUNE 2ND 1865. DIED DECEMBER 1ST 1901.
THIS MONUMENT WAS ERECTED
BY THE SURREY COUNTY CRICKET CLUB
AND FRIENDS IN SOUTH AFRICA
IN MEMORY OF ONE OF THE GREATEST ALL ROUND CRICKETERS
THE WORLD HAS EVER SEEN
A BOWLER OF INFINITE VARIETY
A SPLENDID FIELD AND A RESOLUTE BATSMAN
HE DID EXCELLENT SERVICE FOR SURREY
FROM 1884 TO 1896
AS WELL AS FOR THE PLAYERS AND FOR ENGLAND
HIS WHOLE HEART WAS IN SURREY
AND HE PLAYED THE GAME FROM START TO FINISH
ILL HEALTH ALONE COMPELLED HIM
TO RETIRE FROM THE CRICKET FIELD
WHILE STILL IN HIS PRIME

APPENDIX E: THE MAUD STEVENS CASE

JAMES LOGAN, no stranger to the Courts of Law, was in January 1899 involved in a colourful case, but this time as a defendant in the City Police Court in Cape Town.[1] He did not appear in the dock in person, but hired the powerful advocacy of the Hon T L Graham QC to rebut a charge of attempted rape brought by an eighteen-year-old chambermaid, Maud Stevens. Unsurprisingly, the case aroused all the latent prurience of late nineteenth-century society and the court room was packed on all three days of the case as the movements of the parties concerned were subject to minute legal scrutiny. Maud Stevens was an uneducated coloured girl with a dubious history who, at the instigation of her former employer, Charles Munday, accused Logan of attempted rape in his room at Poole's Hotel.

Logan was proprietor of the hotel, Munday a former manager whose resignation Logan had demanded because of its filthy condition. So, Munday had a grudge against Logan and though he denied it in court, was seemingly using the girl as a pawn in a quest for revenge. Inconsistencies in the evidence and a powerful written rebuttal by the defendant combined to have the case dismissed. The defence centred on the fact that Logan was not even at the hotel at the time of the alleged offence but en route via his office from the Houses of Parliament. The prosecution evidence, though disjointed, suggested that he probably was, but Logan's statement referred to appointments with Rhodes and Sir James Sivewright and was sufficient to persuade the magistrate to dismiss a case which in his native Scotland, might well have led to a verdict of 'not proven'.

Vindictively, he was not prepared to let it rest there. In April, Maud Stevens again appeared in court, this time as defendant on a charge of perjury. She was found guilty and sentenced to six months hard labour. *La raison du plus fort est toujours la meilleure*. All are equal before the law, but some might be more equal than others.

There is no mention of the case in Logan's biography and no record of it in the scrapbook he kept. Given that events such as celebrations at Matjiesfontein to mark the Queen's birthday later in the year are included, that may perhaps be considered surprising, as Logan emerged from the case, if not exactly with his reputation enhanced, then certainly with congratulations from his peers.

> ...The accused is discharged.
>
> General applause greeted the announcement of this decision, but

> was quickly suppressed, and Mr Logan left the court, after numerous handshakings and general congratulations.[2]

Both biography and scrapbook are selective. There is no intention to produce a 'warts and all' picture of Logan and only complimentary material is included. It might be assumed that such hearty congratulations would merit inclusion and the question arises 'Congratulations on what?'. On getting away with it perhaps. A doubt must remain.

However, the part of Logan's defence, which sums up his own status-consciousness and the state of South African society at the time concerns a message to him from Munday conveyed by Maud Stevens,

> ...the girl Stevens came upstairs and said that Munday was very much annoyed that I had rung the bell for her. I told her to ask Munday to come and see me, as I was not in the habit of receiving messages of such a nature from coloured servants... I left word with the barman to tell Munday to let me have full explanation when I arrived on Wednesday morning, as to why he dared to send messages to me by a servant girl.[3]

For Maud Stevens, the pendulum had swung completely. From complainant she was now a victim. The Magistrate summed up as follows,

> He was sorry for the position the accused found herself in, as she did not quite know what she had been doing: but if persons like her were allowed to cast such statements broadcast no man would be safe.[4]

1 *Cape Times* 14,18 January, 1 February 1899; *Cape Argus* 7 April 1899
2 *Cape Times* 1 February 1899
3 Ib
4 *Cape Argus* 7 April 1899

BIBLIOGRAPHY

BOOKS

Allen, D R *Cricket's Silver Lining 1864-1914* Willow 1987
Altham, H S *A History of Cricket* Allen and Unwin 1926
Bailey, Philip; Thorn, Philip and Wynne-Thomas, Peter *Who's Who of Cricketers* Guild Publishing 1984
Barker, Ralph *Ten Great Bowlers* Chatto & Windus 1967
Beldam, G W & Fry, C B *Great Bowlers and Fielders* MacMillan & Co 1906
Bettesworth, W A *Chats on the Cricket Field* Merritt and Hatcher 1910
Birley, Derek *A Social History of English Cricket* Aurum Press 1999
Booth, Keith *The Father of Modern Sport: The Life and Times of Charles W Alcock* Parrs Wood Press 2002
Burman, Jose *Early Railways at the Cape* Human and Rousseau (Cape Town) 1984
Chalke, Stephen & Hodgson, Derek *No Coward Soul* Fairfield Books 2003
Chamberlain, M E *The Scramble for Africa* [Second Edition] Addison Wesley Longman 1999
Coldham, JP *Lord Hawke: A Cricketing Biography* The Crowood Press 1990
A Country Vicar (Rev R L Hodgson) *Cricket Memories* Methuen 1930
Daft, Richard *Kings of Cricket* Arrowsmith 1893
Dorey, H V *Life and Reminiscences of Robert Abel in the Cricket Field* told by himself and edited by... Cricket & Sports Publishers Ltd 1910
Edmonds, Phil *100 Greatest Bowlers* Queen Anne Press 1989
Falloon, Jane *Throttle Full Open: A Life of Lady Bailey, Irish Aviatrix* Lilliput Press (Dublin) 1999
Fry, C B *Life Worth Living* Eyre & Spottiswood 1939
Giffen, George *With Bat and Ball* Ward, Locke and Co 1898
Grace, W G *Cricket* Arrowsmith 1891
Grace, W G *Cricketing Reminiscences and Personal Recollections* James Bowden 1899
Gutsche, Thelma *Old Gold: The History of the Wanderers Club* Howard Timmins (Cape Town) 1966
Harragan, Bob *The History of Llanelli Cricket Club* Llanelli Borough Council 1989
Haynes, B & Lucas, J *The Trent Bridge Battery: The Story of the Sporting Gunns* Willow 1985
Johnson, R L *South Africa: The First Man, the Last Nation* Jonathan Ball (Johannesburg/Cape Town) 2004
Joel, Stanhope *Ace of Diamonds. The Story of Solomon Barnato Joel* Frederick Muller 1958
Kynaston, David *Bobby Abel: Professional Batsman* Martin Secker and Warburg 1982

Knowles, Ray *South Africa v England: A Test Cricket History* New Holland (Publishers) Ltd 1995
Lemmon, David *Cricket's Champion Counties* Breedon Books 1991
Lilley, A A *Twenty-Four Years of Cricket* Mills & Boon 1912
Lodge, Jerry *100 Surrey Greats* Tempus Publishing 2003
Lonsdale, Jeremy *The Army's Grace: The Life of Brigadier General R M Poore* Spellmount Ltd 1992
Lorimer, Rev Malcolm *Johnny Remembered: A Celebration of the life and career of Johnny Briggs* 2005
Low, Robert *W G* Robert Cohen Books 1997
Luckin M W (ed) *The History of South African Cricket* W E Hortor & Co (Johannesburg) 1915
Lyttelton, Hon R H *Giants of the Game* Ward, Lock and Co 1898
Lyttelton, Hon R H *Outdoor Games: Cricket and Golf* J M Dent 1901
McLean, Teresa *The Men in White Coats* Stanley Paul 1987
Meredith, Anthony *The Demon and the Lobster: Charles Kortright and Digby Jephson, Remarkable Bowlers in the Golden Age* The Kingswood Press 1987
Murray, Bruce and Merrett, Christopher *Caught Behind: Race and Politics in South African Cricket* Wits University Press & University of Kwazulu-Natal Press 2004
Nissel, Muriel *People Count* HMSO 1987
Odendaal, André *The Story of an African Game* David Philip (Cape Town) 2003
Pearce, Brian *Cricket at the Crystal Palace: W G Grace and the London County Club* Brian Pearce 2004
Pentelow, J N *England v Australia 1877-1904* Arrowsmith 1904
Ross, Gordon *The Surrey Story* Stanley Paul 1957
Sandiford, Keith A P *Cricket and the Victorians* Scolar Press 1994
Schreiner, Olive *Thoughts on South Africa* Ad Donker 1992
Sheffield Park Garden National Trust 1994
Sheppard, F H H (ed) *Survey of London Vol XXXVII: Northern Kensington* Athlone Press 1973
Sissons, Ric *George Lohmann: The beau ideal* Pluto Press Australia Ltd 1991
Sissons, Ric *The Players: A Social History of the Professional Cricketer* Kingswood Press 1988
Smith, Rick and Williams, Ron *W G Down Under: Grace in Australia 1873-74 and 92-92* Apple Books Tasmania 1994
Standing, Percy Cross *Cricket of Today and Yesterday* T C & E C Jack (Edinburgh) 1902
South African Directory 1883-84 Saul Solomon 1883
Taylor, J B *Lucky Jim: Memoirs of a Randlord* Stonewall Books (Cape Town) 2003
Thomson, A A *Hirst & Rhodes* Epworth Press 1959
Toms, Robert N *Logan's Way: The Life and Times of J D Logan... a Matjiesfontein Chronicle* Mallard (Claremont, South Africa) 1997

Wallace, Edgar *A Short Autobiography* Hodder and Stoughton 1929
Warner, P F *Cricket in Many Climes* Heinemann 1900
Warner, P F *The Book of Cricket* J M Dent & Co 1922
Warner, P F *Long Innings* Harrap 1951
Weinrebb, Ben & Hibberd, Christopher *The London Encyclopaedia* Macmillan 1983
Wilde, Simon *Ranji: A Genius Rich and Strange* Kingswood Press 1990
Williams, Marcus (ed) *Double Century: 200 Years of Cricket in The Times* Willow 1985
Wilton, Iain *C B Fry: An English Hero* Richard Cohen 1999
Woods, S M J *My Reminiscences* Chapman and Hall 1925

ANNUALS AND REFERENCE BOOKS

James Lillywhite's Cricketers' Annual 1872-1900
Oxford Dictionary of National Biography
South African Who's Who
Surrey County Cricket Club Yearbooks 1884–1902, 1973 and 1991
Surrey County Cricket Club – First-Class & Limited Overs Records
Who's Who
Wisden
Wisden Book of Test Cricket
Kelly's Directories; Post Office Directories; Birth, Marriage and Death Certificates, Censuses of Population 1851–1901.

ARTICLES

Allison, Lincoln 'Batsman and Bowler: The Key Relation of Victorian England' *Journal of Sports History* Vol 7 No 2 Summer 1980
Bettesworth, W A 'Chats on the Cricket Field: George Lohmann' *Cricket* 30 July 1896
Elgod, Stuart 'The Search for the Lost Cricket Stamp' *Magazine of the Cricket Memorabilia Society* no 10 March 1991
Caswell, Peter 'Fresh Light on Some 19th Century Bowlers' *Cricket Lore* Vol 4 Issue 8 August 2001
Hall, Bernard and Schulze, Heinrich 'The Cricketing Brothers Tancred' *The Cricket Statistician* Autumn and Winter 2000
Hall, Bernard and Schulze, Heinrich 'A Last Word on the Tancred Brothers' *The Cricket Statistician* Spring 2005
Harris, Lord 'Workers and their Work Interview' in *Daily News* 22 September 1885
Hartland, Peter 'Who was England's Greatest Bowler?' *Cricket Lore* Vol 5 Issue 5 December 2003
Howard, Geoffrey 'Surrey Greats – George Lohmann' *Surrey Yearbook* 1991
Langham-Carter, R R 'A Lonely Grave on the Karoo' *Australian Cricket Journal* Vol 1 No 2 December 1985
Lonsdale, Jeremy 'England's Tour Problems' *Wisden Cricket Monthly* January 1985

Merrett, Christopher 'Sport and Race in Colonial Natal: C B Llewellyn, South Africa's First Black Test Cricketer '*The Cricket Statistician* Winter 2004

Montefiore, David 'Cricket in the Doldrums, the Struggle between Private and Public Control of Australian Cricket in the 1880s' *Australian Society for Sports History* 1992

Parry, Richard 'In A Sense Citizens, But Not Altogether Citizens...' Rhodes, Race and the Ideology of Segregation at the Cape in the Late Nineteenth Century' University of Saskatchewan 1985

'Diamonds, Cricket and Major Warton: Cricket in Kimberley, 1885-1889' *Cricket Lore* Vol 3 Issue 6 July 1998

Rosenwater, Irving 'A History of Wicket-Covering in England' *Wisden* 1970

Sandiford, Keith A P 'The Professionalisation of Modern Cricket' *British Journal of Sports History* Vol 2 no 3 December 1985

Sandiford, Keith A P 'The Cricketers' Fund Friendly Society in the Nineteenth Century' *Journal of the Cricket Society* Vol 15 no 2 Spring 1991

Santall, Sydney 'I like to Remember: First-class Cricket when I was a boy' *The Cricketer Spring Annual* 1940

Stuttaford, Dr Thomas 'D H Lawrence's TB and Lovers' *The Times* 18 March 2005

Vamplew, Wray 'Not Playing the Game: Unionism in British Professional Sport 1870 -1914' *British Journal of Sports History* Vol 2 no 3 December 1985

Webb, G F 'George Lohmann (1865-1901)' *Journal of the Cricket Society* Vol 10 no 3 Autumn 1981

NEWPAPERS AND PERIODICALS

Andover Advertiser, African Review, Athletic Record, Australasian, Australian Cricket Journal, Brimingham Daily Post, Bristol Evening News, British Journal of Sports History, Bulletin (Sydney), Cape Argus, Cape Daily Telegraph, Cape Mercury, Cape Times, The Clarion, Cricket – A Weekly Record of the Game, Cricket and Football Field, The Cricketer, The Cricket Field, Cricket Lore, The Cricket Statistician, Daily Mail, Daily News, Daily Telegraph, Diamond Fields Advertiser, Football & Cricket World, Hobart Mercury, Imvo Zabantsundu, Journal of the Cricket Society, Journal of Sports History, Land en Volk, Llanelly Star, Manchester Guardian, Midland News and Karroo Farmer, Natal Witness, Newcastle Daily Chronicle, The Performer, Punch, Queenstown Free Press, Sheffield Telegraph, South Africa, South African Review, South African Sportsman, South London Press, Sporting Life, Standard and Diggers News, Surrey County Observer, Sydney Referee, later *The Referee, The Star (Johannesburg), The Times, Titbits, Wandsworth and Battersea District Times, Wandsworth Borough News, Worcester Advertiser, Wisden Cricket Monthly*

WEBSITES

Ceres, Wisden Cricinfo, Cricket Archive, Matjiesfontein, Rand Water, Sir Abe Bailey, Union-Castle Line

INDEX

People

Places (including ships)

Grounds

Teams

Events etc

Organisations etc